AppleScripting Adobe InDesign CS5 and CS5.5

Shirley W. Hopkins

AppleScripting Adobe InDesign CS5 and CS5.5

by Shirley Hopkins

Copyright © 2011 by Shirley W. Hopkins

Apple, the Apple logo, AppleScript, AppleScript Studio, Finder, Macintosh and AppleScript Editor are trademarks of Apple Computer, Inc., registered in the U.S. and other countries. Although many of the designations used by manufacturers and sellers to distinguish their products are claimed as trademarks, no attempt has been made to designate as trademarks or service marks any personal computer words or terms in which proprietary rights may exist. The inclusion, exclusion or definition of a word or term is not intended to affect, or to express any judgment on, the validity or legal status of any proprietary right which may be claimed in that word or term. All product names and services identified throughout the book are used in editorial fashion only and for the benefit of such companies. No such use, or the use of any trade name, is intended to convey endorsement or other affiliation with the book.

Every effort has been taken in the preparation of this book and the accompanying scripts provided. No warranty is made of any kind, express or implied, with regard to documentation or programs or data contained in this book. Any implied warranties of merchantability and fitness for a particular purpose with respect to disks, scripts, and/or data contained, listings and/or techniques described are specifically disclaimed, without limitation. The author does not warrant, guarantee or make any representations regarding the use or the results of the use of the scripts in terms of correctness, accuracy, reliability, currentness or otherwise. The entire risk as to the results and performance of the scripts is assumed by the user. The scripts included are written solely to demonstrate applications which the user may develop on his or her own.

In no event shall the author and licensor(s), employees, or others involved in the distribution of this book and software, be responsible or liable for any consequential, incidental or indirect damages (including damages for loss of business profits, business interruption, loss of business information and the like) arising out of the use or inability to use the scripts. The author and licensor(s), employees, or others involved in the distribution of this book and software, assume no liability for any actual damages from any cause whatsoever, and regardless of the form of the action, (whether in contract, tort (including negligence), product liability or otherwise.

Dedicated to the members of my family
to whom I am forever indebted.

Acknowledgements

What makes working with AppleScript a delight is the community that surrounds it. The spirit of sharing information and ideas is remarkable. The names that I could add to the list of people who have shared their knowledge and given encouragement during the course of writing this book is prohibitive. Mention must be made however to those who have volunteered to read sections of the book including William Adams, Nathan Jaynes, and especially Roy McCoy, who put in untiring hours of his valuable time to test scripts, and to give advice and encouragement. Thanks also to Tyler Jaynes for helping test scripts. Additionally, there are the many readers of my earlier AppleScripting books who keep me fired up with their enthusiasm. To all, my sincere thanks and appreciation.

Background

This book is the result of years of working with AppleScript and many pagination programs. It has been expanded and rewritten to include much of what is new in InDesign CS5 and CS5.5.

This is not another learn AppleScript book. Although the basics of AppleScript are covered, the focus is to use and modify pre-written code to automate processes in InDesign. The intent of the book is to complement the many AppleScript reference books on the market and the excellent documentation that comes with InDesign without being redundant. In addition to giving the reader a wealth of information and examples, it strives to give the user ideas on how scripts can be used. Taking advantage of the code included in the robust library of handlers provided, users should be able to build their own custom scripts with a minimum of effort.

Based on the concept that one learns by doing, the approach is to provide plenty of opportunity for learning without a rehash on theory. The reader is encouraged to try out the scripts, experiment with statements, and increase productivity as a result.

There is no end to the benefits one can realize in knowing how to script. Many times, while in the middle of a project, there may arise a situation which can be aided by using a script. Pop into the AppleScript Editor, pull up a handler or two from a library, modify some of the code, and the production problem may be solved. Your scripting efforts may not be examples of impeccable programming, but they may still save hours of time with an investment of a few minutes. It is also possible, however, for complete automated systems to be put together using scripts. Whatever your scope, it is hoped hope is that you will find much satisfaction in scripting and that this book will be a valuable resource for you.

Table of Contents

Proofsheet
Chapter 1

Ruled Form
Chapter 1

Step and Repeat
Chapter 5

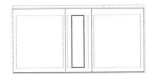

Spread With Spine
Chapter 6

Place Named Images
Chapter 11

Calendar
Chapter 13

Random Snowflakes
Chapter 14

Car Ad
Chapter 15

Recipe
Chapter 16

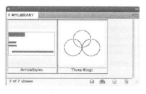

Gradient Fill Flower
Chapter 18

Three Rings
Chapter 19

Biz Card_8up
Chapter 20

Newsletter
Chapter 22

Slideshow
Chapter 23

Interactive PDF
Chapter 23

Welcome

Don't be shy, come on in. Join the growing community of Adobe InDesign users who have discovered scripting to automate many of their repetitive tasks and workflows. The members of this group are diverse, but they have one thing in ccommon: they are enjoying a definite competitive advantage:

- They are able to offer competitive pricing, while realizing more profitability per hour.
- They have more time to be creative and to spend rejuvenating their creative energies.
- They are learning their end product can often be more precise and less error-prone.
- As managers, they discover worker fatigue and repetitive motion disordrs are minimized.

Meet Carl, working for a major newspaper, who has assembled a collection of neat tools that help production artists get their job done faster and more acurately.

Then there is Terry who is a freelance designer. She uses scripts to help build interactive pages.

Mark is an all-around power nut. He uses scripts for everything that involves repetition from real estate booklets to ads.

Faye runs a small copy and printing business. She has set up a scripted system that automates the production of business stationery, invitations, and business cards.

The list goes on. And now, you too, can add your name to the list.

Where You Fit In

How you approach the book and its resources will depend largely on what you want to achieve. With this book as your guide, and the mountains of pre-written code that is at your disposal, you should be well on your way to reaching your particular goal in no time.

New User

If you never write one line of code, you can still benefit from the practical scripts included in the files downloaded from the book's support web site. Additionally, the book will expose you to automation techniques that may help your workflow whether it involves a script or not.

Casual Coder

If you want to learn just enough about scripting so you can put an occasional script together, you will be right at home. The focus of the book is to use pre-written snippets of code (handlers) to build common scripts. A comprehensive library of these handlers is found with the resources that can be downloaded from the book's support web site, or are on the CD that accompanies the book if you ordered the book directly.

Serious Student

You will want to progress through the book from front to back. Follow instructions for entering code into the free AppleScript editor that is part of the Macintosh OS. Spend some time working with the hands-on projects at the end of most chapters.

Power Scripter

Your life is spent putting code together. Pulling syntax off the top of your head is enough to drive you crazy especially if you need to work with several different languages and applications. You know how important code libraries can be in a pinch. The code library included with the book's resource files can be a giant step toward your assembling your own power library for working with InDesign.

Downloadable Scripts and Resources

Most of the code in this book, plus resources for projects, are posted at the book's support site: www.yourscriptdoctor.com. If you ordered the book directly, the CD includes the code plus a few bonus scripts. To download, go to the web site and push the Download button for your particular book.

In the download is a folder containing scripts and projects for each chapter. There is a handlers folder for each InDesign version (CS5 and CS5.5). Handlers in these folders are organized by topic. Follow the instructions in Chapter 1 for placing these resources on your hard drive. Then dig in. Run scripts. Look through the code. Get familiar with handlers. Learn by doing.

While you are at it, join in the conversation at http://tech.groups.yahoo.com/group/applescriptingindesign.

Versions

References in the scripts to the application will be to "Adobe InDesign CS5" but will apply to both versions CS5 and CS5.5. When scripts saved in .non text format (.applescript) are opened in InDesign, the reference will change to the version of the currently active application. A few of the scripts will only work with version CS5.5. In this case the application reference will be specific to CS5.5. If you are copying scripts from the PDF version of the book, you will need to change the references to CS5 to CS5.5 if using the later version. Also look for end line markers (¬) which will need to be removed, and phrases such as end if and end tell which often get split when copied.

Conventions

Angle brackets (>) are used to indicate a progression of selections as with a menu and submenus. To draw attention to terminology used in the book the following conventions have been used.

Italics (*terminology here*) - Bring attention to terminology and variable identifiers.

Bold (**bold**) - References to properties and to highlight specific terminology.

Monospaced (`code and keywords`) - Code and code keywords, including parameters and enumeration values found in text.

Monospaced Bold (**functionName**) -Function identifiers in code.

Script Font (**ScriptName**) - Names of projects, scripts, and script handlers found in text.

Code Conventions

As much as possible the intent was to keep variable identifiers consistent throughout, using ref to indiate a reference to an object, as in docRef to refer to a document.

Handler names use camel case (lower case initial with internal capitalization), while scripts, often having the same name as its principal handler, are capitalized.

Handlers

The first time a handler is introduced in the book, its code will be listed. After that, when used as part of a subsequent script, you will be notified that the handler needs to be added. The entire script will be found in the Chapter Scripts folder for the chapter. The script files, in many cases, are often more complete.

Projects

Projects are scripts that include resources that can be used for testing. They often expect resources to be found at a particular location on your hard drive. To use other locations, you will need to change the paths to the files indicated in the script (see Chapter 7).

File Formats

The InDesign documents for the projects are saved in .indl format. Consequently they have a very small file footprint, and can be opened in either CS5 or CS5.5. A script has been provided to convert these files to the currently active version of InDesign (**Open Indl and Save**). You can use this script to process a folder of files as needed or process the entire AppleScriptingCS5 folder.

Image files included for testing for the most part are saved as low-resolution, low-quality .jpeg files.

A Little History

There must be something about my artistic temperament that has me constantly trying to find a better, maybe faster, way to get a job done. Working better by working smarter became my mantra as I progressed through the evolution of the typesetting industry which began with "hand peg" as soon as I was tall enough to reach the typecases in my father's printing company. So it is no surprise that I became an early adopter of digital technology in the early 1980's. Since then it seems as if I have been running as fast as I can trying to keep up with the constant change (and improvements).

My whole-hearted involvement with scripting began with the first release of AppleScript and Visual Basic. While working with these languages, I kept careful notes and libraries of code snippets. When one of my clients heartily suggested that I write a book, these resources made their way into my first book, AppleScripting Quark XPress (198_). When InDesign was first released as beta, I immediaately took on the task of becoming the InDesign scripting expert for the software development company I was working for at the time.

Since that time, I have been involved in just about every aspect of automation: writing scripts, solving production problems, and helping others become successful with scripting. I am convinced more now than ever that scripting is the hidden key to profitability. Often, I am told by users that they simply could not make deadlines if it were not for the scripts they were using. Many are the comments declaring scripting to be the secret to a user's success. It is my hope that what you gain from this book will become part of your own success story.

--*The Author*

1

Ready, Set, Go

You work with InDesign as a designer or as the head of a design group. You love your work, but time is always a factor. Some of the tasks you do are repetitive and can be practically mind-numbing, consuming precious hours that could be spent otherwise. It would be nice if you could have an assistant to do all of the menial chores for you. Someone who will work for free, tirelessly and accurately. Surprisingly that helper is as close as your computer, and it is part of your Macintosh system. What's more, your favorite application: Adobe InDesign is more than happy to give your helper access to its inner-workings. Your helper is called scripting.

What is a script? A script is nothing more than a set of instructions telling an application what to do and when to do it. The problem is that instructions need to be written in a specific language the application understands. Although scripts can be written for Adobe InDesign in JavaScript (ExtendScript) and Visual Basic, the language of choice here is AppleScript.

Why AppleScript? If your work is on a Macintosh, AppleScript is a natural choice as most of the Apple's "iApps" and some other pretty awesome applications all "talk" AppleScript. This means that there is virtually no limit to what you can do with AppleScript.

Get Ready

Finding time to learn something that will save time is the problem. That is where this book and its resources will prove invaluable. The goal is to get you up and running with usable scripts in the shortest time possible. To start with, Adobe provides some scripts in a folder called Samples. These are ready to use from the Scripts panel in InDesign.

Select Utilities from InDesign's Window Menu and select Scripts from the flyout menu.

To work with the scripts in this book you will want to download the AppleScripting CS5 package from the support web site (www.yourscriptdoctor.com). Included as part of the download are scripts that can be used as is, or modified to fit your needs. For building scripts, there is a library of script modules, called handlers. There is a ;ibrary of handlers for both CS5 and CS5.5. To build scripts using these handlers you will need to become familiar with the basics of the AppleScript language. Working through this book, you will find AppleScript to be very user-friendly and you will soon be thinking of some of your own workflows that could be automated with a script.

Imagine a script that will allow a user to start a project with a keyboard shortcut. Once information is entered into a dialog, the user clicks the OK button to have the structure for the project built in seconds. The document, named and date-stamped, is saved in a folder for the project. Information added to the file can be viewed in Bridge and used for file management (metadata).

Maybe you have a reoccurring project saved as a template. With the template as a base, your script creates a document with resources saved to a specific directory. The script updates and styles the document content. When done, the script leaves the document ready for you to review. The possibilities are endless. So let's get started.

Install Scripts and Resources

1. Copy the resources for the book from the disc if included or download from the book's companion web site:

    `www.yourscriptdoctor.com`

InDesign document resources for the book have been saved in .idml format. To save these as documents (.indd format), a script has been provided for you: **Open IDML and Save**. The script opens .idml files from the chosen folder and its subfolders and saves the documents back into their folders. To use the script, make sure you have your version of InDesign running. Double click on the script and click Run in the dialog presented. When prompted, select the folder you want to process. You can process the entire Applescripting CS5 folder, or individual folders as needed. You will see the documents open and close as the script progresses. The script will prompt you when completed.

2. If you are using AppleScript Editor, place the appropriate Handlers folder (CS5 Handlers or CS55 Handlers folder) into the following location:

    ```
    OS 5: [Hard drive]:Library:Scripts:Script Editor Scripts
    OS 6: [Hard drive]:Library:Scripts:AppleScript Editor Scripts
    ```

Handlers Library

To avoid redundancy, the terminology **Handlers Library** will be used throughout the remainder of the book to reference the files in the CS5 Handlers and CS55 Handlers folders.

---

3. To conform with file paths established in many of the scripts, the Styles and Libraries folders need to be placed inside the Presets folder in InDesign's application folder:

    `[Hard drive]:Applications:Adobe InDesign CS5:Presets:Styles`

    The Templates folder needs to be placed at the same level as the Presets folder:

    `[Hard drive]:Applications:Adobe InDesign CS5:Templates`

    Of course you can change the location of these files, but you would need to change the file path in the scripts accordingly.

4. There are two locations set aside by Adobe for scripts:

    The Application Scripts folder
    `[Hard drive]:Applications:Adobe InDesign CS5 [CS5.5]:Scripts:Scripts Panel`

    Drag the contents of the Scripts Panel folder to this folder.

    The User's Scripts folder
    `[Hard drive]:[[Users]:User Directory][Library]:Preferences:Adobe InDesign:Version 7.0 (7.5):en_US:Scripts:Scripts Panel`

    Drag the contents of the Users Scripts folder into the this folder.

5. Place the contents of the Resources folder inside the Public folder for your user directory.
    `[Hard drive]:Users:[User Name]:Public`

6. Place the Applescripts for CS5 folder at the base level of your User's folder.

Set up a quick access to the Applescripts for CS5 folder by dragging its icon into the PLACES section of Finder's quick access panel. You will use this folder often.

InDesign's Scripts Panel

You will want to verify that your scripts are now in InDesign's Scripts panel.

1. If your version of InDesign is not running, launch it.
2. Open InDesign's Scripts panel from InDesign's Window menu.

   `CS5 and CS5.5: Window > Utilities > Scripts`

Scripts installed in the application's Scripts Panel folder will be listed in InDesign's Scripts panel inside the Application folder. Scripts installed in the User's Library:Preferences folder Scripts folder will be in the User folder (Figure 1.1). The entire paths to these folders is detailed above.

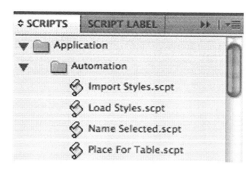

Figure 1.1: Scripts installed in the application's Scripts Panel folder will be in the panel list inside the Application folder. Scripts installed in the user's Library:Preferences folder will be in the User folder (see full path to folder above).

Setup Your Workspace

Set up your own personal workspace to include the Scripts and Script Label panels. Arrange panels as you want them. Click on the current workspace to open the workspace menu. Choose Window > Workspace > New Workspace…. Give your workspace a name and click OK. (Figure 1.2)

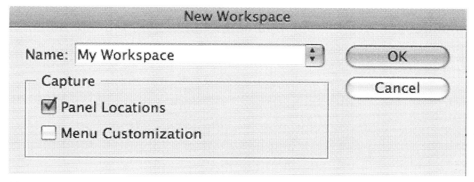

Figure 1.2: Give your workspace a name to help identify it. If you have added menu customizations, you will want to check that option.

Get Set (Set up AppleScript Editor)

The AppleScript Editor is part of the default installation for your Macintosh system. It's name changed from Script Editor to AppleScript Editor in version 10.6 of the operating system. We will use the later name as its reference. It is found at the following directory path:

```
OS 10.5: [Hard drive]:Applications:AppleScript:Script Editor
OS 10.6: [Hard drive]:Applications:Utilities:AppleScript Editor
```

AppleScript provides a folder full of sample scripts. These should be in the Library folder ([hard drive]:Library:Scripts). There is a lot there for you to play with when you are feeling adventurous.

If you do not have the AppleScript Editor pinned to the Dock, you will want to do so. Launch the application. Once launched, control-click on its icon in the Dock and select Keep in Dock from the context menu. When run, AppleScript Editor opens ready for you to enter code into a new Untitled script. AppleScript Editor is a very friendly application. Just a few buttons on the top, with an edit window below. At the bottom are panes: the Result panel shows the result of a script after it is run; the Events panel shows script events and results. as defined in Preferences (application menu:Preferences…). The settings for the Event Log History is one of the settings you can set for the application. Choose Preferences from AppleScript Editor's application menu to become acquainted with the preferences that can be set. For the most part, you can accept the default preferences.

Figure 1.3: Script Editor's Preference Window opens from within its application editor.

Introducing Code

If you have never written a line of code, here is an exercise to whet your appetite.

1. If a new script window is not open, choose New from the AppleScript Editor's File menu.
2. Inside the editor window, enter the following three lines of code:
   ```
   --Displays text defined for variable str in a display dialog
   set str to "Hello World"
   display dialog str
   ```
3. Click the Compile button (hammer). If you made a typing error, you will be alerted. Otherwise you can now run the script.
4. Click the Run button (green circle) to run (or use the keyboard shortcut Command+R.)

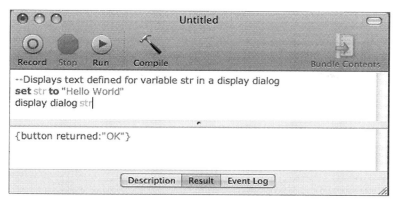

Figure 1.4: Your first script in Script Editor. Notice the Result window at the bottom of the edit window. When activated it displays the result of your script.

5. Review the result of running the script in the Result panel below the Edit window. You can adjust the size of the edit window by dragging on the bottom right corner. The size of the Result panel is adjusted by clicking on the gray divider bar and dragging.

6. Save your script. You might want to set up a folder for your scripts as you go along. You can save your script using a number of formats. For the majority of our scripts, we will use the Script format (.scpt extension).

7. Congratulations, you have created your first script.

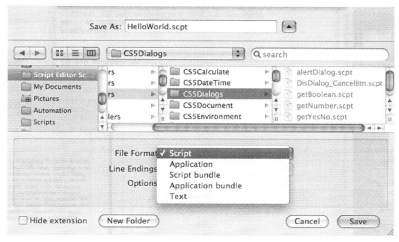

Figure 1.5: Choose Save As... from the File menu. In the Save dialog give the script a name, select Script for File Format. Navigate to the folder in which to save. Click Save.

Standard Additions

Each scriptable application has a dictionary of terminology that is available to AppleScript. This lists the **classes** (object templates), and the **properties** and **commands** the application has exposed to AppleScript. To see the dictionary for an application, choose Open Dictionary... from AppleScript Editor's File menu. Depending on the number of scriptable applications installed, a list of dictionaries is presented. For now you will look at the

StandardAdditions dictionary. Find the dictionary for StandardAdditions in the list and click on its entry. With User Interface selected in the left panel (Suites panel), click on Display Dialog in the second panel. This opens the entry for Display Dialog including a description of the command and a list of its required and optional information. The information required for a command are its **parameters** and provides details to further qualify how the command will perform. The only required parameter for Display Dialog is text. All other parameters are surrounded with square brackets indicating that they are optional. We will explore some of these parameters later.

Go (Working with Scripts)

Running A Script

Now that you are ready to start working with scripts, reward yourself by experimenting with some that have been provided with the resources for this book. See the section "Install Scripts and Resources" above.

Running a script could not be easier. Open the Scripts panel in InDesign if not already open (Option + Command + F11). Double click on an entry for a script and everything bundled into that piece of magic comes alive. Check out the **Tick Marks** script in the Automation folder.

Tick Marks

The **Tick Marks** script creates tick marks to every selected page item using information entered by the user in a simple dialog.

To test, create a document and place some page items on a page (text frames, rectangles, etc.). Select the items. Locate the script in the Automation folder. Double click on its entry to run it. Accept the default values in the dialog presented or experiment with settings. Click OK.

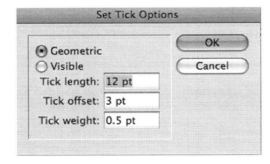

Figure 1.6: Custom dialog for Ticks script. Accept the default values or experiment with your own. Click OK to apply tick marks to selected page items.

Proofsheet

Another, but more involved script, is the **Proofsheet** script (also found in the Automation folder inside InDesign's Scripts panel).

1. Put a number of images into a common folder or use the images found in the Wines folder inside your Public folder (Users:[user name]:Public:Images:Wines). The script

defaults to the Public:Images folder. If you use your own images, you may want to put your folder of images there.

2. Create a document for your Proofsheet (recommended). The document should be letter size and can be vertical or horizontal orientation. If a document is not open, a default document will be created. One advantage of this script is that it can be used with an existing document.

3. If you intend to use captions, you most likely will want to have a paragraph style named Label established in your document. When the script is run the user is presented a dialog in which to select options for the proofsheet. The paragraph style choice in the dialog defaults to a style called Label. If the choice is left at Label and this style is not available, the script creates a style by that name based on text defaults. It is better to choose a style you know is available.

4. By default the script uses the live area of the page (the area inside of margins) for placing the images. If you want to designate another area, create a rectangle (no fill or stroke) and have it selected when the script is run. Double click the Proofsheet listing in the Automation folder of the Scripts panel to run the script.

5. Select the image folder you prepared (see step 1) from within the file browser presented. Once you click the Choose button, you will be presented a dialog. (Figure 1.7).

6. Fill in information as needed (or just use the defaults). The first two fields are for information only. The layout for the items on the page is determined by the number of rows and columns. Gutter indicates spacing between items horizontally. Gap indicates spacing between items vertically.

7. Select Fit options. Options are Fit Proportionally, Center Content, and Frame To Content. Frame to Content sets the images to fit to the frame and then adjusts the horizontal scale to match the vertical scale. Lastly, it fits the frame to the image.

8. Set border width. Border width applies only if fit options are set to Frame to Content.

9. Choose the layer. The layer chosen will be the layer on which both the image and its label (if used) will be placed. Images is the default choice for Layer. If the layer choice is Images and a layer by that name does not exist for the document it will be created.

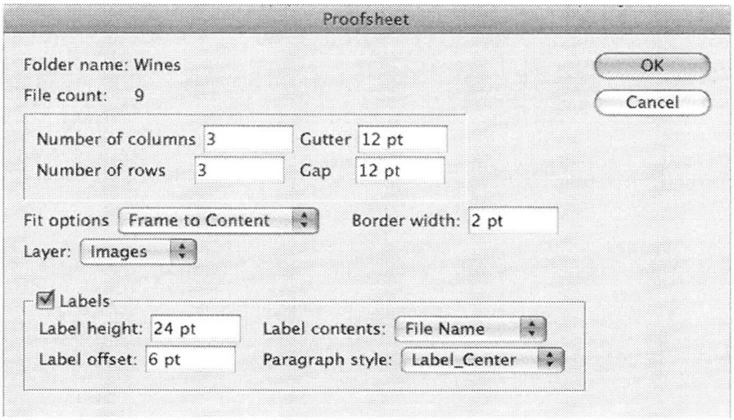

Figure 1.7: Custom dialog for Proofsheet script Accept the default values or experiment with your own. Click OK to create pages for proofing your images.

10. The Labels section is for captions under the images. Check the Labels enabling checkbox if labels are to be included. Label height is the height of the frame for the text. Label offset indicates the spacing between the caption frame and the image.

11. Select options from the dropdowns: Label content and Paragraph style. Click OK.

Depending on the number of images and the speed of your computer, the finished pages are done in no time. (Figure 1.8)

Impressed? This is just the beginning of your journey into the realm of a new working experience. But first we need to cover some basics.

Modify A Script

Two scripts are provided that place tick marks to selected items in a document. The script **Tick Marks**, as with many other scripts in the Application folder of Scripts panel, will run without any modification. Those in the User folder are designed to be customized before becoming useable scripts.

When you ran the **Tick Marks** script you had the option of setting values for the tick marks.

For the majority of times you might want to add tick marks to selected page items, you may not want to be bothered by having to dismiss a dialog. After all, it is likely that you will standardize on the length of your tick marks, the amount of offset, and the width of the line.

For this purpose, the **Ticks** script is provided in the User folder of Scripts panel. To customize the script, locate the script. Control-click on the script to open the context menu. Select Edit Script from the menu. The script will open in AppleScript Editor. Change the values for the variables at the top of the script as needed.

```
--variables
set tickLen to 12 --length of the tick
set ticOffset to 3 --the offset
set lineWt to 0.5 --weight of the line
set layerName to "Furniture"
```

Save the script. Select page items in a document to test the script.

Assign a Keyboard Shortcut to the Script

If you think that you will use this script often, you may want to assign it a keyboard shortcut.

1. Select Keyboard Shortcuts... from InDesign's Edit menu.
2. Create a new set in the Set dropdown by clicking on the New Set button and entering a name for your script set in the Name field. Choose [Default] in the Based On Set dropdown.
3. Select Scripts from the Product Area dropdown.
4. Highlight the script you want to assign from the script list. These are organized by folder.
5. Type your keyboard shortcut in the New Shortcut field. If the shortcut is currently in use it will be indicated in the Currently Assigned to: field. If not available you will need to try again. You may find adding Option+Shift to a keystroke may be an available combination.
6. Leave Default selected for the Context dropdown. Click the Assign button.
7. You can set up any number of keyboard shortcuts. When through, click OK to close.

Now when you want to add ticks to selected items on a page, type your keyboard shortcut.

Camarette_2x3.tif

EdemVinDePay_2x3.tif

Mavette_2x3.tif

StLaurent_2x3.tif

ThreeWines_2x3..tif

WineAndRose_2x3.tif

WinesInARow_2x3.tif

Xavier_2x3.tif

Xavier_Champagne.tif

Figure 1.8: Page created from Proofsheet script. The fit option was set to Fit Frame To Image. This causes the image containers to center within the columns, adding more space between columns than was defined by the user.

Just for Fun

While you are at it, you might want to explore some of the other scripts provided. To illustrate how a script could be used to automate a simple ruled form, the script **Ruled Form** is found in the Automate folder of the scripts panel. When presented the custom dialog, accept the default settings, and click OK. Once you see the result of running the script, you may want to experiment with the settings in the dialog.

Figure 1.9: Form created with Ruled Form script using defaults set in custom dialog.

2

AppleScript Basics

As in any language, AppleScript has its own vocabulary and its own rules for putting words together to create a single thought (*syntax*). A statement in AppleScript is similar to a sentence in English in that it requires a specific structure. A statement is defined by a line return.

Parts of Speech

The Document Editor window in AppleScript Editor will be your new home. Code you will write will include statements that test equality, make comparisons, create objects, and more. To execute code, first click on the Compile button to see if you have made any typographical (or syntactical) errors. If no errors are reported, you can run the script by clicking on the Run button. The Result panel will return the result of the last statement processed. The Event Log panel shows the series of events tracked during execution of the script.

Code Coloring

Enter the following code in the editor.

```
--a simple code example
set str to "Hello World"
set test to length of str
test
```

When you compile the script, the styling of the text changes. Notice that reserved words such as **set, to, of**, and **length** are displayed in a separate style than the rest of the code. This is code coloring. Code coloring can help you by identifying the different "parts of speech" in AppleScript. You can change how your code is colored in the Formatting panel for AppleScript Editor's preferences (Application menu > Preferences). (Figure 2.1) Click on the Formatting icon at the top of the Preference dialog. Here you can set the font, size, and color for language keywords, application keywords, comments, variables, and values. Hint: double click on the color swatch to open the color chooser panel for changing color.

Figure 2.1: Choose Preferences... from AppleScript Editor's application menu to change preference settings.

Try it. Reset some of the colors for the various code elements. Now retype the code introduced at the beginning of the chapter. When you compile the code, notice the difference in the code coloring.

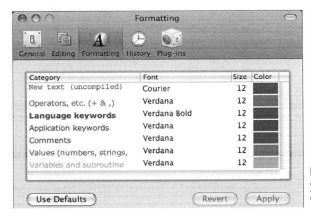

Figure 2.2: Change formatting to help you recognize various parts of speech when your script compiles .

Comments

The first line of the sample script you entered above is a comment. A comment is a note placed in code to help remind yourself, or explain to others, what is happening in the script. Comments are ignored by the computer. A single line comment is preceded by two hyphens.

```
--this is a single line comment
```

A comment that spans more than one line is enclosed in a parenthesis-asterisk pair.

```
(*This is a comment that spans more than one line
Comments are ignored by the computer.*)
```

Variables

A variable identifies a memory location set aside to store data during a script's execution. A variable has a label (identifier) and a value, and is defined by the keyword **set** or **copy**. When you declare a variable you can also give it a value using the keyword **to**.

The second line of your example script declares the variable **str** and gives it a string value. A string is any arrangement of characters within quotation marks--straight quotes only.

```
      assignment    variable keyword    literal string value
          |             |        |              |
        set          str       to      "Hello World"
```

Following are other examples of declaring a variable.

```
set yourName to missing value --variable is declared without a value
set myName to "Mary" --value is a string
set myAge to 21 --value is a number
set amSingle to true --value is boolean (true or false)
copy 16 to yearsOfSchooling --copy used to assign value to variable
```

Variable identifiers are a single word and must begin with a letter, or underscore. All other characters in the variable identifier may be any letter, digit, or underscore. A variable cannot be a word reserved by AppleScript. "Smushing" two words together as in *myVariable* pretty much assures that the identifier will not be a reserved word. Notice how "camel case"—using a capital (hump) in the middle of the identifier—makes it more readable.

Constants and Predefined Variables

AppleScript's predefined variables for the characters **space**, **tab**, and **return** are often mistakenly referred to as constants. The following is a list of constants recognized by AppleScript:

```
all caps, all lowercase, small caps
case, punctuation, diacriticals, white space
plain, bold, condensed, italic, outline, expanded
subscript, superscript
strikethrough, underline, shadow
date and time, such as names of the months and weekdays
true, false
yes, no, ask
application responses, current application
hidden
```

Predefined variables are similar to constants with the exception that their values can be changed. A list of predefined variables follows:

```
return, tab, space
me, my, it
anything
missing value
result
version
pi
```

Properties

Properties are attributes of an object that make the object unique. A string has one property—length. This property is *read only* indicating that the property cannot be assigned by a script.

To get the value for a property the keyword **of** is used, as in:

```
assignment  variable  keyword   property  keyword  variable
    |          |         |          |         |        |
   set       test       to       length      of     myStr
```

You can also use possessive notation to get the value of a property as in:

```
set test to myStr's length
```

Alternatively you can place a statement within a `tell` block to an object to get a value of a property, as in:

```
set myStr to "Hello World"
tell myStr
    set test to length
end tell
```

Reference

When an object is created, a reference to the object (*object reference*) is created. This reference can be assigned to a variable to identify the object later in a script. In addition to its object reference, an object can be identified in a script using one of the following:

- **Index** - The numerical location of the item or range of items within a collection. You can also use the keywords **last, first,** or **middle.**
  In addition to using numbers, the ordinal counterparts such as first, second, up to tenth can be used to reference an object. You can also use any integer followed by its ordinal ending, such as 20th, 13th, and so on.
- **Id** - A unique number assigned the object when it is created; read only.
- **Name** - A unique string value you can assign an object.
- **Arbitrary** - Returned as result of using the keyword **some.**
- **Relative** - Relationship to another object using keywords **before** or **after.**
- **Meeting a Test** - Using the **every** object specifier (with or without a filter).

Data Types

AppleScript is referred to as being "loosely typed" as you do not need to tell a script what kind of data is being stored in a variable. You can designate a value will be stored as a specific type using the keyword **as.** You will see a number of examples of this as you progress in the book.

String

When you place quotes (straight quotes only) around a series of letters, spaces, and other characters, you tell AppleScript the value is data type **string.** As seen previously, a string has a single property, **length,** designating the number of characters in the string. A string contains elements such as characters and words. A text element is determined by AppleScript's text item delimiters which by default is an empty string.

```
set test to AppleScript's text item delimiters --result is {""}
```

Text elements are returned as a list (see discussion of List following).

```
set test to text items of "Now"
```

Elements of a string are character, word, paragraph, text, and text item.

```
set str to "Now is the time to test"
set test to count of words in str --returns 6
```

Change the test statement to:

```
set test to count of characters in str --returns 23
```

To combine strings, the concatenation operator is used:

```
set userName to "Mary"
set testStr to "My name is " & userName
--result is "My name is Mary"
```

The **offset** command indicates where a substring begins within a string:

```
set theOffset to offset of "e" in "Hello"
--result is 2
```

Numbers

Numerical values can be classed as **real**, or **integer**. An integer can hold any number from -536,870,911 to 536,70,911. Placing a decimal after an integer value converts the integer to a real (*automatic coercion*).

```
set testNumber to 123.45
class of testNumber --result is real

set testNumber to 1234567
class of testNumber --result is integer

set testNumber to 123.0
class of testNumber --result is real
```

Date

The **date** keyword converts a compatible string value into a date object.

Enter the following in the editor:

```
set theDate to date "12/26/2010"
```

When you compile the script, the date string is converted to AppleScript's default date format, complete with day of the week and a default time:

```
date "Sunday, December 26, 2010 12:00:00 AM"
```

To get the string value for the current date, the **current date** command is used. (You will find this command in the Miscellaneous Commands suite of Standard Additions.)

To get the individual parts of a date, **month of, day of, weekday of,** and **year of** are some of the qualifiers used.

```
set theDate to current date
set theMonth to month of theDate
set theDay to day of theDate
set theYear to year of theDate
set dateString to (theMonth & " " & theDay & ", " & theYear) as string
```

List

Referred to as an array in other languages, a **list** is a collection of values represented by a single variable. A list can contain a mixture of data types, even other lists.

```
set str to "A list can contain different data types"
set listVar to {str, 12345, {"a", "b"}, pi}
listVar --result is {"A list can contain different data types", 12345,
{"a", "b"}, 3.14159265359}
```

Notice that a list is enclosed by curly braces with a comma separating each list member. Lists have three properties:

- **length** - Returns number of items in the list.
- **rest** - Returns list with all members with exception of the first.
- **reverse** - Returns the list in reverse order.

Members of a list are identified by their position within the list which is one-based (starts with 1, not 0 as in other languages).

Items are added to a list by setting the beginning or end of the list to the value.

```
set listVar to {12, 24, 36, 48}
set end of listVar to 12345
listVar--result is {12, 24, 36, 48, 12345}

set listVar to {12, 24, 36, 48}
copy 12345 to beginning of listVar
listVar--result is {12345, 12, 24, 36, 48}
```

You can also use the concatenation operator to add items to lists and lists to lists.

```
set listVar to {12, 24, 36, 48}
set test to listVar & 12345
test--result is {12, 24, 36, 48, 12345}
```

This is just the tip of the iceberg of what you can do with lists.

Record

A record is similar to a list in that a single variable represents a number of elements. However the elements within a record are labeled, consisting of an identifier followed by a colon and then a value.

```
set bookRecord to {name:"AppleScripting Adobe InDesign CS5", ¬
author:"S.Hopkins", pages:320}
```

Instead of identifying a value by its index as in a list, the value of a record element is returned using its identifier. For the statement above,

```
set numPages to pages of bookRecord --result is 320
```

Continuation Character (¬)

The continuation character symbol is used in printed code listings to indicate that the statement continues to the next line (without a return). If you enter the code into AppleScript Editor, don't place a return at the end of the line; keep typing and let the editor wrap the lines for you.

Testing Equality and Making Comparisons

AppleScript uses mathematical symbols to evaluate and compare values. These work the same in AppleScript as they did in your math classes in school. With comparison operators, the item on the right of the symbol is compared with the item on the left.

Operators

An operator is a reserved token that converts one or more values into a new value. The act of changing values is called an *operation*. The values being acted upon are the *operands*. Some of the more common operators are outlined below.

Mathematical Operators

Mathematical operators in AppleScript work the same as you would expect:

Add (+)   `set myVariable to 2 + 4 --result is 6`

Subtract(-)   `set myVariable to 4 - 2 --result is 2`

Multiply (*)   `set myVariable to 4 * 2 --result is 8`

Divide (/)   `set myVariable to 4/2 --result is 2`

Exponentiation (^) `set myVariable to 2 ^ 2 --result is 4.0`

Integer division (div) `set myVariable to 5 div 2 --result is 2`

Modulo (mod)   `set myVariable to 5 mod 2 --result is 1`

Modulo returns the remainder of a division. To determine if a given number is odd or even modulo comes in handy.

```
set isEvenNumber to 22 mod 2
--returns 0 indicating number is even
```

Comparison Operators

Is, is equal to (=) - `set isEqual to 5 = 4 --result is false`

Is not, is not equal to (≠) - `set notEqual to 5 ≠ 4 --result is true`

Less than (<) - `set lessThan to 5 < 4 --result is false`

Greater than (>) - `set greaterThan to 5 > 4 --result is true`

Less than or equal to (≤) - `set lessOrEqual to 5 ≤ 4 --result is false`

Greater than or equal to (≥) - `set greaterOrEqual to 5 ≥ 4 --result is true`

You can also spell out operators as in

```
set isEqual to 5 is equal to 4 --result is false

set greaterOrEqual to 5 is greater than or equal to 4 --result is true
```

Logical Operators

Logical operators work with true/false values (Boolean algebra).

Logical and - Returns true if all comparisons are true. If even one of the comparisons is false, the result is false,

```
set isTrue to (10 > 5) and (5 > 3) and (7 > 2) --result true
set isTrue to (10 > 5) and (3 > 5) and (7 > 2) --result false
```

Logical or - Returns true if any of the statements are true. Once a comparison evaluates to true, no further evaluations are made.

```
set isTrue to (5 < 10) or (5 > 3) or (2 > 7) --result true
set isTrue to (5 > 10) or (3 > 5) or (2 > 7) --result false
```

Logical not - Negates a comparison (changes false to true; true to false).

```
set isTrue to not (10 > 5) --returns fals
```

You will have plenty of opportunity to see these operators in action as you work with the examples in the book.

Containment

Containment can imply a comparison between two strings, lists, or records. The result is true or false (boolean).

```
set test to ("Hello World") contains "hello" --result is true

set test to {"Hello", "World"} contains "hello" --result is true

set test to {name: "George", age: 42} contains "george" --result is true
```

You can force case consideration by using a **considering case** block

```
considering case
    set test to "Hello World" contains "hello" --result is false
end considering

considering case
    set test to {"Hello World"} contains "hello" --result is false
end considering

considering case
    set test to {name: "George", age: 42} contains "george"
    --result is false
end considering
```

You can test for more than one item in a list, but the items must be in order to evaluate.

```
set test to {1, 2, 3} contains {1, 2} --result is true
set test to {1, 2, 3} contains {1, 3} --result is false
```

Concatenation

The concatenation operator (**&**) joins two or more strings, lists, and records.

```
set myName to "John"
set test to "My name is " & myName -result is "My name is John"
```

You can concatenate values having different classes but the class on the left will change the class of the value on the right if possible (*automatic coercion*). Otherwise the result is a list.

```
set test to "twenty" & 3 --result is "twenty3"

set test to 3 & "twenty" --result is {3, "twenty"}
```

You can add strings to lists, and lists to lists.

```
set test to {"one"} & "two" & "three" --result {"one", "two", "three"}

set test to {"one"} & {"two" & " three"} --result {"one", "two three"}

set test to {name: "John"} & {age: 21} -- result {name:"John", age:21}
```

Exists

Recognized by the Finder, System Events, and in the Standard Suite for Adobe InDesign, **exists** is used to verify an object. The result of an exists statement is a boolean.

Branching

When a script allows two or more options for code execution, we say that it branches. One way to create a branch is using a conditional **if** statement.

If Statement Block

Comparison and equality operators are used in an **if** statement. The result of a comparison operation determines the branch the code will use. Let's test a one-line **if** statement. Enter the following code in the editor. You will need to have sound turned on to hear the beep.

```
if (8 < 10) then beep
```

Note that if statements are more commonly written as blocks of code using **if** to begin and **end if** to end the statement block. More commonly the code above would be written:

```
if (8 < 10) then
    beep
end if
```

If/Else

If the result of an **if** statement is false, an alternative statement inside an **else** block executes. In the following code, the variable *myValue* is assigned the value of 8. If the value of *myValue* is greater than 0, the value of the *myBoolean* variable is true. Otherwise, the code in the **else** statement executes, setting the result value to false. Enter the code in the editor and test. Look for the result in the Result panel.

```
set myValue to 8
if myValue > 10 then
    set myBoolean to true
else
    set myBoolean to false
end if
```

If/Else If

The **else if** clause can serve to perform another **if** test, allowing the statements following the keyword **else if** to execute if the test returns true. Try this script using different values for the variable *age*. Review the result to verify the code that executes based on the value of *age*.

```
set age to 22
if (age ≤ 12) then
    set ageBracket to "youth"
else if (age < 21) then
    set ageBracket to "teenager"
else
    set ageBracket to "adult"
end if
```

You could test just for age being equal to "teenager" using the following. Notice the use of the logical **and** operator:

```
set ageBracket to missing value
set age to 14
```

```
if (age > 12) and (age < 21) then
    set ageBracket to "teenager"
end if
ageBracket
```

Evaluations

Evaluations and operations are performed before any other process within a statement. AppleScript has its own order of precedence to determine the order in which operations take place. Parentheses can be used (as in mathematics) to determine order.

User Interaction

Beep

You have been introduced to the **beep** command as part of the discussion on branching. Beep can be used to give the user an audible indication that a problem has occurred, or that the script has completed. The beep command takes one optional parameter, an integer, that indicates the number of times the beep should occur.

```
beep 2
```

Beep is often used in conjunction with a **return** statement, exiting the script from the current routine. If sound is not enabled on the computer, beep has no effect.

Say

A more friendly way to give the user an audible message is to **say** it. Leave this option for more friendly or non-critical messages as the user may have sound turned down or off. The say command performs text-to-speech, either speaking text or saving synthesized speech as a sound file. There are a number of voices available. The files for these in OS 5 are found in the System:Library:Speech:Voices folder. You will find a fun script, **Say To File**, in Chapter 7 that saves the text of a **say** command to an .aiff file.

Dialogs

AppleScript provides two dialogs for communicating with the user: **display dialog** and **display alert**. These are referred to as *modal* dialogs in that the dialog window must be closed before any other process can be performed in the application. The following discussion provides a brief overview of the dialogs created using the commands **display dialog** and **display alert**.

Display Dialog

Display dialog requires one piece of information: a string value (*text*) that will display to the user. The information used with a command such as *text* for display dialog are called *parameters*. Display dialog has a number of optional parameters which determine if the dialog will act as a message, input, or alert dialog. For a full listing of its optional parameters you will find display dialog listed in the User Interaction section of the Standard Additions dictionary. (Choose Open Dictionary... from AppleScript Editor's File menu and click on Standard Additions in the list of applications presented.)

Parameters enclosed in square brackets are optional. Here are a couple of examples to get your creative juices flowing:

```
--you can define up to three buttons for a display dialog
set str to "Choose Your Option"
display dialog str buttons {"Now", "Later", "Forget It"} ¬
default button "Now" giving up after 2
```

Notice the continuation character in the code listing above.

Try running the previous script without clicking on a button. Verify the result returned when the dialog "gives up." The **giving up after** parameter defines the amount of time, in seconds, for the dialog to wait before giving up. In the example above giving up after has a value of 2.

The **hidden answer** parameter hides the text entered by the user in a display dialog. This can be used for a dialog requiring the user to enter a password.

```
set str to "Enter your password"
display dialog str with title "WELCOME" default answer "" ¬
default button 2 with hidden answer
```

Run the script and enter a password in the text frame presented. Verify the result of the script in the Result panel.

Cancel Button

The **cancel button** parameter gives cancel button behavior to the button indicated within the button list. This can be an index value or string value.

```
set test to display dialog "You have been warned" with title "WARNING" ¬
buttons {"OK", "Not Interested"} cancel button 2 with icon stop
test
```

Notice that when a button with cancel behavior is clicked, there is no result returned to the result window as it throws an error "User Cancelled." With both display dialog and display alert, you can designate a button to be a cancel button. A button with the title "Cancel" is automatically given cancel button behavior. Because of the potential error condition, practice is to provide try/error traps to handle the error (discussion below). If you do not want to handle the user clicking the Cancel button as an error, add a space to the title of the Cancel button as in the example following;

```
set thePrompt to "Enter your first name"
set defaultName to ""
set dialogTitle to "User name dialog"
set userResponse to display dialog thePrompt default answer defaultName ¬
with title dialogTitle buttons {"OK", " Cancel"} default button 1
if button returned of userResponse is " Cancel" then
    display alert "User cancelled"
else if length of text returned of userResponse = 0 then
    display alert "You did not enter your name"
else
    display alert "Hello " & text returned of userResponse
end if
```

Display Alert

Display alert is similar to display dialog. It is designed to be used for sending messages only (not for user input). It has two parameters not available for display dialog: **message** and **as**.

- **Message** - Allows for a second line of text to be displayed in smaller text below the main text.

- **As** - Determines the type of icon that will be displayed in the dialog.

```
set msg to "This is a test, only a test"
set prompt to "Warning you are about to crash"
display alert prompt message msg as warning buttons {"Ouch!", ¬
"Really?", "Not Interested"} default button 2 giving up after 5
```

Error Conditions

There are times within a script an error (*exception*) may occur. When a user clicks a button designated to be a cancel button the error "User Cancelled." number -128 may be generated. Few scripts ever written could get by without code to catch and/or throw an error.

Catching Errors

When an error condition occurs, your script needs to provide some way for the script to gracefully exit while at the same time alerting the user to the problem. The **try/end try** script block provides this functionality. Whenever there is a possibility of code (or the user) producing an error, standard practice dictates that the statements be surrounded with a **try/end try** block.

Within a **try/end try** block any error that occurs will be ignored unless an **on error** statement is included. The on error statement causes script execution to branch to the statements following. You can set up variables to receive the text of the error and the error number. In the example below, the variable *errStr* is used for the error string and *errNumber* for the error number. The second button is set up to be a cancel button, so clicking it will throw the error.

```
try
    set test to display dialog "You have been warned" with title ¬
    "WARNING" buttons {"OK", "Not Interested"} cancel button 2¬
     with icon stop
on error errStr number errNumber
    display alert "Error " & errNumber & ": " & errStr
end try
```

Throwing Errors

The **error** command allows a script to create its own specific error. The parameter supplied the **error** command will be the value of the variable received in the **on error** statement. One way this can be useful is to allow testing for a number of conditions within a single **try** statement block as in the following. This script example requires InDesign to be running. The version of the application is indicated in the first line of code (tell statement). If this does not match the version you are using, change it accordingly. With the application version changed as needed in the `tell` statement, this code should work with every version of InDesign.

```
--checks for a number of conditions within one try/end try statement
tell application "Adobe InDesign CS5"
    try
        if modal state = true then
            error ("Modal state exists")
        end if
        if (count of documents) = 0 then
            error ("Requires an active document")
        end if
    on error errStr
        display alert errStr
    end try
end tell
```

Modal State

If there is a modal dialog open in InDesign, a script will fail to execute. Your script can test for this condition by checking the **modal state** property for the application. If modal state for the application is true, a modal window is open and must be closed before the script can run.

Understanding Handlers

A handler (called a function in other programming languages) is nothing more than a number of statements bundled together to perform a specific set of instructions. A handler can begin with the keyword **on** or **to** followed by the identifier for the handler. A parentheses pair follows the identifier. This can be empty or provide variables and values to be passed to the handler. The code block for a handler ends with the keyword **end** followed by the handler identifier. Between these two statements any number of lines of code performs the desired functionality. To call the handler, its identifier is placed in a line of code followed by a parentheses pair which may contain information to be passed to the handler.

For example, this code calls the handler **getFullName**:

```
set firstName to "George"
set lastName to "Washington"
set fullName to getFullName (firstName, lastName)
```

The handler **getFullName** combines the first and last names passed and passes the result back to the calling statement where it becomes the value for the *fullName* variable.

```
on getFullName (firstName, lastName)
    set fullName to firstName & " " & lastName
    return fullName
end getFullName
```

After the script runs, the Result panel displays "George Washington"

Although this is a simplistic example, you might imagine how this handler could be incorporated into a script that works with information found in a database where the *firstName* and *lastName* are returned as separate values from a database query.

The values passed and received by the handler are called **positional parameters**. The values sent and the receiving variables must be in the same order.

One of the advantages of using handlers is that you can divide a script into separate discrete steps. Each step can be executed by a handler. This way each step of the script can be written and tested individually making the process of script writing much cleaner and easier to manage.

A second advantage, and one we will use throughout the book, is that handlers are reusable. Once you have code that works the way you want it, convert the statements to a handler and add it to a library. These handlers can then be used in any number of scripts. You might think of this methodology similar to building super structures using "Lego" building blocks.

Additionally, because you copied the appropriate Handlers folder (CS5 Handlers or CS5.5 Handlers) to the AppleScript Editor Scripts folder (see Chapter 1), you now have a full library of handlers ready to use. The following discussion provides some examples.

Handlers Library

To avoid redundancy, the terminology **Handlers Library** will be used throughout the remainder of the book to reference the files in the CS5 Handlers and CS5.5 Handlers folders, which ever one you are using.

---

getBoolean

Often your scripts may need to get a true or false response. The handler **getBoolean** found in the Dialogs folder of the Handlers Library can be used. It provides for two parameters: a prompt string, and a boolean indicating if the False button ("No") should be the default.

```
set userPrompt to "Do you want to continue?"
set falseAsDefault to true
set userResponse to getBoolean(userPrompt, falseAsDefault)

--asks for a true false response
on getBoolean(userPrompt, falseAsDefault)
    set defaultButton to 1
    set buttonList to {"Yes", " No"}
    if falseAsDefault then
        set defaultButton to 2
    end if
    activate
    set userResponse to display alert userPrompt buttons buttonList ¬
    default button defaultButton
    return (button returned of userResponse = "Yes")
end getBoolean
```

getDateStamp

Let's say within a project you need to append a six-number date stamp (MMDDYY) to the end of a file name. For this the **getDateStamp** handler is provided in the Date Time folder.

Start a new script. Hold down the control key as you click in the edit window (control-click). In the context menu, locate the folder for your Handlers Library. Hover over this entry to get its flyout menu. Highlight the folder for Date Time and click on the entry for **getDateStamp** in the sub-menu presented. The code is placed in your script window. It will be highlighted until you click inside the window. Compile and then run the script.

Next time you need to add a date stamp to a string, just make sure the **getDateStamp** handler is tucked away somewhere at the bottom of your script. Use the sample code provided to call the handler. Notice that this handler does not need any additional information, so the parentheses pair is empty. Next we will look at an example of a function that requires information (parameters) to be passed as part of its call.

Order of Precedence

If more than one operation is used in a single statement, AppleScript has its own rules as to the order in which the operations are performed. To ensure that operations take place the way you want them, use parentheses. Just as in mathematics, operations take place from the innermost bracketed sets outward. Notice how bracketing is used in the getDateStamp handler. This version of getDateStamp uses a mathematical algorithm based on the number of seconds in an average month to derive the month number. There are other ways of extracting the month number from current date, but this has been a tried and true method we have used for years.

For another method for extracting the month number from current date, you might try the following. This version works depending on the version of AppleScript you (or your user) has installed.

```
set d to (current date)
set theMonth to month of d as number
```

getRandom

The random number command returns a somewhat random number from 0 to 1. Random number is part of the Miscellaneous Commands suite in StandardAdditions. Optional parameters can indicate the range within which the random number will be returned.

Providing a number for the command will define the upper limit for the random number. If using the single number parameter, the parameters **from** and **to** will be ignored.

```
--results in a number from 0 to 6 inclusive
set r to random number 6

--results in a number from 1 to 6 inclusive
set r to random number from 1 to 6
```

You can also provide a seed number, but for most purposes this is not used.

There is not much code involved for generating a random number. When random numbers are involved, chances are your script will need to have a random number generated more than once within a script. For this the **getRandom** handler is provided. In the event you forget how to write a random number generator, you will find the handler in the Calculate folder of your Handlers Library.

```
--declare variables
set minValue to 1
set maxValue to 6
--call handler
set r to getRandom(minValue, maxValue)

--handler
on getRandom(minValue, maxValue)
    set rNumber to random number from minValue to maxValue
    return rNumber
end getRandom
```

roundTo

This handler works with decimals and is found in the Calculate folder of your Handlers Library. (Control-click in AppleScript Editor's edit window and navigate to the Calculate folder. Click on the listing for **roundTo**. In the script change the values for the two variables: *theNumber* and *thePlaces*. Run the script and check the Result panel.

```
--sample call to roundTo handler
set theNumber to 1234.5678
set thePlaces to 2
set roundedNumber to roundTo (theNumber, thePlaces)
(*Rounds a number to nearest decimal given decimal places.*)

on roundTo(theNumber, thePlaces)
    if class of theNumber is not integer then
        set theRound to (round (theNumber * (10 ^ thePlaces)))
        set theNumber to theRound / (10 ^ thePlaces)
    end if
    return theNumber
end roundTo
```

Make Scripts Work for You

This section will have you create a simple script just to get you started using handlers. As part of the procedure for installing the book's support resources, the Handlers Library should be installed in either of the following locations (see Chapter 1):

```
[Macintosh HD]:Library:Scripts:AppleScript Editor Scripts:CS5 Handlers
[Macintosh HD]:Library:Scripts:AppleScript Editor Scripts:CS5.5 Handlers
```

1. Start a new script.
2. Hold the control key down and click inside AppleScript Editor's edit window.
3. Navigate to the handler **getNumber** inside the Dialogs folder in your Handlers Library.
4. Click on the entry for **getNumber** to load it to your script.
5. Click on the Compile button to compile the script. Run the script as is.
6. In the script, change the values for the variables within the call section as follows (or use any values of your own):

```
userPrompt: "What is your favorite number?"
defaultAnswer: "0"
dialogTitle: "GETTING TO KNOW YOU"
```

7. Compile the script and correct any errors.
8. Run the script. Enter a number in the entry field and click OK, or click Cancel. Verify the result in the Result panel.

3

Working With Adobe InDesign

Now that you are familiar with AppleScript's Editor and some basic principles of the AppleScript language, it is time to put your skills to work with your favorite application, Adobe InDesign CS5 (or 5.5). As with many applications, InDesign's structure is hierarchal in nature. This means that each object, with the exception of the application, can be both a parent (container) for other objects as well as a child (element) of another object. This relationship allows a script to reference a particular object based on its hierarchy. Every application that is open to AppleScript, publishes a dictionary that defines its terminology: its objects, their properties, and the commands they understand. To tell AppleScript you will be using the terms belonging to an application's dictionary, you wrap your statements in a **tell** block directed to the application. Be sure to change the application version number as needed.

```
tell application "Adobe InDesign CS5"
--statements that use InDesign's dictionary
end tell
```

Adobe InDesign Versions

All scripts in this book will run in version 5.5 of InDesign. Although the tell statements designate "Adobe InDesign CS5", if CS5.5 is the active application, the tell statement will update to version CS5.5 when the script is compiled. Some scripts for this book will only run in version 5.5. They will be designated as such and will target "Adobe InDesign CS5.5" in the tell statement.

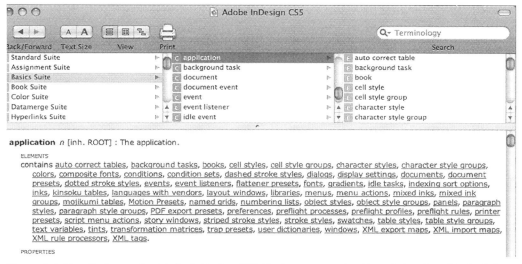

Figure 3.1: The dictionary for Adobe InDesign CS5. Topics are organized into Suites listed in the left hand column. The dictionary opens by default to the Standard Suite.

To understand this concept, let's look at InDesign's Dictionary. From within AppleScript Editor, choose Open Dictionary... from the File menu. Find the version of your application in the list and click on it. The dictionary is pretty big so it may take a second or two to load up.

Once the dictionary is open, you can see the interface looks similar to that for Scripting Additions.(Figure 3-1)/ Topics are categorized in suites listed in the panel on the left. Click on the Basics Suite.

Notice within the Basics Suite you have commands (blue "C" circle icons) and objects (purple "C" square icons). Click on the icon for **application**. There you are presented an extensive list of all of the objects that relate directly to the application (elements). The elements and properties for the application are listed in the far right column. Elements have a brown "E" square icon while properties have a purple "P" square icon.

If you can't find the object you are interested in, type its identifier in the inspect field at top right (magnifying glass icon).

Try it. Type Page in the box. Suddenly you will have every conceivable topic that has to do with a **page**: **active page**, **add page**s, **all page items**, **insert blank page**; and the list goes on.

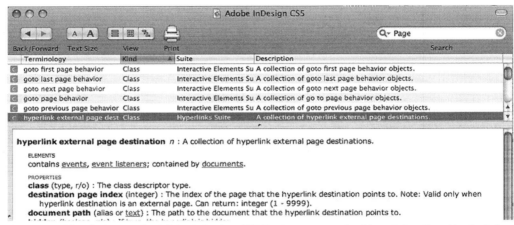

Figure 3.2: The dictionary for Adobe InDesign CS5. Topics are organized into Suites listed in the left hand column. The dictionary opens by default to the Standard Suite.

Click on an item that looks interesting to you. Take a minute to look through its listing.

Click the back arrow at the top left of the interface to return back to the Basics Suite and the application. Notice in the list of properties for the application is **active document**. The data type for active document is, not surprisingly, **document**.

Click on the word **document** inside of the parentheses and you are taken to the document page where you can see its properties. Notice the extensive list of elements that are related directly to the document. At the end of the "contains" list is a "contained by" list. In the case of a document, it can only be contained by application.

Commands

Commands common to objects in InDesign are found in the Standard Suite. Click on the **count** command for example. You will see that count is a command (v for verb) and returns the number of elements for the specified class within the object. Put the information presented into a script. Requires document open containing a story.

```
tell application "Adobe InDesign CS5"
    set theString to paragraph 1 of story -1 of document 1
    tell theString
        count words
    end tell
end tell
```

If there is a document open having a paragraph in story -1 the result of running the script will be an integer. The little arrow pointing to the word integer in the dictionary's description for **count** indicates the class of the result that will be returned.

Instead of using a plural reference as in the above (count words), you can use the keywords **each** or **every**:

```
tell application "Adobe InDesign CS5"
    set theString to paragraph 1 of story -1 of document 1
    set theCount to count each word of theString
end tell
```

Again, if story -1 of document 1 exists, the result of this code will be an integer. Otherwise an error condition will be raised.

You will find the dictionary to be an invaluable aid in working with scripts. So give it "best friend" status.

The following discussion is designed to clarify working with InDesign's hierarchal structure.

Tell

To designate the application that is the object for a statement, a tell block is used. A tell block can be one line as in:

```
tell application "Adobe InDesign CS5" to activate
```

More commonly, a tell block will consist of many lines "blocked" using the word tell at the beginning and end tell at the end

```
tell application "Adobe InDesign CS5"
    activate
    --other statements directed to the application
end tell
```

The command **activate** causes the target application to launch if not already running; otherwise it brings the application to the front.

Nesting Tells

An object within the application's hierarchy can send and receive events relative to its position in the hierarchy. For instance, a document as an element of the application, can be addressed using a tell statement inside of the application's tell statement block (a nested tell block):

```
tell application "Adobe InDesign CS5"
    tell document 1
    --statements directed to the document
    close
    end tell --document
end tell --application
```

Instead of using a nested tell, you can refer to a document as an element of the application using the keyword of, so the script above could be written:

```
tell active document of application "Adobe InDesign CS5"
    close
end tell
```

This could also be written as a one-line statement:

```
tell active document of application "Adobe InDesign CS5" to close
```

Within a tell statement to the application the front-most document can be referenced as active document or document 1. It can also be referenced by its name.

To demonstrate InDesign's object hierarchy, the following **Hello World** script is offered as an example. This script introduces the **geometric bounds** property of a page item. Bounds is a list that describes the item's geometric location within space. In the case of a page item, that space is the page. The items in the bounds list define the object's top vertical, left horizontal, bottom vertical, and right horizontal measurement units as in {top, left, bottom, right}. (More on bounds in the next chapter.)

Hello World

```
--bounds values for the text frame is a list of 4 values
set gBounds to {"3p0", "3p0", "6p0", "12p0"}
tell application "Adobe InDesign CS5"
    make document
    tell document 1
        tell spread 1
            tell page 1
                make text frame
                tell text frame 1
                    set geometric bounds to gBounds
                    set text 1 to "Hello World"
                end tell --text frame
            end tell --page
        end tell --spread
    end tell --document
end tell --application
```

Notice in the above that elements within the application are referenced using an index value (tell document 1, etc.). When an object is created at the beginning of its container it is given an index value of 1. Objects can also be referenced by their name, by id, and using an object reference.

Object Reference

When an object is created, a reference to the object is held in a temporary variable—the **result**. Placing this value into a variable allows the script to refer to the object by means of the variable. As part of creating an object its properties can be defined within a property record as part of the **make** statement. With this in mind, the **Hello World** script could also be written as follows:

```
--bounds values for the text frame is list of 4 values
set gBounds to {"3p0", "3p0", "6p0", "12p0"}
tell application "Adobe InDesign CS5"
```

```
    --place reference to document created in variable docRef
    set docRef to make document
    --refer to the document using the variable
    tell page 1 of spread 1 of docRef
       --define properties for the text frame in a record
       make text frame with properties {geometric bounds:gBounds, ¬
       contents:"Hello World"}
    end tell --page reference
end tell --application
```

Continuation Character

When the text of a statement is longer than the physical length of the printed line, the continuation character (¬) is used. Do not use this character in your scripts. Instead, let your script editor wrap the lines for you.

Terminology

When working with InDesign you will need to be able to define and test objects for their class and properties.

Class

As mentioned in the previous chapter, class is the blueprint from which an object is built. This includes its characteristics (properties) and the commands available to its members. To get the class for an object within an InDesign document, select the object and run the following:

```
tell application "Adobe InDesign CS5"
    if exists selection then
       get class of item 1 of selection
    end if
end tell
```

If no object is selected, nothing will happen. If at least one object is selected, the class of the first object is returned. Go ahead; create an object in an InDesign document. Select it and run the script above. View the result in the Result panel for the editor.

Properties

Properties can be thought of as the attributes of an object. Visible or otherwise, properties can be defined (or changed) using values within a script. The value currently associated with an object's property can be returned using **get**.

```
tell application "Adobe InDesign CS5"
    get properties
end tell
```

Running this script will return an extensive record of all of the properties which are available for the application class. To get a specific property, the property's label is used:

```
tell application "Adobe InDesign CS5"
    get user interaction level of script preferences
end tell
```

The values for **user interaction level** can be one of several enumeration values reserved by InDesign: never interact, interact with self, or interact with all. To set the properties for an object, a script can set its value as in the following:

```
--setting interaction level to never interact disables InDesign's dialogs
tell application "Adobe InDesign CS5"
    set user interaction level of script preferences to never interact
end tell
```

Alternatively, a property can be set as part of a property record:

```
tell application "Adobe InDesign CS5"
    tell script preferences
        set properties to {user interaction level: interact with all}
    end tell
end tell
```

If it is not apparent by now, using a simple script can return a lot of information about an object. This is often a quick way to see just how to write a statement: Create an object, select it, and get its reference and/or properties using a script.

Preferences

If you look through the properties for the application and the document, you will discover that some preferences such as **dictionary preferences, document preferences,** and the various export and import preferences are properties of both the application and document. The difference is that preferences set at the application level are *persistent*. Persistent values remain as set until changed. All documents created thereafter will have these preference values by default. (The same as setting preferences in InDesign manually with no document open.)

Preferences set for the document only apply to the document itself. The document inherits the property values in effect for the application otherwise. An example of setting a default preference is the following that sets measurement units to points. Points are often used as the unit of measurement in scripts as they are an easy base unit to work with mathematically.

```
tell application "Adobe InDesign CS5"
    set properties of view preferences to {horizontal measurement ¬
    units:points, vertical measurement units:points}
end tell
```

Important

For the sake of simplicity some script examples will assume that measurement units have been set to points. If not set specifically, and your current units are set otherwise, the script will most likely error out with a message such as "this operation will place an object off the clipboard." If you get such a message, check your measurement units.

If you need to set a number of preference properties, you may wish to target the preference in a tell statement.

```
tell application "Adobe InDesign CS5"
    tell document preferences
        set properties to {facing pages:false, master text frame:true, ¬
        page height:"11 in", page width:"8.5 in", pages per document:1,¬
```

```
        document bleed top offset:"1p0", document bleed uniform size:true}
    end tell
end tell
```

Caution

In setting preferences at the application level you will want to keep a record of what the original settings were before you changed them. That way you can revert the settings back to the original settings when needed

---

Working With Objects

The following is an overview of some of the objects you may be working with in InDesign. A more complete discussion for many of these objects will be found in subsequent chapters.

Document Preset

A **document preset** is a named collection of document properties whose values are predefined. When it comes to creating documents in InDesign using a script, presets are used extensively. Specific property values not assigned for the preset default to those established for the "[Default]" preset. Some statements to work with presets follow.

```
--get name of all presets
tell application "Adobe InDesign CS5"
    set presetList to name of every document preset
end tell

--determine if a particular preset exists
tell application "Adobe InDesign CS5"
    set itExists to exists document preset "Letter"
end tell

--create document using a preset; insert a valid name for "PresetName"
tell application "Adobe InDesign CS5"
    set docRef to make document with properties ¬
    {document preset: "PresetName"}
end tell
```

Window, Layout Window, Story Window

The **active window** property for the application can be a window, layout window, or story window. If a story window is open and selected, the active window refers to the story window. In this event, the following script would produce an error:

```
tell application "Adobe InDesign CS5"
    set theSpread to active spread of active window
end tell
```

To avoid the possible conflict, you may wish to reference the active layout window as layout window 1. Substitute in the previous script:

```
set theSpread to active spread of layout window 1
```

Properties of the layout window you may use often are **active layer, active page, active spread, selection, transform reference point**, and **zoom percentage**.

You can create a document without its window open and then create the window once all of the processing has completed. This is very efficient as the window does not need to redraw and update itself as items are created.

```
tell application "Adobe InDesign CS5"
    set docRef to make document without showing window
    say "Processing items " using "Junior"
    tell docRef to make window
end tell
```

Caution:

If writing code to run on InDesign Server, avoid statements that include the word "active." InDesign Server has no concept of what "active" is.

Be aware when a document is first created, page 1 is the active page. After that, active page will refer to the page that is currently displayed, not necessarily the page last touched by the user. Try it.

Create a facing page document with 4 pages. Create a page item on page 2 of the document. With the page item selected, use the slider at the bottom of the window to switch to page 3. Run the following:

```
tell application "Adobe InDesign CS5"
    set test to name of active page of layout window 1
end tell
```

Instead, to get a reference to the page for a page item selected, use the item's **parent page** property. The parent page property is new with InDesign CS5.

```
(*Requires page item selection. Will not work with versions prior to 5.0.*)
tell application "Adobe InDesign CS5"
    if exists selection then
        set selRef to item 1 of selection
        set pageName to name of parent page of selRef
    end if
end tell
```

Application/Document Specific

As with preferences, there are some object classes that are shared by both the application and the document. Of note are **text defaults, swatch, color, tint, gradient, character style, paragraph style,** and **ink.** The settings for these classes become defaults when created at the application level (*application context*).

Font

The **font** object at the application level returns a list of all of the fonts available for InDesign. At the document level, the font object is only aware of those fonts used in the document.

```
tell document 1 of application "Adobe InDesign CS5"
    set fontName to name of fonts
end tell
```

Selection

Selection is a property of the application, document, a layout window, story window, or window. The **selection** property returns a list of the objects that are selected. If there is no selection, an empty list is returned.

Before attempting to set a property for a selected object a script needs to check if there is a selection. If there is a selection, then test to see the class of the items in the selection.

```
tell application "Adobe InDesign CS5"
    --if no selection, result for theClass will be missing value
    set theClass to missing value
    --get the selection and test for number of items in list
    set selectList to selection
    if length of selectList > 0 then
        --if items, get the class of the first item
        set theClass to class of item 1 of selectList
    end if
end tell
theClass
```

If there are multiple page items selected, class of selection returns a list of the classes of items within the selection.

Parent

The parent of an object is its container. Should you want to know the page that a selected page item is on, the **parent page** property is now the preferred method. If the object is on the pasteboard, the **parent page** property in CS5 returns the enumeration value nothing.

```
--deletes the first item selected if on the pasteboard
tell application "Adobe InDesign CS5"
    if exists selection then
        set theParent to parent page of item 1 of selection
        if class of theParent is not equal to page then
            delete item 1 of selection
        end if
    end if
end tell
theParent --returns nothing if parent page is pasteboard
```

If an object is nested, the parent property of the object will be its container. The following tests for the parent of a selected object. If the object is nested it is removed from its parent and replaced in the same location on the page (**paste in place**). The object will now move independently of its parent.

```
tell application "Adobe InDesign CS5"
    if exists selection then
        set theParent to parent of item 1 of selection
        if class of theParent is in {rectangle, oval, polygon, ¬
        graphic line} then
            cut item 1 of selection
            select theParent existing selection replace with
            paste in place
        end if
    end if
end tell
```

The parent of a text object is its **story** (text flow). The following script enumerates the text classes that will be allowed for the selection. If the class of the text selected matches one of the values in the *desiredClass* list, an object reference to the text's story is the result.

```
tell application "Adobe InDesign CS5"
    set storyRef to missing value
    set desiredClass to {paragraph, text column, text style range, ¬
    insertion point, word, character}
    set selList to selection
    if (length of selList > 0) and (class of item 1 of selection is in ¬
    desiredClass) then
        set storyRef to parent of item 1 of selection
    end if
end tell
storyRef
```

The parent story property will return a reference to its parent story (text flow).

```
tell application "Adobe InDesign CS5"
    tell page 1 of document 1
        if ((count of text frames) > 0) then
            set frameRef to text frame 1
            try
                set flowRef to parent story of frameRef
            on error errStr
                activate
                display alert errStr
            end try
        end if
    end tell
end tell
```

As a word of caution: If the referenced story is empty, trying to access a property or a text reference within the story will produce an error. To avoid this problem, you can :

1. Check the count of the story or story element reference:

```
set paraRef to missing value
tell application "Adobe InDesign CS5"
    tell page 1 of document 1
        if ((count of text frames) > 0) then
            set frameRef to text frame 1
            set flowRef to parent story of frameRef
            if (count of paragraphs of flowRef) > 0 then
                set paraRef to object reference of paragraph 1 of flowRef
            end if
        end if
    end tell
end tell
paraRef--will be missing value if count of paragraphs = 0
```

2. Check for text class reference.

```
tell application "Adobe InDesign CS5"
    --place reference to selection in variable
    set selList to selection
    --check for length of selection list
    if length of selList > 0 then
        --check for class of item selected
```

```
        if class of item 1 of selList = text then
            set frameRef to parent text frames of selection
        end if
    end if
end tell
```

Text Containers

If you have a story (text flow) reference, its **text containers** property will return a list of the text frames involved in the text flow. Even though the story may be empty the result will be a list of text containers.

```
tell application "Adobe InDesign CS5"
    set selList to selection
    if length of selList > 0 then
        set selItem to item 1 of selList
        if class of selItem is text or class of selItem is ¬
        insertion point then
            set storyRef to parent of selItem
            set frameRef to text containers of storyRef
        end if
    end if
end tell
frameRef
```

Document Specific

Layers

Each document contains at least one named layer by default. The layers are available for every spread of the document. Some designers like to place all of their page marks and guides on one layer, graphics on another layer, and text on another. This way they can activate, hide, and lock layers at their discretion. Layers have been improved in InDesign CS5 in that they now support working with individual items in each layer. Items added to a layer appear in the list disclosed when the small triangle to the left of the layer's name is opened in the Layer panel. Names for items in the layer are shown and can be set in the layers panel.

Section

The **section** class provides the ability to create, count, and delete sections. This class also has properties such as **page number start, page number style,** and **page start** that controls page numbering. **Include section prefix,** when true, places the section prefix before page numbers on all pages of the section.

```
tell application "Adobe InDesign CS5"
    set docRef to make document
    tell docRef
        set facing pages of document preferences to true
        set pages per document of document preferences to 8
        make section with properties {name:"First", page number ¬
        style:arabic, continue numbering:false, page number start:2, ¬
        page start:page 1 of spread 2, marker:"Intro", section prefix:"A",¬
        include section prefix:true}
    end tell
end tell
```

To test this out, run the script. In the document created, open the master page from the Pages panel (F12). Place a text frame at the bottom of the left-facing page. Choose Insert Special Character > Markers > Section Marker from the Type menu. Enter a space, and then select Current Page Number from the same menu. Copy this frame to the second master page. Switch back to page one. It shows only the page number. Switch to page 2 and notice the marker and section prefix that has been added to the page number. Note: Insert Special Character is also part of the context menu presented when you hold the Control key down while clicking with the text tool within a text frame.

To get the number of sections in a document, use either of the following inside a tell block to the application:

```
count sections of document 1
count every section of document 1
```

The Spread

A spread is all of the pages that one would normally want to view or print as a single unit. An example is a facing spread where there is a left and a right page. In this instance, the spread contains two pages. A spread without facing pages is still a spread although containing only one page. Items on the pasteboard are elements of a spread (not a page). If using facing pages, using a document preset to create the document is the preferred method.

The property **allow page shuffle,** when set to false, assures that the pages in the spread will stay together. This property is specific to the spread. Document preferences has a similar property, **preserve layout when shuffling**. This affects all spreads having two or more pages. Multiple-page spreads are changed to two-page spreads if created or changed after the property is turned on. The following code may help you understand this concept. Run the script. Then change values for **allow page shuffle** and **preserve layout when shuffling** and run again to see the how these properties can affect your layouts. Now, that InDesign (as of CS5) allows pages within a spread to be different sizes, you may be using these settings often.

```
tell application "Adobe InDesign CS5"
    set origFacing to facing pages of document preferences
    set facing pages of document preferences to true
    set docRef to make document
    tell docRef
        set pages per document of document preferences to 4
        tell spread 2
            set allow page shuffle to false
            make page at end
        end tell
        set preserve layout when shuffling of document preferences to true
        tell spread 1
            set allow page shuffle to false
            make page at end
        end tell
    end tell
    set facing pages of document preferences to origFacing
end tell
```

The Page

In some ways the page is similar to the spread as they both contain page items, and have the properties **applied master** and **show master items**. If you want to set margins, this needs to be done at the document, master page, or page level. Trapping can be set at the application, document, or page level. **Applied trap preset** is a property of a page.

Name, Index and Document Offset

The **name**, **index**, and **document offset** properties for a **page** can cause some confusion when it comes to writing scripts. The index of a page is its position within its parent spread. As an example, the **index** of the left page in a facing-page spread is 1.

The **document offset** is the physical position of a page within the document. The **name** of a page is its page number expressed as a string value (what you see if a page marker is placed on a page).

To test this concept, run the following script and view the result in the Result panel.

```
tell application "Adobe InDesign CS5"
    set docRef to make document
    tell docRef
        set facing pages of document preferences to true
        set pages per document of document preferences to 4
    end tell
    tell section 1 of docRef to set page number style to lower roman
    tell docRef
        set theIndex to index of page 2
        set theOffset to document offset of page 2
        set theName to name of page 2
    end tell
end tell
{theIndex, theOffset, theName}
```

A page normally is addressed by its index within the spread. It may be addressed as a spread if the spread has only one page.

Page Items

Page items are elements of the document, the spread, the page, and can be elements of any other page or text item. A script can tell the document, page, or spread to make a page item at the beginning or at the end of a page or relative to another item. The following is an example:

```
tell application "Adobe InDesign CS5"
    set docRef to make document
    set objProps to {geometric bounds:{"72 pts", "36 pts", "144 pts", ¬
    "200 pts"}, fill color:"Black", fill tint:30}
    tell docRef
        make rectangle at beginning of page 1 with properties objProps
    end tell
end tell
```

Text

All text items fall within the general classification **text**. Sub-classifications of text include: **story, text style range, text column, paragraph, line, word,** and **character**.

Determining whether the text you wish to address is a story, paragraph, or line can cause some confusion. A story can be thought of as any contiguous block of text. Text that is created as a single entity within a single text frame or within linked text frames is a story. The text in each non-linked text frame is a separate story.

A paragraph is defined by a hard return. This will show up as a paragraph symbol when Show Hidden Characters is enabled in InDesign's Type menu.

Each physical line of a paragraph (where text wraps) is considered a line of text. These can also be delineated in the text by soft returns (shift+return). Run the following sample code with a document open. The document needs to have at least one text frame. The result window will show that the story is referenced as a text flow within the document's hierarchy:

```
tell application "Adobe InDesign CS5"
    set theStory to story -1 of document 1
end tell
```

Contents

For text objects, with exception of the story, a reference to the object will return its contents.

```
tell application "Adobe InDesign CS5"
    set text1 to line 1 of story -1 of document 1
end tell --result is the actual text
```

Should you wish to get the object reference for the text, use its object reference.

```
tell application "Adobe InDesign CS5"
    set textObj to object reference of line 1 of story -1 of document 1
end tell
(*Result is similar to: text from character 1 to character 86 of story id
259 of document "DocumentName" of application "InDesign CS5."*)
```

Insertion Point

The insertion point can be used to define the location for text insertion within a story. To insert text at the beginning of a story, insertion point 1 is used. For the end of a story, a script references insertion point -1. Of course, any other integer from 1 to the length of the story can be used.

```
tell document 1 of application "Adobe InDesign CS5"
    set contents of insertion point 1 of story -1 to "New text"
end tell
```

Make Scripts Work For You

Do you work in an environment where other people use your computer? Have you started a project at the beginning of the day just to find "someone" has reset your document preferences? If you yearn for a solution that would ensure that your settings are the way you want them, our script **Sample Setup** will get you started. Modify it for your own preferences and keep it handy when you need to restore your defaults (and your sanity).

4

InDesign's Geometry

Although some mention has been made in passing concerning lists, bounds, and records, you need to have a solid understanding of these concepts when working with InDesign's document geometry. We will spend some time expanding on these topics in this chapter as we deal with geometric considerations.

Geometric Coordinates

Geometric coordinates for InDesign are not exactly the same as you might expect. Horizontal (*x*) coordinates and vertical (*y*) coordinates are measured from the **zero point** of a page. The zero point is the point at which the page rulers intersect. Points above or to the left of this point are returned as negative values.

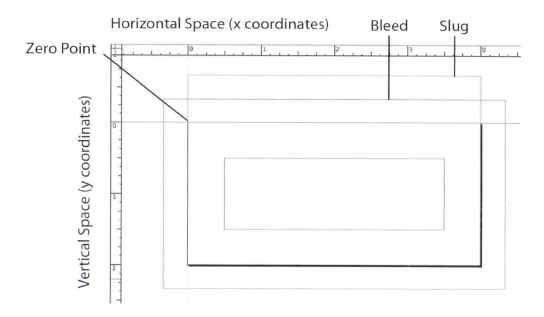

Figure 4.1: InDesign's geometry is based on the Zero Point of the horizontal and vertical rulers. A point within horizontal space is often referred to as the x coordinate, with y referring to a coordinate within vertical space.

InDesign's geometry involves working with lists.

For review, a list can be created by placing values separated by commas inside curly braces:

```
set myList to {"John", "Mary", "Joe"}
```

You can add items to a list using the concatenation operator (&):

```
set myList to {}
set myList to myList & "John"
set myList to myList & "Mary"
--result for myList is {"John", "Mary"}
```

Bounds

The bounds of an object is returned as a list of four items representing the top vertical, left horizontal, bottom vertical, and right horizontal coordinates for the item in that order. Objects within the **page item** class have both a **geometric bounds** and a **visible bounds** property. The geometric bounds ignores any stroke widths that may be applied to the object. The visible bounds considers the stroke width.

As an example, consider a rectangle drawn at the top-left margin of a page where both margins are set at 36 points. The rectangle is 72 points square and has a 12 point stroke that aligns to the outside of the rectangle.

If you run a script to get the values for the rectangle's visible bounds and geometric bounds, you will discover the values are not the same. The geometric bounds property for the object will return {36, 36, 108, 108} as you might expect. The visible bounds for the same object will return {24, 24, 120, 120} because of the stroke.

```
(*Select the rectangle before running the script.*)
tell application "Adobe InDesign CS5"
    set selList to selection
    set rectRef to item 1 of selList
    set gBounds to geometric bounds of rectRef
    set vBounds to visible bounds of rectRef
end tell
{gBounds, vBounds}
```

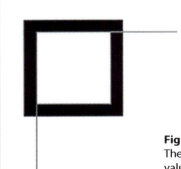

Figure 4.2: Rectangle drawn with a stroke set for outside alignment. The visual bounds and the geometric bounds will return different values because of the stroke.

Point Coordinates

To place an item at a specific location on a page, a two-item list is used to define the point coordinate for the item's top-left corner. Here the order is different from the y,x order of bounds: the first item in the list defines the horizontal coordinate, while the second defines the vertical.

```
--creates a text frame on a page and then duplicates and moves it
tell application "Adobe InDesign CS5"
    tell page 1 of active document
        --notice how properties can be set for an object using a record
        set frameRef to make text frame with properties ¬
        {geometric bounds:{".5 in", ".5 in", "3 in", "2 in"}}
        set dupRef to duplicate frameRef
        move dupRef to {"3 in", ".5 in"}
    end tell
end tell
```

The **place point** parameter is used for placing files in a document. This is expressed as a point coordinate, again a two-item list with the horizontal coordinate as the first item in the list.

```
--requires an open document with a layer named "Images"
set theFile to choose file with prompt "Choose an image file" ¬
without multiple selections allowed
tell application "Adobe InDesign CS5"
    set layerRef to layer "Images" of document 1
    tell page 1 of document 1
        place theFile place point {"3p", "6p"} destination layer ¬
        layerRef without showing options
    end tell
end tell
```

Notice that the syntax for the place command is similar in structure to display dialog in that the parameters for the command are strung together without commas.

Measurements

The values for the bounds of an object in most of the example scripts up to this point have used string values. If your script gets the bounds of an object, the result you will see in the Result panel are number values. These numbers are based on the measurement units currently in effect for the document. For an object placed at 1 inch down from the top of the page, the result will be 1 if the vertical measurement unit is set to inches. However, if set to points the result will be 72. If you know what the measurement units for the document are, you can use number values. Otherwise, play it safe and use string values when entering measurements. Using string values prevents problems in that InDesign converts string values it recognizes to the appropriate numerical internal values required.

With CS5 the list of measurement units supported in InDesign has added pixels (px). You can also tell InDesign what unit of measurement you want to use for text size, strokes, typography, and the print dialog. Our preference is to stick with points for print measurements, with 72 points to an inch. Among the measurement units supported by InDesign are the following:

Measurement Unit	String Value	Example
Centimeters	"cm"	".542 cm"
Millimeters	"mm"	"5.42 mm"
Inches	"i" or "in"	"5 in"
Inches Decimal	"i" or "in"	"1.5 in"
Picas	"p"	"1 p"
Points	"pt"	"9 pt"
Pixels - for Web intent	"px"	"72 px"
You can combine picas and points as in "1p9" for one pica and nine points.		

One common practice in writing a script is to save the current measurement settings in variables, change the measurements to the unit desired for the script, and then change the measurement units back when through. For this you will work with **view preferences**.

View Preferences

Settings for measurement units are part of **view preferences** which can be set for the application as well as for the document. Open InDesign's scripting dictionary. In the Suite listing, click on the Preferences Suite, then Classes in the third column, and finally View Preference in the fourth. The properties of interest are **horizontal measurement units, vertical measurement units, ruler origin, guide snapto zone**, and **show notes**. In the entry for horizontal measurement units, you will see that units can be expressed as points, picas, inches, inches decimal, millimeters, centimeters, and more.

Setting and resetting measurement units is a common task in scripts which makes this functionality an ideal candidate for a handler. For this, you will find an entry in the Handlers Library. Control-click in the Script Editor's edit window and navigate to **setResetMeasures** in the Environment folder. When you click on the listing you will have two handlers added to your script. Place the call to **setMeasures** before you need to work with measurements, and the call to **resetMeasures** when you are through using measurements. Notice that the **setMeasures** handler is written to set units to points and the ruler origin to page origin. You may wish to change these values to your preferred settings for your own scripts. Also, the original values are passed back from the **setMeasures** handler as a list and become the values for variables in the calling statement.

```
--assumes document 1 exists
set docRef to document 1 of application "Adobe InDesign CS5"
--call to handler to set measures to points; ruler origin to page
set {orighm, origvm, origro} to setMeasures(docRef)
--call to handler to reset measures to original values
resetMeasures(docRef, orighm, origvm, origro)

(*Set measures to points, ruler origin to page. Returns original values.*)
on setMeasures(docRef)
    tell application "Adobe InDesign CS5"
        tell view preferences of docRef
            set orighm to horizontal measurement units
            set origvm to vertical measurement units
            set origro to ruler origin
            set horizontal measurement units to points
            set vertical measurement units to points
```

```
                set ruler origin to page origin
            end tell
        end tell
        return {orighm, origvm, origro}
    end setMeasures

    --resets measures to original units
    on resetMeasures(docRef, orighm, origvm, origro)
        tell application "Adobe InDesign CS5"
            tell view preferences of docRef
                set horizontal measurement units to orighm
                set vertical measurement units to origvm
                set ruler origin to origro
            end tell
        end tell
    end resetMeasures
```

See how these handlers are used in the script **Create Rectangle** (in Chapter Scripts folder for this chapter).

Ruler Origin

The fact that the two handlers mentioned above set and reset **ruler origin** requires some discussion on the subject. When working with facing-page documents, ruler origin becomes a critical factor. If ruler origin is set to **page origin,** the ruler zero point for each page is its upper left corner. With **spread origin**, the zero point for both pages is at the upper left corner of the left-facing page. Ruler origin can also be set to **spine origin**.

The following script is designed to illustrate. It creates a document of four facing pages with measurements set to inches and ruler origin set to spread origin. It then tells the left-facing page and right-facing page of spread 2 to create a text frame. This illustrates a problem that can happen when ruler origin is set to spread origin.

Test Ruler Origin

```
tell application "Adobe InDesign CS5"
    set docRef to make document
    tell document preferences of docRef
        set facing pages to true
        set pages per document to 4
    end tell
    tell view preferences of docRef
        set horizontal measurement units to inches
        set vertical measurement units to inches
        set ruler origin to spread origin
    end tell
    --left facing page
    tell page 1 of spread 2 of docRef
        make text frame with properties {geometric bounds:{1, 0.5, 4, 3}}
    end tell
    --right facing page
    tell page 2 of spread 2 of docRef
        make text frame with properties {geometric bounds:{4, 0.5, 8, 3}}
    end tell
end tell
```

Run the script and view the result for pages 2 and 3. The problem is that both text frames end up on page 2 because of the ruler origin setting. (Figure 4.3) This can be corrected by changing the initial setting for ruler origin from spread origin to page origin. Try it.

Figure 4.3: In creating the second text frame the script targeted page 2 of the spread, but the frame ended up on page 1 of the spread. This is due to the fact that the ruler origin was set to spread origin.

Zero Point

If you recall, the zero point for a page is the point at which the zero measurement of the rulers intersect. For the most part you may be able to assume that the zero point is set to {0,0} but if your script is creating page items in an existing document, you might be wise to check the zero point. If you want to add this functionality to your script there is a handler, **checkZeroPoint**, that may work for you. The handler is in the Environment folder in the Handlers Library (see Chapter 1).

```
set docRef to document 1 of application "Adobe InDesign CS5"
--Call to checkZeroPoint
set resetZero to checkZeroPoint(docRef)
(*To reset the zero point later in script
if resetZero is not missing value then
set zero point to resetZero
end if
*)

(*Returns missing value or list*)
on checkZeroPoint(docRef)
    tell application "Adobe InDesign CS5"
        set zPoint to missing value
        set zeroList to zero point of docRef
        if zeroList is not equal to {0, 0} then
            set zPoint to zeroList
        end if
    end tell
    return zPoint
end checkZeroPoint
```

The handler checks the value for the zero point. If not {0,0}, the zero point is set and a list containing the original values is returned. Otherwise a value missing value is returned. The variable *resetZero* acts as a flag to indicate if the zero point needs resetting.

Document Reference

The previous examples assume there is an active document. When writing a script that works with an existing document, your script needs to make sure that a document exists. For this you can use the **getDocRef** handler. You will find this handler in the Documents folder of the Handlers Library. If a document does not exist, the handler creates an error condition. This is trapped in the try statement block that is part of its call. The handler also checks for the modal state of the application.

```
try
    set docRef to getDocRef()
on error errStr
    display alert errStr
end try

(*Returns reference to active document; otherwise throws error.*)
on getDocRef()
    tell application "Adobe InDesign CS5"
        if modal state = true then
            error "Please close dialogs before running script"
        end if
        if not (exists document 1) then
            error "Requires active document"
        else
            return document 1
        end if
    end tell
end getDocRef
```

Transform Reference Point

When you have a page item selected, you may notice a grid of nine small square buttons in the upper left corner of InDesign's control panel. The active button on the grid indicates the reference point from which the selected item may be moved or translated. In CS5, this reference has a few more ways in which it can affect what you do in your documents. This is also true for objects you manipulate with a script.

Transform reference point is a property of the layout window.

```
tell application "Adobe InDesign CS5"
    tell layout window 1
        set transform reference point to center anchor
    end tell
end tell
```

As with measurement units, if your script changes the transform reference point, you will want to reset the point to its original setting. For this there is a file, **setResetEnvironment**, in the Environment folder of your Handlers Library. When you click on its entry from within AppleScript Editor's context menu, two handlers are added to your script: **setEnvironment** and **resetEnvironment**.

SetEnvironment sets measurement units to points, ruler origin to page origin, zero point to {0,0}, and transform reference point to the button indicated by the number value passed as part of the call. The number value corresponds to the cell number for the transform reference point grid (from 1 to 9, left to right, top to bottom). The original values for these settings are returned back to the calling statement in the script.

ResetEnvironment uses the values returned from **setEnvironment** to reset the values back to their original settings.

Page Geometry

In creating page items, geometric bounds are often calculated based on page parameters. The following discussion presents some examples.

Page Bounds

Similar to the geometric bounds for a page item, the page itself has a **bounds** property. To get the bounds for the active page, you can use:

```
tell application "Adobe InDesign CS5"
    set pageRef to page 1 of active spread of layout window 1
    set pBounds to bounds of pageRef
end tell
```

Active Page

Keep in mind that **active page** can be troublesome. If the document is a facing-page document, the active page can actually be the left-facing page even though the right-facing page may be selected. If there is an item selected, get the reference to its page using the **parent page** property for the selected item. If possible, reference a page using its index or its name property. You can test the active page using one of the following statements. within a tell statement to the application.

```
set pName to name of active page of layout window 1
set pageRef to page 1 of spread 1 of layout window 1
```

Page Margins

Margin preferences are properties of the application, the document, and the page. The properties **column count, column gutter, columns positions, left, right, top**, and **bottom** will play a big role in many automation scripts. The bounds of the page area inside its margins are referred to as the *live bounds* of a page. The live bounds of a page for a non-facing page can be represented by the following generalized list:

```
{top margin, left margin, (page height - bottom margin), ¬
(page width - right margin)}
```

For a right-facing page, the left and right margins are the inside and outside margins respectively. For a left-facing page, the margins flip with the left margin value applied to the inside margin, and the right margin value applied to the outside margin.

Side

As of CS3 the page has a **side** property that returns whether the page is a single-sided, left-hand, or right-hand page. This is illustrated in the handler **getLiveBounds**. You will find this handler in the Page folder of the Handlers Library. (Access the handler by control-clicking inside AppleScript Editor's window.)

```
tell application "Adobe InDesign CS5"
    set docRef to document 1
    set pageRef to page 1 of docRef
end tell
set liveBounds to getLiveBounds(docRef, pageRef)

on getLiveBounds(docRef, pageRef)
    tell application "Adobe InDesign CS5"
        if pageRef = missing value then ¬
        set pageRef to active page of layout window 1
        tell document preferences of docRef
            set pageWid to page width
            set pageHgt to page height
        end tell
        tell margin preferences of pageRef
            set py0 to top
            set py1 to bottom
            if side of pageRef is left hand then
                set px1 to left
                set px0 to right
            else
                set px0 to left
                set px1 to right
            end if
        end tell
        return {py0, px0, pageHgt - py1, pageWid - px1}
    end tell
end getLiveBounds
```

Page Columns

The **columns positions** property for a page's margin preferences returns a list representing the beginning and ending horizontal position of columns within a page. The measurements are relative to the left margin with the first column position having a value of 0.

Given the index of any column on a page (that is, which column it is, counting from left to right), its x0 and x1 horizontal coordinate can be returned using the following generalized formulas where *columnPositions* represents the **column positions** of the **margin preferences** for the page, and *colIndex* represents the index of the column:

```
x0 = item ((colIndex * 2) - 1) of columnPositions
x1 = item (colIndex * 2) of columnPositions
```

See how this is used with the following. The script has been pared down for simplicity. Normally, the reference for the document would be returned from our **getDocRef** handler. Depending on the script, the reference to the page would also be generated otherwise. To test the script you will need an active document with at least three columns on the first page with measurements set to points. The **columnCoords** handler is found in the Page folder of the Handlers Library.

Column Frame

```
(*Creates a text frame 200 points high in a column defined by the variable
colIndex. Requires open document with at least 3 columns set for page 1
and measurements set to points.*)
set colIndex to 3 --index of example target column
tell application "Adobe InDesign CS5"
    set docRef to active document
    set pageRef to page 1 of docRef
    set {y0, x0, y1, x1} to my columnCoords(pageRef, colIndex)
    tell pageRef
       make text frame with properties {geometric bounds:¬
       {y0, x0, y0 + 200, x1}}
    end tell
end tell

(*Returns x0, y0, x1, y1 for column given page reference and column index;
also y0, y1 for page live area.*)
on columnCoords(pageRef, colIndex)
    tell application "Adobe InDesign CS5"
       set pageBounds to bounds of pageRef
       tell margin preferences of pageRef
          copy {top, left, bottom, right} to {py0, px0, py1, px1}
          set colPositions to columns positions
          if ((length of colPositions)/2 < colIndex) then
             error "Invalid index for column"
          end if
       end tell
       set x0 to item ((colIndex * 2) - 1) of colPositions
       set x1 to item (colIndex * 2) of colPositions
       return {py0, x0 + px0, ((item 3 of pageBounds) - py1), x1 + px0}
    end tell
end columnCoords
```

To have the text frame fill the entire column, change the bounds list in the statement that creates the text frame to {y0, x0, y1, x1}.

```
tell pageRef
    make text frame with properties {geometric bounds:¬
    {y0, x0, y1, x1}}
end tell
```

Make Scripts Work For You

The following exercise is designed to give you some practice working with page, measurements, and handlers. The resulting script will create a text frame within the live bounds of the designated page. It requires an open document.

To avoid redundancy, all references to a handler folder are for folders inside the Handlers Library for your application version (CS5 Handlers or CS55 Handlers). Again, control-click in AppleScript Editor's editing window to access the handler library.

Start a new script.

1. Add code to make sure there is a document open:

   Add the handler **getDocRef** from the Documents folder to your script. Notice the comment lines dividing the top of the script from the handler. This is only to help organize the script and make it easier to read.

2. Add the following variable declarations to the top of your script:

```
set docOffset to 1
set layerRef to missing value
```

3. Get a reference to the page you will be using.

Add the handler **checkPage** (in the Page folder) to the bottom of your script.

The call to this handler contains an error trap. Since an error trap was added to your script with the **getDocRef** call, you will cut only the line that actually calls the handler and paste it after the line that calls the **getDocRef** handler at the top of the script. Delete the rest of the text that accompanied the call to the handler.

At this point the top portion of your script should look like the following. You may want to test just this much of the script. The result will be a reference to the page.

```
set docOffset to 1
set layerRef to missing value
(*Returns reference to active document; otherwise generates error.*)
try
    set docRef to getDocRef()
    set pageRef to checkPage(docRef, docOffset)
on error errStr
    display alert errStr
end try
```

4. Add code to make sure that measurements will be as expected, and reset the measurements once the script completes.

Add the **setResetMeasures** handlers (Environment folder) to the bottom of your script. Cut and paste the **setMeasures** call to the top of your script below the try statement block. You will come back later to get the call for the **resetMeasures** handler.

5. Set the text frame preferences for the document.

Add the following to your script below the call to **setMeasures**:

```
tell application "Adobe InDesign CS5"
    tell docRef
        set properties of text frame preferences to ¬
        {text column count:1, inset spacing:0}
    end tell
end tell
```

6. Create a property record to define the attributes for the text frame the script will be creating.

Just above the last **end tell** statement added in step 5 above, add the following:

```
set textFrameProps to {fill color:"Black", fill tint:10, ¬
stroke weight:6, stroke color:"Black", ¬
stroke alignment:inside alignment, stroke type:"Solid"}
```

7. Define the bounds for the text frame.

Add the **getLiveBounds** handler (Page folder) to the bottom of your script. Cut the call to the handler and paste to the top of your script (below the tell block added in Step 5).

8. Add code to create the text frame.

Add the **makeTextFrame** handler (Page Items folder) to your script. Cut the call to the handler only and paste to the top portion of the script just below the call to **getLiveBounds**. Remove the rest of the text that accompanied the call.

9.   Find the call to the **resetMeasures** handler that you left above the **setMeasures** handler. Cut the call to the handler and paste it below the call you added in step 8.

10. The top portion of your script should now look like the following:

```
set docOffset to 1
set layerRef to missing value
try
    set docRef to getDocRef()
    set pageRef to checkPage(docRef, docOffset)
on error errStr
    display alert errStr
    return
end try
--call to handler to set measures to points; ruler origin to page
set {orighm, origvm, origro} to setMeasures(docRef)
tell application "Adobe InDesign CS5"
    tell docRef
        set properties of text frame preferences to ¬
        {text column count:1, inset spacing:0}
    end tell
    set textFrameProps to {fill color:"Black", fill tint:10, ¬
    stroke weight:6, stroke color:"Black", stroke alignment:inside ¬
    alignment, stroke type:"Solid"}
end tell
set liveBounds to getLiveBounds(docRef, pageRef)
set frameRef to createTextFrame(pageRef, layerRef, liveBounds, ¬
textFrameProps)
--call to handler to reset measures to original values
resetMeasures(docRef, orighm, origvm, origro)
--=========
--HANDLERS
--=========
```

Compile the script. If all goes well, you can now run the script. If you have problems, refer to the script **Live Bounds TextFrame** in the Chapter Scripts folder for this Chapter.

Challenge: Add a display dialog to have the user enter a number value for the target page. (See handler **getNumber** in the Dialogs folder of the Handlers Library.)

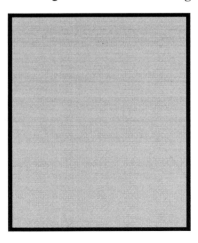

Figure 4.4: Result of running the Live Bounds TextFrame script.

5

Lists and Repeats

The very nature of automating InDesign usually involves processing multiple items. Whether the items are files, documents, pages, or items on a page, some type of repeat structure will be needed to work with the items. In this chapter you will learn how to get lists of object references for your scripts. You will then investigate the different types of repeat structures you can use to process these items. You will also be introduced to the **every** element specifier.

InDesign Object References

In working with object references in InDesign, chances are you will be working with lists. There are several ways that a script can get a list of object references. Top on the list is **selection**.

Selection

Selection returns a list of object references for items selected. Selection can be a property of the application, the document, a window, or a library panel. If no items are selected, the result is an empty list. Work through the following statements. Make sure you have a document open. Test the statements with page items selected, and then without.

```
tell application "Adobe InDesign CS5"
    set selList to selection
    set test to class of selList --result is list
end tell
```

The **length** property of a list can be used to determine if objects are selected.

```
tell document 1 of application "Adobe InDesign CS5"
    set selList to selection
    set selLength to length of selList
end tell
```

The **count** command can also be used but the length property is generally recommended..

```
tell document 1 of application "Adobe InDesign CS5"
    set selList to selection
    set selCount to (count selList)
end tell
```

If the length of the selection list is greater than 0 you can then test for the class of the items in the selection.

```
tell application "Adobe InDesign CS5"
    set selList to selection
    if length of selList > 0 then
```

```
        set test to class of item 1 of selection
    end if
end tell
```

Testing for the class of selection allows you to determine if an object of the type required by your script has been selected. Be aware that class of selection will error if no objects are selected. For this reason the example below tests for the length of selection (*selList*). Although selection is always a list, class of selection returns a single item if only one item is selected. The phrase as list is added to ensure the value of *testList* will be a list.

```
tell application "Adobe InDesign CS5"
    set hasRectangles to false
    set selList to selection
    if length of selList > 0 then
        set testList to class of selection as list
        if rectangle is in testList then
            set hasRectangles to true
        end if
    end if
end tell
hasRectangles
```

Since getting a list of selected objects of a desired class is something many of your scripts might require, let's put this functionality into a handler that returns a list of page items if an item of the desired class (*desiredClass* variable) is in the list of selected items.

Check Selection

```
--call to checkSelection handler
tell application "Adobe InDesign CS5"
    set desiredClass to rectangle
    try
        set selList to my checkSelection (desiredClass)
    on error errStr
        display alert errStr
    end try
end tell

(*Returns list of selected items if the list contains the desired type.*)
on checkSelection(desiredClass)
    tell application "Adobe InDesign CS5"
        set selList to selection
        if length of selList > 0 then
            set test to class of selection as list
            if desiredClass is in test then
                return selList
            end if
        end if
        error "Selection having items of desired class not found."
    end tell
end checkSelection
```

Since this script introduces some new concepts, let's break it down.

Calling a handler within a tell statement

If a word reserved for InDesign's dictionary is part of the values being sent to a handler, the call needs to be within a `tell application "Adobe InDesign CS5"` block. The value for *desiredClass* in the example above is rectangle. The word *rectangle* is known only to InDesign, not AppleScript. Consequently, without the tell block, running the script would generate the error:

```
"The variable rectangle is not defined"
```

My

When you call a handler from within a tell statement, the word **my** needs to precede the call. This tells AppleScript to look in the script for the handler. Without **my** the call to the handler would generate the error:

```
"Can't continue [handler name]"
```

Instead of using the keyword **my** before the call to the handler, **of me** can be placed after the call, but we will stick with using the keyword **my**.

Introducing Raw Codes

While on the subject of application-specific terminology such as **rectangle**, it may be wise to introduce **raw codes**. If you have ever received an error that contains strange four-letter codes inside guillemets («»), you have experienced raw codes. Raw codes are codes specific to an application that define a class or an event. These do not need to be inside a tell statement; instead, when AppleScript encounters a raw code, the compiler looks it up. The lookup table defines the application and the class. Using raw codes, the call to the handler above could read:

```
set desiredClass to «class crec»
try
    set selList to checkSelection (desiredClass)
on error errStr
    display alert errStr
end try
```

The guillemet characters («») are typed using option+backslash and option+shift+backslash respectively.

Parsing a List

The list of items returned from the **checkSelection** handler above can include any number of page items, some of which may not be rectangles. You will, at one point or another, need to filter out the items you want to work with. With this in mind, you can use a **repeat** loop to parse through the list of selected items and filter out those items that meet the required class requirement. Several loop structures come to mind:

- **repeat with** - Uses a counting variable from start value to end value.
- **repeat with...in** - Repeats using a reference to each item in the list as its variable.
- **repeat while** - Repeats while evaluation statement remains true.
- **repeat until** - Repeats until evaluation statement is no longer true
- **repeat** *n* **times** - Repeats a specific number of times

A repeat block begins with a statement starting with the word **repeat** and ends with **end repeat**.

Let's look at each of the above repeat structures individually.

Repeat With

The statement using **repeat with** provides a test for the value of a counting variable, and a method for incrementing the value for this variable. By convention the letter "*i*" is often used for the variable identifier. Generalized, the syntax for the statement is:

```
repeat with variableIdentifier from startInteger to endInteger ¬
[by stepInteger]
```

To see how this works, test the following code fragment:

```
set theList to {"a", "b", "c"}
repeat with i from 1 to length of theList
    display alert "The value of item " & i & " of the list is " & ¬
    item i of theList
end repeat
```

You can work with the items of a list in reverse order.

```
set theList to {1, 2, 3}
repeat with i from length of theList to 1 by -1
display alert "The value of item " & i & " of the list is " & ¬
    item i of theList
end repeat
```

The reserved word **by** allows the counting variable to be incremented by any integer:

```
repeat with i from 10 to 50 by 10
    display alert "The counting value is now " & i
end repeat
```

If an illegal value is provided for the value of **by**, the script does not generate an error; the repeat is ignored.

```
repeat with i from 10 to 12 by -2
    display alert "This will not display"
end repeat
```

Using the **repeat with** structure, you could write a handler that returns a list of selected page items having a desired type. If no items are selected an error is created. If no items of the desired type are found, an empty list is returned. Compare this handler with the **checkSelection** handler.

```
set desiredClass to «class crec»
set desiredList to selectedByClass(desiredClass)

(*Returns list of items selected that match value for desiredClass.*)
on selectedByClass(desiredClass)
    tell application "Adobe InDesign CS5"
        set selList to selection
        if not (length of selList > 0 ¬
        and desiredClass is in class of selection as list) then
            error "Requires selection of class " & desiredClass as string
        end if
        set desiredList to {}
```

```
        repeat with i from 1 to length of selList
            if class of item i of selList = desiredClass then
                set end of desiredList to item i of selList
            end if
        end repeat
    end tell
    return desiredList
end selectedByClass
```

Repeat With...In

This structure is similar to **repeat with**, except that with each repeat loop (*iteration*) the successive item in the list becomes the value of the controlling variable. The following examples use *eachItem* for the variable identifier, however any valid variable identifier could be used.

```
repeat with eachItem in {"a", "b", "c"}
    display alert "The item in the list is now " & eachItem
end repeat
eachItem
```

The tricky part about using **repeat with...in** is that the value of the variable is a **reference** to the object in the list. If the items of the list are literal values, the reference may be dereferenced implicitly as in the example above. Look at the result of running the statements above. The display alert message showed the value of *eachItem* to be a string value. The Result panel, on the other hand, shows a reference: item 3 of {"a", "b", "c"}. Add *as string* to the result test statement (the last statement above) and the value of the result will be dereferenced to a string value.

```
eachItem as string --the result is "c"
```

The subject of dereferencing was introduced in Chapter 2. Because referencing and dereferencing play such an important part in using the **repeat with...in** structure, a number of examples using selection follow:

With text selected, the result of the following will be the actual text.

```
--assumes a text item is selected in document
tell application "Adobe InDesign CS5"
    set selList to selection
    if length of selList is greater than 0 then
        repeat with eachItem in selList
            activate
            display alert "The item selected is " & eachItem
        end repeat
    end if
end tell
```

Try the script with a text frame (not text) selected. An error will be raised which includes four-letter codes (*raw codes*) mentioned earlier.

And yes, you now know that the raw code for text frame is «class txtf» and the code for spread is «class sprd». Should you need to find out the raw code for an object, here is a solution. Select the object for which you want a raw code, and run the script.

Script Debugger

If you have access to Script Debugger, it lets you switch to view your codes as raw (four-letter) codes.

The cause of the error in the example above is due to the fact that AppleScript cannot dereference the list item object (*text frame*) into a string value for the purpose of display alert. If you request a property of the selected item, display alert has no problem.

```
--assumes page items are selected in document
tell application "Adobe InDesign CS5"
    set theList to selection
    if length of theList is greater than 0 then
        repeat with eachItem in theList
            activate
            display alert "The item selected is " & class of eachItem
        end repeat
    end if
end tell
```

Activate

The command *activate* in the example above brings AppleScript's Standard Additions to the front, forcing display alert to display above InDesign. Otherwise, when a display dialog or alert is called within a tell statement to an application it may be hidden.

To set properties for an object, the reference to the object is required. This makes **repeat with...in** an ideal repeat structure for setting (or getting) properties for a list of items.

```
--assumes page items are selected in document
tell application "Adobe InDesign CS5"
    set selList to selection
    repeat with eachItem in selList
        set properties of eachItem to {fill color:"Black", fill tint:10}
    end repeat
end tell
```

In working with a text selection you need to be thinking about whether the items in the selection list are literal text or references to text items. Often a quick test script will do the trick. In the following, the result is a list of the contents (string value) for each word selected.

```
--assumes text is selected
tell application "Adobe InDesign CS5"
    if length of selection is greater than 0 then
        set selList to words of selection
    end if
end tell
```

Should you try to set a property for each item in this list using **repeat with...in**, the script would error. The problem is you can't set properties for literal text. You need a text reference. Change the set statement in the code above to the following to get a list of text references:

```
set selList to a reference to words of selection
--result is an every reference
```

Additionally a **repeat with...in** loop structure will produce an unexpected result should you wish to put specific items from one list into another list.

```
--assumes text is selected containing words defined by the variable str
set str to "time"
tell application "Adobe InDesign CS5"
    if length of selection is greater than 0 then
        set selList to words of selection
        set newList to {}
        repeat with eachItem in selList
            if eachItem = str then
                set end of newList to eachItem
            end if
        end repeat
    end if
end tell
newList --result will be an empty list
```

The result of running the previous code most likely is not what you would expect. If you have words in the selection that match the value assigned to the variable *str* you probably wonder what the problem is. Because repeat with is used, items in *selList* are references, not text. Add the phrase contents of to get the contents of each referenced item. Change the second if statement to read:

```
if contents of eachItem = str
    set end of newList to eachItem
end if
```

Run the script with text selected. Verify the result in the Result panel. The result may not display as anticipated. What it does show is a reference to items in a list.

To get a list of word references that match a particular string value in your selection, add the phrase **a reference to**. This forces the compiler to maintain the reference—not dereference it. So try the following.

```
tell application "Adobe InDesign CS5"
    if length of selection is greater than 0 then
        set selList to a reference to words of selection
    end if
end tell
```

The result is an **every** element specifier.

```
every word of selection of application "Adobe InDesign CS5"
```

The bottom line is, if you have occasion to process every item in a list uniformly, you may be able to use an **every** element specifier and avoid repeat loops all together.

Try the next snippet on for size:

```
(*Be sure the value of colorName matches a swatch in your document.*)
set str to "time"
set colorName to "Red"
tell application "Adobe InDesign CS5"
    try --will generate error if no words matching str are found
        set fill color of words of selection whose it = str to colorName
    on error errStr
        display alert "ERROR: " & errStr
    end try
end tell
```

For more about using the **every** element specifier, see the discussion "Every Element" later in the chapter. Before we get too far off the subject of repeat loops, we should look at the other repeat structures.

Repeat While

The first statement in a **repeat while** loop block includes an evaluation. While the result of the evaluation remains true, the repeat block will loop, and loop... The problem is that if the conditional never changes from true to false, your script will be trapped in a never-ending loop. When first writing a while statement, it is a good idea to include a counting variable that increments by 1 each time through the loop. If the counting variable reaches a maximum number, an **exit repeat** statement will get you out of trouble.

```
set theList to {"one", "two", "three"}
set maxRepeats to 5
set counter to 0
repeat while length of theList > 0
    set counter to counter + 1
    if counter > maxRepeats then
        exit repeat
    end if
end repeat
counter
```

The value of the *counter* variable after running the code above is 6. But there were only three items in the list. When testing a while loop, including a counting variable will give you a way to verify if your loop has a potential problem. In the example above, the list never changes, so the length of the list *theList* is always greater than zero.

What was left out of the loop was a statement to change the list once an item is processed. The list property **rest** throws away the first item of a list. Just before the end repeat statement in the code above, add:

```
set theList to rest of theList
```

Using the **rest** property of a list is very powerful especially with large lists as the processor does not need to look through the list to access the target item. The target item is always item 1. Just remember to add a counting variable test inside your loop just to make sure nothing goes awry.

This discussion brings up another subject worth looking at: how to exit a repeat loop. This will be discussed a little later. For now, let's look at two more repeat loop structures.

Repeat Until

This repeat is similar to **repeat while** with the exception that the test for the conditional is done at the bottom of the statements within the loop block. For the most part, this ensures that the loop is executed at least one time.

```
set theValue to true
repeat until theValue = false
    set theValue to false --value not tested until before end repeat
    display alert "Within the repeat loop"
end repeat
```

Repeat *n* Times

This repeat loop simply allows you to determine the number of times something will happen. Provide an integer for the number of times to loop.

```
repeat 3 times
    beep
    delay 1
end repeat
```

Delay

The delay statement causes the script to pause execution for the number of seconds indicated. Starting with Panther this value can have a decimal value (a *real* value). Without the delay statement in the example script, running the script would sound like only one beep occurred because the beep statement executes in rapid succession.

And, yes the repeat could be eliminated altogether using a one-line beep statement.

```
beep 3
```

But we wanted to have an example of **repeat *n* times**. Besides, the example allowed the introduction of the **delay** command.

Working with Repeats

While we are on the subject of repeats, there are some concepts that need to be covered. First on the list is nesting loops.

Nesting Loops

You can have any number of repeat loops nested inside of another. Just make sure if using **repeat with** you keep the variables used for counting within the loops straight. The following is an example for you in case you have forgotten your 12 and 13 times tables. This little example will display the table for you in the Result panel.

```
set theString to ""
repeat with i from 12 to 13
    repeat with j from 1 to 13
```

```
        set theString to theString & ¬
            ((i as string) & " x " & j & " = " & (i * j) & return)
    end repeat
end repeat
```

Exiting a Loop

There are three methods for exiting a loop.

- **Exit repeat** - This method was mentioned above in discussing the **repeat while** loop.

- **Return** - A return statement exits a loop bringing a value with it

- **Error** - An error statement exits a loop with an error condition

Exit Repeat

This statement simply exits the loop allowing the script to process the next available statements.

```
--only the item "good" will be processed in the repeat.
set theList to {"good", "bad", "better"}
repeat with i from 1 to length of theList
    set test to item i of theList
    if item i of theList = "bad" then
        exit repeat
    end if
    display alert "The item is now " & item i of theList
end repeat
test --returns "bad"
```

Return

The **return** statement exits from a loop bringing a value with it. The value returned will be the value supplied after the word return.

```
return variableOrValue
```

If no variable or value is provided, the value returned will be that of the *result* variable. The *result* variable is a predefined variable that holds the value of the last statement evaluated. To see the return statement in action, change the `if`/`end if` block in the script above to read:

```
if item i of theList = "bad" then
    return i
end if
```

The result is the value of the counting variable (*i*) when execution exited the loop. You can use this idea to find the index of a particular item within a list. Your scripts may require this functionality more than once, making it a good candidate for a handler. The handler **getListMatch** is found in the List folder of the Handlers Library. (Part of the resources installed in Chapter 1. These handlers can be accessed from AppleScript Editor's context menu.)

```
--sample call
set theList to {"one", "two", "three"}
set theItem to "two"
set itemNumber to getListMatch(theItem, theList)
--returns the index of the item within the list.
```

```
(*Returns index of list item that matches data item passed.*)
on getListMatch(theItem, theList)
    set theMatch to 0
    repeat with i from 1 to length of theList
        if item i of theList = theItem then
            set theMatch to i
            exit repeat
        end if
    end repeat
    return theMatch
end getListMatch
```

Error

An **error** statement sets up an error condition that must be handled in a **try/on error** statement block. This can be an effective way to exit a loop, but you need to be aware that error conditions migrate up the execution chain of a script until a **try/on error** statement is found. If not handled correctly, unexpected results can occur.

```
set theList to {40, 20, 10, 15, 25}
try
    repeat with i from 1 to length of theList
        if item i of theList < 20 then
            error item i of theList
        end if
        display alert "The item is now " & item i of theList
    end repeat
on error errStr
    errStr
end try
(*Returns reference to value of item when error occurred. In this example
the value is a reference: item 3 of {40, 20, 10, 15, 25}.*)
```

Examples of Loops with InDesign

Recall that the **selection** property returns a list of items selected. When a **repeat with loop** is used to process each item in the list, the counter variable can be used in a number of creative ways. Below, the script sets the fill color and fill tint for the rectangles selected using the counter variable *i*. For each item referenced in the list, the fill tint changes. To test, have a document open with at least two rectangles selected.

```
--assumes an open document with page items selected
set colorName to "Black"
tell application "Adobe InDesign CS5"
    set propRecord to {fill color:colorName, fill tint:0}
    set selList to selection
    if length of selList > 0 then
        set tFactor to 100 / (length of selList)
        repeat with i from 1 to length of selList
            set fTint to (i) * tFactor
            set fill tint of propRecord to fTint
            set properties of item i of selList to propRecord
        end repeat
```

```
        end if
    end tell
```

A more practical example might be a script that adds an incremented label and name to all page items selected. For this, the **nameItems** handler in the Page Items folder of the Handlers Library is provided. It uses a counting variable *theCounter* to add an incremented number to the value of the *baseName* variable. For all numbers less than 10 it pads the number with a zero. The handler is used in the script **Name Items** found in the Chapter Scripts folder for this chapter.

Name Items

```
(*This script does not work in versions of InDesign prior to CS5.*)
set baseName to "Image"
tell application "Adobe InDesign CS5"
    set itemClass to rectangle
    set selList to selection
    if length of selList > 0 and itemClass is in class of selection then
        my nameItems(selList, baseName, itemClass)
    end if
end tell

(*Sets name and label for items in selList to the baseName to which a
single zero padded increment is added.*)
on nameItems(selList, baseName, itemClass)
    tell application "Adobe InDesign CS5"
        set theCounter to 1
        repeat with everyItem in selList
            if class of everyItem = itemClass then
                set theName to baseName & text -1 thru -2 of ("0" & theCounter)
                set properties of everyItem to {name:theName, label:theName}
                set theCounter to theCounter + 1
            end if
        end repeat
    end tell
end nameItems
```

Because the script sets both the name and the label of the selected items, you can use InDesign's Script Label panel to see that the items were named (and labeled). The name of the page item can be viewed (and changed) in the Layer panel's list for the item's layer. (In version 5.0 the name for items may not display in the layer list.)

Important

One of the biggest "gotchas" in InDesign CS5 is that labels for items take on a slightly different functionality. No longer will your script be able to use the label property as a name reference. You now use the name property. Remember, the name of an object displays in the item list for its layer.

If you have a legacy document (or template) that has items labeled for automation, and now want to use it with CS5 and above, name each item the same as its label. Then have your script reference the objects using the **name** property.

```
tell application "Adobe InDesign CS5"
    tell document 1
        set theList to all page items
        repeat with eachItem in theList
```

```
            if label of eachItem is not "" then
                set name of eachItem to label of eachItem
            end if
        end repeat
    end tell
end tell
```

You can also reference items by the **label** property using the **every** element specifier:

```
tell application "Adobe InDesign CS5"
    tell document 1
        try
            set theList to geometric bounds of every page item where ¬
            label is "Photo"
        end try
    end tell
end tell
```

If the document has page items labeled "Photo" the result of the script above is a list of lists.

Creating Multiple Items

When your script needs to create a number of similar page items, a list of bounds (each set of bounds being a list within a list) can be used. The following script, **Make Rectangles**, establishes the properties for the rectangles in a property record (*propRecord*), and passes the information to the **makeRectangles** handler. The handler parses through the list of lists, adding the **geometric bounds** property to the *propRecord* property record with each iteration. The script allows the name reference to the layer, *layerRef*, to be missing value. If this is the value, the active layer will be used.

Make Rectangles

```
(*Values for propList in order are: fill color, stroke weight, stroke
type, stroke color.*)
set propList to {"None", "1 pt", "Solid", "Black"}
set layerRef to missing value
set boundsList to {{".5 in", ".5 in", "1.5 in", "4 in"}, ¬
{"1.5 in", ".5 in", "4 in", "4 in"}, {".5 in", "4.5 in", "4 in", "7 in"}}
tell application "Adobe InDesign CS5"
    set docRef to document 1
    set pageRef to page 1 of docRef
end tell
set rectList to makeRectangles(docRef, pageRef, propList, boundsList, ¬
layerRef)

(*Creates rectangles using list of lists for bounds; bounds are added to
values in property record propList.*)
on makeRectangles(docRef, pageRef, propList, boundsList, layerRef)
    set frameList to {}
    tell application "Adobe InDesign CS5"
        set propRecord to {fill color:item 1 of propList, stroke ¬
        weight:item 2 of propList, stroke type:item 3 of propList, ¬
        stroke color:item 4 of propList, stroke alignment:inside ¬
        alignment}
        --adds item layer property to property record
```

```
        if layerRef is not missing value then
            set propRecord to propRecord & {item layer:layerRef}
        end if
        tell pageRef
            repeat while length of boundsList > 0
                --add geometric bounds to propRecord
                set newRecord to propRecord & {geometric bounds:item 1 ¬
                of boundsList}
                set end of frameList to make rectangle with properties ¬
                newRecord
                set boundsList to rest of boundsList
            end repeat
        end tell
    end tell
    return frameList
end makeRectangles
```

Adding a Record Item

To add a name: value pair item to a record, use the concatenation operator. See how this is done in the example above.

Step and Repeat

When an item is repeated as a series of columns and rows (*a grid*), this is known as step and repeat. A favorite handler that finds its way into many scripts for this purpose is **calculateGrid**. The handler returns a list of geometric bounds (lists within a list) to be used for creating a grid of items. Step refers to the number of repeats horizontally while repeat refers to the number of repeats vertically. Gutter is the space between items horizontally, gap is the space between items vertically. The space to be divided into the grid is identified by a list of bounds. In the following example, the geometric bounds of a selected object is used.

Calculate Grid

```
--requires a selected page item to identify the target area for grid
set rows to 3
set cols to 4 --columns
set gutter to 12
set gap to 12
try
    set docRef to getDocRef()
    --set measurement units to points; ruler origin to page
    set {orighm, origvm, origro} to setMeasures(docRef)
    set gBounds to pgItemSelectionBounds(docRef)
    if gBounds = {} then
        error "Requires page item selection"
    end if
    set boundsList to calculateGrid(gBounds, rows, cols, gutter, gap)
    resetMeasures (docRef, orighm, origvm, origro)
on error errStr
    activate
    display alert errStr
end try
boundsList
```

```
(*Returns list of bounds for each item to be created in grid.*)
on calculateGrid(areaBounds, rCount, cCount, gut, gap)
    set boundsList to {}
    set fullWid to (item 4 of areaBounds) - (item 2 of areaBounds)
    set fullHgt to (item 3 of areaBounds) - (item 1 of areaBounds)
    set colWid to (fullWid - ((cCount - 1) * gut)) / cCount
    set rowHgt to (fullHgt - ((rCount - 1) * gap)) / rCount
    set x0 to item 2 of areaBounds
    set y0 to item 1 of areaBounds
    repeat with j from 1 to rCount --repeat for rows
        repeat with i from 1 to cCount --repeat for columns
            set x1 to x0 + colWid
            set y1 to y0 + rowHgt
            copy {y0, x0, y1, x1} to end of boundsList
            set x0 to x1 + gut
        end repeat
        set x0 to item 2 of areaBounds
        set y0 to y1 + gap
    end repeat
    return boundsList
end calculateGrid
(*Add handlers: getDocRef, setMeasures, resetMeasures, and
pgItemSelectionBounds (Selection folder) to complete the script.*)
```

I am sure you can see how the **calculateGrid** handler could be combined with the **makeRectangles** handler to create a fully functional script. The section "Make Scripts Work for You" steps you through the procedure.

Removing Multiple Items

When working with items referenced in lists, item reference positions can shift when items are deleted or changed. This can cause unexpected results. To avoid this problem, begin with the last item in the list and work forward. This can be done by using a negative one value (-1) for the optional **by** value in a **repeat with** loop. Alternatively, you may use the **reverse** property of a list to reverse the order of the items in a list.

For an example, the following gets a list of the swatches for a document. The script then parses the list to remove all colors with the exception of those that are specified in the list *lockedList*. Check the swatches panel for the document before and after running the script.

Delete Swatches_List

```
--assumes an open document
--list of colors that won't be removed
set lockedList to {"Black", "Paper", "None", "Registration"}
tell application "Adobe InDesign CS5"
    tell document 1
        set theList to swatches
        repeat with i from length of theList to 1 by -1
            if name of item i of theList is not in lockedList then
                delete item i of theList
            end if
        end repeat
    end tell
end tell
```

In the previous script the names for swatches specified in *lockedList* are reserved by InDesign. An exception will be raised if an attempt is made to delete these swatches. Instead of checking for the reserved colors with an **if** statement as above, a **try block** can be used.

Delete Swatches_Try

```
(*Assumes an open document. Uses try statement to skip reserved items.*)
tell application "Adobe InDesign CS5"
    tell document 1
        set theList to swatches
        repeat with i from length of theList to 1 by -1
            try
                delete item i of theList
            end try
        end repeat
    end tell
end tell
```

Another example is a script that removes all empty text frames found in a document. This uses an **every** element specifier instead of a loop.

Delete Using Every

```
(*Removes items matching criteria of every test. Expects open document.*)
tell application "Adobe InDesign CS5"
    tell document 1
        set theList to every text frame of it where contents = ""
        if length of theList > 0 then
            delete (every text frame of it where contents = "")
        end if
    end tell
end tell
```

Every Element

The **every** element specifier is actually a form of numerical indexing. It points to all items that meet a test or, without a test, all items. In many instances where a repeat loop might be used, an every statement can perform the same function. So before you write a bunch of scripts with a repeat loop, if all items will receive the same treatment, you may consider using an every statement instead.

```
tell document 1 of application "Adobe InDesign CS5"
    set properties of the first paragraph of every story to ¬
    {drop cap characters: 1, drop cap lines: 2}
end tell
```

You may want to look at the project **Drop Caps** that accompanies this chapter. A project is a folder containing a script with a document and/or resources to be used for testing.

Collective Reference

The **every** element specifier can be used as the specifier in a **tell** statement:

```
tell document 1 of application "Adobe InDesign CS5"
    try
        tell every rectangle
```

```
        set properties to {fill color:"None", stroke weight:2, ¬
        stroke color:"Black", stroke style:"Solid"}
    end tell
  end try
end tell
```

The plural form of an **every** reference can be used in place of the keyword **every**. In the example above, the tell statement using the every specifier could be changed to:

```
tell rectangles
```

Filtering

Filtering provides the test to qualify the **every** specifier using a **where** or **whose** clause. Suppose you want to apply a special type font to every occurrence of the name of your company in a document. This can be done easily by using a filter statement with an **every** specifier.

Apply Font_Every

```
(*Change values for fontName and style in call to testFont; also findStr
to values applicable to your document*)
try
    set fontRef to testFont("Herculanum", "Regular")
on error errstr
    display alert errstr
end try

set findStr to "Quintessential" --must be a single word
tell application "Adobe InDesign CS5"
    set docRef to document 1
    tell docRef
        try
            set properties of every word of every story whose contents is ¬
            findStr to {applied font:fontRef}
        end try
    end tell
end tell
(*Add handler testFont from Environment folder of Handlers Library to
complete the script.*)
```

The previous example will only work if the value for *findStr* is a single word. A more robust way to set attributes for text is using find/change. This will be covered in Chapter 16.

Remember to surround statements using a filtered **every** specifier with a **try/end try** trap. If no object is found meeting the specifications given, the script could error.

Make Scripts Work for You

The script you will put together in this section, **Step and Repeat Rectangles**, will create a grid of rectangles within a given area. The area can be defined either by the user having a page item selected or for a page whose page offset may be designated by the user. In Chapter 17 you will discover how to create a custom dialog to allow your user to define values for the variables in your scripts.

You may also want to check out the script **Page Item Grid** in the Chapter Scripts folder for this chapter.

Plan Your Script

When starting a script, it is good to think through the functionality by jotting down a flow chart of some type before you start to code. The flow for this script will be as follows:

1. Make sure there is a document open.
2. Set measurement units to points, ruler origin to page origin.
3. Get the bounds for the grid.
    - 3a. If there is a page item selected, get the bounds of the item.
        - Else.
    - 3b. If there is more than 1 page in the document.
        - Get the page number for the target page from the user.
        - Else.
        - Reference page 1.
    - 3c. Get live bounds for the page.
4. Calculate bounds for grid items using gBounds from selected item, or if no item selected the live bounds for the page..
5. Create the rectangles using the bounds calculated.
6. Reset measurement units and ruler origin.

Verify Handlers to be Used

Next verify the handlers that can be used for each step in your script. If a handler is not to be found, create the handler and test with dummy information. Luckily for this project, all of the handlers are in folders in the Handlers Library. Handlers listed for each step follow:

1. **getDocRef** - Returns reference to document 1 if it exists; else throws error. In Document folder.
2. **setResetMeasures (setMeasures)** - Saves current measures, and changes measurement units to points, ruler origin to page origin. In Environment folder.
3. 3a. **pgItemSelectionBounds** - Returns bounds for page item selection. Returns empty list if valid page item not selected. In Selection folder.
    - 3b. **parentPageofSelection** - Returns reference to parent page of selected page item. In Selection folder.
    - 3c. **pageRefByNumber** - Returns reference to target page. If more than one page in the document, a display dialog asks for the number of the target page. Returns reference to page. Will throw error if valid answer not entered by user or user cancels. In Dialogs folder.
    - 3d. **getLiveBounds** - Returns bounds for area inside margins for page referenced. In Page folder.
4. **calculateGrid** - Returns list of geometric bounds for area defined. In Calculate folder.
5. **makeRectangles** - Creates rectangles given bounds list returned from step 4. In Page Items folder.
6. **getSetMeasures (resetMeasures)** - Resets measures using values saved in step 2. See step 2 above.

Assemble the script

1. Start a new script. Add the first item from your list of handlers to the script, **getDocRef**. Optional: Place a divider comment between the call to the handler and the handler. This has been done for you in the **getDocRef** handler.

2. Acquire the handlers in order, one by one, using your workflow outline and add them to the bottom of your script. As you do so, cut the call to the handler along with variable declarations (if included). Paste and arrange as needed at the top of your script.

3. Refer back to your outline to place calls to handlers where needed.

4. Add code necessary and make sure variables needed for handlers match variables used to hold values returned from previous handlers.

   Your script needs to test if there is a page item selected to identify the bounds to be used. Test for an empty list returned from **pgItemSelectionBounds**. If the value for *pageItemBounds* is an empty list, your script will need to get the bounds for the target page. The target page reference is returned from the handler **pageRefByNumber**. Use this reference to call **getLiveBounds** to get the bounds of the page inside of its margins. Set this up with an if/end if block:

   ```
   if pageItemBounds = {} then
       set pageRef to pageRefByNumber(docRef)
       set pageItemBounds to getLiveBounds(docRef, pageRef)
   else
       set pageRef to parentPageOfSelection
   end if
   ```

5. Make sure variables used to hold values returned from handlers use the same identifier if used later in a call to a handler. The only change required for this script is the variable used to identify the area to be calculated for a grid. The value returned from the handler **pgItemSelectionBounds** is *pageItemBounds*. This variable is also used in the code for Step 4 above that checks for the value returned from **getLiveBounds** .

   The call to **calculateGrid** uses the variable *gBounds* for the same value. It doesn't matter if you use *pageItemBounds* or *gBounds* for the variable, just make sure you are consistent.

Compile Your Script

The top portion of your script should look similar to the following when finished:

```
(*StepAndRepeatRectangles -
Creates grid of rectangles in area defined by either page item selected or
the live area for a page if no selection.*)

--variables
set rows to 3 --step
set cols to 4 --repeat
set gutter to 12 --in point units
set gap to 12 --in point units
set layerRef to missing value
(*Values for propList in order are: fill color, stroke weight, stroke
type, stroke color.*)
set propList to {"None", "1 pt", "Solid", "Black"}
try
    set docRef to getDocRef()
    --call to handler to set measures to points; ruler origin to page
    set {orighm, origvm, origro} to setMeasures(docRef)
```

```
        --get bounds to use for grid
        set pageItemBounds to pgItemSelectionBounds()
        if pageItemBounds = {} then
            set pageRef to pageRefByNumber (docRef)
            set pageItemBounds to getLiveBounds (docRef, pageRef)
        else
            set pageRef to paerntPageOfSelection()
        end if
        --calculate bounds list for grid
        set boundsList to calculateGrid(pageItemBounds, rows, cols, gutter, ¬
        gap)

        --create the rectangles
        set frameList to makeRectangles(docRef, pageRef, propList,¬
        boundsList, layerRef)

        --call to handler to reset measures to original values
        resetMeasures(docRef, orighm, origvm, origro)
    on error errStr
        display alert errStr
    end try
```

Test Your Script

Try to run your script. If you receive an error saying a variable is not defined, make sure the variables required for handlers match those returned from previous handlers. Use Find (command + F) in Script Editor to locate the variable(s) undefined.

The complete script, **StepAndRepeat Rectangles**, is in the Chapter Scripts folder for this chapter.

Figure 5.1: Grid of rectangles created with StepAndRepeat Rectangles script.

6

Document Structure

Now that you have some basics under your belt, your attention needs to turn to creating documents with emphasis on structure: guides, grids, layers, and the master page. In the process you will become acquainted with a number of handlers provided as part of the downloadable resources at this book's support site (see Chapter 1).

Document Preset

There are a number of reasons using a document preset is the preferred method for creating a document with a script. First, and foremost, it just seems to work better and more conveniently. Settings for facing pages and master text frame work consistently. You also have the ability to set margins (top, left, bottom, right), column count, plus a slug of other settings (including slug) with one preset. And presets are easy to manage.

You may wish to look at the property listing for **document preset** in InDesign's dictionary. (Choose Dictionary... from AppleScript Editor's File menu and select the listing for your version of InDesign.)

To make your presets more reusable, set **pages per document** for your preset to 1 for non-facing pages and 4 for facing (unless you consistently need some other number of pages for your preset). If you need more pages for an individual project, just override using **pages per document** for the document's **document preference**. As an example, the following uses the handler **docFromPreset** from the Document folder of the Handlers Library. As part of the parameters for this handler, the number of pages for the document can be passed to override the number of pages established in the document preset. If missing value is passed as the value for the number of pages (*numPages* variable), the preset's **pages per document** value is used.

Change the values for the *presetProps* record in the code below as desired.

Document From Preset

```
set presetName to "8x10_Facing"
tell application "Adobe InDesign CS5"
    set presetProps to {name:presetName, page width:"8i", page height: ¬
    "10i",intent:print intent, top: "60 pt", left:"24 pt", bottom:"48pt",¬
    right:"36 pt", column count:2, master text frame:false, ¬
    pages per document:4, slug top offset:"36 pt", document slug uniform ¬
    size:false, document bleed top offset:"12 pt", document bleed ¬
    uniform size: true}
    set numPages to missing value
    set docRef to my docFromPreset(presetName, presetProps, numPages)
    set mSpreadRef to master spread 1 of docRef
    set pageRef to page 1 of mSpreadRef
```

```
            set column count of margin preferences of pageRef to 2
        end tell
    (*Creates document using preset. Creates preset if not found.*)
    on docFromPreset(presetName, presetProps, numberPages)
        tell application "Adobe InDesign CS5"
            if exists document preset presetName then
                set presetRef to document preset presetName
            else --create the preset
                set presetRef to make document preset with properties presetProps
            end if
            set docRef to make document with properties {document preset: ¬
            presetRef}
            if numberPages is not missing value then
                tell document preferences of docRef
                    set pages per document to numberPages
                end tell
            end if
        end tell
        return docRef
    end docFromPreset
```

If values for **document bleed** are to be uniform for all sides of the document, set the value for **document bleed top offset** and then set **document bleed uniform size** to true. The same holds true for **slug top offset**. If you want slug offsets to be uniform, establish the setting for **document slug uniform size** to true. Most commonly slug offset is set for the top of the document only as in the preset example above.

Layers

A layer is an element (child) of the document. Every document has one layer by default. Page items and guides are associated with layers by virtue of their **item layer** property. To get a list of all layers in a document you can use the following.

```
    tell document 1 of application "Adobe InDesign CS5"
        set nameList to name of layers
    end tell
```

In working with an existing document, if your script does not specify the layer on which page items will be created, the items will be associated with the currently active layer.

A layer can return a list of all page items to which it is associated using its **all page items** or **all graphics** properties. Specific object classes associated with a layer can be targeted using the **every** element specifier. If no items of the type specified are associated with the layer, an empty list is returned.

```
    tell application "Adobe InDesign CS5"
        if exists layer "Images" of document 1
            tell layer "Images" of document 1
                set rectList to rectangles
                --alternatively can be written: set rectList to every rectangle
            end tell
        end if
    end tell
```

Working with Layers

When a layer is created, it is placed by default at the top of the document's layer stack. As with other objects that are identified by name, you must verify that a layer does not exist before attempting to create one by the same name. The handler **getLayerRef** checks for the existence of the layer before attempting to create it. If a layer already exists by the name specified, it is unlocked if needed, and a reference to the layer and its previous locked state are returned. If no layer as named is found, the layer is created. When set to true, the **toBack** parameter for the handler moves the layer to the bottom of the layer stack. The value for the variable *clr* (layer color) can be `missing value` in which case a default color is assigned by the application. The handler returns a reference to the layer, a boolean indicating if the layer existed and was locked, and the index of the active layer prior to creating the new layer (*activeIndex* variable). When a new layer is created, it becomes the active layer. The *activeIndex* variable can be used to restore the original layer as the active layer.

Get Layer Reference

```
set layerName to "Furniture"
set clr to {0, 255, 0} --layer color can be a list of 3 values (RGB)
set toBack to true
set docRef to document 1 of application "Adobe InDesign CS5"
set {layerRef, wasLocked, activeIndex} to getLayerRef(docRef, ¬
layerName, clr, toBack)

(*Checks for existence of layer named. If found, a reference to the layer
and previous locked state is returned. Otherwise new layer is created.*)
on getLayerRef(docRef, layerName, clr, toBack)
    set wasLocked to false
    tell application "Adobe InDesign CS5"
        tell docRef
            set activeIndex to index of active layer
            if exists layer layerName then
                set layerRef to layer layerName
                set wasLocked to locked of layerRef
                set locked of layerRef to false
            else
                set layerProps to {name:layerName, visible:true, ¬
                locked:false}
                if clr is not missing value then
                    set layerProps to layerProps & {layer color:clr}
                end if
                set layerRef to make layer with properties layerProps
                if toBack then
                    move layerRef to after layer -1 of docRef
                end if
            end if
        end tell
    end tell
    return {layerRef, wasLocked, activeIndex}
end getLayerRef
```

A handler to reset the layers if needed, called **resetLayers**, is also provided. Use this handler at the end of a script to reset the active layer when the **getLayerRef** handler (above) is used. Both handlers are found in the Document Structure folder of the Handlers Library.

```
resetLayers (docRef, layerRef, wasLocked, activeIndex)

(*Resets active layer and relocks layer referenced if existing.*)
on resetLayers(docRef, layerRef, wasLocked, activeIndex)
    tell application "Adobe InDesign CS5"
        tell docRef
            if index of layerRef is not activeIndex then
                set active layer to layer activeIndex
            end if
            if wasLocked then
                set locked of layerRef to true
            end if
        end tell
    end tell
end resetLayers
```

The handler **getLayerRef** is combined with **resetLayers** in a script that creates ruler guides for a document. This script, **Ruler Guides**, is found in the Chapter Scripts folder for this chapter. More about ruler guides will be found later in this chapter.

Layer Methods

Layers can be duplicated, merged with other layers, or removed using commands provided for the layer class. Below is a handler that merges all layers to the first layer. The **mergeLayers** handler is in the Document Structure folder of the Handlers Library (see Chapter 1).

Merge Layers

```
set docRef to document 1 of application "Adobe InDesign CS5"
mergeLayers(docRef)

(*Merges the top layer with remaining layers.*)
on mergeLayers(docRef)
    tell application "Adobe InDesign CS5"
        tell docRef
            set layerList to layers
            if length of layerList > 1 then
                set targetLayer to item 1 of layerList
                set layerList to rest of layerList
                tell targetLayer to merge with layerList
            end if
        end tell
    end tell
end mergeLayers
```

Notice how the **rest** property for a list is used in this handler.

Master Spread

Similar to a document spread, the master spread has properties and commands, and acts as the parent of the pages contained. Objects created on a page of the master spread are reflected on all pages to which it is applied. The default master spread ("A-Master") is applied to all pages of a document by default. The master spread is used primarily to define the foundation for its assigned pages. Headers, footers, repeating elements, guides, slug information, and page numbering are some of the more common elements placed on master pages.

The **master text frame** property for **document preferences,** creates a text frame for pages of the master spread. When **master text frame** is set to true, a reference to text frame 1 for the document targets the master text frame. With **facing pages** set to true, the default text frames for the master spread pages are linked. To reference the linked text frames, the index reference needs to be text frame 2 for the document reference. Try the following with an open document with facing pages and master text frame set to true, opened to the master spread.

```
tell application "Adobe InDesign CS5"
    tell document 1
        set contents of text frame 2 to "THIS WILL BE ON MASTER PAGE 1"
    end tell
end tell
```

To create page items on a master page, reference the page by its index within the master spread. With facing pages, the left and right margins switch for the left-facing page.

Folio Frames

```
(*Assumes facing-page document with layer "Furniture", paragraph
style"Folio", measurements set to points.*)
set marginOffset to 10
set folioHgt to 24
set footerStr to ""
set masterName to "A-Master"
tell application "Adobe InDesign CS5"
    set docRef to document 1
    set styleRef to paragraph style "Folio" of docRef
    set layerRef to layer "Furniture" of docRef
    set masterRef to master spread masterName of docRef
    set rAlign to right align
    set lAlign to left align
end tell
set lFootRef to doFooter(docRef, masterRef, 1, layerRef, marginOffset, ¬
folioHgt, footerStr, styleRef, 1, lAlign)
set rFootRef to doFooter(docRef, masterRef, 2, layerRef, marginOffset, ¬
folioHgt, footerStr, styleRef, 1, rAlign)

on doFooter(docRef, masterRef, pgNumber, layerRef, marginOffset,¬
folioHgt, footerStr, styleRef, pageInsert, alignVal)
    tell application "Adobe InDesign CS5"
        tell docRef
            set pageWid to page width of document preferences
            set pageHgt to page height of document preferences
            set pageRef to page pgNumber of masterRef
            set bm to bottom of margin preferences of pageRef
            set y0 to (pageHgt - bm) + marginOffset
            set x0 to left of margin preferences of pageRef
            set x1 to (right of margin preferences of pageRef)
            set y1 to y0 + folioHgt
            set textFramePrefs to {text column count:1, inset spacing:0, ¬
            first baseline offset:cap height}
            tell pageRef
                if side = left hand then
                    set gBounds to {y0, x1, y1, pageWid - x0}
                else
                    set gBounds to {y0, x0, y1, pageWid - x1}
                end if
                set frameRef to make text frame with properties ¬
```

```
            {geometric bounds:gBounds, fill color:"None", stroke ¬
            weight:0, stroke color:"None", itemLayer:layerRef, ¬
            text frame preferences:textFramePrefs, contents:footerStr}
            set contents of insertion point pageInsert ¬
            of frameRef to auto page number
        end tell
        tell text 1 of frameRef
            apply paragraph style using styleRef with clearing ¬
            overrides
            set justification to alignVal
        end tell
    end tell
end tell
return frameRef
end doFooter
```

Most of this script should be fairly self-explanatory. Notice that the automatic page number is added using the enumeration value auto page number. It is added to an insertion point identified by the variable *pageInsert*. For the right-facing page, text is justified to align right.

Properties for master pages such as columns and gutters are inherited from the **margin preferences** for the application unless overridden by the document. To override these settings, the margin preferences for the individual master pages can be set. If you ran the script **Document From Preset** at the beginning of the chapter, you should have a preset named "8x10_Facing." With this in place, the following script creates a document using the preset. A color swatch is added using the handler **createProcessColors** (see Chapter 8). The document will also have a single column for left-facing pages and a double column for right-facing pages. You will want to save this document as it will be used for testing master spread concepts. The script in its entirety is found in the Chapter Scripts folder for this chapter.

Master Pages

```
(*Creates document with color. Assumes document preset "8x10_Facing."*)
set colorList to {{"Red", {0, 100, 100, 0}}}
set numPages to 6
tell application "Adobe InDesign CS5"
    set presetRef to document preset "8x10_Facing"
    set docRef to make document with properties ¬
    {document preset:presetRef}
    set existingColors to my createProcessColors(docRef, colorList)
    tell docRef
        set pages per document of document preferences to numPages
        set masterSpreadRef to master spread 1
    end tell
    set pageRef to page 1 of masterSpreadRef
    set column count of margin preferences of pageRef to 1
end tell

(*Add handler createProcessColors from Colors folder to complete script.*)
```

Save the document created for further testing.

Master Page Items

The **master page items** property for a document page returns a list of page item references associated with its master page. This will include objects such as guides as well as page items. With the document created using the script above open, run the following:

```
tell application "Adobe InDesign CS5"
    tell document 1
        tell page 2 of master spread 1
            make guide with properties {location:"1i", orientation:vertical}
            set masterFrame to make text frame with properties {geometric ¬
            bounds:{"1i", "1i", "4i", "7i"}, fill color:"Black", ¬
            fill tint:50}
        end tell
        set pageRef to page 1
        set masterPageItems to master page items of pageRef
    end tell
end tell
masterPageItems
```

Verify the value of *masterPageItems* in AppleScript Editor's Result panel includes a reference to the text frame. Revert this document to its last saved version (File > Revert) for further testing.

Override/Overridden

Unless overridden, an item created on the master page cannot be accessed by default from a document page. To override a master page item, the **override** command is targeted to the item on the master page with a reference to the document page on which it will be overridden.

```
tell masterFrame to override destination page pageRef
```

To determine if a page item in question is overridden, its **overridden** property is used. To see this in action, find the statement that declares the variable *masterPageItems* in the previous script:

```
set masterPageItems to master page items of pageRef
```

Add the following statement before the statement above, so it reads:

```
tell masterFrame to override destination page pageRef
set masterPageItems to master page items of pageRef
```

Make sure you revert the test document to its original saved state before running the modified script. Verify the value of *masterPageItems* after running the script. Notice that the text frame is not in the list. Keep the document open for the next test.

To get a list of all overridden page items on a page, an **every** object specifier can be used. Try the following with your test document.

```
tell application "Adobe InDesign CS5"
    tell page 1 of document 1
        set testList to every page item where overridden is true
    end tell
end tell
testList
```

Detach

Overriding a master page item allows settings made at the page level to override those of the item on the master page. Once overridden, the item no longer appears in the list of **master page items** for the page. However, if you later make changes to the item on the master page, these changes will be inherited by the page item even though overridden. To avoid this, you must also **detach** the overridden master page item. To illustrate, run the following with your test document.

Detach

```
tell application "Adobe InDesign CS5"
    tell document 1
        set pageRef to page 1
        set mSpread to applied master of pageRef
        tell page 2 of mSpread
            set rectRef to make rectangle with properties ¬
            {geometric bounds:{"1i", "4i", "2i", "5i"}, fill color:"Red"}
            set oRef to override rectRef destination page pageRef
            detach oRef
        end tell
        tell page item 1 of pageRef
            --value of overridden master page item is nothing if overridden
            set isOverridden to overridden master page item is nothing
        end tell
        set fill color of rectRef to "Paper"
    end tell
end tell
isOverridden
```

After running the previous script, the item created on the master page should have a fill color of "Paper" while its corresponding item on page 1 retains its original fill color of "Red." The script is found in the Chapter Scripts folder for this chapter.

Unlink

In older versions of InDesign the command to detach a page item from its master page was **unlink**. Unlink now works with links, severing the link to the source file while embedding the image in the document.

Master Spread Commands

Some of the more common commands you may incorporate in your scripts when working with master spreads follow.

Load Masters

If you have a template from which you want to replicate master spreads in your document, you can use the **load masters command** for the document. This requires a file path or alias reference to the template you wish to use. An optional parameter, **global strategy for load masters,** dictates the action to take when existing master pages have the same name as those being imported. The default for this is load all with overwrite. To rename the master pages use the value load all with rename. (See Chapter 7 for sample code.)

Create Master Spread

To create a master page, if you want to set both the base name and prefix for a master spread you must first verify that a master page having the same base name and prefix does not exist. Otherwise, if you supply only the base name, the next alpha character available will be supplied for its prefix. If you supply neither the base name nor the name prefix, the name will default to the next available alpha character followed by "-Master."

To test for the existence of a master page, use its base name and prefix. The code below creates master spread "B-Master" and applies it to spread 1 of the document

```
tell application "Adobe InDesign CS5"
    tell document 1
        if not (exists master spread "B-Master") then
            set masterB to make master spread with properties ¬
            {base name:"Master", name prefix:"B", show master items:true}
        else
            set masterB to master spread "B-Master"
        end if
        --apply the master to the spread
        set applied master of spread 1 to masterB
    end tell
end tell
masterB
```

Applied Master

You can create any number of master spreads based on another. For this the **applied master** **property** is used. This requires a reference to the master spread on which the new master will be based. In the following script, a document is created with a master spread added based on "A-Master." When an object such as a master page is created based on another, it inherits the properties of the object it is based on.

Master Based On

```
(*Assumes document preset 8x10_Facing exists; will error otherwise.*)
tell application "Adobe InDesign CS5"
    set presetRef to document preset "8x10_Facing"
    set docRef to make document with properties ¬
    {document preset:presetRef}
    tell docRef
        set masterA to master spread 1
        tell page 2 of masterA
            make guide with properties {location:"1i", ¬
            orientation:vertical}
            set rectRef to make rectangle with properties ¬
            {geometric bounds:{"1i", ".5i", "2i", "6i"},¬
            fill color:"Black", fill tint:-1}
        end tell
        set masterB to make master spread with properties ¬
        {applied master:masterA}
        tell masterB
            set frameRef to make text frame with properties ¬
            {geometric bounds:{"2i", "1i", "5i", "6i"}, ¬
            fill color:"Black", fill tint:20}
        end tell
        --assign master spread to document spread
```

```
        set applied master of spread 2 to masterB
    end tell
end tell
```

Master Page Overlay

New to CS5 is the ability to have pages with different sizes in one document. Because of this, the master page and its associated pages can be different. **Master page overlay** determines how the master page is positioned on its associated pages. This is powerful stuff especially because scripts give you additional capability for applying page transformations. You will work with transformations in Chapter 18. The following creates a three-page spread and resizes the center page as with a spine for a book cover..

Spread With Spine

```
tell application "Adobe InDesign CS5"
    set presetRef to document preset "8x10_Facing"
    set docRef to make document with properties ¬
        {document preset:presetRef}
    tell docRef
        set masterB to make master spread with properties ¬
        {base name:"Master", name prefix:"B"}
        set centerPage to page 2 of spread 2
        tell spread 2
            set allow page shuffle to false
            make page at end
        end tell
        set applied master of centerPage to masterB
    end tell
    tell page 2 of masterB
        make rectangle with properties {geometric bounds: ¬
        {"36 pt", "215 pt", "667 pt", "348 pt"}, fill color:"None", ¬
        stroke weight:8, stroke color:"Black"}
    end tell
    --changes size of page 2 of spread 2
    resize centerPage in inner coordinates from center anchor ¬
    by replacing current dimensions with values {288, 720}
end tell
```

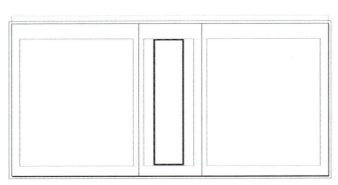

Figure 6.1: Spread created with Spread With Spine script.

Guides

InDesign provides ruler, margin, column, and slug guides to aid in aligning and positioning objects.

Column guide locked, column guide color, and **margin guide color** are part of the properties found in **document preferences**. **Guide preferences** is a property of the application and the document. Properties for guide preferences include **guides in back, guides locked, guides shown, guides snapto, ruler guides color**, and **ruler guides view threshold**. This last property determines the minimum view percentage at which the guides will be visible.

You can assign a guide to a layer using its **item layer** property. The **locked** and **visible** state for the guides are controlled using the **lock guides** and **show guides** properties for the associated layer.

Ruler Guides

To create a ruler guide manually, you drag from the ruler onto the page. Using a script, you supply values for the **location** (measurement units) and **orientation** (`horizontal` or `vertical`). If not set specifically for the guide, the ruler guide inherits properties set for **guide preferences**. When a guide is created at the document level, even though it may be assigned to Layer 1, it is only visible on the first page of the document. To have the guide visible on all pages assigned to a master spread, you need to target the master spread. The script below demonstrates. It assumes an active document. A more complete version of this script, **Ruler Guides**, is found in the Chapter Scripts folder for this chapter.

Ruler Guides

```
--assumes document 1 exists
set masterName to "A-Master"
set vertPos to {"1i", "2i", "4.5i"} --positions for vertical guides
set horizPos to {"2 in", "6 in"} --positions for horizontal guides
tell application "Adobe InDesign CS5"
    set docRef to document 1
    tell guide preferences of docRef
        set guides locked to false
        set ruler guides view threshold to 30
        set ruler guides color to orange
    end tell
    set layerRef to layer 1 of docRef
    --this guide will only show on page 1
    tell page 1 of docRef
        make guide with properties {item layer:layerRef, ¬
        orientation:vertical,location:"3p"}
    end tell
    --guides created on master page are on all associated pages
    set masterRef to master spread masterName of docRef
end tell
createRulerGuides(masterRef, layerRef, vertPos, horizPos)

(*Creates ruler guides on layer referenced of master spread.*)
on createRulerGuides(masterRef, layerRef, vertPos, horizPos)
    tell application "Adobe InDesign CS5"
        tell masterRef
            repeat with i from 1 to length of vertPos
```

```
            make guide with properties {item layer:layerRef, ¬
                orientation:vertical, location:item i of vertPos}
        end repeat
        repeat with i from 1 to length of horizPos
            make guide with properties {item layer:layerRef, ¬
                orientation:horizontal, location:item i of horizPos}
        end repeat
    end tell
  end tell
end createRulerGuides
```

Examine the result of running the script. Notice when no page is designated for the master spread and ruler spread origin is page origin, the guide is placed on the right-facing page.

Create Guides

Intended to be used with a spread reference, **create guides** is a core InDesign command. It creates even-spaced guides given the number of columns and rows. The parameters for **create guides** are labeled (similar to those used for display dialog). You just string the name/value pairs in one long statement with no commas between. All parameters for the command are listed as being optional but can include the **row gutter, column gutter,** and **guide color**. If the value for **remove existing** is true, existing guides are removed. If a reference for the layer is not supplied, the guides will be created on the active layer. The following demonstrates. It assumes that you now have a document preset for "8x10_Facing."

Create Guides

```
--assumes document preset "8x10_Facing" exists
set vertPos to {"1i", "2i", "4.5i"}
tell application "Adobe InDesign CS5"
    set presetRef to document preset "8x10_Facing"
    set docRef to make document with properties ¬
    {document preset:presetRef}
    set spreadRef to spread 2 of docRef
    set layerRef to layer 1 of docRef
    tell spreadRef
        create guides number of rows 2 number of columns 3 ¬
        row gutter ".5 in" column gutter "1p0" guide color gray ¬
        layer layerRef with fit margins without remove existing
    end tell
end tell
```

Grids

InDesign has two kinds of grids:

- **document grid** - the document grid encompasses the entire pasteboard.
- **baseline grid** - the baseline grid displays across the spread.

Grids display on every spread but cannot be assigned to a master spread.

Attributes for the grids are set using properties for **grid preferences**. Grid preferences can be set at both the application and document level. To toggle grids on and off with a script, the **not** operator can be used.

```
tell application "Adobe InDesign CS5"
    tell grid preferences of document 1
        set baseline grid shown to not baseline grid shown
    end tell
end tell
```

If you plan to set **grid preferences,** you will want to refer to InDesign's dictionary to see all of the properties that can be set for the document and baseline grid.

Color for Guides and Grids

The values that can be supplied for guides and grids can be either an RGB value supplied as a list of three numbers ranging in value from 0-255 or UI color values: light blue, red, green, blue, yellow, magenta, cyan, gray, black, or orange.

Make Scripts Work for You

Create Document

This project walks you through the process of creating a script by modifying a script template. A script template is a collection of related handlers that serve a common purpose. Instead of looking up an entire list of handlers for your project, open a script template. Hopefully much of what you want may be included. Make the necessary changes to variable values, and comment out handlers that you won't be using. You may also need to add a handler or two not included in the template.

The template you will be using for this project is **Document Template.** You will find this template inside the **Create Document** project folder for this chapter. Open the template to view the handlers included. You will see there are a number that could be used in just about any script that involves creating a document.

testFont - Returns reference to font named if installed. Otherwise, an error condition is created.

docFromPreset - Checks for a preset by name. If preset is not found it is created using property record. Returns reference to document created using preset.

createLayers - Designed for a new document, allows for a number of layers to be created. Using a list of layer names, the layers are created in order so the first item in the list is the top layer. Returns reference to layer designated.

createProcessColors - Uses list of lists to define swatch names and process color values.

getParastyle - Checks for paragraph style. If the style is not found, it is created based on the default paragraph style with font size and first line indent values defined.

doFooter - Creates footer text frames for page referenced. Bounds are calculated using margin settings, page width, and page height.

setDocMeasures - Similar to **setMeasures**, this handler sets measurement units and ruler origin and is designed for a new document rather than one that is active.

getNumber - Displays a dialog prompting user to enter a number. If entry is not valid, an error is thrown.

getMasterSpread - Returns reference to master spread. Includes option to create spread based on a master spread.

Sample values for the variables required are assigned and found at the top of the template. Calls to the handlers needed to create the document are also included. The template can be run as is.

The **checkFont** handler will error if the font designated is not found. The **getNumber** handler requests a page number entry from the user. If the number entered is valid, the document is built.

Run the script and examine the document created.

Your task is to use the script template to build a similar document, perhaps one that is a different size, or one that requires a second master page. For the purpose of the following discussion it will be assumed you want to change functionality to post a message if the font is not found. The user is asked if she wants to continue by using the font for the default paragraph style. For this you will need to replace the **testFont** handler with a handler called **testFontWPrompt**. It is found in the Environment folder of the Handlers Library.

1. If not open, open the script **Document Template** in AppleScript Editor.
    Run the script to test.
2. Save the script under a new name. This will now be your script.
3. Make changes to values for variables as needed. For instance, change the names for layers to be created to the names of those layers that you will want.
4. If a paragraph style named "Folio" is not found, one is created in the **getParastyle** handler using the property record *parastyleProps* which includes a definition for the font referenced. This may not be what you want. If so, either change the name of the style designated in the variable *paraStyleName* to a default style, or change the values in the property record.
5. At the bottom of your script, add the **testFontWPrompt** handler. (Control-click at the bottom of your script, and navigate to the Environment folder in the Handlers Library. Click on the entry for **testFontWPrompt**.)
    In addition to the **testFontWPrompt** handler, this file adds two handlers:
    getBoolean - asks user to respond yes or no
    getDefaultFont - gets reference to the applied font for text defaults
6. Copy the statement that calls **testFontWPrompt** at the top of the code added in Step 5. Delete the other sample call information.
7. Replace the call to the **testFont** handler with the line you just copied. (The call will be the first statement in the first try block.)
8. Test your script. You may wish to change the font name to one you know does not exist just to see how your new code works.

You will find the final script, **Create Document_Final**, along with **Document Template** script in the **Create Document** project folder for this chapter.

Challenge: Add metadata to your document by adding the **addMetadata** handler to your script. This handler is in the Document folder in the Handlers Library.

7

Files and Folders

The subject of files and folders is essential to most automation projects. Files are often the principal means of providing data for a project. Templates and style sheets stored in the file system can provide valuable resources for creating and styling documents.

Access to the file system is provided by the Macintosh operating system itself (via Standard Additions) and by applications which are part of the system such as Finder and System Events. Listings of the objects and methods supported are found in the dictionaries for these items. For working with image files you will also want to check out Image Events.

File System Paths

The absolute path to a file or folder is represented by a colon-delimited string:

```
set myPath to [folder]:[user directory]:[filename.extension]
```

The path to a file or folder can also be represented as a POSIX path, which delimits path items with slashes rather than colons.

```
tell application "System Events"
    set thePath to POSIX path of library folder
end tell
--the result is "/Library"
```

You can build a path to a specific file by concatenating string references to paths with that of reserved folders. For instance, to get the path to the application support folder on the Macintosh, use the following. The result is an alias reference to the folder.

```
set appPath to path to application support folder
--result: alias "Macintosh HD:Library:Application Support:"
```

To convert the alias reference to a string value, add the phrase **as string**:

```
set appPath to path to application support folder as string
```

Other fixed folder paths of interest are:

- **desktop** - `set myDesktop to path to desktop from user domain`
- **home folder** - `set myHome to path to home folder from user domain`
- **public folder** - `set pubFolder to path to public folder`
- **temporary items folder** - `set tempPath to path to temporary items folder`

For a complete listing of reserved folders, look in the dictionaries for both Standard Additions and System Events.

When working with Standard Additions, use the **path to** command to get the paths to reserved folders, as in the previous examples. **Path to** allows optional parameters:

from -Indicates domain in which to look for the folder. You can use user domain, system domain, local domain, network domain, and Classic domain.

```
set docFolder to path to documents folder from user domain
```

as - Determine the class type: alias or string.

```
set docFolder to path to documents folder from user domain as string
```

folder creation - Creates the folder if it doesn't exist. Defaults to true.

Reserved folders are properties of the Systems Events application.

```
tell application "System Events"
    set libPath to library folder
end tell
--result: folder "Macintosh HD:Library:" of application "System Events"
```

As you can see, the result is an object reference for the folder. You can get an alias reference to the folder by adding **path to**:

```
tell application "System Events"
    set libPath to path to library folder
end tell --result is an alias reference
```

Inside a tell statement to System Events or the Finder, the result of the following is a slash-delimited reference to the system Library folder.

```
tell application "System Events"
    set libFolder to path to library folder
    set pPath to POSIX path of libFolder
end tell --result is "/Library"
```

File Path

The **file path** property for the InDesign application returns a file reference to its folder.

```
tell application "Adobe InDesign CS5"
    set appFolder to file path
end tell --result:file "Macintosh HD:Applications:Adobe InDesign CS5:"
```

Active Script

When a script is run from the Scripts panel, the **active script** property of the application object returns the script's file path. For a script in the Users folder of InDesign's Scripts panel (installed as part of the procedure in Chapter 1), the result will be similar to:

```
Macintosh HD:Users:[user name]:Library:Preferences:Adobe InDesign:Version
7.0:en_US:Scripts:Scripts Panel:[name of script]
```

System References

Notice in the discussion above, a reference to a file or folder within the system can be returned as an alias reference, a path (string value), or an object reference (file or folder). In using the **path to** command, the value is returned as an alias. To change it to a path (string) reference add the phrase as string:

```
set test to path to desktop folder as string --returns string
set test to path to desktop folder --returns alias reference
```

Exists

Within a tell statement to the Finder or System Events, you can use the **exists** command to
discover if a file is in a designated path.

```
set publicFolder to path to public folder from user domain as string
set filePath to publicFolder & "Test:TestFile.aiff"
tell application "Finder"
    set fileExists to exists file filePath
end tell
```

On occasion your script may need to create a designated folder if it does not exist.

```
set homePath to path to home folder from user domain as string
tell application "Finder"
    if not (exists folder (homePath & "Test")) then
        set folderRef to make folder at homePath with properties ¬
        {name:"Test"}
    else
        set folderRef to folder (homePath & "Test")
    end if
end tell
folderRef --result is object reference to the folder
```

Object Reference

If you run the example above you will find the result will begin with the word *folder*. This is a third
reference method used for files and folders: its object reference. When the keyword *folder* or *file*
is used in a Finder or System Events statement (as in the example above), an object reference is
returned if the object exists.

User Interaction

Standard Additions for AppleScript provides a number of commands which allow your scripts
to interact with the user. In working with files, **choose folder, choose file**, and **choose file
name** may be used often.

Choose Folder

There are a number of optional parameters that can be supplied to the **choose folder**
command. You will undoubtedly be using all of these some time as part of your scripts. These
options are self-explanatory. To experiment, you may wish to change the values for some of the
parameters in the following:

```
(*The keyword as string changes the alias reference to a string.*)
set userFolder to path to home folder from user domain as string

--default location needs to be a folder or alias reference
set testFolder to alias (userFolder & "Test")
```

```
set theFolder to choose folder with prompt "Choose desired folder(s):" ¬
default location testFolder without invisibles and ¬
multiple selections allowed
```

Choose File

The result of a **choose file** command is an alias reference to a file. When you have an alias or file reference to a file, you can use the **container** property for System Events or Finder's **container** class to discover its parent folder.

```
set fileRef to choose file
tell application "System Events"
    set parentFolder to container of fileRef
end tell
parentFolder --result is an object reference to the folder
```

Choose file has the same optional parameters as **choose folder**. Unique to choose file is the ability to filter the file type using the optional **of type** parameter. The file type supplied requires a list even if only one file type is requested. You could decide to include image file types in your list:

```
set dPath to path to desktop folder from user domain
set theFile to choose file with prompt "Choose an image file" of type ¬
{"8BPS", "JPEG", "TIF", "PNG ", "PDF ", "EPSF"} default location dPath ¬
with multiple selections allowed without invisibles
```

If you wish to discover the file type for a specific file, the following script can be used. Run the script and respond by selecting the file of choice. The type of the file will be displayed in the Result panel.

```
set fileChoice to choose file
tell application "Finder"
    set theType to file type of fileChoice
end tell
theType
```

Sadly, some files do not have a file type and will return `missing value` for the script above.

Info for returns other information about a file including its creation and modification date (date object), size, whether the item chosen is a folder or package, and name extension. To see all of the properties of a file that is known to info for, run the following script and select a file from the file chooser:

```
set theFile to choose file with prompt "Choose a file" without multiple ¬
selections allowed and invisibles
set theInfo to info for theFile
theInfo
```

Alias Reference

When using a choose folder or choose file command, the reference returned is an alias reference. To add a string to the alias reference you need to coerce the alias reference to a string using *as string*.

You can coerce a string reference to an alias reference using as `alias`. If the file does not exist, an error will occur. This is one way you can test for the existence of a file.

```
set publicFolder to path to public folder from user domain as string
set filePath to publicFolder & "Test:TestFile.aiff"
```

```
try
    set fileAlias to filePath as alias
on error errStr --file not found
    display alert "File not found."
end try
```

Choose File Name

The command **choose file name** is often associated with writing information to a file. This command creates a file reference with the chosen name but without actually creating the file. It has three parameters: **with prompt**, **default name**, and **default location**.

An example of creating a file using **path to** and **choose file name** is the script **Say To File**. This also demonstrates using the **say** command which converts text to speech and can be saved as a sound file (.aiff).

Say To File

```
set theString to "This is a test, only a test"
set thePath to (path to public folder from user domain as string) & ¬
"Test:" as alias
set theFileRef to choose file name with prompt ¬
"Select location for recording" default name "TestFile.aiff" ¬
default location thePath
say theString using "Junior"
say theString using "Junior" saving to theFileRef
```

Listing Files

There may be times your script will need to present a list of files found in a designated folder to your user. You can use an **every** reference to get a reference to the files as an alias.

```
set folderRef to choose folder
tell application "Finder"
    set fileList to name of every file of folderRef whose name ¬
    extension is "txt" or file type is {"TEXT"}
end tell
```

Choose file may be used with a repeat loop to create a list of files of a designated type or types. In the following the **kind** property is examined for each file within a loop.

```
set kindList to {"Portable Network Graphics image", ¬
"Adobe PDF document", "Adobe Photoshop EPS File", ¬
"Adobe Photoshop JPEG file", "TIFF image", "JPEG image", ¬
"Adobe Photoshop document"}
set validList to {}
set fileChoice to choose file with multiple selections allowed ¬
without invisibles
repeat with i from 1 to length of fileChoice
    set theInfo to info for (item i of fileChoice)
    if kind of theInfo is in kindList then
        set the end of validList to item i of fileChoice
    end if
end repeat
validList
```

Should you wish to list all items in a folder, including folders, **list folder** can be used:

```
set theFolder to choose folder
set theList to list folder theFolder without invisibles
```

To present just the names of files without the name extension, you can use string manipulation to remove the extension from the name. The following uses **info for** to determine the **file type**, and **name extension** for the files in a folder. It creates a list of names for the desired files.

Get File Names
```
--parameters: file kind, file extension
set fileNames to getFileNames ("Plain text", "txt")

on getFileNames (fileKind, fileExt)
    set validList to {}
    set folderRef to (choose folder)
    set fileList to list folder folderRef without invisibles
    set folderPath to folderRef as string
    repeat with i from 1 to length of fileList
        set fullName to item i of fileList
        set theInfo to info for file (folderPath & fullName)
        if folder of theInfo is false then
            try
                if kind of theInfo = fileKind or name extension of theInfo = ¬
                fileExt then
                    set theOffset to offset of fileExt in fullName
                    set fileName to text 1 thru (theOffset - 2) in fullName
                    set end of validList to fileName
                end if
            end try
        end if
    end repeat
    return validList
end getFileNames
```

Choose From List

Once you have a valid list of file names, you can use **choose from list** to have the user choose the file. This might be more convenient for the user than working with the file browser.

```
--add this code after line 2 in the script above
set userChoice to choose from list fileNames with prompt ¬
"Choose file to process:" without multiple selections allowed
```

The result of **choose from list** is a list even though only one item may be selected. If the user cancels from the list, the result is false.

InDesign Documents

Now that you have some experience with files, folders, and file paths, the next step is to work with InDesign documents as they relate to them. In this section you will start by creating a simple document and saving it as a template. Using this document, you will work with handlers for saving and opening InDesign documents.

Save and Close

The following script, **Simple Template**, creates a document you can use for testing. The script saves the document as a template in the Templates folder (Applications:InDesign CS5 [or CS5.5]:Templates). It introduces a new handler which assumes there is a folder named Templates in InDesign's application folder.

saveAsTemplate - Saves document in Templates folder given a reference to the document, the name for the template, and a boolean value indicating if the template should be written over if found. In Documents folder of Handlers Library.

Simple Template

```
set presetName to "Letter_Single"
set templateName to "Letter Single.indt"
set saveOver to false
tell application "Adobe InDesign CS5"
    set presetProps to {name:presetName, pageWidth:"8.5 in", ¬
    pageHeight:"11 in", intent:print intent, pages per document:1,¬
    facing pages:false, master text frame:false}
    --last parameter is number of pages for document; can be missing value
    set docRef to my docFromPreset(presetName, presetProps, missing value)
end tell
--parameters: document, name for template, save over option
saveAsTemplate(docRef, templateName, saveOver)

--saves document as template with save over option
on saveAsTemplate(docRef, templateName, saveOver)
    tell application "Adobe InDesign CS5"
        set appPath to file path as string
        set templatePath to appPath & "Templates:" & templateName
        try
            set templatePath to templatePath as alias
            if saveOver then
                close docRef saving in templatePath with force save
            else
                activate
                display alert "Template " & templateName & " already exists."
            end if
        on error --template does not exist
            close docRef saving in templatePath
        end try
    end tell
end saveAsTemplate
(*Add handler: docFromPreset to complete script.*)
```

A complete version of this script can be found in the Chapter Scripts folder for this chapter.

Open/Save

To create a document from the template above, the following script opens the template and saves the document at location chosen by the user.

Document From Template

```
set templateName to "Letter Single.indt"
try
    set templatePath to checkTemplate(templateName)
    set docRef to docFromTemplate(templatePath, false)
end try
(*Opens designated template and saves document to path chosen by user.*)
on docFromTemplate(templatePath, doClose)
    tell application "Adobe InDesign CS5"
        set docRef to open file templatePath
        activate
        set savePath to choose file name with prompt ¬
        "Select file and folder for save"
        --tests to make sure name of file ends with ".indd"
        if savePath as string does not end with ".indd" then
            set savePath to (savePath as string) & ".indd"
        end if
        if doClose then
            close docRef saving yes saving in savePath without force save
        else
            save docRef to savePath without force save
        end if
    end tell
    return docRef
end docFromTemplate
(*Returns alias reference to template if it exists; else throws error.*)
on checkTemplate(templateName)
    tell application "Adobe InDesign CS5"
        set appPath to path to file path as string
        set filePath to appPath & "Templates:" & templateName
        set templateAlias to filePath as alias
    end tell
    return templateAlias
end checkTemplate
```

The script is in the Chapter Scripts folder for this chapter.

Check for Open Document

Your script may need to determine if the user has a particular document open. If not open, one option would be to ask the user to find the file and then have the script open it. In the script below, if the document is open, the script will make it the active document. The handler **getDocNamed** allows the user to choose the file if needed. If a file is chosen, the handler checks the name of the file. If not the same as the name designated in the script, the user is given the option to use the chosen file instead.

Check Open Document

```
set docName to "MyDocument.indd" --change name as needed
try
    set docRef to getDocNamed(docName)
on error errStr
    activate
    display alert errStr
end try
```

```
(*If document exists it is brought to the front; otherwise user is given
an option to select the document.*)
on getDocNamed(docName)
    tell application "Adobe InDesign CS5"
        if (not (exists document docName)) then
            set fileRef to choose file with prompt "Find document " & docName
            set fileTest to fileRef as string
            (*If user does not choose file as named, given option to use
                another file.*)
            if fileTest does not end with docName then
                set userPrompt to "File chosen is not " & docName & ¬
                ". Do you want to substitute?"
                set userResponse to my getBoolean(userPrompt, true)
                if userResponse = false then return
            end if
            open fileRef
        else
            if name of document 1 is not docName then
                set active document to document docName
            end if
        end if
        return document 1
    end tell
end getDocNamed

--asks for a true or false response
on getBoolean(userPrompt, falseAsDefault)
    set defaultButton to 1
    set buttonList to {"Yes", " No"}
    if falseAsDefault then
        set defaultButton to 2
    end if
    activate
    set userResponse to display alert userPrompt buttons buttonList ¬
    default button defaultButton
    return (button returned of userResponse = "Yes")
end getBoolean
```

The script is found in the Chapter Scripts folder for this chapter.

Load Resources

For many automation projects you will need to borrow resources such as styles, or master spreads from other documents. These documents will need to be saved in a fixed location such as in the Presets folder of the InDesign application folder. Establish the file path to such a document by adding its name to the string reference of its parent folder. From there, you can load the resources needed. The following loads the master spreads from the referenced file into the active document. It relies on two handlers:

chooseTemplate - Presents user with list of templates found in Templates folder from which to choose.

loadMasters - Loads master pages from template chosen with option of master spreads being renamed in the event of name clash.

Load Masters

```
set docRef to document 1 of application "Adobe InDesign CS5"
try
    set templatePath to chooseTemplate ()
(*Boolean if false indicates master spreads should be renamed in case of
name clash.*)
    loadMasters (docRef, templatePath, false)
on error errStr
    display alert errStr
    return
end try

(*Presents user with list of templates from which to choose.*)
on chooseTemplate()
    tell application "Adobe InDesign CS5"
        set appPath to file path as string
        set templatePath to appPath & "Templates:"
    end tell
    tell application "Finder"
        set templateNames to name of every file of folder templatePath ¬
        whose file type is in {"ID7t", "IDd7", "IDd2", "ID2t"}
    end tell
    set fileChoice to choose from list templateNames with prompt ¬
    "Select template:" without multiple selections allowed
    if fileChoice = false then
        error "No file chosen."
    end if
        return (templatePath & fileChoice)
end chooseTemplate

(*Loads master spreads from referenced document.*)
on loadMasters(docRef, filePath, doOverwrite)
    tell application "Adobe InDesign CS5"
        tell docRef
            if doOverwrite = true then
                load masters from filePath global strategy for ¬
                master page load all with overwrite
            else
                load masters from filePath global strategy for ¬
                master page load all with rename
            end if
        end tell
    end tell
end loadMasters
```

If the page size of the master document does not match the active document, the user will be presented with a warning.

InDesign File Properties

Some document properties you will use in working with the system file structure are reviewed briefly in the following discussion.

Full Name

If you are not sure how to describe the path to a document file, open the document and use the following.

```
tell application "Adobe InDesign CS5"
    set fullName to full name of document 1
end tell --result is object reference to file
```

If you try this with a document that has not been saved, you will get an error.

Saved, Modified, Converted

Trying to get the full name or file path of a document that has never been saved or has been converted will produce an error condition. You can test if a document has been saved by using its **saved** property. The **modified** property indicates that the document has been modified since its last save. If **converted**, the document was saved in a previous version of InDesign. In the following, the active document is checked to see if it has been saved, converted, or modified. If it has not been saved, or has been converted the **saveDoc** handler has the user determine the name and file path for the document to which it will be saved. If it has been saved, but since modified, the document is saved normally.

Save Document

```
try
    set docRef to document 1 of application "Adobe InDesign CS5"
    set saveName to saveDoc(docRef)
on error errStr
    activate
    display alert errStr
end try

(*If not saved user is prompted for file path and name for save.*)
on saveDoc(docRef)
    tell application "Adobe InDesign CS5"
        if saved of docRef = false or modified of docRef = true then
            activate
            set savePath to choose file name with prompt ¬
            "Select file name and path for file."
            --tests to make sure name of file ends with ".indd"
            if savePath as string does not end with ".indd" then
                set savePath to (savePath as string) & ".indd"
            end if
            save docRef to savePath
        end if
        set docName to name of docRef
    end tell
    return docName
end saveDoc
```

Activate

Notice the use of the activate statement before the choose file name statement. This brings the dialog to the front with the file name entry field active. Otherwise, the user would need to select the text in the field in order to enter the name for the file.

Read, Write to File

Before you can read or write to a file, the file must be opened. The AppleScript **open for access** command is used for this. **Open for access** returns a file reference number for the file to be opened. If the indicated folder exists but not the specified file, the file will be created. If the folder does not exist, the script generates an error.

Once you have opened a file, and performed the desired operations you must close it using the **close access** command. It is a good idea to use the same variable returned from the **open for access** statement for the **close access** statement.

The **get eof** [file reference] command returns the length of the file. This is a good way to determine if the file is empty.

Read [file reference] has a number of optional parameters. For the entire list look in the dictionary for Standard Additions in the File Read/Write suite (where open for access, close access, and get eof are also described). The most common parameters you will use are:

from...to - Designates the byte in file to read from and optionally to.

for - Designates the number of bytes to read.

as - Designates the form in which to read and return data (as string or as list).

using delimiter(s) - Designates delimiter(s) (see below). Use the plural form (delimiters) if a list is provided.

before - Allows designation of a character to read up to. Does not include the character in the read.

until - Similar to **before**, but includes the character designated in the read.

The following reads entire text from the file designated and opened using **open for access**. The file is closed inside a try statement, just to make sure the file gets closed even if an error condition is encountered.

```
set publicFolder to path to public folder from user domain as string
set filePath to publicFolder & "Text Files:Article.txt"
set textStr to ""
--filePath is a string, so word file is needed as part of reference
set fileRef to open for access file filePath
set fileSize to (get eof fileRef)
try
    set textStr to read fileRef as string from 1 to fileSize
    close access textStr
on error
    close access fileRef
end try
textStr
```

Delimiter

Specifies the character to be used to separate chunks of text. In reading a file, specifying a character for the optional **using delimiter** parameter splits the text into a list of strings. The **as** class (as in *as text*) parameter is required if you use a delimiter.

In the event you want a list of paragraphs returned from the read command, you can use return for the delimiter as part of the read file statement. The handler **readTextFile** takes a delimiter as one of its parameters. If no delimiter is to be used, `missing value` should be supplied.

Read Text File

```
set publicFolder to path to public folder from user domain as string
set filePath to "TextFiles:Article.txt"
set fileAlias to (publicFolder & filePath) as alias
set delimChar to return --can be missing value
set fileList to readTextFile(fileAlias, delimChar)
length of fileList

(*Parameters: file alias, delimiter character can be missing value.*)
on readTextFile(fileAlias, delimChar)
    set textStr to ""
    set fileRef to open for access fileAlias
    set fileSize to (get eof fileRef)
    try
        if delimChar = missing value then
            set textStr to read fileRef as string from 1 to fileSize
        else
            set textStr to read fileRef as string from 1 to fileSize ¬
            using delimiter delimChar
        end if
        close access textStr
    on error
        close access fileRef
    end try
    return textStr
end readTextFile
```

You can use more than one delimiter to generate a list of values, as in:

```
read fileRef using delimiters {tab, return} as text
```

If the text in the file to be read can be interpreted as integers, you can use the **as** class to coerce the text to integers as part of the read. If the part of the file to be read as numbers includes a character that cannot be coerced to a number, attempting to read will cause an error. The script **Read Numbers** included with the scripts for this chapter demonstrates. It first reads the file using return as a delimiter to get the count of lines in the file. After closing and reopening the file, it reads each line of the file within a repeat loop using **before** to eliminate reading return characters. Closing and reopening the file resets the file read pointer back to the beginning of the file.

To write to a file you must open the file with write permission. The only required parameter for the **write** command is **to** which can be a reference to the file, a file alias, or the file reference number returned from the open for access command. The optional parameters are **starting at**, **for**, and **as** [type class].

You can remove the bytes in a file opened with open for access using the **set eof** [file reference] command and setting the value to zero which clears the file. To append text to a file set the end of file (eof) to its current size plus 1. You will also want to make sure there is a line return before the text to be added. The following demonstrates:

Write To File

```
set appendStr to true
set textStr to ¬
"Just testing" & return & "This is sample text for testing."
set publicFolder to path to public folder from user domain as string
set filePath to (publicFolder & "Test:JustTesting.txt")
set bytesWritten to writeToFile(filePath, textStr, appendStr)

(*Parameters: path to file, string to write. Returns bytes written.*)
on writeToFile(filePath, textStr, appendStr)
    try
        set fileRef to open for access file filePath with write permission
        set fileSize to (get eof fileRef)
        if appendStr = true and fileSize > 0 then
            set eof fileRef to (fileSize + 1)
            set textStr to (return & textStr)
        else
            set eof fileRef to 0
        end if
        write textStr to fileRef starting at eof
        set fileLength to (get eof fileRef)
        close access fileRef
    on error
        close access fileRef
    end try
    return fileLength
end writeToFile
```

Do Script

The **do script** command for the application allows an AppleScript script to run a script written in AppleScript or ExtendScript (JavaScript). The command has only one required parameter, a reference to the script to execute. This can be literal text or a file on disk. The **language** parameter is optional when the targeted script is written in AppleScript, but required when in JavaScript. Do script requires that a script executed as literal text (rather than as a file) be enclosed within quotes. Also a backslash needs to precede each occurrence of a quotation mark inside the quotes. For JavaScript you can use a single quote instead of the backslash quote.

```
set theScript to "alert (\"Hello world!\")"
tell application "Adobe InDesign CS5"
    do script theScript language javascript
end tell
```

You can pass arguments to a do script script using the **arguments** parameter. Define the parameters as you would for passing parameters to a handler, with the exception that the parameters are elements of a list.

```
--create a list of parameters
set scriptParams to {"Enter your name:", ""}
--enter code for script using backslashes or single quotes
set jScript to "prompt(\"\" + arguments[0], arguments[1])"
tell application "Adobe InDesign CS5"
```

```
    set retValue to do script jScript language javascript with arguments¬
    scriptParams
end tell
```

Notice the empty quotes in the prompt statement. This is necessary to make sure that the first argument (arguments[0]) is coerced to a string value. When the script is run, the value of the variable *retValue* will contain the value of the text entered by the user.

There is no advantage to using do script for creating an alert or prompt dialog as in the above example. The goal here was to acquaint you with the idea of writing a script as a string. Later you will discover some of the exciting ways that do script can be used to advantage.

It may interest you to know the handlers you have been using in the Handlers Library (added in Chapter 1) are all written as strings. The strings are passed to AppleScript Editor, which in turn places the handler in your script.

Make Scripts Work for You

When you save a document, the settings for the active window such as **view percentage** are retained. The next time you open the document, this value will be used. This may not be what you want. A quick script, **Open to Zoom**, can be used to open your documents with your desired settings in place.

The script works with properties for the active window. To see these properties along with your ideal values, open a typical document and set the scale and position of the document for your ideal.

With this document positioned exactly as you would wish all your documents to be opened, run the following script:

```
tell application "Adobe InDesign CS5"
    tell layout window 1
        get properties
    end tell
end tell
```

The result window will give you the information you will want to use for your **Open to Zoom** script.

The example script below starts by having the user select the document(s) to open. For this the **getFiles** handler is used. If the user cancels out of the choose file dialog, an error condition will be raised. For this reason the call to the handler is placed inside a try/end try trap. If using a version of InDesign other than CS5 or CS5.5, change the value for the *fileType* variable.

```
set defaultLocation to ((path to public folder from user domain ¬
as string) & "Test:") as alias --change folder default location as desired
set fileType to {"IDd7", "IDd2"}
set selectMultiple to true
try
    set aliasList to getFiles(defaultLocation, fileType, selectMultiple)
on error errStr
    display alert errStr
    return
end try

(*Returns alias list of files chosen.*)
on getFiles(defaultLocation, fileType, selectMultiple)
    set defaultLocation to defaultLocation as alias
```

```
          set fileList to choose file with prompt "Select files" ¬
          default location defaultLocation of type fileType ¬
          multiple selections allowed selectMultiple without invisibles
          return fileList as list
     end getFiles
```

With the value returned for the variable *aliasList* containing file references, you can have the application open the documents and set layout window preferences. The handler **openDocuments** provides this functionality. You will want to set the values for the properties to your own desired settings, perhaps copied or adapted from the script at the beginning of this section.

```
     --call to the openDocument handler
     if length of aliasList > 0 then
     set docList to openDocuments(aliasList)
     docList --this statement provided for testing
     end if

     (*Opens documents in aliasList and sets properties of window 1 to values.*)
     on openDocuments(aliasList)
         set docList to {}
         tell application "Adobe InDesign CS5"
             repeat with i from 1 to length of aliasList
                 open item i of aliasList
                 tell document 1
                     set layerRef to layer 1
                     set spreadRef to spread 1
                     set windowProperties to {zoom percentage:100,¬
                     screen mode:preview off, active layer:layerRef, ¬
                     view display setting:typical, active spread:spreadRef, ¬
                     bounds:{111, 206, 855, 1446}}
                     set properties of layout window 1 to windowProperties
                 end tell
                 set end of docList to document 1
             end repeat
         end tell
         return docList
     end openDocuments
```

Assign a keyboard shortcut for this script and save yourself some fussing when you open documents.

The complete script, **Open to Zoom**, is found in the folder for this chapter.

8

Page Item Properties

In this chapter you will explore some of the properties that can be set for page items such as rectangles, text frames., ovals, and polygons. One of the properties that changes in CS5 from earlier versions of InDesign is **label**.

Label vs Name

In previous versions, scripts used an object's **label** as a form of reference. With CS5 the **name** property has been added and is now the preferred way to identify objects within InDesign. When a page item is named, its name is used for identification in the item list for its layer. Run the following and verify its name in Layer 1.

```
tell application "Adobe InDesign CS5"
    set gBounds to {"1 in", "1 in", "2 in", "4 in"}
    tell page 1 of document 1
        set rectRef to make rectangle with properties ¬
        {geometric bounds: gBounds, label: "myLabel", name:"Photo_1"}
        set rectRef to rectangle "Photo_1" --"myLabel" would raise an error
    end tell
end tell
```

You can use the label property as part of a test to identify a page item. After creating the rectangle with the preceding script, try the following:

```
tell document 1 of application "Adobe InDesign CS5"
    set rectRef to every rectangle whose label is "myLabel"
end tell
```

There may be times you may want to use the same identifier for both the **label** and **name** properties. You can verify the label of the page item by selecting it and looking in the Script Label panel (Window > Utilities > Script Label).

Labels are now being used for more specific tasks. Because a label can store a large amount of text, labels can be used to store data, scripts written as text, or just plain text.

Page Item Defaults

When you create a page item, many of its properties are set by default depending on the values for **page item defaults** currently in effect. By default, the object styles [Basic Graphics Frame] and [Basic Text Frame] are assigned to the page item defaults property. But you can create your own object styles and use them instead. Assume that you have created your own object style named "Default Graphic." You can assign this object style as the **applied graphic object style** for page item defaults.

```
tell application "Adobe InDesign CS5"
    tell document 1
        set objstyleRef to object style "Default Graphic"
        tell page item defaults
            set applied graphic object style to objstyleRef
        end tell
    end tell
end tell
```

When you create a page item, the properties assigned to this style will now be applied by default:

```
tell application "Adobe InDesign CS5"
    tell document 1
        tell page 1
            set rectRef to make rectangle with properties ¬
            {geometric bounds:{"3p", "3p", "12p", "24p"}}
            --for testing
            tell rectRef
                set test to name of applied object style
            end tell
        end tell
    end tell
end tell
--result: "Default Graphic"
```

In addition to the **applied graphic object style**, and **applied text object style**, page item defaults provides settings for fill, stroke, corner options, and transparency. Check out the listing for page item defaults in InDesign's dictionary.

Color and Swatches

When a color is selected from the color panel (Window > Color), an unnamed color is applied to the object selected. Just for testing, create a document with a page item such as a rectangle or text frame. Open the colors panel. From the panel's menu select one of the color modes (Lab, CMYK, or RGB). With your page item selected, select a color with the fill icon active. Now run the following test script:

```
tell application "Adobe InDesign CS5"
    tell document 1
        set selList to selection
        if length of selList > 0
            set test to name of fill color of item 1 of selection
        end if
    end tell
end tell
```

The result is an empty string. You can get the properties of the color by substituting the statement requesting the name of the fill color in the test statement above with the following:

```
set test to properties of fill color of item 1 of selection
```

To continue with the example above, open the Colors panel. Your color should be selected. Choose Add to Swatches from the panel's menu. Again, with your page item selected, run the test script above.

The color will have a name consistent with its color value. As you can see, a swatch is simply a color that has been given a name. Swatches inherit the properties of colors including **space** (RGB, CMYK, LAB, or MixedInk), **color value** (ink values), and **model** (spot, process, registration, or mixed ink model).

Unnamed Colors

The problem with unnamed colors is they don't show up in the swatch palette. As demonstrated above, InDesign makes it easy to add any unnamed colors to the swatch palette in the UI. Should you want to do it with a script, the script **Unnamed Colors** finds all unnamed colors and creates a color swatch for each with that color's values. You will find the script in the Chapter Scripts folder for this chapter.

Swatches

Creating a Swatch

The subject of setting color for fill and stroke may be central to many projects working with page items. If you use a standardized set of colors, you might want to create a default set by targeting the application as the specifier for statements creating swatches. For colors you use periodically, you can create swatches at the document level, and save as part of a template. Additionally, you might want to save a document with the colors to use as a style sheet and load swatches as needed. You can test for the existence of a swatch by name

```
set swatchName to "Puce"
set itExists to false
tell document 1 of application "Adobe InDesign CS5"
    if exists swatch swatchName then
        set itExists to true
    end if
end tell
itExists
```

If the swatch does not exist, you can then create the swatch. To allow for the creation of a number of swatches, the following handler is provided. It is in the Colors folder of the Handlers Library (see Chapter 1). Notice that the variable *colorList* is a list of lists with each item of the list consisting of the swatch name and a list of CMYK color values.

Create Process Colors

```
(*Creates colors from list of lists {swatch name, color values}.*)
set colorList to {{"Red", {0, 100, 100, 0}}, {"Blue", {100, 50, 0, 0}}}
set docRef to document 1 of application "Adobe InDesign CS5"
--existingList is a list of colors not created as they already exist
set existingList to createProcessColors(docRef, colorList)

on createProcessColors(docRef, colorList)
    set existingList to {}
    tell application "Adobe InDesign CS5"
        tell docRef
            repeat with i from 1 to length of colorList
```

```
                    set theColor to item i of colorList
                    set newName to item 1 of theColor
                    set valueList to item 2 of theColor
                    if not (exists swatch newName) then
                        set newcolor to make color with properties{name:¬
                        newName,model:process, space:CMYK, color value: ¬
                        valueList}
                    else
                        set end of existingList to newName
                    end if
                end repeat
            end tell
        end tell
        return existingList
    end createProcessColors
```

Changing Color

An **every** element reference statement can be used to find all items having a particular color fill for finding and changing. For more complex find and change operations, you will want to use the find/change capability in InDesign (see Chapter 16).

```
    tell application "Adobe InDesign CS5"
        tell document 1
            try
                set oldSwatch to swatch "C=100 M=0 Y=0 K=0"
                set newSwatch to swatch "Red"
                set fill color of rectangles where fill color is oldSwatch ¬
                to newSwatch
            on error errStr
                display alert errStr
            end try
        end tell
    end tell
```

Swatch Reference Required

Important: When working with statements that work with swatches, make sure you test to make sure the swatch exists. You can then use its object reference in the script.

Merging Swatches

The **merge** command deletes swatches and allows each of the applied colors to be replaced with another. The following merges all spot colors into the color "Black." It uses an every element reference. You need to be careful in using an every element reference to get a list of spot colors. If no objects meet the filter requirements the list will be empty.

Merge Swatches

```
    tell application "Adobe InDesign CS5"
        tell document 1
            set blackColor to swatch "Black"
                set spotColors to (colors where model is spot)
            if length of spotColors > 0 then
                merge blackColor with spotColors
```

```
        end if
    end tell
end tell
```

Unused Swatches

The unused swatches property for a document can be used to clean up your swatch list. This becomes especially handy when default swatches add unneeded colors to your document.

```
tell application "Adobe InDesign CS5"
    tell document 1
        set swatchRef to swatch "Black"
        set testList to unused swatches as list
        if length of testList > 0 then
            merge swatchRef with testList
        else
            display alert ("No unused swatches found")
        end if
    end tell
end tell
```

Deleting a Swatch

When deleting a swatch you can specify the color to use as its replacement. All objects assigned the color deleted will now have the replacement color specified. For testing, the handler passes back a list of the color names that were not found. If all colors specified were found and removed, *notFoundList* will be an empty list.

Replace Swatches

```
set replaceColor to "Black"
set docRef to document 1 of application "Adobe InDesign CS5"
set deleteList to {"Purple", "TestRed", "Orange"}--colors to be deleted
set notFoundList to deleteWithReplace(docRef, replaceColor, deleteList)

(*Deletes swatches in deleteList replacing with replaceColor.
Returns list of swatch names not found.*)
on deleteWithReplace(docRef, replaceColor, deleteList)
    set notFoundList to {}
    tell application "Adobe InDesign CS5"
        tell docRef
            set baseColor to swatch replaceColor
            repeat with i from 1 to length of deleteList
                if exists swatch (item i of deleteList) then
                    delete swatch (item i of deleteList) ¬
                        replacing with baseColor
                else
                    set end of notFoundList to item i of deleteList
                end if
            end repeat
        end tell
    end tell
    return notFoundList
end deleteWithReplace
```

Load Swatches

The trick to managing swatches in an automation project is to have the color palette established in the template to be used, or to load the swatches from a style sheet. Style sheets are documents saved in a pre-determined location. The location used for the scripts in this book is a folder called Styles inside the Presets folder in InDesign's application folder. This folder should be added as part of the book's resources downloaded from its support site (see Chapter 1).

When you want to use swatches from a style sheet, these can be manually loaded to a new project using the Swatches panel menu. For an automated solution, the **load swatches** command is used. This command is supported by both the application and the document. Either an alias or path (string) reference to the target document may be used.

Load Swatches

```
set stylesheetName to "Colors.indd"
set docRef to document 1 of application "Adobe InDesign CS5"
set wasSuccess to loadSwatches(docRef, stylesheetName)

(*Loads swatches from style sheet named into document.*)
on loadSwatches(docRef, stylesheetName)
    tell application "Adobe InDesign CS5"
        set appPath to file path as string
        set stylePath to appPath & "Presets:Styles:" & stylesheetName
        try
            set styleAlias to stylePath as alias
        on error errStr
            activate
            display dialog "Style sheet not found"
            return false
        end try
        tell docRef
            load swatches from styleAlias
        end tell
    end tell
    return true
end loadSwatches
```

Fill and Stroke

To apply color to a page item such as a rectangle, text frame, or text, its fill color or stroke color can be set using the swatch name or reference. If a swatch is to be used repeatedly in a script, it may be a good idea to place its reference in a variable.

For **fill tint** and **stroke tint**, number values representing percentages are used. Notice in the following how a property record sets these properties as part of the object being created.

```
tell application "Adobe InDesign CS5"
    tell document 1
        set cyanColor to swatch "C=100 M=0 Y=0 K=0"
        set rectProp to {geometric bounds:{"1i", "1i", "4i", "5i"}, ¬
        fill color:cyanColor, fill tint:50, stroke color:"None"}
        tell page 1
            set rectRef to make rectangle with properties rectProp
            set geometric bounds of rectProp to {"4.5i", "1i", "6i", "8i"}
```

```
        make rectangle with properties rectProp
      end tell
    end tell
  end tell
```

Assuming that the default fill or stroke color for an item will be "None" can produce unexpected results. If the user has either the fill or stroke in the interface assigned to a color, objects created by a script, if not assigned a stroke or fill color otherwise, can default to the values set in the user interface.

Negative 1 Value (-1)

In a script for InDesign the value negative one (-1) for fill tint will default to 100% if the color is defined; otherwise it will use the value currently in effect in the user's interface.

Tint

A tint is a tinted version of a swatch and is displayed in the Swatches panel. Tints are often used to make additional colors from a spot color. Tints of a spot color are all printed on the same plate. Because colors and tints update together, editing a swatch causes all objects using a tint of the swatch to update. Values of tints are similar to the **fill tint** property in that the color value becomes darker as the tint value property increases in value.

Creating a tint requires a reference to a swatch along with the tint value to be assigned. The name of the tint is automatically assigned using the name of the swatch followed by the tint value.

Create Tints

```
set docRef to document 1 of application "Adobe InDesign CS5"
set swatchName to "Black"
set tintList to {20, 30, 40, 50, 60, 80}
set tintNames to createTints(docRef, swatchName, tintList)

(*Creates series of tints for defined swatch. Returns list of tint names
created.*)
on createTints(docRef, swatchName, tintList)
    set tintNames to {}
    tell application "Adobe InDesign CS5"
        tell docRef
            if exists swatch swatchName then
                set swatchRef to swatch swatchName
                repeat with i from 1 to length of tintList
                    try
                        set tintRef to make new tint with properties ¬
                        {base color:swatchRef, tint value:item i of tintList}
                        set end of tintNames to name of tintRef
                    end try
                end repeat
            end if
        end tell
    end tell
    return tintNames
end createTints
```

Gradients

Most people think of a gradient as being a graduated blend between two or more colors. In InDesign you can also blend between two tints of the same color. Gradients can be radial or linear.

Setting gradient stops is where the creativity begins. When you create a gradient, two gradient stops are created by default: one at 0 and the other at 100. A gradient stop is the point at which a gradient changes from one color to the next. The midpoint of a gradient stop is a point between the stop and the one to its left. The first stop of a gradient does not have a midpoint. A midpoint is defined as a percentage of the gradient stop's length (from 13 to 87). If you don't designate the midpoint, a default of 50 will be used.

If you define a gradient having different color models (RGB and CMYK for instance), all colors will be converted to CMYK. To avoid color shifts that occur when colors are converted, it is best to define colors for gradients as either CMYK or RGB. An example of creating a gradient is the script **Two Stop Gradient**. The handler that does the work is shown below. It requires a reference to the document, the name for the gradient, and a string "linear" or "radial." If the value for the variable *midPt* (mid point) is missing value, the mid point will default to 50. The script is in the Chapter Scripts folder for this chapter.

```
set gradRef to twoStopGradient(docRef, gradName, gradtypeStr, color1,
color2, midPt)

(*Creates a two-stop gradient for document referenced.*)
on twoStopGradient(docRef, gradName, gradtypeStr, color1, color2, midPt)
    tell application "Adobe InDesign CS5"
        tell docRef
            if (exists gradient gradName) then return gradient gradName
            --verify swatches; will error if swatches not found
            set stop1 to swatch color1
            set stop2 to swatch color2
            if gradtypeStr = "linear" then
                set gradType to linear
            else
                set gradType to radial
            end if
            set gradRef to make gradient with properties {name:gradName, ¬
            type:gradType}
            tell gradRef
                set stop color of gradient stop 1 to stop1
                set stop color of gradient stop 2 to stop2
                if midPt is not missing value then
                    set midpoint of gradient stop 2 to midPt
                end if
            end tell
        end tell
    end tell
    return gradRef
end twoStopGradient
```

Ink

The ink object allows a color to be changed for the purpose of output without changing the color in the document. If you want to output all spot colors in your document as process colors, you can do so manually by checking the All Spots to Process checkbox at the bottom of the Ink Manager dialog (Swatches panel menu). To change spot inks to process in a script, you need to loop through the list of inks and convert those that are not process. Remember, this does not change the color itself, only its profile as part of output.

To see a list of the inks for a document, the following returns the name of each ink and whether it is a process ink.

```
set testList to {}
tell document 1 of application "Adobe InDesign CS5"
    set inkList to inks
    repeat with eachItem in inkList
        tell eachItem to set end of testList to {name, is process ink}
    end repeat
end tell
testList
```

Trapping

Color trapping is a subject that should be discussed between yourself and your output provider. InDesign provides the Trap Preset object which can be used to assign settings for trapping at the document and application level. By default InDesign provides two trap presets. The trap presets can be applied to pages using the page's **applied trap preset** property. The properties that can be set for trap presets are self explanatory.

```
tell application "Adobe InDesign CS5"
    set propList to properties of trap preset 1
end tell
```

Check Out Adobe® Kuler®

Pronounced "cooler," Kuler is a web-hosted application for creating color themes. You can access the application from the Window > Extensions menu item. Select Kuler from the flyout menu, or go on line to www.adobe.com/products/kuler/.

Make Scripts Work For You

Open the Colors.indd style sheet. This file (and others) should be in the Presets:Styles folder for InDesign as part of the files installed in Chapter 1. Set the swatches for this file to correspond to those that you use consistently. You may wish to make this process a breeze by using the **Create Process Colors** script in the Chapter Scripts folder for this chapter. Save the document when you are through. You will use this document as a style sheet for creating a new document.

Open the Script Template **Choose Style** (in the **Choose Style** project for this chapter). Examine the handlers provided and see how they are used to create a functioning script. As written, the script creates a document using the "Letter" document preset. This preset is created if it does no exist. You will modify the script to have the user choose the preset from a list. This will use the handler **docFromChosenPreset** in place of the handler **docFromPreset**.

1. Save the **Choose Style** script template with a new name, **Doc From Chosen Preset**.

2. Instead of using a fixed value for the document preset, your script will have the user choose the preset from a list.

3. Add the handler **docFromChosenPreset** to the bottom of your script. The handler is in the Documents folder as part of the Handlers Library (see Chapter 1).

4. Instead of using the variables provided with the sample call, you will place the values for the variables in the statement that calls the handler. This line should read similar to:

```
set docRef to docFromChosenPreset ("Select document preset", ¬
"New Document", {"Letter"})
```

5. Now that values are used, you no longer need the variables. Delete the four lines that define the variables you just replaced.

6. Cut the statement that calls **docFromChosenPreset** and paste it in place of the call to **docFromPreset** in the PROCESS section.

7. The PROCESS section of your script should look similar to the following:

```
--===============
--PROCESS
--===============
try
    --returns file alias for stylesheet chosen; otherwise throws error
    set stylesheetFile to chooseStyleFile(promptStr, dialogTitle, ¬
    defaultChoice)
    --create document
    (*Presents user with list of document presets from which to choose.*)
    set docRef to docFromChosenPreset("Select document preset",¬
     "New Document", {"Letter"})
    --load swatches from stylesheet
    set wasSuccess to loadSwatchFile(docRef, stylesheetFile)
on error errStr
    display alert errStr
end try
wasSuccess
```

8. Compile the script, and run. Accept default values in dialogs presented.

9. Save the document created as a template in the Templates folder for the application. Name it "Letter.indt."

In Chapter 17 you will discover how the two user interaction dialogs used above can be replaced with one custom dialog.

9

Adding Style

In Chapter 8 you were introduced to the idea of working with styles in discussing page item defaults. This chapter will expand on the idea of working with styles in scripts for automation.

In essence, a style is nothing more than a named collection of predefined property values. Apply the style to an object, and all of the properties are assigned. In this chapter you will be introduced to text and text object styles with emphasis on paragraph and character styles. Table styles and cell styles will be reserved for a chapter of their own.

Text Styles

The list of properties that can be set for text is huge. Imagine having to define all of the properties individually for every paragraph or character style change within a document. The task would be prohibitive. Fortunately, the hierarchal nature of InDesign simplifies the task.

Start by defining the properties for the document's text defaults **applied paragraph style**. This will be the applied style for all text that is not otherwise assigned a style. From there, individual paragraph styles can take care of specific text styling at the paragraph level. Character styles then override styling for text objects within a paragraph. Take advantage of the fact that you can base a paragraph style on another, associate styles, and create nested styles.

Paragraph Styles

You can get the names of the paragraph styles available for the application using the every element specifier. Within the listing returned will be an entry for [No Paragraph Style] and [Basic Paragraph].

```
tell application "Adobe InDesign CS5"
    get name of every paragraph style
end tell
```

If you request the name of the applied paragraph style for application's text defaults, the [Basic Paragraph] style will be returned unless it has been set otherwise.

```
tell application "Adobe InDesign CS5"
    get name of applied paragraph style of text defaults
end tell
```

Each document created will inherit the styles established for the application. For this reason you need to be particularly careful to make sure that any styles set for the application will be supported by every workstation. Most default paragraph styles will use a font such as Minion Pro as the type font for the default style. You could change the properties for the [Basic Paragraph] style but a better idea would be to create a style that can be used consistently and make it the applied paragraph style for text defaults. For this you will need two handlers: **testFont** and **defaultParastyle**.

In testing for the existence of a font do not try to use **exists**. Instead get the **status** of the font. If the status returns the enumeration value `installed` you are good to go.

```
set familyName to "Myriad Pro"
set fontStyle to "Regular"
try
    set fontRef to testFont (familyName, fontStyle)
on error errStr
    display alert errStr
end try

on testFont(familyName, fontStyle)
    tell application "Adobe InDesign CS5"
        set fontStr to familyName & "\t" & fontStyle
        if status of font fontStr = installed then
            return font fontStr
        end if
        error "Font " & fontStr & " not found"
    end tell
end testFont
```

The handler **testFont** is found in the Environment folder of the Handlers Library (see Chapter 1).

In testing for a paragraph style, you have three options should the style not exist: (1) Throw an error, (2) Create the style based on the default style [Basic Paragraph], (3) Create the style using properties provided.

For demonstration, we will create a style having all properties of "[Basic Paragraph]" with the exception of the applied font. This takes advantage of the based on property for a style.

```
set parastyleName to "Default Style"
set fontRef to testFont ("Myriad Pro", "Regular")
set parastyleRef to defaultParastyle(parastyleName, fontRef)
on defaultParastyle(parastyleName, fontRef)
    tell application "Adobe InDesign CS5"
        if exists paragraph style parastyleName then
            set styleRef to paragraph style parastyleName
        else
            set defaultStyle to paragraph style "[Basic Paragraph]"
            set styleRef to make paragraph style with properties ¬
            {name:parastyleName, based on:defaultStyle}
            set applied font of styleRef to fontRef
        end if
        return styleRef
    end tell
end defaultParastyle
(*Add the testFont handler from above to complete the script.*)
```

The handler **defaultParastyle** is found in the Styles folder of the Handlers Library.

With the two handlers, **testFont** and **defaultParastyle** in place, the following creates the default paragraph style and assigns it to the application's text defaults.

Default Paragraph Style

```
(*Check for font and create paragraph style if needed using the font.*)
set parastyleName to "DefaultStyle"
set fontName to "Minion Pro"
set fontStyle to "Regular"
try
    set fontRef to testFont(fontName, fontStyle)
    set parastyleRef to defaultParastyle(parastyleName, fontRef)
on error errStr
    display alert errStr
end try
--apply the paragraph style referenced to text defaults
tell application "Adobe InDesign CS5"
    set applied paragraph style of text defaults to parastyleRef
end tell
(*add handlers testFont and defaultParastyle here.*)
```

Text defaults is not exclusive for the application. When a document is created, it inherits text defaults from the application and can override it. Suppose your script needs to create a document using Adobe Caslon Pro instead of Minion Pro. You could create a paragraph style unique for the document. Better, you can change the font designation for the text defaults inherited from the application as shown below.

```
try
    --call to testFont handler
    set fontRef to testFont("Adobe Caslon Pro", "Regular")
end try
tell application "Adobe InDesign CS5"
    tell (make new document)
        set defaultStyle to applied paragraph style of text defaults
        set applied font of defaultStyle to fontRef
    end tell
end tell
(*Add handler testFont here.*)
```

Based On

The **based on** property for a paragraph style allows any number of styles to inherit properties from another. Most documents will use a common type font for all body copy and perhaps a different type font for headlines. If all paragraph styles for text are based on a common style, changing the font designation for the "parent" style will change the designation for all styles based on this style. For this reason, you could have a set of text styles defined for the document or application where all properties are the same with the exception of a specific list of values such as **size, leading, first line indent, space before**, and **space after**. The following demonstrates.

```
(*Properties for styles: name, size, leading, first line indent, space
before, space after.*)
set pList to {{"Text_10", "10 pt", "12 pt", "12 pt", 0, 0}, ¬
{"Text_12", "12 pt", "14 pt", 0, "6 pt", 0}, ¬
{"Text_18", "18 pt", "18 pt", 0, "6 pt", 0}}
parastylesBasedOn("DefaultStyle", pList)

(*Repeats through list of parameter values and creates styles based on style
named. Change the name as needed.*)
on parastylesBasedOn(parentStyleName, pList)
```

```
tell application "Adobe InDesign CS5"
    tell document 1
        set parentStyle to paragraph style parentStyleName
        repeat with i from 1 to length of pList
            copy item i of pList to {styleName, styleSize, styleLead, ¬
            flIndent, spBefore, spAfter}
            if not (exists paragraph style styleName) then
                set styleRef to make paragraph style with properties ¬
                {name:styleName}
            else
                set styleRef to paragraph style styleName
            end if
            set properties of styleRef to {basedOn:parentStyle, ¬
            point size:styleSize, leading:styleLead, ¬
            first line indent:flIndent, space before:spBefore, ¬
            space after:spAfter}
        end repeat
    end tell
end tell
end parastylesBasedOn
```

You might decide to set up a number of styles as defaults. To make the paragraph styles created in the example above application defaults, comment out the lines targeted to document 1 (tell document 1 and end tell).

Chained Styles

If you have documents where styles consistently follow a given order (such as Headline followed by Byline, the Dateline, and finally Body), you will find style chaining invaluable. The idea is to designate the **next style** property for each style to the next style in the pattern. In the script **Chained Styles**, a paragraph style is established for Headline, Byline, Dateline, and Body. Each style designates the next style in the chain as its next style. With styles chained in this manner, the user needs only to select the first style in the chain when entering copy (Headline). When the user enters a paragraph return, the next style (Byline) is activated. With each successive paragraph return the next style in the "chain" becomes the applied style.

The following lines from that script set up the chain of styles.

```
set next style of paragraph style "Headline" to paragraph style "Byline"
set next style of paragraph style "Byline" to paragraph style "Dateline"
set next style of paragraph style "Dateline" to paragraph style "Body"
```

You will find the script in the Chapter Scripts folder for this chapter.

New for CS5

My top "hurrah!" for CS5 is a new set of properties for paragraph styles that support spanning and splitting a text frame. Gone are the days when you need to create a separate text frame for a headline in order to span multiple columns. Set the paragraph style for the headline to span the columns and put the headline in the same text frame as the multiple-column text. For scripted solutions this is huge. Also, should you want to have a number of lines within a paragraph split into columns, you don't need to add a text frame, and anchor it. Just set the paragraph style for the lines to split the column using **span column type:split columns**, and **span split column count**. **Span split column count** can take a number value or the enumeration value all. The following script demonstrates using **span column**. The script creates a default document, creates paragraph styles, establishes the default paragraph style, adds a text frame, populates the text frame with placeholder text, adds a headline, sets the paragraph style for the headline, and resets the geometric bounds for the frame.

Span Column

```
--test for fonts
try
    set headFont to testFont("Myriad Pro", "Bold")
    set bodyFont to testFont("Adobe Caslon Pro", "Regular")
on error errStr
    display alert errStr
    return
end try

tell application "Adobe InDesign CS5"
    tell (make document)
        set properties of text frame preferences to {text column count:3}
        set headStyle to make paragraph style with properties ¬
        {name:"Headline", applied font:headFont, point size:24, ¬
        leading:24, space after:"12 pt", span column type:span columns, ¬
        span split column count:all}
        set bodyStyle to make paragraph style with properties ¬
        {name:"Body", applied font:bodyFont, point size:10, leading:12}
        set next style of paragraph style "Headline" to bodyStyle
        tell page 1
            set frameRef to make text frame with properties ¬
            {geometric bounds:{"36 pt", "36 pt", "9 in", "8 in"}, ¬
            contents:placeholder text}
                tell frameRef
                    set applied paragraph style of text 1 to bodyStyle
                    set insertion point 1 to ("Headline Will Span Columns" ¬
                    & return)
                    set applied paragraph style of paragraph 1 to headStyle
                    --reset size of text frame to avoid overset
                    copy geometric bounds to {y0, x0, y1, x1}
                    set geometric bounds to {y0, x0, "9.5 in", x1}
                end tell --frame reference
        end tell --page
    end tell --document
end tell
(*Add handler testFont here to complete script.*)
```

Other properties that work in conjunction with **span column type** are **span column min space after, span column min space before, split column inside gutter,** and **split column outside gutter.** These properties should be self-explanatory.

Character Styles

The way that InDesign uses character styles may be somewhat different than what you are used to (for instance if you are a convert from Quark or MultiAd Creator). Character styles should be reserved for overriding text within a paragraph and for creating nested styles. For this reason, properties for a character style may be limited to defining the font style only, such as Bold, Italic, or Bold Italic. For nested styles, Superscript and Subscript are often used.

For automation, you may decide to add a set of character styles automatically to every document using the application's default set. This is demonstrated in the following which uses the **createCharacterStyles** handler. Notice that the handler checks for an existing style before attempting to create the style.

Create Character Styles

```
(*Each item in list is name of character style, and style designation.*)
set charstyleList to {{"Bold", "Bold"}, {"Italic", "Italic"},¬
{"Bold Italic", "Bold Italic"}}
set charStyles to createCharacterStyles(charstyleList)

(*Creates character styles if not found.*)
on createCharacterStyles(charstyleList)
    set charRefList to {}
    tell application "Adobe InDesign CS5"
        repeat with i from 1 to length of charstyleList
            copy item i of charstyleList to {charstyleName, charStyle}
            if exists character style charstyleName then
                set styleRef to character style charstyleName
            else
                set styleRef to make character style with properties ¬
                {name:charstyleName, font style:charStyle}
            end if
            set end of charRefList to styleRef
        end repeat
        return charRefList
    end tell
end createCharacterStyles
```

Object Styles

Object styles are one of the best things to be added to InDesign. Object styles default to [Basic Graphics Frame] for non-text containers and [Basic Text Frame] otherwise. Creating and implementing object styles is similar to working with paragraph styles. Object styles are applied to page items instead of to text. If you have never used object styles before, you may want to set one up manually just to see the process. For creating an object style programmatically, the following is an example. It creates a text frame style that defines a paragraph style for the frame. It assumes that the paragraph style "Headline" exists. A more robust version of this script is in the Chapter Scripts folder for this chapter.

Caution

Notice the property for text wrap preferences changes as of CS4. The property is now called **text wrap mode** and is enumerated in the text wrap preference class.

Create Frame Style

```
set parastyleName to "Headline"
set objstyleName to "Headline"
set doChain to false
set basedOnStyle to missing value
tell application "Adobe InDesign CS5"
    set framePrefs to {text column count:1, text column gutter:¬
    "12 pt", inset spacing:0, vertical justification:top align}
```

```
        set frameProps to {fill color:"None", fill tint:0,¬
        stroke color:"None", stroke tint:0}
        set docRef to document 1
        --assumes paragraph style named exists
        set parastyleRef to paragraph style parastyleName of docRef
        set frameStyle to my createFrameStyle(docRef, objstyleName, ¬
        basedOnStyle, parastyleRef, doChain, framePrefs, frameProps)
    end tell

    (*Creates object style if not found; otherwise returns reference to existing
    style.*)
    on createFrameStyle(docRef, objstyleName, basedOnStyle, parastyleRef, ¬
    doChain, framePrefs, frameProps)
        tell application "Adobe InDesign CS5"
            tell docRef
                if basedOnStyle = missing value then
                    set basedOnRef to object style 1
                end if
                if exists object style objstyleName then
                    return object style objstyleName
                else
                    set objstyleRef to make object style with properties ¬
                    {name:objstyleName, basedOn:basedOnStyle, applied ¬
                    paragraph style:parastyleRef, apply next paragraph style:
                    doChain, properties:frameProps, text frame preferences: ¬
                    framePrefs, enable fill:true, enable stroke:true, ¬
                    enable frame fitting options:false, enable stroke and ¬
                    corner options:false, enable paragraph style:true, ¬
                    enable text frame general options:true, ¬
                    enable anchored object options:false}
                end if
            end tell
        end tell
        return objstyleRef
    end createFrameStyle
```

The script assumes there is a document active, and that the paragraph style named exists. To make the script robust, you will want to add handlers to verify the existence of the document, the paragraph style, and optionally the object style used for based on. For an example of how this would be done, check out the script **Create Frame Style** in the Chapter Scripts folder for this chapter. This demonstration script is just the beginning of what you can do with an object style. For the full list of properties that can be set, look up object style in the dictionary for InDesign. As you will see there is an abundance of properties that can be set as part of an object style. That is the power of working with styles.

Text Frame Style Options

When working with object styles for text frames, take advantage of the **apply next paragraph style** property (*doChain* variable in the example above). If you have set up a chain of paragraph styles (see "Chaining Styles" section of this chapter), the paragraphs for the text frame will be styled using the styles in the chain.

Our sample script does not support frame fitting options, this can be a very powerful feature which you may want to add to your object style script especially when working with page items that act as containers. You will work with some of these properties in Chapter 11.

Apply Object Style

To apply an object style to an object, you can set its **applied object style** property or use the **apply object style** command. The advantage of the latter is the ability to determine if overrides are to be cleared using the parameters **clearing overrides** and **clearing overrides through root**.

Import Styles

Once you establish documents with paragraph and object styles for a document, you can then import these styles into any new project using **import styles**. Import styles can be used to import paragraph, character, table of contents, stroke, object, table, and cell styles. To designate the style format to import use one of the following enumeration values: **paragraph styles format**, **character styles format**, **text styles format**, **object styles format**, **table styles format**, **cell styles format**, **table and cell styles format**, TOC **styles format**, or **stroke styles format**. Using **text styles format** imports both paragraph and character styles. As with importing colors, the **from** parameter requires either a file or file path reference to the file. **Global strategy** indicates the process to use in the event styles with the same name exist in the target document.

The following script demonstrates by importing text styles from a given style sheet. It includes the handler **testStylesheet** to verify the existence of the named style sheet. The file should be in the Styles folder inside the Presets folder for the application (see Chapter 1).

Import Styles

```
set styleFileName to "ArticleStyles.indd"
try
    set stylesheetRef to testStylesheet(styleFileName)
    set docRef to document 1 of application "Adobe InDesign CS5"
    (*Booleans indicate styles to import: objectStyles, text styles, table
styles.*)
    importStyles(docRef, stylesheetRef, false, true, false)
on error errStr
    display alert errStr
    return
end try

(*Imports styles from style sheet referenced given boolean values for
object, text, and/or table styles.*)
on importStyles(docRef, stylesheetRef, doObject, doText, doTable)
    tell application "Adobe InDesign CS5"
        tell docRef
            if doObject is true then
                import styles format object styles format from stylesheetRef
            end if
            if doText is true then
                import styles format text styles format from stylesheetRef
            end if
            if doTable is true then
                import styles format table styles format from stylesheetRef
            end if
        end tell
    end tell
end importStyles
```

```
(*Returns alias reference to style sheet if found.*)
on testStylesheet(styleFileName)
    tell application "Adobe InDesign CS5"
        set appPath to file path as string
    end tell
    set stylePath to appPath & "Presets:Styles:"
    try
        set aliasRef to (stylePath & styleFileName) as alias
        return aliasRef
    end try
    error "Style sheet " & styleFileName & " not found"
end testStylesheet
```

Make Scripts Work for You

It is easy to see from the examples in this chapter that using styles can add immeasurably to the efficiency of an automated project. The following exercise will have you combine two of the scripts introduced in this chapter to create a style sheet you will use in the next chapter. These scripts will be found in the **Chained Frame Style** project folder for this chapter.

The scripts you will use will be:
- Chained Styles
- Create Frame Style

The result will be a script that creates a frame style supporting chained paragraph styles.

Procedure:

1. Open the script **Chained Styles** from the **Chained Frame Style** project folder for this chapter. With a new document open, run the script.

2. This script creates a chain of paragraph styles. Verify this functionality:
   a. Create a text frame in the document.
   b. Select the Headline paragraph style.
   c. Type four lines of copy ending each with a paragraph return.

3. Open the script **Create Frame Style** from the project folder.

4. Save this script using the name "Chained Frame Style."

To establish an object style with chained paragraph styles you need a reference to the first style in the chain. For our styles this will be the style defined in the variable *parastyleName* ("Headline"). You also need to make sure that the value for *doChain* is true.

5. Copy the handlers **parastylesBasedOn** and **testFont** from the **Chained Styles** script and paste to the bottom of your **Chained Frame Style** script (created in step 4 above).

6. Create a handler wrapper at the bottom of your **ChainedFrameStyle** script.
   ```
   on setStyles ()
   end setStyles
   ```

7. Copy the entire code from the top of the **Chained Styles** script and paste it inside the handler wrapper established in step 6 above.

8. Your script will need to set the value for the variable *parastyleRef* to the first paragraph style of the paragraph style chain (paragraph style "Headline").
   a. Add the following at the end of the statements inside the tell document 1 block which is now inside the **setStyles** handler:

```
set headStyle to paragraph style "Headline"
```

b. Before the `end setStyles` closing statement, add:

```
return headStyle
```

c. Replace the statement that sets the variable *parastyleRef* inside the try block at the top of the script with:

```
set parastyleRef to setStyles()
```

9. To make the chained paragraph styles part of the object style, set the variable *doChain* to true (at the top of the script).

10. Copy the handlers from the bottom of the **Chained Styles** script to the bottom of your script (**parastylesBasedOn** and **testFont**).

11. Test your script.

    Run the script. Create a text frame in your document. With the frame selected, click on the entry for "Headline" inside the Object Styles panel (Window > Styles > Object Style). Enter four paragraphs of text in the text frame and watch the styling for the paragraphs change with each paragraph return.

12. Save the document created in the Presets:Styles folder in InDesign's application folder. Name the document "Chained Styles.indd".

Your next project (Chapter 10) will need the style sheet ("Chained Styles.indd") to take advantage of the text frame style. You may wish to save the script you just created with your favorite scripts. You will find the completed script in the **Chained Frame Style** project folder for this chapter.

10

Placing Text

In this chapter you will be introduced to a number of handlers that can be used for placing text in a document. These handlers should be found in the Handlers Library which is part of the book's resources (see Chapter 1). In working with placing text, the concepts of linked text frames and linking files will be covered.

Place

The **place** command is available for the document, spread, page, image, graphic, page items, and even text or media items. If the page is the object used to place, a text frame is created for the placed object. If no parameters are provided for the place command, the containing object will be placed to the top/left of the page and will be the front-most page item (item 1 of the page or spread reference).

The following code places the file chosen at the 0,0 place point for the active spread.

```
set theFile to choose file
tell application "Adobe InDesign CS5"
    set theSpread to spread 1 of document 1
    tell theSpread
        place theFile
    end tell
end tell
```

You saw in Chapter 7 that **choose file** has a number of parameters that can be used, and that file type and file name extension can be used to determine if the file chosen was of the type or extension needed. The next script, **Place File_Placeable**. will let InDesign determine if the file chosen can be used for placement. This will use the **placeable file types** and **placeable file extensions** properties for the application. For this InDesign will need to know the file type and file name extension for the file chosen. The handler **chooseFileWithInfo** returns an alias reference to the file chosen, its file type, and file name extension. If the user cancels out of the **choose file** dialog an error condition will be thrown.

```
set thePrompt to "Choose text file to place"
--change the path for the default location as needed
set publicFolder to path to public folder from user domain as string
set dLocation to (publicFolder & "Text Files") as alias --default location
set fileInfo to chooseFileWithInfo (thePrompt, dLocation)

(*Returns file reference, its type, and name extension.*)
on chooseFileWithInfo (thePrompt, dLocation)
    set theFile to choose file with prompt thePrompt default location ¬
    dLocation without invisibles and multiple selections allowed
    set theInfo to info for theFile
    set theType to file type of theInfo
```

```
        set theExt to name extension of theInfo
        return {theFile, theType, theExt}
    end chooseFileWithInfo
```

As part of the place command, you can determine if you want file placement options to be shown, and whether to use autoflow. Using the **chooseFileWithInfo** handler to verify the file, the following script then places it using a handler, **placeFile_placeable**.

Place File_Placeable

```
set thePrompt to "Choose file to place"
--change default location path as needed
set dLocation to (path to Public folder from user domain) as alias
set placePoint to {"36 pt", "36 pt"}
set showOptions to false
set doAutoflow to false
try
    set {fileRef, fileType, fileExt} to chooseFileWithInfo(thePrompt, ¬
    dLocation)
    tell application "Adobe InDesign CS5"
        set objRef to page 1 of document 1
        set layerRef to layer 1 of document 1
    end tell
    placeFile_placeable(objRef, layerRef, placePoint, fileRef, fileType,¬
    fileExt, showOptions, doAutoflow)
on error errStr
    display alert errStr
    return
end try

(*Uses application's placeable file type to determine if valid file is
chosen.*)
on placeFile_placeable(objRef, layerRef, placePoint, fileRef, fileType, ¬
fileExt, showOptions, doAutoflow)
    set canPlace to false
    tell application "Adobe InDesign CS5"
        if (fileType is not "" and fileType is in placeable file types) ¬
        or (fileExt is not "" and fileExt is in placeable file ¬
        extensions) then
            set canPlace to true
        end if
        if canPlace = false then
            error "Invalid file chosen"
        end if
        if class of objRef is in {page, spread} then
            tell objRef to place fileRef showing options showOptions ¬
            autoflowing doAutoflow place point placePoint ¬
            destination layer layerRef
        --if text frame or insertion point place point and layer are not used
        else if class of objRef is in {text frame, insertion point} then
            tell objRef to place fileRef showing options showOptions ¬
            autoflowing doAutoflow
        end if
    end tell
end placeFile_placeable
(*Add chooseFileWithInfo handler here.*)
```

Place Point

Place point is a list of two measurement values with the horizontal (x) coordinate as the first item in the list. If a page or spread with text columns places a text file, the containing text frame will be sized to the column width. The vertical coordinate will be used as indicated. Try the script above with a spread having two or three columns. Change the value of the variable *placePoint* so that it falls within a column.

Test the previous script with the variable *doAutoflow* set to true. If the file has sufficient text, the story will flow to all subsequent columns and will override the vertical place point coordinate using the top margin for the page instead. If the original document does not have sufficient pages, additional pages will be added as needed.

Text Import Preferences

To disallow the user from setting text import options as part of placing the text file, the example above sets the variable *showOptions* to false. You may want to make sure the options are as needed by the script. For this, you may want to set the **text import preferences** properties for the application. If your script consistently uses the same preferences for text import you might consider setting this up as a handler. The following is a example.

```
textImportPrefs()

(*Sets text import preferences as might be used consistently.*)
on textImportPrefs()
tell application "Adobe InDesign CS5"
        tell text import preferences
            set convert spaces into tabs to true
            set spaces into tabs count to 5
            set strip returns between paragraphs to true
            set strip returns between lines to false
            set use typographers quotes to true
            set platform to macintosh
        end tell
    end tell
end textImportPrefs
```

Objects Used for Placing

The story object does not support the place command. To place text using a text object you can use an insertion point, a text frame, or text reference. When a text frame or text object is used for placing, two properties control whether the text frame will overset or allow multiple text frames and pages to be created.

autoflowing - Parameter of the place command determines autoflow for the text. Accepts a boolean value. If autoflowing is set to true, using a text frame to place determines place point for text.

on - Can be spread, page, master spread, page item, or graphic. Test for the overset condition of a text frame using its **overflows** property.

Insertion Point

The **insertion point** marks the location of text within a text object. There is an insertion point before and after each character. Using a reference to insertion point 1 for a story object will insert the placed text at the beginning of the story. To append text to the end of a story use the insertion point reference index of -1 for the story. Use one of the references below in the **Place File_Placeable** script above.

```
set objRef to insertion point 1 of story 1 of document 1
set objRef to insertion point -1 of story 1 of document 1
```

When using a text object other than an insertion point, the content within the object is replaced with the content from the file. Change the statement that sets variable *objRef* in the **Place File_Placeable** script to read as follows and try running the script.

```
set objRef to text frame 1 of document 1
```

Text Containers

When it comes to placing text, the text frame is often the target object. Text frames and text paths are referred to collectively as text containers. To reference all of the text containers for a story, the **text containers** property of the story can be used. If there is no story 1 in a document, the following test script will throw an error.

```
tell application "Adobe InDesign CS5"
    tell story 1 of document 1
        set containerList to text containers
        set theCount to length of containerList
    end tell
end tell
theCount
```

Fit Text

The only fit option that applies to a text frame is **frame to content**. This only works if the text frame has a single column and is unlinked. The **fit** command will shrink or expand the frame to fit the contained text as demonstrated in the following which requires a text frame selection.

```
set theFile to choose file
tell application "Adobe InDesign CS5"
    set selList to selection
    if length of selList > 0 and class of item 1 of selList is ¬
    text frame then
        set frameRef to item 1 of selList
        tell frameRef
            place theFile
            fit given frame to content
        end tell
    end if
end tell
```

If the text frame is wider than the text and the text does not contain a line return, the text frame will shrink in both the horizontal as well as the vertical direction.

Master Text Frame

If **master text frame** is set to true when a document is created, a reference to story 1 is a reference to the story on a master page. Any reference to a text object within story 1 will fail if there is no story in the master text frame.

The master text frame has its own set of rules when it comes to placed text. Even though autoflowing may be set to true, pages will not be created to accommodate the text if the master text frame is used for placing. Try the following with a document having a master text frame.

```
set theFile to choose file with prompt "Select a long file."
tell application "Adobe InDesign CS5"
    tell text frame 1 of document 1
        place theFile place point {"36 pt", "72 pt"} with autoflowing
    end tell
end tell
```

If master text frame is set to true, the index reference to a story or text frame at the document level begins with the stories and text frames on the master page. Change the reference above to the following. Run the script again to see the difference.

```
tell spread 1 of document 1
```

The master text frame can also present a problem if you want to target the first "non master" story of the document. The following is one approach to the problem.

Story Index

```
set testList to {}
tell application "Adobe InDesign CS5"
    set storyList to stories of document 1
    set masterList to every page of every master spread of document 1
    repeat with i from 1 to length of storyList
        set firstFrame to item 1 of text containers of item i of storyList
        if parent page of firstFrame is not in masterList then
            set end of testList to id of item i of storyList
        end if
    end repeat
    set firstIndex to my minFromList(testList)
    set storyRef to story id firstIndex of document 1
    index of storyRef
end tell

--returns minimum number from list of numbers
on minFromList(theList)
    set theMin to item 1 of theList
    set thisList to rest of theList
    repeat with i from 1 to count of thisList
        set theNumber to item i of thisList
        if theNumber < theMin then
            set theMin to theNumber
        end if
    end repeat
    return theMin
end minFromList
```

As you can see, having master text frames set to true can add some extra work to a script. For this reason you may wish to avoid using them unless needed for a specific purpose.

Document

If the document is used as the object for the place command, you must use the **on** parameter as in the following:

```
set theFile to choose file
tell application "Adobe InDesign CS5"
    tell document 1 to place theFile on page 1 place point¬
    {"36 pt", "72 pt"}
end tell
```

Linked Text Frames

When the **next text frame** and/or **previous text frame** property for a text frame returns the reference to another text frame, the frames are linked. You cannot place text into an existing text frame that is linked to other frames unless it is the first frame in the linked list and contains no text. To determine if a frame is linked, check its **previous text frame** and **next text frame** properties. Since this is something that your scripts may do often, the **checkUnlinked** handler is provided. It is found in the Page Items folder of the Handlers Library.

```
tell application "Adobe InDesign CS5"
    set selList to selection
    if length of selList > 0 then
        set selectedItem to item 1 of selection
        if class of selectedItem = text frame then
            set isUnlinked to my checkUnlinked(selectedItem)
            isUnlinked
        end if
    end if
end tell

(*Returns true if frame referenced is unlinked; or if linked, is empty.*)
on checkUnlinked(frameRef)
    tell application "Adobe InDesign CS5"
        set prevItem to previous text frame of frameRef
        set nextItem to next text frame of frameRef
        if (prevItem = nothing and nextItem = nothing) then
            return true
        else if (prevItem = nothing) and (text 1 of frameRef = "") then
            return true
        else
            return false
        end if
    end tell
end checkUnlinked
```

Checking for previous text fame and next text frame plays an important role in the script **Break Link** which is part of the scripts found in the folder for this chapter. This script breaks the story flow in linked frames at the frame following the text frame selected.

Name Linked Frames

When working with a document that will have a number of text frames designed to be containers for multiple stories, you will want to name the frames for reference. Should the text frames be linked, you will only want to name the first text frame for each linked set. The following test script demonstrates. It names the text frames that are selected using the text returned from a display dialog and increments the name with a padded number. If a selected text frame is linked, only the first frame is named. This script will work for CS5 and above only. For earlier versions use the label property to reference the text frame.

Name First Frame

```
(*Name text frames selected; if linked, only the first text frame of link is
named.*)
set userResponse to display dialog ¬
"Enter base name for the selected text frames" default answer "text"
set nameBase to text returned of userResponse
if length of nameBase = 0 then
    display alert "Invalid entry"
    return
end if
set theCounter to 1
tell application "Adobe InDesign CS5"
    set selList to selection
    repeat with i from 1 to length of selList
        set thisItem to item i of selList
        if (class of thisItem = text frame) and (previous text frame of ¬
        thisItem is nothing) then
            set padNumber to "0" & theCounter
            set name of thisItem to text 1 thru -1 of (nameBase & "_" & ¬
            padNumber)
            set theCounter to theCounter + 1
        end if
    end repeat
end tell
activate
display alert "" & theCounter - 1 & " items named"
```

In working with linked text frames, you can fit the last text frame to the last column of its text by getting the baseline of the last line of the story reference. If your text frames use inset spacing, you will need to add that to your calculations. The following script should get you started. It takes advantage of the **vertical balance columns** property of text frame preferences.

Fit Linked Frame

```
--assumes measurements set to points, text or insertion point selection
set storyRef to getStoryOfSelection()
tell application "Adobe InDesign CS5"
    set textFrames to text containers of storyRef
    set lastFrame to item -1 of textFrames
    tell lastFrame
        set vertical balance columns of text frame preferences to true
    end tell
    if overflows of lastFrame = true then
        my correctOverflows (lastFrame)
    else
        set lastLine to a reference to line -1 of lastFrame
        set textBase to baseline of lastLine
        set gBounds to geometric bounds of lastFrame
        set geometric bounds of lastFrame to {item 1 of gBounds, ¬
        item 2 of gBounds, textBase, item 4 of gBounds}
    end if
    if overflows of lastFrame = true then
```

```
            my correctOverflow(lastFrame)
        end if
    end tell

    (*Adjusts height of text frame to correct overflow.*)
    on correctOverflow(lastFrame)
        tell application "Adobe InDesign CS5"
            set lineSpace to leading of paragraph -1 of lastFrame
            if class of lineSpace is not number then
                set autoLead to (auto leading of paragraph -1 of lastFrame * .01)
                set adjSpace to (point size of paragraph -1 of lastFrame) * ¬
                autoLead
            else
                set adjSpace to lineSpace
            end if
            set gBounds to geometric bounds of lastFrame
            copy gBounds to {y0, x0, y1, x1}
            repeat while overflows of lastFrame = true
                set y1 to y1 + adjSpace
                set geometric bounds of lastFrame to {y0, x0, y1, x1}
            end repeat
        end tell
    end correctOverflow
    (*Add handler getStoryofSelecion to complete script. You will find the entire
    script in the Chapter Scripts folder for this chapter.*)
```

Linked Text

As of InDesign CS3, you have the option of linking a text file when importing. By default the value for this property, **link text files when importing**, is false. There are instances, however, when you might want this to be true. When a text file is linked, the text of the document will update whenever the text file is modified. This can be a good thing. But beware, you lose all local text formatting when this happens. On the other hand, if all of the text relies on object and text styles, the document can automatically have its text updated without losing styling.

Create Document With Linked Text

The script **Doc With Linked Text** demonstrates using linked text. It is part of the **Linked Text** project. The script expects a document (style sheet) named "Chained Styles.indd" to be in the Presets:Styles folder for the application (see Chapter 9). Other than that, it is a fairly standard script that creates a document preset. The following is a cut down version of the script. Select the file "Ten Things.txt" in the project folder when prompted.

Doc With Linked Text

```
set filename to "Chained Styles.indd"
set chainName to "Headline"
try
    set stylesheetRef to getStylesheet(filename)
    set fileRef to choose file with prompt "Select text file"
on error errStr
    activate
    display alert errStr
    return
end try
```

```
tell application "Adobe InDesign CS5"
    set docRef to make document
    my importStyles(docRef, stylesheetRef, true, true, false)
    tell docRef
        --this is where the text linking is established
        set link text files when importing of text preferences to true
        set objStyleRef to object style chainName
    end tell
    tell page 1 of docRef
        set frameRef to make text frame with properties {geometric bounds:¬
        {"72 pt", "36 pt", "4 in", "6 in"}, applied object style:¬
        objStyleRef}
    end tell
    tell frameRef
        place fileRef
        clear object style overrides
    end tell
end tell
(*Add handler importStyles which includes handler getStylesheet from Styles
folder. The complete script is found in the project folder.*)
```

When the user opens a document with linked text that has been updated, there is a dialog that must be dismissed before the text is updated and formatting lost. A better idea would be to have a script open the document.

Open Document With Linked Text

When you open a document that has linked text your script can disable the out of date links dialog. It then can check the links and update as needed. If styling is controlled by an object style, it can be reapplied. The following script demonstrates. Before running the script, close and save the document created with the **Doc With Linked Text** script. Move the file "Ten Things.txt" to the Original Text folder and replace with the one in the Updated Text folder.

Open Linked Text Doc

```
set homeFolder to path to home folder from user domain as string
set dLocation to (homeFolder & ¬
"AppleScripts for CS5:Chapter 10:Linked Text") as alias
try
    set fileRef to chooseFileExtTest("Select InDesign Document", {"indd"},
dLocation)
on error errStr
    activate
    display alert errStr
    return
end try
tell application "Adobe InDesign CS5"
    set linkList to {}
    set origLevel to user interaction level of script preferences
    set user interaction level of script preferences to never interact
    set docRef to open fileRef
    try
        set linkList to links of docRef where status is link out of date
    end try
    repeat with i from 1 to length of linkList
        if link type of item i of linkList = "Text" then
```

```
            set theObj to parent of item i of linkList
            set theFrames to text containers of theObj
            tell item i of linkList to update
            tell item 1 of theFrames to clear object style overrides
        end if
    end repeat
    set user interaction level of script preferences to interact with all
end tell
(*Add handler chooseFileExtTest to complete the script.*)
```

Make Scripts Work for You

Up to this point you have worked with some of the ways you can automate a part of a workflow. With this project you will begin to see how these pieces can be put together to create a complete workflow. Once you have templates and style sheets in place, a script can create a document using the template, and style stories placed using object and text styles imported from style sheets. If you create an alias to your script, you can run the script from Adobe's Script panel while retaining a pointer to its location in the project's folder. The file path to the script can then be used to provide a path to the project's resources if in the same folder. The **Article** project included with this chapter demonstrates. It uses a number of handlers that you should be familiar with.

The project assumes the following:

- You saved the document created with the **Doc From Chosen Preset** script (Chapter 8) in the Templates folder for InDesign. It should be saved as "Letter.indt."
- You saved the document created with the **Chained Frame Style** script (Chapter 9) in the Presets:Styles folder for InDesign under the name "Chained Styles.indd."

Procedure

1. Open the script **Place Article** in the Article folder for this chapter. Familiarize yourself with the script and its handlers. Use AppleScript Editor's **find** command (Command-F) to locate the **addMetadata** handler. Change the values of the variables in this handler as desired. It is assumed the values in the handler, after once being set, will not need to be changed and should be self-explanatory.

2. Change the values for the variables *metaDesc*, *metaKeys*, *docTitle*, and *metaName* at the top of the script as needed. These values may change from time to time. Save the script making sure that it is saved in the **Article** folder. Close the script.

3. Create an alias for the script you saved in Step 2 above. Install the alias in the Application Scripts folder for InDesign (Adobe InDesign CS5 (or CS5.5):Scripts:Scripts Panel:Automation).

4. Bring InDesign to the front and find the listing for the script in the Scripts panel. Double-click on the script. Sit back and watch the magic:
   a. A document is created using the template named in the script.
   b. Styles are imported from the style sheet named.
   c. A live bounds text frame is created on page 1 of the document and assigned an object style that includes chained paragraph styles.
   d. The text from the text file is placed and styled as established for the object style.
   e. The file is saved with a date stamp in the same folder as the script alias.
   f. Metadata is added to the document and the document is saved.

5. Use Bridge to locate your document and view its metadata.

11

Placing Images and PDFs

In this chapter you will be introduced to a number of handlers that involve placing images and PDF files in a document. Since wrapping text is often associated with image containers, we begin with a discussion of text wrap.

Text Wrap

Text wrap is set for a page item using its **text wrap preferences** property. This property has changed between versions of InDesign. In InDesign CS3, **text wrap type** defined the way wrap would affect text items. This became **text wrap mode** in CS4, but the enumeration values remained the same. Another problem you need to be aware of is with the issue of setting **text wrap offset** values. This is one place that you may need to set values as a separate property. With some modes of text wrap, InDesign ignores the text wrap offset if set as part of a property record.

```
(*THIS DOES NOT SET TEXT WRAP OFFSETS.*)
tell application "Adobe InDesign CS5"
    set docRef to document 1
    set pageRef to page 1 of docRef
    set wrapPrefs to {text wrap mode:bounding box text wrap,¬
    text wrap offset:{"12 pt", "6 pt", "6 pt", "6 pt"}}
    tell pageRef
        set rectRef to make rectangle with properties ¬
        {geometric bounds:{"1i", "1i", "2i", "4i"}}
        set properties of text wrap preferences of rectRef to wrapPrefs
    end tell
end tell

(*THIS ESTABLISHES TEXT WRAP OFFSETS.*)
tell application "Adobe InDesign CS5"
    set docRef to document 1
    set pageRef to page 1 of docRef
    tell pageRef
        set rectRef to make rectangle with properties ¬
        {geometric bounds:{"1i", "1i", "2i", "4i"}}
        tell text wrap preferences of rectRef
            set text wrap mode to bounding box text wrap
            set text wrap offset to {"12 pt", "6 pt", "6 pt", "6 pt"}
        end tell
    end tell
end tell
```

Placing Images

As with placing text, a graphic file can be placed using a page, spread, master spread, a page item, an imported page, or media item. In CS4 the document could issue a **place** command in which case the files were loaded to the cursor for placement by the user. This has changed with CS5. There is now a **place gun** object that can be loaded with one or more files (**load place gun** command). This loads the cursor, so the user can manually place the files as needed. (See "Processing Multiple Files" later in this chapter.)

The **place** command requires a text or alias reference to the file. Optionally the parameters **on, place point, destination layer**, and **showing options** can be used to define the placement further. The following script demonstrates by placing an image chosen by the user. The handler **checkLayer** is added to identify the layer on which the image will be placed.

Place Image

```
--define default location for choose command
set dLocation to path to public folder from user domain

--returns reference to file chosen, file type, and file extension
set {fileRef, fileType, fileExt} to chooseFileWithInfo ¬
("Select image file for placing", dLocation)

(*Identify objects and call placeImageWithTest.*)
tell application "Adobe InDesign CS5"
    try
        set docRef to document 1
        (*If last parameter is true, the layer is created if not found.*)
        set layerRef to my checkLayer(docRef, "Images", true)
        set pageRef to page 1 of docRef
        tell margin preferences of pageRef
            set placePt to {left, top}
        end tell
        --boolean indicates if place options are shown
        set imageRef to my placeImage_placeable(pageRef, layerRef, ¬
        placePt, fileRef, fileType, fileExt, false)
    on error errStr
        display alert errStr
        return
    end try
end tell
imageRef

(*Uses file type and extension to test to make sure file can be placed.*)
on placeImage_Placeable(objRef, layerRef, placePt, fileRef, fileType, ¬
fileExt, showOptions)
    set canPlace to false
    tell application "Adobe InDesign CS5"
        if (fileType is not "" and fileType is in placeable file types) ¬
        or (fileExt is not "" and fileExt is in placeable file extensions)¬
        then
```

```
            set canPlace to true
        end if
        if canPlace = false then
            error "Invalid file chosen"
        end if
        tell objRef
            set imageRef to place fileRef showing options showOptions ¬
            place point placePt destination layer layerRef
        end tell
    end tell
    return imageRef
end placeImage_placeable

(*Returns reference to file, its type, and its extension.*)
on chooseFileWithInfo(thePrompt, dLocation)
    set theFile to choose file with prompt thePrompt default location ¬
    dLocation without invisibles and multiple selections allowed
    set theInfo to info for theFile
    set theType to file type of theInfo
    set theExt to name extension of theInfo
    return {theFile, theType, theExt}
end chooseFileWithInfo

(*Returns reference to layer. If not found and createIt is true, the layer is
created; else an error is thrown.*)
on checkLayer(docRef, layerName, createIt)
    tell application "Adobe InDesign CS5"
        tell docRef
            if exists layer layerName then
                set layerRef to layer layerName
            else
                if createIt is true then
                    set layerRef to make layer with properties ¬
                    {name:layerName}
                    move layerRef to after layer -1
                else
                    error "Layer " & layerName & " not found"
                end if
            end if
        end tell
    end tell
    return layerRef
end checkLayer
```

Fit image

If you look at the Result for the previous script you will see that the image reference includes a reference to its parent rectangle. This rectangle is created by default when a graphic is placed to a page using a place point. When placed to a page item, your script can fit the image to the page item using the **fit** command.

Options for fitting images are listed under **fit** in the Layout Suite of InDesign's dictionary and include **content to frame, center content, proportionally, frame to content, fill proportionally,** and **apply frame fitting options**. To test this, create a rectangle on a page. With the rectangle selected run the following test script:

```
set theImage to choose file
tell application "Adobe InDesign CS5"
    set selList to selection
    if length of selList > 0 then
        set rectRef to item 1 of selList
        tell rectRef
            place theImage without showing options
            fit given frame to content
        end tell
    end if
end tell
```

Fill Proportionally

When working with columnar material, the width of the image container is often controlled by column widths. To fit an image into a column-wide container you can use the **fill proportionally** option. Substitute the following at the end of the test script above and test:

```
fit given fill proportionally
```

If the scale of the image vertically is larger than the frame, the image will crop at the bottom. If the horizontal scale is larger than the frame, the image will crop at the right. You can force the image to crop on both sides by adding a fit given center content statement. For more control over fitting, you may wish to resort to using **frame fitting option**s.

Frame Fitting Options

The **frame fitting option** class provides a number of options for fitting an image or pasted content into a frame. In addition to allowing the image to be cropped to a given measurement (**top crop, left crop, bottom crop, right crop**), it allows the frame to apply **auto fit** when the frame is resized. You will want to look at this class in the Layout Suite of InDesign's dictionary. The following will give you some ideas for using this option.

```
set theImage to choose file
tell application "Adobe InDesign CS5"
    set selList to selection
    if length of selList > 0 and class of item 1 of selList is in ¬
    {rectangle, oval, polygon} then
        set rectRef to item 1 of selList
        tell rectRef
            set properties of frame fitting options to ¬
            {auto fit:true, fitting alignment:center anchor, ¬
            fitting on empty frame:fill proportionally}
            place theImage without showing options
            fit given apply frame fitting options
        end tell
    end if
end tell
```

Try this script with a rectangle, oval, or polygon selected. After placing the image, drag on a corner of the container to resize. Notice that the image automatically resizes proportionally with the frame.

Don't forget that you can specify frame fitting options for the application, the document, a frame, or object style. Page item defaults can be assigned an object style for graphics using the **applied graphic object style** property. This object style can have frame fitting options defined.

With these in place, your scripts should need to address fitting issues only when there is a need to override your defaults.

Place Image Preferences

In the previous scripts the **with options** parameter of the **place** command was set to false. If set to true, the user would be presented with a dialog box to designate import options. These options change depending on the file type chosen. Check out **IO preferences** in the Preferences Suite of InDesign's dictionary.

Processing Multiple Images

Few automation workflows will be content to import just one file. Whether selected by the user or grouped in a specified folder, your script will need to have some way to determine how multiple files will be placed. One way is to have page items named to correspond with the name of the files. Containers can be created by a script using a list that designates the geometric bounds for each container and the name of its corresponding file. Your script would then place the files using a repeat loop.

You might even consider allowing the user to place the images using a document's **place gun**. The following expects a folder of tiff or jpeg files to be in the user's public folder. Change the folder reference as needed and run the script with a document open. The images from the folder will be gathered and ready for placement using the place gun.

Place Gun

```
set validList to {}
--change values for folder path as needed
set publicFolder to path to public folder from user domain as string
set folderPath to (publicFolder & "Images:Wines:")
set folderRef to folderPath as alias
set fileList to list folder folderRef without invisibles
repeat with i from 1 to length of fileList
    set fileAlias to (folderPath & item i of fileList) as alias
    set theInfo to info for fileAlias
    if name extension of theInfo is in {"tif", "jpg"} or ¬
    kind of theInfo is in {"TIFF image", "JPEG image"} then
        set end of validList to fileAlias
    end if
end repeat
tell application "Adobe InDesign CS5"
    tell document 1
        if loaded of place gun 1 is false then
            tell place gun 1
                load place gun validList without showing options
            end tell
        end if
    end tell
end tell
```

Links

Image files are automatically linked to the document as part of their being placed. As with linked text files, the information about the file is found in its related link. The **link status** property of a link indicates if the link is missing, out of date, needed, or embedded.

To get a list of links where the status is link missing, the every element reference can be used.

```
--assumes active document
tell application "Adobe InDesign CS5"
    tell document 1
        set missingList to every link where status is link missing and ¬
        (link type = "Photoshop" or link type = "JPEG")
    end tell
end tell
missingList
```

Link Commands

For an automation script that works with images, there are a number of commands available for a link which may prove invaluable. Of particular interest are **update**, **unlink**, **relink**, and **show**. When given the show command, the script turns the document pages, zooms, and scrolls to the center of the specified linked object. The script **Show** in the project folder of the same name uses this command to display consecutively images where link status is missing. From this we have the following statements:

```
set missingList to links where status = link missing
repeat while missingList is not {}
    show item 1 of missingList
    delay 3
    set missingList to rest of missingList
end repeat
```

When updating, unlinking, or relinking, be sure to modify items from back to front as in the script below which uses the handler **updateOutdatedLinks** to check link type and status of links before updating.

Update Links

```
(*Updates links that are out of date for document referenced. Returns number
of links updated.*)
set docRef to document 1 of application "Adobe InDesign CS5"
set linksUpdated to updateOutdatedLinks(docRef)
linksUpdated

on updateOutdatedLinks(docRef)
    set linkCounter to 0
    tell application "Adobe InDesign CS5"
        tell docRef
            set linkList to links where link type = "Photoshop" or link type ¬
            = "TIFF" or link type = "JPEG" or link type = "EPS"
            repeat with i from length of linkList to 1 by -1
                if status of item i of linkList = link out of date then
                    update item i of linkList
                    set linkCounter to linkCounter + 1
                end if
            end repeat
        end tell
```

```
        end tell
        return linkCounter
    end updateOutdatedLinks
```

Another task that may find its way into an automation workflow is image replacement. The project **FPO** (For Placement Only) uses relinking to switch low-resolution images to corresponding high-resolution images.

When you replace images you may want to make sure that the image retains its original crops. For this, the application has the **preserve bounds** property for **image preferences**. This is set to true by default, but you will want to make sure its setting is as anticipated. The **FPO** script saves the original value for preserve bounds in a variable which is then used to restore the setting at the end of the script.

FPO

```
set preserveBounds to true

tell application "Adobe InDesign CS5"
    set origImagePref to preserve bounds of image preferences
    set preserve bounds of image preferences to preserveBounds
    set docRef to document 1
    set searchFolder to ":LoRes:"
    set replaceFolder to ":HiRes:"
    set imagesReplaced to my relinkImages(docRef, searchFolder, ¬
    replaceFolder)
    set preserve bounds of image preferences to origImagePref
end tell

(*Relinks images to images found in the path defined by newPath.*)
on relinkImages(docRef, findStr, replaceStr)
    set replaceCounter to 0
    tell application "Adobe InDesign CS5"
        tell docRef
            set picList to all graphics
            repeat with i from length of picList to 1 by -1
                set linkRef to item link of item i of picList
                set origStr to file path of linkRef
                set newPath to my replaceStr(origStr, findStr, replaceStr)
                if newPath is not equal to "" and (exists file newPath) then
                    try
                        relink linkRef to file newPath
                        set replaceCounter to replaceCounter + 1
                    end try
                end if
            end repeat
        end tell
    end tell
    return replaceCounter
end relinkImages

(*Uses string manipulation to replace a portion of one string with another.*)
on replaceStr(origStr, findStr, replaceStr)
    if findStr is in origStr then
        set strOffset to (offset of findStr in origStr) - 1
        set strLen to (length of findStr) + 1
        if strOffset + strLen > length of origStr then
            set newStr to (text 1 thru strOffset of origStr) & replaceStr
        else if strOffset = 0 then
```

```
            set newStr to replaceStr & (text strLen thru -1) of origStr
        else
            set newStr to (text 1 thru strOffset of origStr) & replaceStr¬
            & (text (strOffset + strLen) thru -1 of origStr)
        end if
    else
        set newStr to ""
    end if
    return newStr
end replaceStr
```

To test the script, open the document "LowResImagesPlaced.indd" in the **FPO** folder for this chapter. Run the script. The image on page 3 is purposely resized. Revert the document or close without saving and reopen. Change the value for the variable *preserveBounds* at the top of the script to false. Run the script with this change to verify how this setting affects replacing an image that has been resized.

Link Metadata

Link metadata provides information about the image file, which may be valuable to an automation script. Some workflows will define the caption and author as part of the image file's metadata. This way, the credits and caption for the file can be added automatically as part of the image being placed. The project **Place With Caption** found in the folder for this chapter demonstrates this workflow. This project uses a fairly lengthy script that calls on a number of handlers you should be familiar with. It does introduce some new handlers, of which **placeImageWCaption** should be of particular interest. The following code is excerpted from this handler. Test the script with the document provided and select an image with author and description metadata defined.

```
tell frameRef
    place fileRef
    fit given fill proportionally
    set imageRef to image 1
end tell
--get image metadata
set linkRef to item link of imageRef
set linkMeta to properties of link xmp of linkRef
if author of linkMeta is not "" then
    set capStr to author of linkMeta & return
    set hasCredit to true
end if
set capStr to capStr & description of linkMeta
```

Alert

How link metadata is handled in CS5 is greatly improved from earlier versions. The script for this project will not work with earlier versions of InDesign.

Image Properties and Commands

Don't overlook the many properties and commands that can be applied to images. The list is quite extensive. Only a few will be discussed here.

Although InDesign's preflight capability is greatly expanded, you may want to check image information as part of a script. Of interest may be image type (**image type name**), resolution (**actual ppi**), and whether the image has been flipped (**flip**, and **absolute flip**).

Fill Color, Fill Tint

Fill color and **fill tint** can be set for one bit and grayscale images to achieve a colored or tint effect. Additionally, the **overprint fill** property dictates if the fill color will overprint. To determine an image's type, the property **image type name** is used. The **space** property returns a string value indicating if the image is Grayscale, Black and White, RGB, or CMYK. In the following, the handler **colorImage** tests to see if the image is grayscale or black and white before applying fill color and fill tint. To see this in action, look at the **Color Image** project for this chapter. It includes the complete script and a document for testing.

```
(*Adds color to a one bit or grayscale image.*)
on colorImage(docRef, imageRef, colorName, colorTint, doOverprint)
    tell application "Adobe InDesign CS5"
        if image type name of imageRef is not in ¬
        {"Photoshop", "TIFF", "JPEG"} then
            error "Wrong image type"
        end if
        if space of imageRef is not in ¬
        {"Grayscale", "Black and White"} then
            error ("Wrong color space for image")
        end if
        tell docRef
            if not (exists swatch colorName) then
                error "swatch " & colorName & " not found"
            end if
            set fill color of imageRef to colorName
            set fill tint of imageRef to colorTint
            set overprint fill of imageRef to doOverprint
        end tell
    end tell
end colorImage
```

Bounds

As with its container, images also have **bounds** properties: **geometric bounds**, and **visible bounds**. This can be used for moving the item within its container. Changing an image's bounds can also affect the scale of the image.

Image Events

Image Events is an AppleScript application that gives you added capability in working with image files. You may want to spend some time looking through its dictionary. Select Open Dictionary…from Script Editor's File menu. You should see the application listed. It may be well to note that some of the image file properties will not return a value unless the file is opened. Here is an example:

```
set theFile to choose file
set theDesc to ""
tell application "Image Events"
    set fileRef to open theFile
```

```
        set theProp to properties of fileRef
        set theType to file type of theProp
        set theSize to dimensions of theProp
        set theResolution to resolution of theProp
        close fileRef
    end tell
    {theType, theSize, theResolution}
```

It is advised to put properties of the file into a variable, as above, before trying to extract values. Otherwise, missing values can cause your script to error.

Apple provides a number of scripts that demonstrate using Image Events as part of routines to batch process folders of files dropped onto a Folder Action script. The path to these scripts changes with the version of the OS. You will also find some sample scripts for working with Image Events in the Image Manipulation folder that is part of the AppleScript Editor Scripts collection. These can be accessed through the AppleScript Editor's contextual menu (Control-click inside an editing window).

Place PDFs

Placing a PDF file is the same as placing an image file with the exception that the script will need to set the **PDF place preferences** for the application.

Properties that can be set for PDF place preferences are fairly self-explanatory:

- **open document password** - Password text required for access to file.
- **page number** - The page of the PDF to place.
- **PDF crop** - Enumeration value; can be crop art, crop PDF, crop trim, crop bleed, crop media, crop content visible layers, or crop content all layers.
- **transparent background** - Indicates if the background of the PDF is transparent.

You may find the most used preference in this collection to be **page number**. The **open document password** property is used only when the PDF has been saved with a password.

The **Place Multipage PDF** script demonstrates by creating a document and then placing a multiple page PDF in the document. You will find the script in the project folder of the same name for this chapter. The handler that does the heavy-lifting for this script is shown below:

```
on placeMultipagePDF(docRef, pdfFileRef, placePt, pageWid, pageHgt)
    set pageCounter to 1
    tell application "Adobe InDesign CS5"
        set curPageRef to page 1 of docRef
        set pdfPlacePrefs to {PDF crop:crop PDF, page number:pageCounter, ¬
        transparent background:true}
        set doRepeat to true
        repeat while doRepeat = true
            if pageCounter > 1 then
                tell docRef
                    set curPageRef to make page at after curPageRef
                end tell
            end if
            set page number of PDF place preferences to pageCounter
            try
                tell curPageRef
                    set placedObj to place pdfFileRef place point placePt
```

```
                    set pdfPage to item 1 of placedObj
                end tell
                set pageAttrib to properties of PDF attributes of pdfPage
                if pageCounter = 1 then
                    set firstPage to page number of pageAttrib
                else
                    if page number of pageAttrib = firstPage then
                        set doRepeat to false
                    end if
                end if
                set pageCounter to pageCounter + 1
            on error errStr
                activate
                display alert errStr
            end try
        end repeat
        --delete the last page
        tell docRef to delete page -1
    end tell --application
end placeMultipagePDF
```

Make Scripts Work for You

For practice working with images, this chapter includes a project that may prove to be the start of an automation workflow for you. The project **Place Named Images** involves two scripts: **Image Template** and **Place Images_Named**.

Image Template creates a document that will later be used in the project. The document is created using a document preset after which object and text styles are imported from a style sheet. The document created consists of a grid of rectangles named incrementally (as in "Image_01") to match the file names for images in a folder to be chosen by the user when the **Place Images_Named** script is run.

Place Images_Named expects a document created with the **Image Template** script to be open. The handler that places the images needs a little explanation. It starts by getting a list of all of the rectangles on the referenced page. Within a loop that parses the list, a rectangle named to match the name for an image file will place the file. The handler also matches a rectangle named *Banner* for placing a banner image at the top of the page.

Procedure:

1. Open the **Image Template** script in the project folder. Look through the script to make sure you understand it. Run it.

2. Save the document created in the project folder. The name is not important. Were you to want to use the document as a template for similar projects, you could save it as a template in InDesign's Template folder.

3. With the document created in step 2 open, run the **Place Images_Named** script. From the top of the script we read:

```
set folderName to "Images"
set publicFolder to path to public folder from user domain as string
set imageFolder to publicFolder & "Images:CapitolReef"
tell application "Finder"
    set thefiles to (every file of folder imageFolder) as alias list
end tell
```

```
if length of thefiles > 0 then
    set validList to validFileNames(thefiles, fileType, fileExt)
end if
```

The Image files have been named incrementally to correspond to the container names in the document. The script assumes that file extensions for the image files will be consistent and will match the value set for the variable *fileExt* in the script.

The handler that places the files is shown below.

```
on placeImages_named(docRef, pageNum, nameBase, fileExt, folderPath)
    tell application "Adobe InDesign CS5"
        tell page pageNum of docRef
            set rectList to rectangles where name begins with nameBase
            repeat with i from 1 to length of rectList
                set fileName to name of item i of rectList & "." & fileExt
                try
                    set fileRef to (folderPath & ":" & fileName) as alias
                    place fileRef on item i of rectList
                on error
                    activate
                    display dialog "Not found: " & folderPath & fileName
                end try
            end repeat
        end tell
    end tell
end placeImages_named
```

Make sure you understand how the script works. Many automation projects are based on a workflow similar to this.

12

Lines and Borders

Although some of the scripts up to this point have unavoidably involved lines and borders (generally as stroke properties), this chapter will expand on the subject. To differentiate between lines of text and lines drawn on the page, InDesign refers to the latter as graphic lines. For the purpose of the discussion here, the word *line* can refer to a graphic line while the word *border* will be used to refer to a stroke applied to a shape. In the process of the discussion, **corner options**, which have changed dramatically as of CS5, will be covered.

Graphic Lines

Graphic lines, like other page items, inherit many of their properties from the generic **page item** class. Unique to graphic lines are the properties **end cap**, **left line end**, and **right line end**. The latter two properties define the arrowhead that may be used at the end of lines. The different types of arrowheads are listed in InDesign's dictionary (**graphic line** class). This listing includes the enumeration value none which is the default.

Stroke Style

The various stroke styles available can be discovered using the following code:

```
tell application "Adobe InDesign CS5"
    get name of stroke styles
end tell
```

Little known to many working with InDesign is that there are a number of hidden stroke styles. These are dashed and striped styles named Woof, Feet, Lights, Happy, and Rainbow. All but Rainbow are dashed stroke styles; Rainbow is a striped stroke style.

Here is a script that will add the dashed stroke styles to your list:

```
set dashList to {"Woof", "Feet", "Lights", "Happy"}
tell application "Adobe InDesign CS5"
    set styleList to name of every dashed stroke style
    repeat with i from 1 to length of dashList
        set styleName to item i of dashList
        if styleName is not in styleList then
            make dashed stroke style with properties {name:styleName}
        end if
    end repeat
end tell
```

Doing the same for Rainbow will be similar; just change the value of the *dashList* variable to {"Rainbow"} and use striped stroke style instead of dashed stroke style.

Once you have added the styles to the application, you can access the styles by name. The following example code illustrates. It assumes that there is a document open created after the styles were added to the application. Measurement units must be set to points; ruler origin to page origin.

Special Line Styles

```
set x0 to 36
set x1 to 336
set ytop to 69
set y0 to 72
set strokeWid to 18
tell application "Adobe InDesign CS5"
    tell document 1
        set stroke color of page item defaults to "Black"
        set dashList to name of every dashed stroke style
        set stripeList to name of every striped stroke style
        set styleList to dashList & stripeList
        set pageRef to page 1
    end tell
    (*Repeats through list of styles to create sampling.*)
    tell pageRef
        repeat with i from 1 to length of styleList
            set styleName to item i of styleList
            make graphic line with properties {geometric bounds:¬
            {y0, x0, y0, x1}, stroke weight:strokeWid, ¬
            stroke alignment:center alignment, stroke type:styleName}
            if i = 1 then
                set styleNames to styleName
            else
                set styleNames to styleNames & return & styleName
            end if
            set y0 to y0 + 36
        end repeat
        set frameRef to make text frame with properties¬
        {geometric bounds:{ytop, x1 + 12, y0, x1 + 100},¬
        fill color:"None", stroke type:"None", contents:styleNames}
        set properties of text 1 of frameRef to {leading:36, point size:12}
    end tell
end tell
```

This script is a good exercise in working with items in lists. Notice how the value for y0 is incremented with each loop iteration. Also, see how the string *styleNames* is created as part of the repeat process.

Graphic Line Properties

If you look at the properties for a graphic line you will notice the properties **fill color, fill tint,** and **overprint fill**. These are inherited from the page item class but have no affect on graphic lines. The properties you will use with graphic lines are **stroke color, stroke tint,**

gap color, **gap tint**, **overprint stroke**, and **overprint gap**. Gap refers to the space between dashes for dashed styles and the space between lines for striped line styles. With styles such as Wavy, Dotted, White Diamond, and Japanese Dots, defining a value for gap will affect the background behind the stroke design. If you fail to designate a stroke color, stroke tint, gap color, or gap tint, your line can pick up unexpected values set in the user interface. You may want to experiment with the following to see how **gap color** and **gap tint** affect graphic lines. Measurements are in point units.

```
tell application "Adobe InDesign CS5"
    tell page 1 of document 1
        make graphic line with properties {geometric bounds:¬
        {372, 36, 372, 336}, stroke weight:18, stroke type:"Wavy", ¬
        stroke color:"Paper", stroke tint:50, ¬
        gap color:"C=100 M=0 Y=0 K=0", gap tint:50}
    end tell
end tell
```

Stroke Dash and Gap

The property **stroke dash and gap**, which can define up to six values for alternating dash and gap widths, is only available when stroke type is Dashed. If you try to add stroke dash and gap to any other style, an error will be raised. The following script will display the error "The property is not applicable in the current state."

```
tell application "Adobe InDesign CS5"
    tell page 1 of document 1
        try
            make graphic line with properties {geometric bounds:¬
            {372, 36, 372, 336}, stroke weight:18, stroke type:"Dotted", ¬
            stroke color:"Paper", stroke tint:50, gap color:¬
            "C=100 M=0 Y=0 K=0", gap tint:50, ¬
            stroke dash and gap:{12, 3, 12, 6}}
        on error errStr
            activate
            display alert errStr
        end try
    end tell
end tell
```

Change the stroke type to "Dashed" and the script will not produce the error.

Overprint

Setting the properties for **overprint stroke** and **overprint gap** to true ensures that the color will overprint colors below. Be aware that setting either property without a corresponding color for **stroke color** or **gap color** will raise an error.

End Cap

The **end cap** property for a graphic line can be set to `butt end cap`, `projecting end cap`, or `round end cap`. The round end cap is often used with a Dashed line style to create specialized styles. One application for a rounded end cap is to produce a dotted line style where spacing between the dashes (dots, with a rounded end cap) can be controlled programmatically. The following script demonstrates in creating the display in Figure 12.1. Measurements need to be in points.

Using End Caps

```
set sAndGList to {{}, {}, {12, 18}, {0, 24, 0, 12}, {0, 24}}--dash and gap
set sLabels to {"Dotted", "Japanese Dots", "Dashed (12 18)",¬
"Dashed (0 24 0 12)", "Dashed (0 24)"}
set x0 to 36
set x1 to 240
set y0 to 72
set dy to 24
set starty to 69
tell application "Adobe InDesign CS5"
    tell page 1 of document 1
        repeat with i from 1 to length of sLabels
            try
                if (i < 3) then
                  set lineProps to {stroke type:item i of sLabels}
                else
                  set lineProps to {stroke type:"Dashed", ¬
                  stroke dash and gap:item i of sAndGList, ¬
                  end cap:round end cap}
                end if
                if i = 1 then
                  set typeStr to item 1 of sLabels
                else
                  set typeStr to typeStr & return & item i of sLabels
                end if
                set lineRef to make graphic line with properties ¬
                {geometric bounds:{y0, x0, y0, x1}, stroke color:"Black", ¬
                stroke weight:6, gap color:"None"}
                set properties of lineRef to lineProps
                set y0 to y0 + dy
            end try
        end repeat
        set frameRef to make text frame with properties ¬
        {geometric bounds:{starty, x1 + 12, y0, x1 + 150},¬
        fill color:"None", stroke type:"None", contents:typeStr}
        set properties of text 1 of frameRef to {point size:12, leading:dy}
    end tell
end tell
```

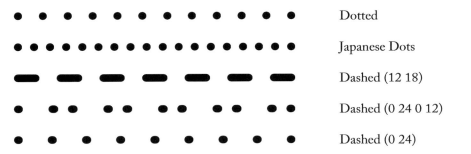

Figure 12.1: Dotted stroke styles created with UsingEndCaps script

Stroke Alignment

Your script can designate whether the stroke for a graphic line will be made centered on the geometric bounds, above (outside), or below (inside). Failure to designate stroke alignment will default to the alignment currently set in the user's interface or page item defaults.

```
tell application "Adobe InDesign CS5"
    set testIt to stroke alignment of page item defaults
end tell
```

Line Object Styles

Creating an object style for a line is similar to creating any other object style. You may decide to organize your line styles in a style group, perhaps named "Lines." Styles and style groups can be created for the application as well as for documents. The following script demonstrates.

Line Object Style

```
(*Creates line object style within style group named "Lines."*)
set groupName to "Lines"
set styleName to "White Dots"
tell application "Adobe InDesign CS5"
    if not (exists object style group "Lines") then
        set lineGroup to make object style group with properties ¬
        {name:groupName}
    else
        set lineGroup to object style group groupName
    end if
    if not (exists object style styleName of lineGroup) then
        tell lineGroup
            set objStyle to make object style with properties ¬
            {name:styleName}
            set enable stroke of objStyle to true
            set stroke type of objStyle to "Dotted"
            set stroke weight of objStyle to 8
            set stroke color of objStyle to "Paper"
            set gap color of objStyle to "Black"
            set gap tint of objStyle to 100
        end tell
    end if
end tell
```

Remember:

A style added to the application is not available to existing documents, only those created after the style is added to the application. An attempt to use a style that does not exist can cause an error that could cause InDesign to crash.

Always check for the existence of a style before attempting to use it. Placing styles within groups aids organization, but adds a level of difficulty to your scripts as you need to verify the existence of the style within its group. as in the following script.

Get Grouped Style

```
set styleName to "White Dots"
set groupName to "Lines"
(*Verifies if style within a style group exists.*)
```

```
try
    set styleRef to getGroupedStyle(groupName, styleName)
on error errStr
    activate
display alert errStr
end try

on getGroupedStyle(groupName, styleName)
    tell application "Adobe InDesign CS5"
        if exists object style group groupName then
            set groupRef to object style group groupName
        else
            error "Style group " & groupName & " not found"
        end if
        tell groupRef
            if not (exists object style styleName) then
                error "Object style " & styleName & " of group " & ¬
                groupName & " does not exist"
            end if
            set styleRef to object style styleName
        end tell
    end tell
    return styleRef
end getGroupedStyle
```

Alternatively, you can take advantage of the **all object styles** property for the application or document to get a list of all object style references. The script could then use a repeat to parse through the list until the style is found. Caution is advised in using this method as there could be more than one style of the same name residing in different groups. If this is a possibility, you would then need to verify the group to which the style belongs using its **parent** property. See the script **Group Style By Name** in the Chapter Scripts folder for this chapter.

Border

Most of what has been said about graphic lines is true for strokes applied to shapes. When a shape is involved, the properties having to do with **end join, stroke corner adjustment**, and corner options now come into play. Version CS5 added new capability for working with corners while making your scripts written for earlier versions obsolete. Now, instead of **corner option** (corner effect in CS3 and CS4) and **corner radius**, there is a separate property for each corner of the page item. In the following example, only the top left corner is rounded, all others are squared.

```
(*The following will not work with a version of InDesign prior to CS5.*)
tell application "Adobe InDesign CS5"
    tell page 1 of document 1
        set rectRef to make rectangle with properties {geometric bounds:¬
        {"72 pt", "36 pt", "200 pt", "400 pt"}, stroke color:"Black", ¬
        stroke weight:8, stroke type:"Solid", top left corner option:¬
        rounded corner, top left corner radius:"36 pt"}
    end tell
end tell
```

The problem is, as of this writing, this functionality is broken for the bottom right corner when set directly with a script. There are workarounds. One workaround that is part of the sample scripts provided by Adobe, works with path manipulation. The subject of working with paths will be covered in Chapter 18. The easiest workaround is to manually create object styles that include your desired corner options. When you need to create a page item that has rounded corners (or other corner options) you apply the appropriate object style. You can always override the object style settings including the bottom right corner radius.

Rounded Corner

```
(*Assumes document 1 has an object style "Rounded Corner."*)
tell application "Adobe InDesign CS5"
    tell document 1
        if exists object style "Rounded Corner" then
            set styleRef to object style "Rounded Corner"
        else
            return beep
        end if
    end tell
    tell page 1 of document 1
        set rectRef to make rectangle with properties {geometric bounds:¬
        {"2p0", "3p0", "12p0", "36p0"}, applied object style:styleRef}
        --override object style settings
        tell rectRef
            set stroke weight to 12
            set bottom right corner radius to "48 pt"
        end tell
    end tell
end tell
```

This may prove to be your favorite way of creating page items even disregarding the problem with the right corner option.

For any non-rectangular polygon (not having four sides), the corner option and corner radius will apply to all corners when the top left corner option and top left corner radius properties are set.

```
(*Will not work with versions of InDesign prior to CS5.*)
tell application "Adobe InDesign CS5"
    set properties of polygon preferences to {number of sides:3,¬
    inset percentage:0}
    tell page 1 of document 1
        set polyRef to make polygon with properties {geometric bounds:¬
        {"72 pt", "36 pt", "200 pt", "400 pt"}, stroke color:"Black", ¬
        stroke weight:8, stroke type:"Solid", top left corner option:¬
        rounded corner, top left corner radius:"36 pt"}
    end tell
end tell
```

For a rectangle, you have another option for corners if all corners will be uniform: **convert shape**. This is limited to only three corner styles: Rounded Rectangle, Beveled Rectangle, and Inverse Rounded Rectangle.

Rounded Rectangles

```
set boundsList to {{"1i", "1i", "3i", "4i"}, {"4i", "1i", "6i", "4i"}}
tell application "Adobe InDesign CS5"
    set docRef to make document
    tell page 1 of docRef
```

```
        repeat with eachItem in boundsList
            set rectRef to make rectangle with properties {geometric bounds:¬
            eachItem, stroke weight:6, stroke type:"Solid", stroke ¬
            alignment:inside alignment}
                tell rectRef to convert shape given convert to ¬
                rounded rectangle corner radius 36
        end repeat
    end tell
end tell
```

Stroke Corner Adjustment

When working with dash and gap, you will be pleased to know there is a stroke corner adjustment property that allows you to set a value for how dashes and gaps will be altered (or not) to make corners meet. The values you can use are none, dashes, gaps, and dashes and gaps. The following script demonstrates how the different values affect the length of the strokes and gaps. This script may be used as a testing ground for experimenting.

Stroke Corner Adjust

```
set x0 to 36
set y0 to 36
set dAndg to {12, 6, 12, 6, 12, 6}
tell application "Adobe InDesign CS5"
    tell page 1 of document 1
        set cornerAdjust to {none, dashes, gaps, dashes and gaps}
        repeat with i from 1 to length of cornerAdjust
            set gBounds to {y0, x0, y0 + 72, x0 + 300}
            make rectangle with properties {geometric bounds:gBounds,¬
            stroke weight:6, stroke color:"Black", stroke type:"Dashed",¬
            stroke dash and gap:dAndg, end cap: butt end cap, ¬
            stroke corner adjustment:item i of cornerAdjust}
            set y0 to y0 + 90
        end repeat
    end tell
end tell
```

Make Scripts Work for You

To Group or Not to Group

A script you might find handy is **Fence It**. It draws a border around the combined geometric bounds of the page items selected. It does this by temporarily grouping the items, acquiring the geometric bounds of the group, and then ungrouping once the dimensions have been recorded.

In creating a group, all items are moved to a common layer. This may not be advisable for your script. Compare the code for **Fence It** with that for **Fence It_NoGroup**. Both scripts are found in the Chapter Scripts folder for this chapter. If you would have occasion to use either of these scripts, change values for the border properties and save in one of InDesign's script folders.

13

Tables

Tables are story elements having cells within rows and columns. They flow with the text. This means that in addition to being able to be used for displaying tabular data, they have a relationship with text flow that can be used to an advantage as part of an automated project. This chapter will explore some of these options as part of the discussion on cells, tables, cell styles, and table styles.

Table Properties and Elements

A quick look at the list of properties available to a table may cause a mild case of property record shock. Most of the properties have to do with setting stroke and fill attributes that are, for the most part, self-explanatory. The discussion here will only scratch the tip of the iceberg in regard to the available options.

The **parent** property of a table can be a text item (story, paragraph, or other). The dimensions of the table may be defined using its **height** and **width** properties. The **space before** and **space after** properties add space between the table and adjacent text.

Divisions of the table across are columns, the number of which is returned using the **column count** property. Divisions of the table vertically are rows, for which there are three subclassifications: header rows, body rows, and footer rows.

```
tell application "Adobe InDesign CS5"
    tell page 1 of document 1
        set frameRef to make text frame with properties ¬
        {geometric bounds:{"72 pt", "36 pt", "300 pt", "436 pt"},¬
        contents:"Text before table"}
        tell frameRef
            set tableRef to make table with properties {column count:4, ¬
            header row count:1, body row count:5, width:"400 pt", ¬
            height:"200 pt", space before:"10 pt"}
        end tell
    end tell
    set test to parent of tableRef
end tell
test --returns reference to text frame
```

Rows are referenced using their row index within the table. The number of rows, however, is independently returned in each classification using the **header row count**, **body row count**, and **footer row count** properties.

Within rows and columns are the basic table elements: cells.

Cells

A script can reference cells by their index within a table, as a cell within a row, or as a cell within a column. The **name** property of a cell is a string value containing its column index followed by a colon and then its row index. For example, the first cell of the third row of a table is named 1:3.

Replace the test line at the bottom of the script above with the following:

```
set test to name of cell 1 of row 3 of tableRef
```

When the script is run, the result will be "1:3".

Accordingly, with the table created using the script above, all of the following statements reference the same cell (the first cell of the second row). Replace the test line at the bottom of the script above with:

```
tell tableRef
    set text 1 of cell 5 to "Cell 2"
    set fill color of cell "1:2" to "C=100 M=0 Y=0 K=0"
    set fill tint of cell 1 of row 2 to 20
    set vertical justification of cell 2 of column 1 to center align
    set test to name of cell 1 of row 2
end tell
```

Creating Tables

Converting Text to Table

A table can be created as an element within a text frame, as in the example above. Another way to create a table is to convert text to a table using the text object's **convert to table** command. This requires that the text be delimited using a column and row separator. A delimiter can be a comma, a tab, or a paragraph return. Within a script, paragraph returns and tabs can be designated alternatively using the escaped characters: "\r" and "\t" respectively.

Convert Text to Table

```
set theText to ¬
"column one\tcolumn two\tcolumn three\tcolumn four"
set theText to theText & return
set theText to theText & "row 2\tcell 2:2\tcell 2:3\tcell 2:4"
tell application "Adobe InDesign CS5"
    tell page 1 of document 1
        set frameRef to make text frame with properties ¬
        {geometric bounds:{"72 pt", "36 pt", "300 pt", "436 pt"}, ¬
        contents:theText}
    end tell
    tell text 1 of frameRef
        convert to table column separator "\t" row separator "\r"
    end tell
end tell
```

Converting Placed Text

The **convert to table** command can also be used to convert a placed text file that is properly delimited. The principal idea for the following script is to style an empty paragraph at the end of the text with a paragraph style named *Table*. This will identify all of the text placed as a text style range. (Text style range is covered in Chapter 14.). To see how this works, create a text frame with a few lines of text styled with any paragraph style other than *Table*. With the text frame selected, run the script **Place For Table** in the Chapter Scripts folder for this chapter. Select a tab-delimited text file when prompted. (You will find a file "TextForTable.txt" in the Public:Text Files folder, which is the default location for the script's Choose File command.) By styling the text that is imported with a unique paragraph style, the script is able to use a text style range for the table conversion. From the script:

```
tell text style range -1 of storyRef
    set tableRef to convert to table column separator tab ¬
    row separator return
end tell
```

Creating a Table Using Text Reference

You can create a table using a text object as the target for the tell statement. Just make sure that the reference is an object reference (not actual text). Without an **at before** parameter, the table will be created by default after the text object referenced.

```
--assumes word 4 of text frame 1 of document 1 exists
tell application "Adobe InDesign CS5"
    set textRef to object reference of word 4 of text frame 1 ¬
    of document 1
    tell textRef
        set tableRef to make table at before (a reference to it) ¬
        with properties {body row count:4, column count:3, ¬
        header row count:1, footer row count:0}
    end tell
end tell
```

Adding a Table to a Text Frame

When a text frame is the target of the tell statement that creates a table, the table width defaults to the width of the text frame if the table width is not specified.

```
--assumes text frame 1 of document 1 exists
tell application "Adobe InDesign CS5"
    tell text frame 1 of document 1
        set tableRef to make table with properties {body row count:4, ¬
        column count:5}
    end tell
end tell
```

If the table width is specified and is less than that of the frame, the table will align using the alignment of the paragraph style in effect. You can override the justification of the existing paragraph style by setting the justification for the insertion point at which the table is to be created or inserted. The following example centers the table within the text frame.

```
--assumes text frame 1 of document 1 exists
tell application "Adobe InDesign CS5"
```

```
    set frameRef to text frame 1 of document 1
    set justification of insertion point -1 of frameRef to center align
    tell frameRef
        set tableRef to make table with properties {body row count:4, ¬
        column count:5, width:"4 in", height:"2.5 in"}
    end tell
end tell
```

Creating a Table with Scripted Text

Instead of converting placed text to a table you can use a list of text items for the table's
contents property.

```
--assumes text frame 1 of document 1 exists
set theText to {"One", "Two", "Three", "Four", "Five", "Six", ¬
"Seven", "Eight", "Nine", "Ten"}
tell application "Adobe InDesign CS5"
    set frameRef to text frame 1 of document 1
    set justification of insertion point -1 of frameRef to center align
    tell frameRef
        set tableRef to make table with properties {body row count:2, ¬
        column count:5, width:"4 in", height:"1.5 in", contents:theText}
    end tell
end tell
```

This is the method used for the **Calendar** project you will find in the folder for this chapter.

Working with Cells

To place an image file in a table cell, an insertion point in the cell, usually insertion point 1 or
insertion point -1, is used.

```
--assumes a text frame that contains a table is selected
tell application "Adobe InDesign CS5"
    set selList to selection
    if length of selList > 0 and ¬
    class of item 1 of selList is text frame then
        set frameRef to item 1 of selList
        --assumes user selects an image file
        set fileRef to choose file with prompt "Select an image"
        set tableRef to table 1 of frameRef
        set cellRef to cell 1 of tableRef
        set auto grow of cellRef to true
        tell insertion point 1 of cellRef
            place fileRef
        end tell
    end if
end tell
```

You will likely set the **auto grow** property for the cell to true, as in the above example. This
property allows the cell to grow vertically to fit the height of the image. The property **clip
content to cell** may also be considered to prevent the image from overlaying adjoining cells
horizontally. Without **clip content to cell**, your script could adjust the width of the cell to
accommodate the image, but this will change the overall width of the table. The script **Place
Image** is a more complete script that demonstrates this concept. Make sure a text frame is
selected when you run the script. Select the file "Sedona.psd" when prompted.

Setting Cell Properties

You can set properties for any cell, or use a range reference. This is true also for rows and columns.

```
--assumes text frame 1 exists for active document
tell application "Adobe InDesign CS5"
    tell document 1
        set yellowColor to swatch "C=0 M=0 Y=100 K=0"
        set frameRef to text frame 1
    end tell
    tell frameRef
        set tableRef to make table with properties {body row count:4, ¬
        column count:4}
    end tell
    tell tableRef
        set cellRef to cell "3:2"
        set fill color of cellRef to "Black"
        set fill color of row 1 to yellowColor
        set cellRange to cells 1 thru 2 of row 2
        set fill color of cellRange to yellowColor
        set properties of rows 3 thru 4 to {fill color:"Black", ¬
        fill tint:20}
    end tell
end tell
```

Styling Text In Cells

The text for a table defaults to the styling for text in effect when the table is created. To style text in individual cells, you can take advantage of the every element reference. This can be combined with range references for rows or columns as demonstrated in the following:

```
set textList to {"Head Here"}
repeat with i from 1 to 16
    set end of textList to ("" & i)
end repeat
--assumes a text frame selection
tell application "Adobe InDesign CS5"
    set selList to selection
    if length of selList > 0 and ¬
    class of item 1 of selList = text frame then
        set frameRef to item 1 of selList
    else
        return beep --ends script with beep
    end if
    tell frameRef
        set tableRef to make table with properties {body row count:5, ¬
        column count:4}
    end tell
    tell tableRef
        tell row 1 to merge (cells 1 thru -1)
        set contents to textList
        set headProps to {applied font:"Minion Pro", font style:"Bold", ¬
        point size:16, justification:center align}
        set bodyProps to {applied font:"Minion Pro", font style:"Regular",¬
        point size:12, justification:center align}
        tell row 1
```

```
        set properties of text 1 of every cell to headProps
    end tell
    tell rows 2 thru -1
        set properties of text 1 of every cell to bodyProps
    end tell
end tell
end tell
```

Cell and Table Styles

Creating cell and table styles in a script is fairly straight forward. The thing to remember is that cell styling, if used, can override settings in the table style. Because of this, consider the following two main options:

- Avoid defining stroke properties for cell styles (including stroke type: "*None*") if you don't want your table strokes to be overridden. Rely on stroke settings in the table style such as start and end stroke settings to define row and column strokes. An example of using this option is the script **ColorHead Table Style** in the project folder **Table and Cell Styles**.

  The table style defines the border stroke weight and type as well as the stroke properties for rows and columns. It uses two cell styles: ColorHead for the header region, and Body for the body region. (See discussion of "Table Regions" following.) The header region cell style defines the properties for fill color, bottom edge stroke, and text styling (applied paragraph style and vertical justification). The body region cell style defines properties for text styling only.

- Set up a cell style for each region of the table and rely on styling for all regions. With this option, cell style properties can define the border for the table. The script **GrayHead Table Style** demonstrates this option.

Remember:

For those table style properties that you do not set, the values will default to those of "[Basic Table]". For "[Basic Table]" the default start row and column stroke count is 0; stroke weight is "1 pt", and stroke type is "Solid."

Table Regions

A table is divided into five regions: header region, footer region, body region, left column, and right column regions. Corresponding region styles, to which cell styles can be assigned, are properties of a table style.

If you browse through the listing of properties that can be set for a cell style, don't panic. For most purposes, your script can create a basic style to base your styles on. This style can be used to define the properties for the majority of the cell styles, using **based on**. Properties not defined default to cell style "[None]" which sets property values to nothing).

The script **Based On Cell Styles** following uses a limited set of properties for demonstration. The cell styles created will be used in a script that creates a table style. The script and a sample document for testing can be found in the **Table and Cell Styles** project folder for this chapter.

Based On Cell Styles

```
tell application "Adobe InDesign CS5"
    set docRef to document 1
    try
        tell docRef
            set parastyleRef to applied paragraph style of text defaults
            set headStyleRef to paragraph style "Head_14"
            set bodyStyleRef to paragraph style "Text_10"
        end tell
        set basicProps to {name:"Basic", applied paragraph style:¬
        parastyleRef, top inset:"0p1", left inset:"0p6", ¬
        vertical justification:center align}
        set basicStyle to my createCellStyle(docRef, "Basic", basicProps,¬
        missing value)
        --create style for head region
        set headProps to {name:"Head", applied paragraph style:¬
        headStyleRef, fill color:"Black", fill tint:20}
        set headStyle to my createCellStyle(docRef, "Head", ¬
        headProps, basicStyle)
        --create style for body region
        set bodyProps to {name:"GrayHead Body", applied paragraph style:¬
        bodyStyleRef}
        set bodyStyle to my createCellStyle(docRef, "GrayHead  Body", ¬
        bodyProps, basicStyle)
        --create style for left region
        set leftProps to {name:"LeftCol", applied paragraph style:¬
        bodyStyleRef, left edge stroke color:"None", ¬
        left edge stroke weight:0}
        set leftStyle to my createCellStyle(docRef, "LeftCol", ¬
        leftProps, basicStyle)
        --create style for right region
        set rightProps to {name:"RightCol", applied paragraph style:¬
        bodyStyleRef, right edge stroke color:"None", ¬
        right edge stroke weight:0}
        set rightStyle to my createCellStyle(docRef, "RightCol", ¬
        rightProps, basicStyle)
    on error errStr
        display alert errStr
    end try
end tell

(*Creates cell style if it does not exist; returns cell style reference.*)
on createCellStyle(docRef, styleName, styleProps, basedOnRef)
    tell application "Adobe InDesign CS5"
        tell docRef
            if (exists cell style styleName) then
                set styleRef to cell style styleName
            else
                if basedOnRef is not missing value then
                    set cellRecord to styleProps & {based on:basedOnRef}
                else
                    set cellRecord to styleProps
                end if
                set styleRef to make cell style with properties cellRecord
            end if
        end tell
    end tell
end tell
```

```
        return styleRef
    end createCellStyle
```

Using existing cell styles to define regions, creating a table style is fairly easy. With a document having the cell styles established, the following creates a table style called "GrayHead."

GrayHead Table Style

```
set tablestyleName to "GrayHead"
try
    set docRef to getDocRef()
    --supply name of cell styles for each region; can be missing value
    set regionList to {"Head", "GrayHead Body", missing value, "LeftCol",¬
    "RightCol"}
    set tablestyleRef to my createTableStyle(docRef, tablestyleName, ¬
    regionList)
on error errStr
    display alert errStr
end try

on createTableStyle(docRef, tablestyleName, regionList)
    set errStr to ""
    tell application "Adobe InDesign CS5"
        tell docRef
            if exists table style tablestyleName then
                error "table style " & tablestyleName & " already exists"
            end if
            --check for cell styles
            repeat with i from 1 to length of regionList
                if item i of regionList is not missing value then
                    set cellStyleName to item i of regionList
                    if not (exists cell style cellStyleName) then
                        set errStr to "missing " & cellStyleName & return
                    end if
                end if
            end repeat
            if length of errStr > 1 then
                error errStr
            end if
            set tablestyleRef to make table style with properties ¬
            {name:tablestyleName}
            if item 1 of regionList is not missing value then
                set header region cell style of tablestyleRef to cell style ¬
                (item 1 of regionList)
            end if
            if item 2 of regionList is not missing value then
                set body region cell style of tablestyleRef to cell style ¬
                (item 2 of regionList)
            end if
            if item 3 of regionList is not missing value then
                set footer region cell style of tablestyleRef to cell style ¬
                (item3 of regionList)
            end if
            if item 4 of regionList is not missing value then
                set left column region cell style of tablestyleRef to ¬
                cell style (item 4 of regionList)
            end if
            if item 5 of regionList is not missing value then
```

```
                    set right column region cell style of tablestyleRef to ¬
                    cell style (item 5 of regionList)
                end if
            end tell --document
        end tell --application
    end createTableStyle
    (*Add handler getDocRef here.*)
```

Create Table using Table Style

With a table style in your active document, creating a table manually or programmatically is a breeze. The following creates a table on the first page of the active document using the table style "GrayHead."

GrayHead Table
```
set tablestyleName to "GrayHead"
set textList to {"Header Here"}
repeat with i from 1 to 20
    set end of textList to ("" & i)
end repeat
tell application "Adobe InDesign CS5"
    tell document 1
        if not (exists table style tablestyleName) then
            return beep
        end if
        set styleRef to table style tablestyleName
        set frameRef to make text frame with properties ¬
        {geometric bounds:{"72 pt", "36 pt", "500 pt", "576 pt"}, ¬
        fill color:"None", stroke color:"None"}
        tell frameRef
            set tableRef to make table with properties {width:"464 pt", ¬
            height:"10p0", header row count:1, body row count:4, ¬
            column count:5, applied table style:styleRef}
        end tell
        tell row 1 of tableRef
            merge (cells 1 thru -1)
        end tell
        set contents of tableRef to textList
        tell cells of tableRef to clear cell style overrides
    end tell
end tell
```

Read File for Table

Seldom will your scripts have the contents for the table created as was done in the sample script above. The information will more likely come from either a database, a standing text file, or a table created in another application. The script **Read File for Table** in the Chapter Scripts folder for this chapter demonstrates reading a tab return delimited file for placing in a table. Below is the handler **readForTable** and its calling statement from the script.

```
set rowDelim to return
set colDelim to tab
set {dataList, numRows, numCols} to readForTable(fileChoice, rowDelim, ¬
colDelim)

on readForTable(fileChoice, rowDelim, colDelim)
    set numCols to 0
```

```
        set fileRef to open for access fileChoice
        if ((get eof fileRef) is not equal to 0) then
            set theData to read fileRef as list using delimiter {rowDelim}
        end if
        --close the file
        close access fileRef
        set numRows to length of theData
        --parse the list
        set dataList to {}
        set AppleScript's text item delimiters to colDelim
        repeat with i from 1 to length of theData
            set thisList to (text items of item i of theData)
            if length of thisList > numCols then
                set numCols to length of thisList
            end if

            set dataList to dataList & thisList
        end repeat
        set AppleScript's text item delimiters to ""
        return {dataList, numRows, numCols}
    end readForTable
```

Importing Table and Cell Styles

In Chapter 9 you were introduced to the **importStyles** handler (in Styles folder of the Handlers Library). This handler provides three parameters which can be set to true or false to indicate the type of styles to be imported. Set the last parameter to true to have table and cell styles imported to the document referenced by the *docRef* variable.

Import Table Styles

```
set fileName to "TableStyles.indd"
try
    set stylesheetRef to getStylesheet(fileName)
    set docRef to document 1 of application "Adobe InDesign CS5"
    importStyles (docRef, stylesheetRef, false, true, true)
on error errStr
    display alert errStr
    return
end try

on importStyles(docRef, stylesheetRef, doObject, doText, doTable)
    tell application "Adobe InDesign CS5"
        tell docRef
            if doObject is true then
                import styles format object styles format from stylesheetRef
            end if
            if doText is true then
                import styles format text styles format from stylesheetRef
            end if
            if doTable is true then
                import styles format table styles format from stylesheetRef
            end if
        end tell
    end tell
end importStyles
(*Add handler getStylesheet (Styles folder) to complete script.*)
```

Make Scripts Work For You

You will find a number of fun projects in the folder for this chapter. Be sure to read the instructions in scripts for these projects:

Box Text. Creates a single column table to create a box around text selected in a story flow. The variables that establish values such as spacing and stroke are placed at the top of the script. Once these values are established, it is assumed that they will not need to be changed. Use with document "BoxText.indd" for testing.

Inline Sidebar. While an anchored frame for a sidebar is the more common practice, using a table makes it possible to edit the text in the sidebar and have it expand as needed. Text for this is set to have a left indent the same width as the sidebar. To use this script, the operator selects two paragraphs, the first of which will be the inline sidebar. Give this script a keyboard shortcut to make quick work of sidebar heads. "TestSidebar.indd" is provided for testing.

Image With Caption_Table. This script creates a single-column table to contain a graphic file and its caption. Because a table flows with the text, this is an ideal way to place images with captions in text that may change. Use "TestDocument.indd" for testing.

Total Table Columns. Designed to work with the document "TableDoc.indd." If this document is not open, the user will be prompted to select the file. Requires that text frame for table is named "TableFrame." The document "TableDoc.indd" is provided in project for testing.

Calendar. Creates a twelve-month calendar using a template with containers named for the month name "MonthName", the images "Image", and the calendar table "ThisMonth." This script includes a do script call to a JavaScript that creates a non-modal dialog to indicate the script is processing. Once processing is complete the document creates its window. A screen shot of a page from the calendar is shown on the front cover of the book.

Photo by S. Hopkins

Temple of the Moon is one of the outstanding monoliths found in Cathedral Valley. This valley is just one corner of the back country beckoning the adventurer in Capitol Reef National Park.

Figure 13.1: Single-column table with two rows: one for image, the other for caption and credit.

Exerum sunt dolupta temporrum fugit quo dolorio qui ut dusandi gnihicium am id eost fuga. Itas dem alitatios milla verum hit ut pori cus.

```
I used the BoxText script to bring attention to
this text.
```

Rum aceptat ecturis autaeru nditae occabor sunditium faci occab ilibus maio. Nos magnam fugita pedit eos digendit.

Figure 13.2: Single-column Box Text table creates box around selected text.

Il magnim eos autem sum liti doloratquid qui renesciiscit autectatem. Offic temporem res asim harciunt volupti vene cus.

Sidebar head   At parionsed magnihillore pos di quam sant laute ped qui net am etur, ni aut mi, nullora quae. Tiuste simus doloris eos moditat odignis nonse iliam lique quod quuntesequia doluptatquas simillorero doluptiant laborit asperuptat et omnienestrum labo. Eventiu sament vit, ut optae odiae core velitate rem ipsam num endeliquas dolupta nihil ius.

Figure 13.3: Hanging sidebar head created with Inline Sidebar script.

First	Second	Third	Fourth
125	432	576	333
463	595	212	474
321	497	884	432
457	422	386	394
872	212	999	497
686	632	621	364
2924	2790	3678	2494

Figure 13.4: Total Table Columns script creates table and totals the column contents.

14

Text Considerations

Although the subject of styling text has been touched on in the discussion of paragraph and character styles, this chapter will cover some other concepts that have to do with working with text. As part of the discussion, you will discover ways special characters and tabs can be used advantageously in an automated project.

Text, References, Text Style Range

InDesign provides a wealth of text objects, properties, and commands for working with text. From story to character and with every text object in between, text objects all have one thing in common: text. The classification **texts** represents a collection of all text objects contained by a parent object. Let's look at some sample code to help clarify the concept. For this you will need a document with some placeholder text.

Placeholder Text

Placeholder text is a member of the contents property of a text frame. Here is a sample script demonstrating the addition of placeholder text to a default document:

Create Test Document

```
tell application "Adobe InDesign CS5"
    set docRef to make document
    tell docRef
        if not (exists paragraph style "Text_14") then
            make paragraph style with properties {name:"Text_14",¬
            point size:14}
        end if
    end tell
    set framePrefs to {text column count:1, text column gutter:"12 pt", ¬
    vertical justification:top align, ignore wrap:false}
    set pageRef to page 1 of docRef
    set liveBounds to my getLiveBounds(docRef, pageRef)
    tell pageRef
        set frameRef to make text frame with properties ¬
        {geometric bounds:liveBounds, fill color:"None", stroke weight:0,¬
        stroke color:"None", contents:placeholder text}
        set properties of text frame preferences of frameRef to framePrefs
    end tell
end tell
(*Add handler getLiveBounds (Page folder) to complete script.*)
```

The entire script is found in the Chapter Scripts folder for this chapter. Use the document created for testing the following statements.

Text References

Text can be referenced by story, paragraph within a story, text within a story or paragraph, or text range. The following example demonstrates referencing a paragraph within a story reference. To set the paragraph style, it uses the command **apply paragraph style**. If the paragraph does not exist, an error will be thrown.

Test Story

```
--requires active document with paragraph style "Text_14"
tell application "Adobe InDesign CS5"
    set docRef to document 1
    tell docRef
        if (count of stories) is greater than 0 then
            set storyRef to story -1 of docRef
            set textRef to object reference of paragraph 1 of storyRef
            set parastyleRef to paragraph style "Text_14"
            tell textRef to apply paragraph style using parastyleRef ¬
            with clearing overrides
        end if
    end tell
end tell
```

The reference to the first story of a document (story 1) yields varying results, depending on whether a master text frame exists. If the document is created with **master text frame** set to true, the first story is a reference to the story in the master text frame. Using a reference to story -1 assures that the most recent story created is used as the target story.

Paragraphs can be referenced by range. Substitute the highlighted code in the test script above with the following and test.

```
tell storyRef
    if (count of paragraphs) > 2 then
        set textRef to object reference of (text from paragraph 2 ¬
        to paragraph 3)
    end if
end tell
```

A text reference is often used to reference text ranges within a text object. A reference to text 1 references the entire text.

Substitute for the highlighted code in the script above with the following and test:

```
tell storyRef
    if (count of paragraphs) > 3 then
        set textRef to object reference of (text 1 of paragraph 4)
    end if
end tell
```

Applying a paragraph style to a range of words (or characters) will apply the style to the parent paragraphs. Test the script with the following code substituted as above.

```
tell storyRef
    try
        set textRef to object reference of (text from word 300 to word 400)
    on error
        return beep
    end try
end tell
```

To style only the words referenced, not the entire paragraph, use a character style. The following uses the command **apply character style** to set styling. To test, make sure your document has a character style named "Bold."

Apply Character Style

```
--requires active document with character style "Bold"
tell application "Adobe InDesign CS5"
    set docRef to document 1
    tell docRef
        set boldRef to character style "Bold"
        if (count of stories) is greater than 0 then
            set storyRef to story -1
        else
            return beep
        end if
    end tell
        try
            set textRef to object reference of (text from word 10 to ¬
            word 100) of storyRef
            tell textRef to apply character style using boldRef
        end try
end tell
```

You can mix text object references in establishing a text reference.

```
set textRef to object reference of (text from character 10 to ¬
paragraph 3 of storyRef)
```

Text Style Range

Text style ranges define text within a text object that has a different set of attributes than the surrounding text. If a paragraph has more than one text style range, it indicates that styling within the paragraph has been overridden at the word or character level. To demonstrate, the following sets the fill color for every other text style range in a story to "C=0 M=100 Y=0 K=0." The test document you have been using might be a good subject for this test.

```
set colorName to "C=0 M=100 Y=0 K=0"
tell application "Adobe InDesign CS5"
    tell document 1
        if (count of stories) > 0 then
            set storyRef to story -1
        else
            return beep
        end if
        tell storyRef
            repeat with i from 1 to count of text style ranges by 2
                set fill color of text style range i to colorName
            end repeat
        end tell
    end tell
end tell
```

Selection

Often your script will need to work with the text the user has selected. Remember that the selection property returns a list. When text is selected, the class of item 1 of the selection list is **text**.

```
tell application "Adobe InDesign CS5"
    set selList to selection
    if length of selList > 0 then
        set test to class of item 1 of selList
    end if
end tell
```

If the text cursor is placed with no text selection, the result of the previous test would be **insertion point**.

To get the individual class member of a text selection, reference the selection directly. This can also return the class **text** if a text range is selected. Otherwise, paragraph, character, word, or other text class will be returned.

```
tell application "Adobe InDesign CS5"
    if length of selection > 0 then
        set test to class of item 1 of selection
    end if
end tell
```

A handler you may use often is **getStoryOfSelection** (Selection folder). It returns a reference to the parent story (text flow) for a selected text object or text frame.

```
try
    set theStory to getStoryOfSelection()
on error errStr
    activate
    display alert errStr
end try

on getStoryOfSelection()
    set errMsg to "Requires text or insertion point selection."
    tell application "Adobe InDesign CS5"
        set selList to selection
        if length of selList > 0
            if class of item 1 of selList is in {text, insertion point} then
                set storyRef to parent story of item 1 of selList
            else if class of item 1 of selList = text frame then
                set storyRef to parent story of text 1 of item 1 of selList
            end if
        else
            error errMsg
        end if
    end tell
    return storyRef
end getStoryOfSelection
```

Iterating Through Text

Often your script will need to work with elements within a text object. Most likely, this will involve some type of repeat loop structure. For this, it is best to work from back to front to prevent dynamic text references from interfering with the intent of the script.

Delete Empty Paragraphs

```
try
    (*Returns reference to parent story if text or text frame selected.*)
    set storyRef to textOrFrameSelected()
on error errStr
    display alert errStr
    return
end try
tell application "Adobe InDesign CS5"
    tell storyRef
        set paraList to object reference of paragraphs of storyRef
        repeat with i from length of paraList to 1 by -1
            if length of item i of paraList = 1 then
                delete item i of paraList
            end if
        end repeat
    end tell
end tell
(*Add handler textOrFrameSelected to complete script.*)
```

Apply Multiple Styles

If you have a repeating paragraph style pattern and are not using chained paragraph styles, you can set up a list of style names and apply them to paragraphs using a repeat loop. For this there must be a paragraph for each paragraph style in the list, and the same number of paragraphs in each text grouping. An empty paragraph can stand in for a missing paragraph in a text grouping if needed.

The script **Style Paragraphs_Loop** uses a handler that takes advantage of a handy mathematical formula using the AppleScript **mod** function to style paragraphs in a repeating loop. We will examine this script in the "Make Scripts Work for You" section of this chapter. You can see how the looping formula works using the following test script.

```
set styleList to {"Make", "Description", "Price"}
set numParagraphs to 6
set styleLen to length of styleList
repeat with i from 1 to numParagraphs
    set modIndex to ((i + numParagraphs - 1) mod styleLen) + 1
    display dialog "modIndex " & item modIndex of styleList
end repeat
```

Special Characters

Some of the scripts in earlier chapters used enumeration values for defining special characters. A list of special characters available is offered when you select **Insert Special Character**, **Insert White Space**, or **Insert Break Character** from InDesign's text context menu (control-click with the text cursor in a text frame).

Enumeration values for special characters present a specific problem for scripts in that they cannot be concatenated to a string. Instead, the **contents** property of an insertion point can be used. To see how this works, select a text frame in an open document and run the following:

```
tell application "Adobe InDesign CS5"
    set selList to selection
    if length of selList > 0 and class of selection = text frame then
        set frameRef to item 1 of selection
        set text 1 of frameRef to "Page "
        set contents of insertion point -1 of frameRef to auto page number
    end if
end tell
```

Copy Special Characters

For someone coming from a traditional typesetting background, two special characters can be welcome substitutes for an insert space. **Right Indent Tab** can be used with left aligned or justified text. **Flush Space** is effective only with fully justified text where it fills out the last line of a paragraph. The following discussion demonstrates one use for the Right Indent Tab.

In Chapter 6 you were introduced to a handler **doFooter** which creates a folio frame at the bottom of the master pages. The idea behind this handler is to define the insertion point for the page number and use the insertion point to insert the **current page number** special character. Justification for the folio is one of the parameters passed to the handler.

For our next script, we will take the **doFooter** handler one step further by adding the name of the publication, the date of publication, as well as the page number to the folio frames. This will require a white space character (en space) as well as the current page number character. To force the last element of the folio string to the right, a right indent tab will be used.

To create a string that includes special characters for a script, one way is to start in InDesign and create the folio string there using fixed spaces for elements that will change. Then, paste the string into your script.

The sample pattern for the left folio (*leftFooterStr*) will be:

```
"Page [en space for Page Number][Right Indent Tab]"pubDate
```

For the right folio (*rightFooterStr*) the pattern will be:

```
pubName"[Right Indent Tab]Page [en space for Page Number]"
```

Copy the text from InDesign and paste it to define variables. In code this would now look like the following. Be sure to change quotes to straight quotes if needed.

```
set leftFooterStr to "Page   " & pubDate
set rightFooterStr to pubName & "  Page "
```

Add variables at the top of the script to define the publication name (*pubName*), *marginOffset*, *folioHgt*, and *masterName*. With a call to the handler **getDateString** for the publication date (*pubDate*), the top of the script should now read as follows:

```
set marginOffset to 10 --offset from bottom margin
set folioHgt to 24 --height of folio frame
set pubName to "MY PUBLICATION"
set pubDate to getDateString ()
set leftFooterStr to "Page   " & pubDate
set rightFooterStr to pubName & "  Page "
set masterName to "A-Master"
```

To define the document and its objects, add the following:.

```
tell application "Adobe InDesign CS5"
    set docRef to document 1
    set styleRef to paragraph style "Folio" of docRef
    set layerRef to layer "Furniture" of docRef
    set masterRef to master spread masterName of docRef
    set lAlign to left align
end tell
```

The call to the **doFooter** handler requires a number to define the insertion point for the page number. The insertion point for the current page number for the left folio will be 6 and for the right folio will be -1. Notice that the justification for both is left align (*lAlign*). With this the calls to the **doFooter** handler will be:

```
set lFootRef to doFooter(docRef, masterRef, 1, layerRef, marginOffset, ¬
folioHgt, leftFooterStr, styleRef, 6, lAlign)

set rFootRef to doFooter(docRef, masterRef, 2, layerRef, marginOffset, ¬
folioHgt, rightFooterStr, styleRef, -1, lAlign)
```

All that is left is to add the handlers: **doFooter** and **getDateString**. The latter handler is shown below. If the active document has facing pages, measurements set to points, a paragraph style named Folio and a layer named Furniture, the script can be run as is. For a complete script that takes care of measurements and verifies the layer and paragraph style, check out the **Folio** script in the Chapter Scripts folder for this chapter.

```
(*Returns current date in form Month Day, Year.*)
on getDateString()
    set d to (current date)
    set wDay to (weekday of d as string)
    set theMonth to (month of d as string)
    set theDay to day of d as string
    set theYear to (year of d as string)
    return wDay & ", " & theMonth & " " & theDay & ", " & theYear
end getDateString
```

ASCII Text

Unlike enumeration values for special characters, ASCII character values can be concatenated to a string as demonstrated in the following.

```
--assumes there is a text frame in an open document
set theText to "testing"
tell application "Adobe InDesign CS5"
    set frameRef to text frame 1 of document 1
    set text 1 of frameRef to ((ASCII character 9) & theText)
end tell
--ASCII character 9 is a tab character.
```

The problem is ASCII numbers often cannot be relied on. This depends on the font, and is especially true for "high ASCII" numbers above 126. Care must therefore be exercised when designating characters in this way.

For some fonts such as Zapf Dingbats you can use ASCII numbers to designate special characters. To get the ASCII number for a character, add it to an InDesign document manually, as needed. Select the character and run the following script:

Get ASCII Number

```
tell application "Adobe InDesign CS5"
    if (exists selection) and (class of item 1 of selection = character) ¬
    then
        set selChar to item 1 of selection
        set ASCIINum to (ASCII number selChar)
    end if
end tell
```

A fun demonstration script for working with a designated list of ASCII character numbers is **Random Snowflakes**. This script creates a document with a background of random snowflake characters from the Zapf Dingbats font. It relies on a list of random numbers to define the character and a list of random sizes to define the character's point size. This is accomplished using the **getRandom** handler (Calculate folder).

```
set num to 10 --number of random choices
set rndCharList to getRandom(num, 100, 107) --list of random character numbers
set rndSizeList to getRandom(num, 30, 80) --list of random sizes

(*Returns list of random numbers based on values passed.*)
on getRandom(numtimes, theMin, theMax)
    set rndList to {}
    repeat numtimes times
        copy (random number from theMin to theMax) to the end of rndList
    end repeat
    return rndList
end getRandom
```

Fortunately for the script the ASCII numbers of the desired characters were within a set range of numbers. To designate a random ASCII character from a list of disparate numbers instead, use statements like the following:

```
set rndCharList to (99, 100, 103, 105, 107)

set theNum to some item of rndCharList
```

You will find the script in the Chapter Scripts folder for this chapter.)

Unicode Values

You can identify special characters also by using their Unicode character number. Unicode numbers consist of four numerical values. You can get this value from the Glyphs panel. With the appropriate text font active, hover your cursor over the special character in the palette to see its Unicode values. Its enumeration value and OpenType feature (if applicable) are also displayed in the tool tip.

If you try the following, you will discover Unicode values display as literal text.

```
tell application "Adobe InDesign CS5"
    set storyRef to story -1 of document 1
    set contents of insertion point -1 of storyRef to ¬
    "Not equal to <2260>" & return
end tell
```

The solution requires AppleScript's **data** value type. The data value type is used for data that does not fit within other established classes (boolean, integer, string, etc.). The data value type can be used to define Unicode values that display correctly.

```
tell application "Adobe InDesign CS5"
    set storyRef to story -1 of document 1
    --entering special characters by their Unicode glyph ID value:
    set contents of insertion point -1 of storyRef to "Not equal to: "¬
    & «data utxt2260» & return
end tell
```

If you don't mind typing guillemets («»), you may find working with AppleScript's Data value type is the way to go for working with special characters. In addition to enabling entry of a vast range of characters, they can be concatenated to text. Using Unicode values for the footer strings in the **Folio** script, you can substitute the following.

```
set leftFooterStr to "Page" & «data utxt2002» & «data utxt0018» & ¬
«data utxt0008» & pubDate
set rightFooterStr to pubName & «data utxt0008» & "Page" & ¬
«data utxt2002» & «data utxt0018»
```

You will also need to remove the statement that sets the contents of the insertion point in the **doFooter** handler.

Character	Unicode	Character	Unicode
carriage return	«data utxt000D»	soft return	«data utxt000A»
commercial at	«data utxt0040»	flush space	«data utxt2001»
section character	«data utxt00A7»	en space	«data utxt2002»
registered trademark	«data utxt00AE»	em space	«data utxt2003»
copyright symbol	«data utxt00A9»	figure space	«data utxt2007»
trademark symbol	«data utxt2122»	punctuation space	«data utxt2008»
middle dot	«data utxt00B7»	thin space	«data utxt2009»
degree symbol	«data utxt00B0»	hair space	«data utxt200A»
bullet	«data utxt2022»	character space	«data utxt0020»
ellipse	«data utxt2026»	zero space	«data utxt200B»
auto page number	«data utxt0018»	hard space	«data utxt00A0»
section marker	«data utxt0019»	right indent tab	«data utxt0008»
ff ligature	«data utxtFB00»	non-breaking space	«data utxt00A0»
fi ligature	«data utxtFB01»	no break hyphen	«data utxt2011»
fl ligature	«data utxtFB02»	en dash	«data utxt2013»
ffi ligature	«data utxtFB03»	em dash	«data utxt2014»
ffl ligature	«data utxtFB04»		

Figure 14.1: Special character table created with script Special Characters in Chapter Scripts folder for chapter.

OpenType Ornaments

Have you often wondered how you could display an OpenType ornament using a script? Here's how. Use the Unicode value to define the character, and set the **OpenType features** property for the text using the value shown within parentheses in the Glyphs panel.

Ornamental Character

```
(*Requires active document with text frame.*)
set spChar to «data utxt2022»
tell application "Adobe InDesign CS5"
    set fontRef to font ("Minion Pro" & tab & "Regular")
    set textProps to {applied font:fontRef, point size:18, ¬
    justification:center align, OpenType features:{{"ornm", 3}}}
    set docRef to document 1
    set frameRef to text frame -1 of page 1 of docRef
    set myText to ""
    repeat 5 times
        set myText to myText & spChar
    end repeat
    set contents of insertion point 1 of frameRef to myText
    set textRef to object reference of text 1 of frameRef
    set properties of textRef to textProps
end tell
```

Figure 14.2: Ornament created with Ornamental Character script in Chapter Scripts folder for chapter.

Font Type

A font's **font type** property returns whether it is **OpenType, type 1, TrueType,** or any one of the other types of fonts that may be installed. In working with **OpenType** you may want to also check whether it supports any one of a number of **OpenType** features. The script **Fractions_OTF** styles instances of numbers having a virgule (fraction slash) to a real fraction using the **OpenType fractions feature**. It supports up to two numbers before and after the fraction slash (virgule). Only part of the script is shown below. For more about find and change (see Chapter 16).

```
--from the script Fractions_OTF
set theType to font type of fontRef
if theType is in {OpenType CFF, OpenType CID, OpenType TT} then
    set doFractions to check OpenType feature fontRef using ¬
    fractions feature
end if
if doFractions is true then
        --do a search and replace to style fractions
        set whole word of find change text options to true
        set include locked layers for find of find change text options to ¬
        true
        set case sensitive of find change text options to true
        try
            my findChangePrefs("^9^9/^9^9", "")
            tell storyRef to set changedText to change text
        end try
        try
```

```
        my findChangePrefs("^9/^9^9", "")
        tell storyRef to set changedText to change text
    end try

    try
        my findChangePrefs("^9/^9", "")
        tell storyRef to set changedText to change text
    end try
    end if
end tell
```

(*Add handlers: **getStoryOfSelection** (Selection folder), **testFont** (Environment folder), **findChangePrefs** (Find Change folder).*)

Metacharacters

Wild cards and metacharacters can be used in a find what statement. Only non-wild card metacharacters and literals can be used in a change to statement. The **Fractions_OTF** script uses metacharacters to search for number-slash combinations to change to a "real" fraction. A table of metacharacters and wild cards you can use follows.

Character	Metacharacter	Character	Metacharacter
auto page number	^#	em space	^m
section marker	^x	en space	^>
bullet	^8	flush space	^f
caret	^^	hair space	^|
copyright	^2	nonbreaking space	^s
carriage return	^p	thin space	^<
forced line break	^n	white space	^w
inline graphic maker	^g	discretionary hyphen	^-
paragraph symbol	^7	nonbreaking hyphen	^~
registered trademark	^r	left quotation mark	^{
section symbol	^6	right quotation mark	^}
tab character	^t	single left quote	^[
end nested style	^h	single right quote	^]
right indent tab	^y	any character	^?
indent to here	^i	any number	^9
em dash	^_	any letter	^$
en dash	^=		

Figure 14.3: Metacharacter table created with script Special Characters in Chapter Scripts folder..

Tabs

Working with tabs is fairly straightforward in InDesign. The **tab list** is a property of text defaults, paragraph, paragraph style, and other text objects. The result of getting the tab list for a text reference is a list of records. The items of this list define for each tab the position, alignment, alignment character, and leader (if used). To see the tab list in effect for text defaults, you can use the following:

```
tell application "Adobe InDesign CS5"
    tell document 1
        set tabList to tab list of text defaults
    end tell
end tell
tabList
```

An example of setting tab positions using the tab list is seen in the following example that requires a selected text frame:

```
set theText to "just " & tab & "for testing" & tab & " last text"
tell application "Adobe InDesign CS5"
    set selList to selection
    if length of selList > 0 and ¬
    class of item 1 of selection = text frame then
        set frameRef to item 1 of selection
        set contents of frameRef to theText
        set textRef to object reference of paragraph 1 of frameRef
        set tabRecord to {{position:"1.5 in", alignment:left align, ¬
        leader:"."}, {position:"4 in", alignment:left align}}
        set tab list of textRef to tabRecord
    end if
end tell
```

Make Scripts Work for You

This chapter introduced a number of concepts involving text references. including styling text using paragraph styles within a repeat loop structure. In this exercise you compare the two scripts **Style Paragraphs_Loop** and **Style Paragraphs_Dlg**. The scripts open the door to two topics that will be covered in the next few chapters: nested paragraph styles (Chapter 15) and custom dialogs (Chapter 17). The paragraph styles Price and cPrice in the sample document use a nested paragraph style to style the dollar sign ($) to superscript. Both scripts are found in the **Style Paragraphs** project. Open the test document, "MakeDescPrice.indd", included with the project and follow the directions included at the top of the document.

The paragraph styles used for **Style Paragraphs_Loop** are defined by the *styleList* variable in the script. The user selects the text or the text frame for the text to be styled.

The **Style Paragraphs_Dlg** script presents the user with a dialog in which to select a paragraph style for each paragraph in a set. A maximum of four paragraphs per set is allowed. The user selects the paragraphs for one of the sets before running the script. The user is presented a dialog from which to select a paragraph style for each paragraph. When the user clicks OK, the paragraphs in the selected flow are styled using the styles designated. Try the script once using the styles Make, Description, and Price; and then with cMake, cDescription, and cPrice.

Both scripts expect the text groups to have a uniform number of paragraphs.

15

Text Style Revisited

This chapter takes you outside of the ordinary when it comes to styling text. We will look at paragraph rules, underscore, strike through, list styles (bullets and numbering), drop caps, and, best of all, nested styles. Although for demonstration some of the sample code assigns values to text properties directly, establishing paragraph styles is generally recommended.

Paragraph Rules

If you need a rule under or over a paragraph, paragraph rules are the way to go. Some unique text styling such as reverse text and text over a background can also be achieved using paragraph rules. Paragraph rules can be part of the properties assigned to a paragraph style, supporting most of the properties available for graphic lines.

To enable paragraph rules, the **rule above** and/or **rule below** properties for a paragraph or paragraph style need to be set to true. From there, let your creativity be your guide. Below is a script snippet that will allow you to experiment. Create some text in a document and select before running the script. Change values for some of the properties to experiment.

Rule Below

```
--requires paragraph selection
tell application "Adobe InDesign CS5"
    set selList to selection
    if length of selList > 0 and class of item 1 of selection = ¬
    paragraph then
        set textRef to object reference of item 1 of selection
        tell textRef
            set rule below to true
            set rule below line weight to 10
            set rule below offset to "4 pt"
            set rule below color to "Black"
            set rule below left indent to "-12 pt"
            set rule below right indent to "-12 pt"
            set rule below tint to 100
            set rule below type to "Dashed"
            set rule below overprint to true
            set rule below gap color to "Black"
            set rule below gap tint to 50
            set rule below gap overprint to false
            set rule below width to text width
        end tell
    end if
end tell
```

Width vs Weight

Confusing to some are the properties **weight** and **width** when working with rule above and rule below. Weight determines the heaviness of the rule. Width has to do with the length of the rule. For a paragraph rule, width can be defined as being the same as the text (`text width`) or the width of the text container (`column width`). This can be further modified by setting **left indent** and **right indent** values.

Paragraph Rule Offsets

Values for paragraph rule offsets can lead to some confusion. Remember, for rule above **offset** is measured from the bottom of the rule to the baseline of the first line of the paragraph. A positive value moves the rule up. For rule below, offset is measured from the top of the rule to the paragraph's text baseline. A positive value moves the rule down.

Reverse Text

If you are not using rule above (or rule below) to produce reverse text, now is a good time to get started. The concept is simple: You can use either rule below or rule above, setting the rule weight the same (or larger) than the text point size. For rule above, use a negative value for the offset value. A good rule of thumb is to use an offset value one-sixth the text point size. Set the fill color of the text to Paper (or any color other than that used for the rule) and you have reversed type (or colored type on a colored background).

```
Reverse Text
(*Requires paragraph selection.*)
tell application "Adobe InDesign CS5"
    try
        set fontRef to my testFont("Verdana", "Bold")
        set textRef to my textByClass(paragraph)
        tell textRef
            set applied font to fontRef
            set point size to 24
            set justification to center align
            set fill color to "Paper"
            set rule above to true
            set rule above overprint to false
            set rule above width to text width
            set rule above line weight to 25
            set rule above offset to "-4 pt"
            set rule above left indent to "-1p0"
            set rule above right indent to "-1p0"
            set rule above color to "Black"
            set rule above tint to -1
        end tell
    on error errStr
        display alert errStr
    end try
end tell
(*Returns object reference to text if it meets criteria for class.*)
on textByClass(textClass)
    tell application "Adobe InDesign CS5"
        set selList to selection
```

```
            if length of selList > 0 and class of item 1 of selection = ¬
            textClass then
                set textRef to object reference of item 1 of selection
            else
                error ("Requires " & textClass as string) & " selection"
            end if
            return textRef
        end tell
    end textByClass
    (*Add handler testFont (Environment folder) here to complete script*)
```

Underline, Strike Through

The properties for **underline** and **strike through** are similar in that they can be assigned values for offset, weight, type, color, tint, overprint, gap color, gap tint, and gap overprint. The property identifiers are the same for underline and strike through with the exception they are prefaced with the word *underline* or *strike through* as in **underline color** and **strike through color**. Both rules center on the baseline of the text when the values for their respective offsets are set to zero:

```
        set underline offset of textRef to 0
        set strike through offset of textRef to 0
```

The difference between underline and strike through is that a negative value for **underline offset** raises the rule above the text baseline. A negative value for **strike through offset** lowers the rule below the text baseline. With underline, the rule is behind the text; with strike through the rule is in front.

Both underline and strike through can be toggled on and off by setting the **strike thru** and **underline** properties for a text reference or paragraph style to true or false. Try changing the offset values in the following and observe the difference when the script is run.

Underline and Strike Through
```
--Requires active document
tell application "Adobe InDesign CS5"
    set ulineProps to {point size:16, underline:true, underline weight:1,¬
    underline offset:-6, underline type:"Sold", underline color:¬
    "C=100 M=0 Y=0 K=0"}
    set sthruProps to {point size:16, strike thru:true, strike through ¬
    weight:1, strike through offset:-6, strike through type:"Solid", ¬
    strike through color:"C=0 M=100 Y=0 K=0"}
    tell page 1 of document 1
        set frameRef to make text frame with properties ¬
        {geometric bounds:{"3p0", "3p0", "12p0", "36p0"}, ¬
        contents:"Testing for underline and for strikethrough"}
        set textRef to object reference of paragraph 1 of frameRef
        set properties of (text from word 1 to word 3 of textRef) to ¬
            ulineProps
        set properties of text from word 4 to word -1 of textRef to ¬
            sthruProps
    end tell
end tell
```

Drop Caps

A drop cap is established for a paragraph or paragraph style using the properties **drop cap characters**, **drop cap lines**, **drop cap style**, and **drop cap detail**. With the exception of **drop cap detail** which takes a number value, these properties are self-explanatory. The user interface shows two values for **drop cap detail** labeled Align Left Edge and Scale for Descenders.

Working with drop caps is another place that experimenting with values is the best way to become familiar with the settings. Select a paragraph and change the values in the following to test.

Drop Cap_Charstyle

```
--assumes paragraph selected in document; swatch "C=100 M=0 Y=0 K=0"
tell application "Adobe InDesign CS5"
    set selList to selection
    if length of selList > 0 and class of item 1 of selection = ¬
    paragraph then
        set textRef to object reference of item 1 of selList
        tell document 1
            if not exists character style "Color" then
                set charstyleRef to make character style with properties ¬
                {name:"Color", fill color:"C=100 M=0 Y=0 K=0", fill tint:100}
            else
                set charstyleRef to character style "Color"
            end if
        end tell
        set properties of textRef to {drop cap characters:1, ¬
        drop cap lines:2, drop cap style:charstyleRef, dropcap detail:1}
    end if
end tell
```

Using a character style for the drop cap is optional, but its use opens the door to an almost limitless number of possibilities.

Case and Capitalization

The **capitalization** property for text was once the **case** property. According to InDesign's dictionary, capitalization can be set to small caps, normal, all caps, and cap to small cap. Problem is, you may have difficulty finding a font that supports cap to small cap. So, unless you know the font is accommodating, stick to all caps or small caps. A script for testing, **Capitalization**, is found in the Chapter Scripts folder for this chapter. A cut down version of the script follows. It assumes the font designated is installed.

```
set headstyleName to "AllCap24"
set fontName to "Myriad Pro"
set fontStyle to "Bold"
set headLine to "My headline here for testing" & return
tell application "Adobe InDesign CS5"
    set docRef to make document
    set fontRef to font (fontName & tab & fontStyle)
    set parastyleProps to {name:headstyleName, applied font:fontRef,¬
    point size:24, leading:24, first line indent:0, justification:center¬
    align,capitalization: all caps, span column type:span columns, ¬
    span split column count:all, space after:"24 pt"}
```

```
        set parastyleRef to my getParastyle(docRef, headstyleName, ¬
        parastyleProps)
        tell page 1 of docRef
            set frameRef to make text frame with properties {geometric ¬
            bounds:{"72 pt", "24 pt", "500 pt", "516 pt"}, contents:headLine}
            set contents of frameRef to placeholder text
            set applied paragraph style of paragraph 1 of frameRef to ¬
            parastyleRef
        end tell
    end tell
    (*Add handler getParastyle (Styles folder) to complete script. A more robust
    version is found in the Chapter Scripts folder for this chapter.*)
```

Notice that capitalization is a property of a text object or text style. **Changecase**, on the other hand, is a command. The specifier for the command can be any text object. It has one parameter; **using**, which can be one of the following: uppercase, lowercase, titlecase, and sentencecase. For the headline in the document created in the script above to display as cap to normal, remove the capitalization property from the *parasyleProps* record. Then add the following just before the next to last end tell statement:

```
    tell paragraph 1 of frameRef to changecase using titlecase
```

Just in case you have ever looked up to see the last two paragraphs of text have been typed with the caps lock key on, don't retype. Keep the next little script handy.

Sentence Case

```
(*Changes case of selected text to sentencecase.*)
tell application "Adobe InDesign CS5"
    set selList to selection
    if length of selList > 0 and class of item 1 of selList = text then
        tell item 1 of selList
            changecase using sentencecase
        end tell
    end if
end tell
```

Bullets and Numbers

The bullets and numbering capability in InDesign does not need much explanation. For setting up a paragraph style that supports these capabilities, you might want to start in the user interface. Once you have the style the way you want it, add it to a document to be used as a style sheet for importing as needed to a project. There may be occasion you would want to see how the style is created programmatically. To get the values you would set for the style, identify the name of the paragraph style for the variable *styleName* at the top of the following script and run.

Get Bullet Properties

```
--assumes measurements are set to points
set styleName to "Bullet List"
tell application "Adobe InDesign CS5"
    set bText to missing value
    tell document 1
        set styleRef to paragraph style styleName
    end tell
    tell styleRef
```

```
set bulletChar to bullet char
set charProps to {bullets font:bullets font of bulletChar, ¬
bullets font style:bullets font style of bulletChar, ¬
charactertype:character type of bulletChar, character ¬
value:character value of bulletChar}
set bType to bullets and numbering list type
set lIndent to left indent
set flIndent to first line indent
try
    set tabPosition to position of item 1 of tab list
    if alignment of item 1 of tab list = left align then
        set tabAlign to left align
    else if alignment of item 1 of tab list = right align then
        set tabAlign to right align
    else
        set tabAlign to center align
    end if
    set alignChar to alignment character of item 1 of tab list
    set tabProps to {{position:tabPosition, alignment character:¬
    alignChar, alignment:tabAlign}}
on error
    set tabProps to {}
end try
try
    set bText to bullets and numbering result text
end try
set bCharstyle to name of bullets character style
set bTextAfter to bullets text after
end tell
set bulletRecord to {name:styleName, bullets and numbering list type:¬
bType, bullets text after:bTextAfter, bullets alignment:bullets ¬
alignment of styleRef, left indent:"" & lIndent & " pt", first line ¬
indent:"" & flIndent & " pt", tab list:tabProps}
if bText is not missing value then
    set bulletRecord to bulletRecord and ¬
    {bullets and numbering result text:bText}
end if
set bulletRecord to bulletRecord & {bullet char:charProps}
end tell
bulletRecord
```

Use the record returned from the script for the property record for your bullet style. You can add other properties to the record such as **applied font**, **fill color**, and **point size**, as needed.

Nested Styles

The ability to nest character styles within a paragraph style is one of the big features of later versions of InDesign and a boon to automation. Where the character style is applied within the paragraph is determined by a character delimiter. The delimiter need not be an actual character, but can be an enumeration value such as any character or any word. To get a listing of all of the delimiters allowed, look up the nested style class in InDesign's dictionary. The delimiter entry is fairly complete.

Unless you are setting up a number of nested styles, there is little advantage to creating the style programmatically. Either way, create the styles once, save them in a style sheet and import the styles as needed to your project.

Your approach to creating a nested style within a script may be as individual as the way you approach creating a script. My preference includes four steps.

1. Create a paragraph style to act as the parent style.
2. Create character styles for each element that overrides the parent style (*nested styles*).
3. Set up a list of lists to define the rules to govern each character style (*nestedStylesList*). Each list includes a reference to the character style, the delimiter to use, a boolean indicating inclusive (*doInclude*), and a value for repeat.
4. Create the nested paragraph style based on the parent paragraph style using the handler **createNestedStyle**. Parameters for the handler include a reference to the document, the name for the style, a reference to the based on style, and the list of nested style parameters.

The project **Program** included with this chapter demonstrates creating a nested paragraph style to set the styling for a typical program. Open the document, "Program.indd." Select the text (Command+A) and run the **Style Program** script. Code from the script that creates a nested paragraph style follows:

```
(*Requires active document with paragraph style "Text_10" and character style
"Italic."*)
set doInclude to true
set nestedName to "Program"
tell application "Adobe InDesign CS5"
set docRef to document 1
    set baseStyleRef to paragraph style "Text_10" of docRef
    set nestedRegularRef to character style "Italic" of docRef
end tell
--nested style list{character style ref, delimiter, inclusive, repeats
set nestedStyleLists to {{nestedRegularRef, "    ", doInclude, 1}}
set nestedstyleRef to createNestedStyle(docRef, nestedName, baseStyleRef,
nestedStyleLists)

(*Creates nested style based on parent style.*)
on createNestedStyle(docRef, nestedName, basedOnStyle, nestedStyleLists)
    tell application "Adobe InDesign CS5"
        tell docRef
            if exists paragraph style nestedName then
                set nestedstyleRef to paragraph style nestedName
            else
                set nestedstyleRef to make paragraph style with properties ¬
                {name:nestedName, based on:basedOnStyle}
                tell nestedstyleRef
                    repeat with i from 1 to length of nestedStyleLists
                        copy item i of nestedStyleLists to ¬
                        {charstyleRef, delimChar, doInclude, numRepeat}
                        make nested style with properties {applied character ¬
                        style:charstyleRef, delimiter:delimChar, ¬
                        inclusive:doInclude, repetition:numRepeat}
                    end repeat
                end tell
            end if
        end tell
    end tell
```

```
        end tell
        return nestedstyleRef
    end createNestedStyle
```

The project is a good example of how nested paragraph styles can automate something that would otherwise involve a fair amount of hand work.

Song "Story of the Glory" .... *SFMS Chorus*

Figure 15.1: Line from program showing nested style.

Nested Line Styles

Nested line styles were introduced in InDesign CS4. If you think nested styles are great, start experimenting with nested line styles and prepare to get blown away. Nested line styles work the same as other nested styles with the exception that character styles designated can apply to an entire line (or lines) or to specific delineated text within a line.

As with nested styles, you can set up two or more nested line styles to work together, and you can create a repeating sequence.

Because a paragraph style can have both nested styles and nested line styles, setting up a paragraph style having both is much easier in the user interface than trying to create the style with a script. Put your styles in a template or a style sheet for import. Another idea is to put your nested styles in a library (see Chapter 19). Either way, just remember that all lines within each text group to be styled must end with a soft return, as a paragraph return ends the style.

See the project **Car Ad** for a script that utilizes a nested line style. After running the script, open the Drop Caps and Nested Styles panel for paragraph style *NestedCar* to see how the style was created.

Nested styles can be used for a wide variety of tasks in your automation projects. The biggest problem you may encounter is to ensure text is supplied as required by the style (forced line returns instead of paragraph returns, and so forth). The next time you are tempted to style mixed text manually, create a nested paragraph or nested line style. Save your style in a style sheet or in a library, and apply using a script.

GREP Styles

Another nested style introduced with CS4 is GREP styles. The GREP style provides the ability to apply a text style using regular expressions. For instance, should you wish to apply a particular attribute to text within a paragraph based on a GREP pattern, you can now do it with a GREP paragraph style. This is powerful.

You can establish a GREP paragraph style manually in the user interface or with a script. Doing so programmatically is similar to setting up any other nested style. If you look up the properties for **nested grep style**, you will see that it has very few properties. The project **Style Markup** for this chapter sets up a paragraph style that applies a character style to every character string included in angle brackets (as with HTML markup). The style is based on the designated paragraph style (*parastyleName*) and is named the same with a "*g_*" added. You can use any naming convention that works for you. The majority of the script is shown here as it introduces some new handlers.

Style Markup

```
set grepPattern to "<.+?>"
set parastyleName to "Text_12"
set charStyleName to "Color"
try
    set textRef to textSelection()
    set docRef to getDocRef()
    set parastyleRef to getTextStyle(docRef, "paragraph", parastyleName)
    set charstyleRef to getTextStyle(docRef, "character", charStyleName)
on error errStr
    display alert errStr
    return
end try
set gParastyleRef to createGrepStyle_basedOn(docRef, parastyleRef, ¬
charstyleRef, grepPattern)
tell application "Adobe InDesign CS5"
    tell textRef
        set applied paragraph style to gParastyleRef
    end tell
end tell

(*Creates a grep paragraph style based on style referenced.*)
on createGrepStyle_basedOn(objRef, parastyleRef, charstyleRef, grepPattern)
    tell application "Adobe InDesign CS5"
        tell objRef
            set styleName to name of parastyleRef
            if styleName = "[Basic Paragraph]" then
                set gstyleName to "g_Basic"
            else
                set gstyleName to "g_" & styleName
            end if
            if not (exists paragraph style gstyleName) then
                set gParastyleRef to make paragraph style with properties ¬
                {name:gstyleName, based on:parastyleRef}
                tell gParastyleRef
                    make nested grep style with properties {applied character ¬
                    style:charstyleRef, grep expression:grepPattern}
                end tell
            else
                set gParastyleRef to paragraph style gstyleName
            end if
        end tell
    end tell
    return gParastyleRef
end createGrepStyle_basedOn

(*Returns reference to paragraph or character style as named.*)
on getTextStyle(docRef, styleType, styleName)
    tell application "Adobe InDesign CS5"
        tell docRef
            try
                if styleType = "paragraph" then
                    set styleRef to paragraph style styleName
                else
                    set styleRef to character style styleName
                end if
            on error
```

```
                 error "Cannot find " & styleType & " style " & styleName & "."
          end try
       end tell
     end tell
     return styleRef
  end getTextStyle
  (*Add handlers getDocRef (Documents folder) and textSelection (Selection
  folder) to complete script.*)
```

Make Scripts Work for You

Another common application of a GREP style is to assign Open Type features to a paragraph style which will apply only to text matching a GREP expression. For instance, you may want to apply ordinals to all occurrences of *th*, *st*, *nd*, and *rd* that follow a number. For practice working with GREP styles, you will modify the **Style Markup** script to create a GREP style for styling ordinals. Refer to the **Formal Invitation** project in the folder for this chapter.

1. Open the document "Formal Invite.indd." Double-click on the Body style in the Paragraph Styles panel. Take note of the settings used for this style, particularly in the OpenType Features tab.

2. Open the **Style Markup** script. Save it as **Grep Style_Ordinals**.

3. Change the values for the variables at the top of the script as follows:

```
set grepPattern to "(?<=\\d)(th|st|nd|rd)\\>"
set parastyleName to "Body"
set charStyleName to "Ordinals"
```

4. Add code to make sure the character style Ordinals exists in the document. For this you will add the handler **getCharstyle** (in Styles folder of Handler Library).

5. To call the handler, we will need to make a few changes inside the first try statement block. Change the code to read:

```
set textRef to textSelection()
set docRef to getDocRef()
tell application "Adobe InDesign CS5"
   set charstyleProps to {name:charstyleName, OTF ordinal:true}
end tell
set parastyleRef to getTextStyle(docRef, "paragraph", paraStyleName)
set charstyleRef to getCharstyle(docRef, charstyleName, ¬
charStyleProps)
```

6. Compile your script and correct any problems.

7. Select the text in the invitation and run your script. Notice that all occurrences of *th*, and *nd* are styled as ordinals.

8. Add a description to the top of your script, rename it, and save.

9. In InDesign's Paragraph Styles panel, double-click on the paragraph style created (g_Body). Open the GREP Style tab to see how the style is represented.

10. Add some text to the document and experiment with some GREP settings of your own.

Perhaps you have a document that uses a variety of paragraph styles and you want all occurrences of ordinals set ordinal style irrespective of its applied paragraph style. Instead of setting a GREP style for each of your paragraph styles, you will want to use **find and change**. This is the subject of the next chapter.

16

Find and Change

Although find and change can be used with most objects in InDesign, it is most often used with text. Working with find and change in InDesign is one place where scripting has a definite advantage over the user interface. With a script, the scope of a find and/or change operation can be established for just about any text object. The process can be as broad as working with the entire text of a document, or as limited as working with characters in a word.

Text searches can be conducted using a text reference, a glyph reference, or GREP (Regular Expressions). To set the properties for each of these, the find and change preferences of the application are first cleared using the nothing enumeration. Since clearing the find and change preferences needs to be done before and after each find or find/change operation, you may be wise to set this up as a handler.

```
(*initializes text preferences to nothing for find/change.*)
on initTextPrefs()
    tell application "Adobe InDesign CS5"
        set find text preferences to nothing
        set change text preferences to nothing
    end tell
end initTextPrefs
```

You can use the same structure for initializing glyph preferences and GREP preferences.

```
(*Initializes glyph preferences to nothing for find/change.*)
on initGlyphPrefs()
    tell application "Adobe InDesign CS5"
        set find glyph preferences to nothing
        set change glyph preferences to nothing
    end tell
end initGlyphPrefs

(*Initializes grep preferences to nothing for find/change.*)
on initGrepPrefs()
    tell application "Adobe InDesign CS5"
        set find grep preferences to nothing
        set change grep preferences to nothing
    end tell
end initGrepPrefs
```

When a preference is set with a script, the preference setting is added to the current settings. This explains why it is necessary to clear the find and change preferences before setting. You don't want settings from a previous find or change operation to affect the current process.

Options can also be set to narrow the parameters for a find/change operation. The following sections take a brief look at using all three types of find and change operations: text, glyph, and GREP.

iteral Text

e following sample code returns a list of all text meeting the given criteria. It introduces the handler **findText**. For testing, the document "GoodDocument.indd" is provided with the files for this chapter.

Find Text

```
set textStr to "good"
set caseSensitive to false
set wholeWord to true
try
    set textRef to textSelection()
on error errStr
    display alert errStr
    return
end try
tell application "Adobe InDesign CS5"
    set findChangeOptionProps to {case sensitive:caseSensitive, ¬
    whole word:wholeword, include footnotes:false, include hidden ¬
    layers:false, include locked layers for find:false, ¬
    include locked stories for find:false,include master pages:false}
end tell
set foundSet to findText(textRef, textStr, findChangeOptionProps)
foundSet
on findText(objRef, textStr, findChangeOptionProps)
    --clear find text preferences
    initTextPrefs()
    tell application "Adobe InDesign CS5"
        set properties of find change text options to findChangeOptionProps
        set find what of find text preferences to textStr
        tell objRef
            set foundSet to find text
        end tell
    end tell
    initTextPrefs()
    return foundSet
end findText

(*Returns reference to text selected; otherwise throws error.*)
on textSelection()
    tell application "Adobe InDesign CS5"
        set selList to selection
        if length of selList > 0 then
            set objRef to item 1 of selList
            if class of objRef is in {insertion point, text, story, ¬
            paragraph, word, text column, text style range, line} then
                return objRef
            end if
        end if
        error "Requires text selection"
    end tell
end textSelection
(*Add handler initTextPrefs (Find Change folder) to complete script.*)
```

Find and Change Text

To find and change literal text, the **Find Change Text** script is the same as **Find Text** with the exception the script uses a handler called **findChangeText**. Make the following changes to the **Find Text** script. The complete script is included with the chapter scripts folder for this chapter.

Find Change Text

```
--change variables as needed
set findText to "good"
set changeText to "bad"
set caseSensitive to true
set wholeWord to true
set textRef to textSelection()
set findChangeOptionProps to getOptionProps (wholeWord, caseSensitive)
set foundSet to findChangeText (textRef, findText, changeText, ¬
findChangeOptionProps)

on findChangeText(objRef, findText, changeText, findChangeOptionProps)
    --clear find text preferences
    initTextPrefs()
    tell application "Adobe InDesign CS5"
        set properties of find change text options to findChangeOptionProps
        set find what of find text preferences to findText
        set change to of change text preferences to changeText
        --boolean value, if true, returns references in reverse order
        tell objRef
            set textChanged to change text          — runs Find/Change operation
        end tell                                        and creates reference to
    end tell
    initTextPrefs()
    return textChanged      — returns reference to main script
end findChangeText
(*Add handlers textSelection (Selection), initTextPrefs (Find Change) and
getOptionProps (Find Change) to complete script.*)
```

Find/Change Text by Attribute

Finding and changing text that meets a given criteria for style or other attributes can use syntax similar to the scripts above. In this case, **find text preferences** and **change text preferences** can define any number of text properties. Take a brief look at the properties provided for a text object in InDesign's dictionary. In the example below, the **fill color** of the subject text is the only attribute changed. The handler **findChangeByAttribute** for this script can be used for finding text by attribute as well as changing. It can apply the find/change to specific text or any text having a set of attributes. If the variable *findAttrib* is an empty record, the find criteria is limited to literal text. This also applies to the variable *changeAttrib*. You may want to experiment with the values for these variables. See the script **Find Change by Attribute** in the Chapter Scripts folder for this chapter for the complete code. The sample document "GoodDocument.indd" contains a number of text scenarios for testing.

```
set wholeWord to true
set caseSensitive to false
```

```
set findText to "good"
set changeText to "bad"
set findAttrib to {«class flcl»:"C=100 M=0 Y=0 K=0"} --fill color
set changeAttrib to {} --can be empty list
set textRef to textSelection()
findChangeOptions(wholeWord, caseSensitive)

--call the findChangeByAttribute handler
set {foundList, changedList} to findChangeByAttribute(textRef, findText, ¬
changeText, findAttrib, changeAttrib, findChangeOptionProps)

(*All purpose find/change text handler; returns list of text found and text
changed.*)
on findChangeByAttribute(objRef, findText, changeText, findAttrib, ¬
changeAttrib)
    set foundSet to {}
    set changedText to {}
    initTextPrefs()
    tell application "Adobe InDesign CS5"
        if findAttrib is not {} then
            set properties of find text preferences to findAttrib
        end if
        if findText is not missing value then
            set find what of find text preferences to findText
        end if
        tell objRef
            set foundSet to find text
        end tell
        if changeText is not missing value or changeAttrib is not {} then
            if changeAttrib is not {} then
                set properties of change text preferences to changeAttrib
            end if
            if changeText is not missing value then
                set change to of change text preferences to changeText
            end if
            tell objRef
                set changedText to change text
            end tell
        end if
    end tell
    initTextPrefs()
    return {foundSet, changedText}
end findChangeByAttribute
(*Add handlers: textSelection (Selection folder), findChangeOptions (Find
Change folder), initTextPrefs (Find Change folder.*)
```

To find a reference to all text that is styled with a specific character style, you could change the variables in the **Find Change by Attribute** script to the following:

```
set findText to missing value
set changeText to missing value
tell application "Adobe InDesign CS5"
    set findStyle to character style "Color" of document 1
    set changeStyle to character style "RedColor" of document 1
    set findAttrib to {applied character style: findStyle}
    set changeAttrib to {applied character style: changeStyle}
end tell
```

You might want to use a script dedicated to the task of just returning text references that have a specified character style applied.

Find by Charstyle

```
--assumes character style "Color" exists in active document
try
    set objRef to textSelection()
    tell application "Adobe InDesign CS5"
        set docRef to document 1
        set charStyle to character style "Color" of docRef
    end tell
on error errStr
    activate
    display alert errStr
    return
end try
--parameters are for whole word and case sensitive
findChangeOptions(true, false)
--change objRef to docRef to get all references in document
set foundList to textByCharStyle(objRef, charStyle)

--returns text references meeting attribute criteria
on textByCharStyle(objRef, charStyle)
    set foundSet to {}
    tell application "Adobe InDesign CS5"
        set applied character style of find text preferences to charStyle
        tell objRef
            set foundSet to find text
        end tell
    end tell
    return foundSet
end textByCharStyle
(*Add handlers: textSelection (Selection folder), findChangeOptions (Find
Change folder), and initTextPrefs (Find Change folder) to complete script.*)
```

Metacharacters and Wild Cards

Your script can use the same metacharacters and wild cards provided in the user interface. Wild cards can only be used for find, but metacharacters can be used for both find and change. A script can also use enumeration values for special characters for both find and change. (See Chapter 14 for more about special characters.)

An example of parameter values that could be used for both the **Find Change Text** and **Find Change by Attribute** scripts follows. You will also want to make sure the value for **whole word** option is false.

```
--change paragraph returns to forced line returns
set findText to "^p"
set changeText to "^n"
```

Wildcards and metacharacters can also be used when working with attributes. For many scripts, you may prefer to use a paragraph or character style instead of setting property values directly. The following metacharacter string could be used to apply a designated character style to any number sequence following a dollar sign having two digits before and after a dot. For this you would want the value for the **whole word** option to be true.

```
set findText to "$^9^9.^9^9"
```

The **Metacharacters** script in the project of the same name uses a handler similar to **findChangeByAttrib**. It does not allow for the literal text to be changed, just its attributes. This is ideal for working with metacharacters as they cannot be used for a change string. Using metacharacters may be just the ticket for you, especially if GREP (regular expressions) is still a foreign language for you. (See the discussion of GREP styles later in this chapter.)

Find/Change Glyphs

Finding and changing glyphs is similar to text but the properties available are limited. Properties for **find change glyph preferences** are the **applied font**, the **font style**, and the **glyph ID**. To ensure that you have the right glyph ID values, use InDesign's Glyph panel. (Figure 16.1).

Make sure the font you want to use is active, and open the Glyph panel (Type > Glyphs). The name of the font and its style are displayed and can be changed at the bottom of the panel. Hovering the cursor over the glyph desired will display its information in the tool tip. The GID (first line of the tool tip) is the number to use for the glyph ID.

If you want to change attributes for glyphs, get a list of references using find and then parse the list to change attributes. The following example gets a list of the copyright symbols (glyphID 87) for font Adobe Caslon Pro. It then changes each glyph to a colored character style Find the project **Find Glyphs** in the folder for this chapter.

Glyph_Apply Style

```
set glyphID to 87 --copyright symbol
try
    set docRef to getDocRef()
    set fontName to "Adobe Caslon Pro"
    set fontStyle to "Regular"
    set fontRef to testFont(fontName, fontStyle)
    set textRef to textSelection()
on error errStr
    display alert errStr
end try
tell application "Adobe InDesign CS5"
    set findChangeOptionProps to {include footnotes:false, include ¬
    hidden layers:false, include locked layers for find:false, ¬
    include locked stories for find:false, include master pages:false}
    set styleProps to {name:"Color", fill color:"C=100 M=0 Y=0 K=0"}
    set charstyleRef to my getCharstyle(docRef, "Color", styleProps)
    my initGlyphPrefs()
    set properties of find change glyph options to findChangeOptionProps
    set applied font of find glyph preferences to fontName
    set font style of find glyph preferences to fontStyle
    set glyph ID of find glyph preferences to glyphID
    tell textRef
        set foundSet to find glyph
    end tell
    my initGlyphPrefs()
    --to change attributes glyphs in foundSet, use a repeat loop
```

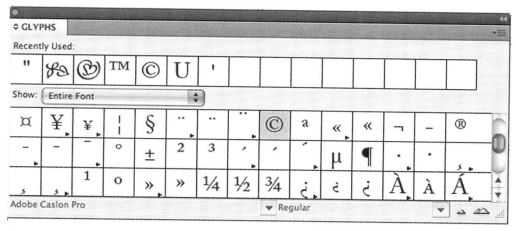

Figure 16.1: Hold he cursor over a glyph in the Glyph panel to see information about the glyph in the tool tip.

```
      repeat with i from 1 to length of foundSet
          set applied character style of item i of foundSet to charstyleRef
      end repeat
end tell
```
(*Add handlers to complete script: **getDocRef** (Documents), **initGlyphPrefs** (Find Change), **testFont** (Environment), **textSelection** (Selection), and **getCharStyle** (Styles).*)

Find/Change GREP

GREP (Global Regular Expression Print) brings the real power to find and change in that text patterns can be used instead of actual text or metacharacters. The problem is that you need to understand GREP. Once you have the GREP expression defined for the find and/or change, the syntax for finding and changing is pretty much the same as with text. The following styles occurrences of email addresses in selected text to character style "Color." A document "TestGrep.indd" is provided for testing.

Find Change Grep_Attrib

```
(*Expects active document. Character style "Color" is created in script.*)
set findStr to "(?i)[A-Z0-9]*?@[A-Z0-9]*?[.]..."
try
    set docRef to getDocRef()
    set textRef to textSelection()
on error errStr
    display alert errStr
    return
end try
initGrepPrefs()
tell application "Adobe InDesign CS5"
    set findChangeOptionProps to {case sensitive:false, whole word:true, ¬
    include footnotes:false, include hidden layers:false, include locked ¬
    layers for find:false, include locked stories for find:false, ¬
    include ¬master pages:false}
    set charstyleProps to {name:"Color", fill color:"C=100 M=0 Y=0 K=0"}
```

```
        set charstyleRef to my getCharstyle(docRef, "Color", charstyleProps)
        set changeAttrib to {applied character style: charstyleRef}
        set find what of find grep preferences to findStr
        set properties of change grep preferences to changeAttrib
        tell textRef
            change grep
        end tell
    end tell
end tell
initGrepPrefs()
```
(*Add handlers to complete script:**initGrepPrefs** (Find Change folder),
getDocRef (Documents folder), **textSelection** (Selection folder), **testFont**
(Environment folder) and **getCharstyle** (Styles folder).*)

GREP OTF Fractions

If you are working with an OpenType type font that supports the **Fraction feature,** you
can change improper fractions to a fraction simply by using the following settings for the
Find Change Grep_Attrib script above. Make sure you comment out the line that defines
changeAttrib to the applied character style. This works for the fraction combinations
supported by the particular font.

```
set findStr to "([0-9]+)/([0-9]+)"
```
(*Inside the tell statement to application replace the set changeAttrib
statement with:*)
```
set changeAttrib to {OTF fraction:true}
```

Fractionator

For working with non OpenType fonts, the **Fractionator** script can be used. It is part of the
Fractions project found in the folder for this chapter. It uses GREP expressions to find and
change number-slash-number GREP expressions to a "real" fraction. The **createFractions**
handler for the script is shown below.

```
(*Uses three find/change operations to create fractions from numbers before
and after a forward slash.*)

on createFractions(docRef, textRef)
    initGrepPrefs()
    setGrepOptions()
    tell application "Adobe InDesign CS5"
        set upperstyleRef to my getCharstyle(docRef, "Super", ¬
        {position:superscript})
        set lowerstyleRef to my getCharstyle(docRef, "Sub", ¬
        {position:subscript, baseline shift:4})
        set normalstyleRef to my getCharstyle(docRef, "Normal", ¬
        {position:normal})
        --set style for numerator
        set find what of find grep preferences to "([0-9]+)/"
        set properties of change grep preferences to {change to:"$1/", ¬
        applied character style:upperstyleRef}
        tell textRef to change grep
        my initGrepPrefs()
        --set style for denominator
        set find what of find grep preferences to "/([0-9]+)"
```

```
            set properties of change grep preferences to {change to:"/$1", ¬
            applied character style:lowerstyleRef}
            tell textRef to change grep
            my initGrepPrefs()
            --change forward slash to virgule and style to "Normal"
            my initTextPrefs()
            my setTextOptions()
            set find what of find text preferences to "/"
            --virgule and character style
            set properties of change text preferences to {change to:"/",¬
            applied character style:normalstyleRef}
            tell textRef to change text
            my initTextPrefs()
        end tell
    end createFractions
```

Run the **Fractionator** script with the sample document in the **Fractions** project. While on the subject of fractions, you might also want to look at the **Recipe** script in the **Recipe** project. This script uses the **OTF Fractions feature** to style text matching a GREP pattern. Additionally it shows how a range of text can be converted to a table to supply a background color for the text. Select all of the text in the document "RecipeForOTF.indd" and run the script. This is a good example of how a script can be used to style stories that have a consistent styling pattern.

Make Scripts Work for You

If you have a production problem that can be solved by using any one of the handlers in this chapter, see if you can now build on the code supplied to make a script of your own. For instance you might want to build a script that finds all occurrences of text styled with a designated character style and writes the contents to a text file. The following builds on an existing script to perform this functionality.

1. For this, start with the **Find By Charstyle** script (Chapter Scripts folder). Save it under a new name (this will be your new script). Make sure the object reference in the call to **textByCharStyle** is *docRef*. Also the parameters for **findChangeOptions** is (false, false). Test the script as is with a document having text styled with character style "Color."

2. Place the following declarations at the top of the script:

```
--for WriteToFile
set doAppend to true --appends text to bottom of existing file
set publicFolder to path to public folder from user domain as string
set filePath to (publicFolder & "Text Files:TestFind.txt")
```

3. Add the **parseToString** handler (List folder) to the bottom of the script:

```
(*Creates a delimited string from a list of text references.*)
on parseToString(theList, theDelimiter)
    set textStr to contents of item 1 of theList
    repeat with i from 2 to length of theList
        set theContent to contents of item i of theList
        if theContent is not in {"", " "} then
            set textStr to textStr & theDelimiter & theContent
        end if
    end repeat
    return textStr
end parseToString
```

4. Add the **writeToFile** handler (File Folder folder) to the bottom of your script.

```
(*Parameters: path to file, string to write, boolean, appendStr, indicates if
text will be appended to file. Returns length of file.*)
on writeToFile(filePath, textStr, appendStr)
    try
        set fileRef to open for access file filePath with write permission
        set fileSize to (get eof fileRef)
        if appendStr = true and fileSize > 0 then
            set eof fileRef to (fileSize + 1)
            set textStr to (return & textStr)
        else
            set eof fileRef to 0
        end if
        write textStr to fileRef starting at eof
        set fileLength to (get eof fileRef)
        close access fileRef
    on error
        close access fileRef
    end try
    return fileLength
end writeToFile
```

5. Add a call to **parseToString** and **writeToFile** at the end of the top portion of your script. Modify the sample calls provided with the handlers to read as follows:

```
set theDelimiter to return
set bytesWritten to 0
if length of foundList > 0 then
    set textStr to parseToString(foundList, theDelimiter)
    set bytesWritten to writeToFile(filePath, textStr, doAppend)
end if
```

6. Follow this with a display alert to report the success (or failure) of your script:

```
activate
display alert ("Bytes Written: " & bytesWritten)
```

7. Test your script with the document as before.

If you have problems, check out the script **Write Found Text** in the Chapter Scripts folder for this chapter.

Challenge:

Change the script so that it looks for email addresses using a GREP pattern instead of the character style.

17

InDesign Dialogs

Up to this point, the scripts presented have purposely avoided the need for user interface other than the dialogs provided by AppleScript. The scripts now shift into second gear with user interface created using InDesign's dialog object. By way of introduction your attention is initially turned to a subject that can be somewhat confusing: **scope**.

Scope

Scope is the range over which AppleScript recognizes declared variables. Until now, our script examples have declared variables at the top level of the script and passed their values to handlers as part of the call to the handler. Values created within handlers were passed back to the calling statement by virtue of the **return** keyword. If values are not passed as needed, the script will error. This is because the variable is implicitly treated as being **local**.

```
--THIS WILL PRODUCE AN ERROR (The value of x is not defined.)
set x to 20
set returnVal to incrementX()
display alert "X is now " & returnVal
on incrementX()
    set x to x + 1
    return x
end incrementX
```

In order for the handler to use the variable, you must either pass the value to the handler as we have done in the past, or you can establish the variable as being global.

Global Scope

When a variable is defined as being **global**, it is visible from the point where it is declared in the script and in *every* handler *subsequently* defined. A global variable can be declared and initialized (given its initial value) anywhere within a script.

```
global myValue
set myValue to "Hello"
myHandler()
on myHandler()
    display alert "MyValue is " & myValue
end myHandler
```

This can be very convenient in that all of your script's handlers have access to values of variables defined as global. Having global variables in code can be very powerful—and potentially dangerous in their ability to be used, changed, and possibly abused anywhere within the script. This can have a side effect that can keep you up at night trying to trace where the value was changed unexpectedly, as the value of x does in the following snippet.

```
--THIS WILL PRODUCE AN UNEXPECTED RESULT
set x to 20
incrementX()
on incrementX()
    global x
    set x to 1
    set x to x + 1
end incrementX
```

If your script does use global variables, make sure you do not assume your other variables are local by default. Declare the variables as local. Be advised you can declare the scope of more than one local or global variable in a single statement.

```
local x, y, z
set x to 20
incrementX()
squareX(x)

on incrementX()
    global x
    set x to 1
    display alert "x plus 1 is " & x + 1
    set x to x + 1
end incrementX

on squareX(x)
    set x to x ^ 2
    display alert "x squared is " & x
end squareX
```

Run the code above and take note of the value of x when squared. Comment out the first line of the code and run the script again. What happened to the value of x?

Remember

A global can be declared and/or initiated anywhere within a script. But a global variable must have a value (be initiated) before it can be used.

Script Property

A script property is a variable with global scope that is given its initial value when declared. It looks similar to a **property** in a property record in that it has a name value followed by a colon and then the value:

```
property propertyName:initialValue
```

A property can only be initialized at the top of a script. Not only is a property global within the script, its value can be persistent. Save the following code as a script (.scpt) or application (.app).

```
property countValue: 1
set countValue to countValue + 1
activate
display dialog "The count value is now " & countValue
```

Run the script again, and again. You can see that the value of a script property is persistent between runs. This can be used to an advantage when you want a script to remember the last value for a variable. More often, a property is used to hold a value that will remain constant within the script. You will see several examples of this in the scripts that follow.

Script Property Persistence

The value of a script property persists until the script is re-compiled at which time the value established in the script is re-initialized.

Creating a Custom Dialog

Creating a custom dialog is not the simplest task. In fact, depending on its complexity, creating a custom dialog can end up being more work than writing the rest of the script. Never fear. There is help at hand. In the Script Templates folder for this chapter are a number of scripts you will want to use to take much of the work out of putting a script with a custom dialog together. Before you start your dialog-dependent script, you may find a script in this folder with a dialog similar to the one you want to create. You can modify the script template, or cut and paste portions of it into your script.

Custom dialogs can vary widely in their scope. The one thing that InDesign dialogs have in common is that they are **modal**. As with display dialog and display alert, modal dialogs require the dialog to be dismissed before other operations can take place. Modal dialogs are designed specifically to get input from the user. For this there are a variety of user interface objects, called widgets, that can be added to the dialog.

Modal Dialog

A dialog that must be dismissed before any other action can take place in the application.

The Dialog Object

The object at the top of the InDesign dialog model is **dialog**. It has a limited number of properties that can be set: **name**, **canCancel**, and **label**. Your script makes a dialog using the **make** command, as with any other object. When your script creates a dialog, it is not displayed (shown) until the **show** command for the dialog is invoked. If the user cancels out of the dialog, the result of the **show** command is false. Otherwise, the values found in the dialog's interface objects can be used by the script. To clear memory of the information used to create the dialog and its widgets, the **destroy** command for the dialog must be used.

There are a number of ways that the syntax for a dialog can be written. The code structure used in the following examples creates variables to reference parent objects (containers). The variable is then used to create child objects. Variables are also assigned to objects that will hold user input.

Parent Objects

The hierarchy of a dialog can be a little confusing. The only child object that a dialog can have is a column (**dialog column**). Also, a row (**dialog row**) can only be a child of a column. Other objects can be children of either a dialog column or a dialog row. Container objects such as **border panel** and **enabling group**s, require their parent to be a dialog column.

The following example creates a simple dialog with all widgets contained by a single row.

Dialog With Row

```
try
    (*Supply name, can cancel, and label for dialog.*)
    set userResponse to dialogWRow("Dialog Name", true, "Label Here")
    userResponse
on error errStr
    activate
    display alert "ERROR " & errStr
end try

on dialogWRow(dlgName, cancelIt, dlgLabel)
    set wasCancelled to false
    tell application "Adobe InDesign CS5"
        --make sure user interaction level will allow a dialog
        set origLevel to user interaction level of script preferences
        set user interaction level of script preferences to interact with all
        set dlgRef to make dialog with properties {name:dlgName, ¬
        canCancel:cancelIt, label:dlgLabel}
        tell dlgRef
            tell (make dialog column)
                set rowRef to make dialog row
                --add widgets to row
                tell rowRef
                    make static text with properties {static label:¬
                    "Your name here:"}
                    set nameField to make text editbox with properties ¬
                    {min width:144}
                end tell
            end tell
        end tell
        --show the dialog and capture the result
        set userResponse to show dlgRef
        if userResponse = true then
            set nameFieldVal to edit contents of nameField
        else --user cancelled
            set wasCancelled to true
        end if
        destroy dlgRef
        set user interaction level of script preferences to origLevel
        --if cancelled, throw error; otherwise return values
        if wasCancelled then error "User cancelled"
        return nameFieldVal
    end tell --application
end dialogWRow
```

More rows could be added to the script to add more widgets to the dialog window. However, you may wish to align the widgets vertically. For this you will need to set up dialog columns.

Substitute the following handler for the **dialogWRow** handler in the previous script. (Make sure to also change the call to the handler.)

Dialog With Columns

```
on dialogWColumns(dlgName, cancelIt, dlgLabel)
    set wasCancelled to false
    tell application "Adobe InDesign CS5"
    --make sure user interaction level will allow a dialog
        set origLevel to user interaction level of script preferences
        set user interaction level of script preferences to interact with all
        set dlgRef to make dialog with properties {name:dlgName, ¬
        canCancel:cancelIt, label:dlgLabel}
        tell dlgRef
            tell (make dialog column)
                set rowRef to make dialog row
                --add widgets to row
                tell rowRef
                    set col1 to make dialog column
                    tell col1
                        make static text with properties {static label:¬
                        "Your name here:"}
                        make static text with properties {static label:"Age:"}
                    end tell
                    set col2 to make dialog column
                    tell col2
                        set nameField to make text editbox with properties ¬
                        {min width:144}
                        set ageField to make integer editbox with properties ¬
                        {min width:72}
                    end tell --col 2
                end tell --rowRef
            end tell --column
        end tell --dialog
        set userResponse to show dlgRef
        if userResponse = true then
            set nameFieldVal to edit contents of nameField
            set ageFieldVal to edit value of ageField
        else --user cancelled
            set wasCancelled to true
        end if
        destroy dlgRef
        set user interaction level of script preferences to origLevel
        --if cancelled, throw error; otherwise return values
        if wasCancelled then error "User cancelled"
        return {nameFieldVal, ageFieldVal}
    end tell --application
end dialogWColumns
```

Border Panels

The border panel object is used to organize groupings of interface objects within a dialog. This is a specialized container that acts like a row in that it can contain widgets, enabling groups (see below), and dialog columns. A row within a border panel needs to be contained by a column. Substitute the following handler in the **Dialog With Row** script using dialogWPanels in the handler call. The script is in the Chapter Scripts folder for this chapter.

Dialog With Panels

```
on dialogWPanels(dlgName, cancelIt, dlgLabel)
    set wasCancelled to false
    tell application "Adobe InDesign CS5"
        --make sure user interaction level will allow a dialog
        set origLevel to user interaction level of script preferences
        set user interaction level of script preferences to interact with all
        set dlgRef to make dialog with properties {name:dlgName, ¬
        canCancel:cancelIt, label:dlgLabel}
        tell dlgRef
            tell (make dialog column)
                set mRow to make dialog row
                tell mRow
                    set panel1 to make border panel
                    set panel2 to make border panel
                end tell
                tell panel1
                    set pcol1 to make dialog column
                    set pcol2 to make dialog column
                end tell
                tell pcol1
                    make static text with properties {static label:¬
                    "Your name here:"}
                    make static text with properties {static label:"Age:"}
                end tell --pcol1
                tell pcol2
                    set nameField to make text editbox with properties ¬
                    {min width:144}
                    set ageField to make integer editbox with properties ¬
                    {min width:72}
                end tell --pcol2
                tell panel2
                    set ppcol1 to make dialog column
                    set ppcol2 to make dialog column
                end tell
                tell ppcol1
                    make static text with properties {static label:"Division:"}
                    make static text with properties {static label:"Extension:"}
                end tell --ppcol1
                tell ppcol2
                    set divfield to make text editbox with properties ¬
                    {min width:72}
                    set extfield to make integer editbox with properties ¬
                    {min width:48}
                end tell --ppcol2
            end tell --column
        end tell --dialog
        set userResponse to show dlgRef
        if userResponse = true then
            set nameFieldVal to edit contents of nameField
            set ageFieldVal to edit value of ageField
            set divVal to edit contents of divfield
            set extVal to edit value of extfield
        else --user cancelled
            set wasCancelled to true
        end if
        destroy dlgRef
```

```
            set user interaction level of script preferences to origLevel
            --if cancelled, throw error; otherwise return values
            if wasCancelled then error "User cancelled"
            return {nameFieldVal, ageFieldVal, divVal, extVal}
        end tell --application
end dialogWPanels
```

Enabling Groups

Enabling groups are similar to border panels with the exception that they include a checkbox and can have a label (**static label**). Objects within the enabling group are enabled when the **checked state** property of the checkbox is true. Compare the code for the following with that for **Dialog With Panels**. This handler introduces a dropdown object which allows a user to select an item from a list. Notice that the list (*divisionList*) is defined as a script property, as its value will not change within the script.

Dialog With Enable Group

```
property divisionList : {"Sales", "Support", "QandA", "Production"}
try
    (*Supply name, can cancel, and label for dialog.*)
    set userResponse to dialogWEnableGroup("Dialog Name", true, "Departments")
    userResponse --places result of dialog in result variable
on error errStr
    activate
    display alert "ERROR " & errStr
end try

on dialogWEnableGroup(dlgName, cancelIt, dlgLabel)
    set wasCancelled to false
    tell application "Adobe InDesign CS5"
        --make sure user interaction level will allow a dialog
        set origLevel to user interaction level of script preferences
        set user interaction level of script preferences to interact with all
        set dlgRef to make dialog with properties {name:dlgName, ¬
        canCancel:cancelIt, label:dlgLabel}
        tell dlgRef
            tell (make dialog column)
                set panel1 to make border panel
                tell (make dialog row)--acts as spacer
                    make static text with properties {static label:""}
                end tell
                set egroup to make enabling group with properties ¬
                {static label:"Division Member", checkedState:false}
                --panel group
                tell panel1
                    set pcol1 to make dialog column
                    set pcol2 to make dialog column
                end tell
                tell pcol1
                    make static text with properties {static label:¬
                    "Your name here:"}
                    make static text with properties {static label:"Age:"}
                end tell --pcol1
                tell pcol2
                    set nameField to make text editbox with properties ¬
                    {min width:144}
```

```
                    set ageField to make integer editbox with properties ¬
                    {min width:72}
                end tell --pcol2
                --enabling group
                tell egroup
                    set ecol1 to make dialog column
                    set ecol2 to make dialog column
                end tell
                tell ecol1
                    make static text with properties {static label:"Division:"}
                    make static text with properties {static label:"Extension:"}
                end tell --ecol1
                tell ecol2
                    set divfield to make dropdown with properties {min width:¬
                    120, string list:divisionList, selectedIndex:1}
                    set extfield to make integer editbox with properties ¬
                    {min width:48}
                end tell --ecol2
            end tell --column
        end tell --dialog
        set userResponse to show dlgRef
        if userResponse = true then
            set divVal to missing value
            set extVal to missing value
            set nameFieldVal to edit contents of nameField
            set ageFieldVal to edit value of ageField
            if checked state of egroup = true then
                set divVal to item ((selected index of divfield) + 1) of ¬
                divisionList
                set extVal to edit value of extfield
            end if
        else --user cancelled
            set wasCancelled to true
        end if
        destroy dlgRef
        set user interaction level of script preferences to origLevel
        --if cancelled, throw error; otherwise return values
        if wasCancelled then error "User cancelled"
        return {nameFieldVal, ageFieldVal, divVal, extVal}
    end tell --application
end dialogWEnableGroup
```

Editboxes

The previous scripts introduced you to two editboxes available for the dialog: **text editboxes** and **integer editboxes**. There are a number of other editboxes available which determine the type of information they can receive and display.

real editboxes - Can accept a number with a decimal value.

percent editboxes - Shows entry as a percent when user exits the field.

angle editboxes - Shows entry as an angle when user exists the field.

measurement editbox - Allows measurements unit to be designated.

For all classifications of editboxes with exception of the **text editbox**, and **measurement editbox** the properties that can be set are the same:

edit value - Use to supply a default value (use **edit contents** for text editbox).

maximum value and **minimum value** - Use to determine range for valid numbers.

min width - The maximum width for the widget.

small nudge - The amount to increment/decrement the value when the user presses an arrow key.

large nudge - The amount to increment/decrement the value when the user holds the shift key down while pressing an arrow key.

The text editbox has only two properties that can be set: **edit contents** and **min width**.

If your script gets the **edit contents** of an editbox, the value received is a string value. If, on the other hand, the script asks for the **edit value**, a number value is returned. Of special interest in this regard is the measurement editbox.

Measurement Editbox

The **measurement editbox** has an additional property which requires some explanation: **edit units**. Setting this property to anything other than `points` may cause some confusion. This is because whatever value is entered is converted internally into points. The following example code demonstrates. Notice that the edit units value for the measurement editbox is set to inches. The default edit value is set to 72 (1 inch in points). When the script is run, the display shows "1 in" in the editbox. But the script returns 72. In code, if you mistakenly set the edit value to 1 with a minimum value of 72, the dialog will produce an exception. If you set the minimum value to 1 (thinking inches), it will actually be 1 point (.0139 inches).

Dialog With Measure

```
set userResponse to dialogWMeasure ("Measurements", true, "Label here")

on dialogWMeasure(dlgName, cancelIt, dlgLabel)
    set wasCancelled to false
    tell application "Adobe InDesign CS5"
        --make sure user interaction level will allow a dialog
        set origLevel to user interaction level of script preferences
        set user interaction level of script preferences to interact with all
        set dlgRef to make dialog with properties {name:dlgName, ¬
        canCancel:cancelIt, label:dlgLabel}
        tell dlgRef
            tell (make dialog column)
                tell (make dialog row)
                    make static text with properties {static label:¬
                    "Width (inches):"}
                    set widField to make measurement editbox with properties ¬
                    {min width:108, maximum value:(22 * 72), large nudge:12, ¬
                    small nudge:1, edit units:inches}
                end tell --row
            end tell --column
        end tell --dialog
        set userResponse to show dlgRef
        if userResponse = true then
            set widVal to edit value of widField
        else --user cancelled
            set wasCancelled to true
```

```
            end if
            destroy dlgRef
            set user interaction level of script preferences to origLevel
            --if cancelled, throw error; otherwise return values
            if wasCancelled then error "User cancelled"
            return widVal
        end tell --application
    end dialogWMeasure
```

Widgets that Provide Choices

For providing choices, you have been introduced to the **dropdown** which allows the user to select from a list of string values (see **Dialog With Enable** script). Comboboxes, checkboxes (**checkbox controls**), and radio buttons (**radiobutton controls**) can also be used to provide the user optional choices.

Combobox

Similar to the dropdown are the various comboboxes: **angle combobox, integer combobox, measurement combobox, percent combobox**, and **real combobox**. Comboboxes provide a text entry field in addition to the dropdown. A combobox has an **edit value** and an **edit contents** property, but does not have a **selected index** property as the dropdown does. Use either the **edit contents** or **edit value**, but not both. With a combobox, the user is not restricted to choices in the list, but can enter any value in the text entry field provided it meets the optional minimum and or maximum value criteria set for the edit value.

Checkbox

Checkboxes (**checkbox controls**) give the user the opportunity to make selections by checking any one or a combination of boxes. Properties to set for the checkbox control are **min width, static label**, and **checked state** (true or false).

Radiobutton

Similar to a checkbox is a radio button. Radio buttons (**radiobutton controls**) are contained by a **radiobutton group**. Only one button within a radio button group can be checked at any one time. The initial checked state needs to be set to true for only one item in the group, with all others assumed to be false.

The following sample script demonstrates adding a measurement combobox, a checkbox control, and radiobutton group to a dialog.

Dialog With Choices

```
property sizeList : {"2 in", "4 in", "6 in", "8 in", "10 in"}
try
    (*Supply name, can cancel, and label for dialog.*)
    set userResponse to dialogWChoices("Document Settings", true, ¬
    "Unit Measurements")
    userResponse
end try

on dialogWChoices(dlgName, cancelIt, dlgLabel)
    set wasCancelled to false
    tell application "Adobe InDesign CS5"
```

```
                --make sure user interaction level will allow a dialog
                set origLevel to user interaction level of script preferences
                set user interaction level of script preferences to interact with all
                set dlgRef to make dialog with properties {name:dlgName, ¬
                canCancel:cancelIt, label:dlgLabel}
                tell dlgRef
                    tell (make dialog column)
                        tell (make dialog row)
                            make static text with properties {static label:¬
                            "Choose width:"}
                            set widField to make measurement combobox with properties ¬
                            {min width:72, edit units:inches, edit value:144, ¬
                            string list:sizeList, minimum value:72, maximum ¬
                            value:720, large nudge:4, small nudge:4}
                        end tell
                        set checkField to make checkbox control with properties ¬
                        {static label:"Show Guides", checked state:false}
                        set radioGroup to make radiobutton group
                        tell radioGroup
                            make radiobutton control with properties {static label:¬
                            "Geometric Bounds", checked state:true}
                            make radiobutton control with properties {static label:¬
                            "Visible Bounds"}
                        end tell
                    end tell --column
                end tell --dialog
                set userResponse to show dlgRef
                if userResponse = true then
                    set widValue to edit value of widField
                    set checkValue to checked state of checkField
                    set radioValue to selected button of radioGroup
                else --user cancelled
                    set wasCancelled to true
                end if
                destroy dlgRef
                set user interaction level of script preferences to origLevel
                --if cancelled, throw error; otherwise return values
                if wasCancelled then error "User cancelled"
                return {widValue, checkValue, radioValue}
            end tell --application
    end dialogWChoices
```

Notice that the value returned for the checkbox (*checkValue*) is either true or false. The value for *radioValue* (value for selected button of the radiobutton group) is an integer indicating the index (0-based) of the button selected.

Timeout

By default AppleScript waits two minutes (120 seconds) for the user to respond to a modal dialog. If the dialog is not closed in this time, a timeout error will be raised. Give your user more time to respond to your dialog by surrounding the call to a custom dialog handler with a **timeout** statement block:

```
with timeout of 300 seconds --5 minutes
--call to custom dialog handler here
end timeout
```

Non-Modal Dialogs

You can use Apple Xcode to develop non-modal dialogs as well as complete AppleScript applications (see Apple Developer website: http://developer.apple.com). Other than that, you can use ExtendScript to create a non-modal dialog for InDesign that you can call using do script. An example is the script **Floating Window** found in the Chapter Scripts folder for this chapter. It calls two handlers: the first to show the floating window; the second to hide the window. It also demonstrates creating a document without a window and then creating the document's window once processing is complete.

Make Scripts Work for You

Some of the script templates provided in the Script Templates folder for this chapter are fully functioning scripts which include a dialog. They can be used as is, modified, or used as a template for building scripts requiring a similar user interface. One such template is **Border It**.

The template **Border It** provides a fairly comprehensive handler for creating a dialog: **getBorderProps**. The dialog involves values having to do with object style and stroke. The script depends on the active document having an object style for each border type stored in the object style group "Borders." If this style group is not found, it is loaded from a stylesheet. In addition to the usual handlers **getLiveBounds**, **setMeasures**, and **resetMeasures**, other handlers include:

calculateBounds - Calculates bounds from selected item or page bounds given an inset value which can be a positive or negative value.

createBorder - Pulls data from list passed, *dialogResult*, to establish properties for the border and layer references. Creates a rectangle with stroke as defined.

getStyleNames, **getStrokeNames**, **getColorNames**, and **getLayerNames** - Each handler returns an array of string values for the appropriate style names to be used in dropdowns.

testStyles - Tests for style group named. If group is not found, it is loaded from the stylesheet referenced. Parameters provide options for loading swatches, object styles, text styles, and table styles.

With a document open, run the template to test its functionality. Try adding widgets to the script to add more functionality for your script.

Challenge:

See if you can create a custom dialog of your choice using the **Border It** template as a starting point.

You may also want to look at the script **StepAndRepeat Rect_Dlg** in the Chapter Scripts folder for this chapter. See how the **Step and Repeat** script template was used to provide the custom dialog for this script.

18

Graphic Concepts

As the title suggests, this chapter will focus on working with objects that act as graphics. More than just working with the graphic objects, you will be introduced to a number of concepts that can be beneficial in many automation situations. Some of the handlers introduced, although associated with graphics, can also be applied to other page items. Along the way you will look at paths, translation, transparency, and special effects such as drop shadows and feathering. So, buckle up! You may find yourself wanting to spend a little time with some of these concepts.

Content Type

When it comes to page items, most of our effort to this point has been involved with text frames and rectangles, principally in their role as containers for text and images. Rectangles containing an image or other page item have a **content type** of **graphic type**. The content type of text frames is **text type**. Any shape, however, can have a content type of text type, graphic type, or unassigned depending on its contents.

Many users don't make a distinction between a rectangle created with the Rectangle Frame Tool (tool icon has intersecting lines) and one created with the Rectangle Tool. The same goes for ellipses and polygons. But there is a difference. Page items created manually with one of the "Frame" tools expect to be filled with a graphic and, by default, have a content type value of graphic type. and are assigned the object style "[None]" by default. Otherwise, the **content type** is unassigned and the **applied object style** is "[Basic Graphics Frame]." When created with a script, the **content type** of page items, other than text frames, is unassigned and the **applied object style** is "[Basic Graphics Frame]" unless designated otherwise in the script.

Once you place an insertion point inside of a page item created manually with either tool, its content type changes to text type but the **applied object style** does not change. Placing text manually inside a page item created with a script changes its **content type** but not its **applied object style**.

Because graphic type page items are designed to be used for frame-first layouts (where frames are created and placed ahead of their content), you may want to set the **content type** for these items to graphic type. The following assigns the **content type** of the rectangle created to graphic type.

Content Type

```
--assumes document 1 exists
set gBounds to {"3p", "3p", "12p", "24p"}
tell application "Adobe InDesign CS5"
    set pageRef to page 1 of document 1
```

```
            set pageItemProps to {content type:graphic type}
            set itemRef to my createPageItem (pageRef, rectangle, gBounds, ¬
            pageItemProps)
        end tell
        (*Creates page item of type identified by itemClass.*)
        on createPageItem(objRef, itemClass, gBounds, itemProps)
            tell application "Adobe InDesign CS5"
                tell objRef
                    set itemRef to make itemClass with properties ¬
                    {geometric bounds:gBounds} & itemProps
                end tell
            end tell
            return itemRef
        end createPageItem
```

Assigning text type as the **content type** of a page item does not allow a script to set its **contents** to text as part of a property record. However, you can set the contents as part of a separate statement.

```
        --assumes document 1 exists
        set gBounds to {"3p", "3p", "12p", "24p"}
        tell application "Adobe InDesign CS5"
            set pageRef to page 1 of document 1
            set pgItemProps to {content type:text type, fill color: "None"}
            set itemRef to my createPageItem(pageRef, rectangle, gBounds, ¬
            pgItemProps)
            set contents of insertion point 1 of itemRef to "Hello"
        end tell
        (*Add createPageItem handler here.*)
```

To discover the content type for a selected item, you first need to verify that the object is a page item, not a group, text item, or a path.

```
        tell application "Adobe InDesign CS5"
            set pageItemList to {rectangle, text frame, oval, polygon, graphic line}
            set selList to selection
            if length of selList > 0 and class of item 1 of selList is in ¬
                pageItemList then
                set objType to content type of item 1 of selList
            end if
        end tell
```

Once a graphic or image is placed in a page item, its **content type** changes to graphic type.

When you get the **all graphics** property for an object, a list of references to all images, EPSs, PDFs, and so on, is returned. To get all objects having a **content type** of graphic type, you can use an every object specifier:

```
        tell application "Adobe InDesign CS5"
            tell document 1
                set graphicItems to every page item where content type = graphic type
            end tell
        end tell
```

All vs. Every

When your script uses an "all" property (all page items or all graphics), the result includes nested items (items contained by other items). The every object specifier does not include nested items.

Working from Center

Often in working with graphics, the ability to describe an object's bounds calculated from a center coordinate is required. The following creates an oval using this concept.

Oval From Center

```
(*Assumes document open with measurements set to points.*)
set xRad to 72
set yRad to 60
set cx to 300
set cy to 200
set objstyleName to "[Basic Graphics Frame]" --change as needed
set docRef to document 1 of application "Adobe InDesign CS5"
set ovalRef to ovalFromCenter(docRef, cx, cy, xRad, yRad, objstyleName)

(*Creates oval from cx,cy center coordinates.*)
on ovalFromCenter(docRef, cx, cy, xRad, yRad, objstyleName)
    set x0 to cx - xRad
    set y0 to cy - yRad
    set x1 to cx + xRad
    set y1 to cy + yRad
    tell application "Adobe InDesign CS5"
        set objstyleRef to object style objstyleName of docRef
        tell page 1 of docRef
            set ovalRef to make oval with properties {geometric bounds:¬
            {y0, x0, y1, x1}, applied object style:objstyleRef}
        end tell
    end tell
    return ovalRef
end ovalFromCenter
```

Polygons

A **polygon** is any shape that is not a rectangle, oval, or graphic line. A polygon can have any number of sides. When working with polygons you need to set **polygon preferences** which is a property of the application. This preference has two properties that can be set: **inset percentage**, and **number of sides**.

number of sides - The number of sides in range from 3 to 100.

inset percentage - The star inset percentage in range from 0 to 100.

The following script creates a sampling of polygons shown below. (Figure 18.1) A more complete version of this script is found in the Chapter Scripts folder for this chapter.

Figure 18.1: Polygons created using Polygons_5to9Sides script.

Polygons_5to9 Sides

```
(*Demonstrates creating multiple polygons from center.*)
property numSides : 5 --number sides for polygons
property inPcent : 50 --star inset percent
(*assumes measurement units for existing document are set to points.*)
set cx to 100 --center horizontal coordinate
set cy to 100 --center vertical coordinate
set xRad to 50 --horizontal radius
set yRad to 50 --vertical radius
set dx to 100 --move distance horizontal
set dy to 100 --move distance vertical
setPolyPrefs(numSides, inPcent)
set x0 to cx - xRad
set x1 to cx + xRad
set y0 to cy - yRad
set y1 to cy + yRad
tell application "Adobe InDesign CS5"
    set itemProps to {fill color:"Black", fill tint:50, stroke color:¬
    "Black", stroke tint:100, stroke weight:2, content type:graphic type}
    set pageRef to page 1 of document 1
    repeat with i from 1 to 5
        my createPageItem(pageRef, polygon, {y0, x0, y1, x1}, itemProps)
        set x0 to x0 + dx
        set x1 to x1 + dx
        set numSides to numSides + 1
        my setPolyPrefs(numSides, inPcent)
    end repeat
end tell

(*Sets polygon preferences.*)
on setPolyPrefs(sideCount, inPcent)
    tell application "Adobe InDesign CS5"
        tell polygon preferences
            set number of sides to sideCount
            set inset percentage to inPcent
        end tell
    end tell
end setPolyPrefs
(*Add handler createPageItem to complete script.*)
```

Convert Shape

An object can be converted to a polygon using its **convert shape** command. As an example, the following creates a rectangle and then converts it into a triangle.

Convert Shape

```
--assumes active document
tell application "Adobe InDesign CS5"
set pageRef to page 1 of document 1
tell pageRef
    set rectRef to make rectangle with properties {geometric bounds:¬
    {"3p", "3p", "15p", "15p"}, stroke weight:2, stroke color:"Black",¬
    fill color: "None"}
    set dupRef to duplicate rectRef
    move dupRef to {"18p", "3p"}
```

```
            tell dupRef to convert shape given convert to triangle¬
                inset percentage 0 corner radius 0
        end tell
    end tell
```

Convert shape gives us another option for creating a rectangle with rounded corners. Start with a rectangle and then convert it. For a rectangle there are only three corner options supported: rounded rectangle, beveled rectangle, and inverse rounded rectangle.

Rounded Rectangle

```
--assumes active document
tell application "Adobe InDesign CS5"
    set pageRef to page 1 of document 1
    tell pageRef
        set rectRef to make rectangle with properties {geometric bounds:¬
        {"3p", "3p", "15p", "15p"}, stroke weight:2, stroke color:"Black"}
        tell rectRef to convert shape given convert to rounded rectangle ¬
        corner radius "24 pt"
    end tell
end tell
```

Also supported as part of the **convert to** parameter are oval, triangle, polygon, line, straight line, open path, and closed path, as in given convert to oval.

Note

Even though the page item has been converted, its class remains as original and its geometric bounds have not changed.

Paths

Most page items, including graphic lines, are made up of paths. Paths can be simple to very complex. When created, a page item such as a rectangle will only have one path. A path can be either closed or open. The value for this is returned using the **path type** property. The **path points** property of a path is a list of lists that describe the path. Points in a path can be one of four point types: corner, line type, smooth, or symmetrical. You can target individual points within a path using their index reference within the path points list. A list of all of the path points for a path is returned using the **entire path** property.

When you want to construct a polygon or work with all of the points in a path, using the **entire path** property is the most direct (simplest) method. For a shape that consists entirely of points that are either corner or line type, the **entire path** property for a path returns a list in which each element is a list representing the {x, y} coordinates for the path point. As an example, the following script returns a path list for a selected triangle. Create a 3-sided object with the pen tool. With the item selected, run the following:

Entire Path

```
(*Assumes polygon is selected; measurements are set to points.*)
tell application "Adobe InDesign CS5"
    set selList to selection
    if length of selList > 0 and class of item 1 of selList = polygon then
        set objPath to paths of item 1 of selList
        set pathPoints to entire path of item 1 of objPath
```

```
        end if
    end tell
    pathPoints
```

To create a polygon, the **entire path** property can do the trick. The following uses a list returned from the **Entire Path** script to recreate the triangle. Your list values will be different.

Recreate Triangle

```
(*Assumes active document with measurements set to points.*)
set thePath to {{134, 79}, {46, 233}, {221, 233}}--put your list values here
tell application "Adobe InDesign CS5"
    tell page 1 of document 1
        set polyRef to make polygon with properties {geometric bounds:¬
        {79, 46, 233.5, 221}, stroke weight:2, fill color:"None", ¬
        stroke color:"Black"}
        tell path 1 of polyRef
            set entire path to thePath
            set path type to closed path
        end tell
    end tell
end tell
```

The number of items for each item of an entire path list is not limited to two; and this is where an element of complexity steps in. When the **point type** of a path point is either smooth or symmetrical, it takes a list of three two-item lists to describe the point (a Bezier curve).

item 1 - Contains the x,y coordinates of the anchor point.

item 2 (left-direction point) - Contains a set of x,y coordinates that control the curve of the line segment before the point.

item 3 (right-direction point.) - Contains a set of x,y coordinates that control the curve of the line segment after the anchor point.

The following script creates the shape illustrated in Figure 18.2. Note that points 1 and 3 are corner points while point 2 is smooth.

Curve Points

```
(*Assumes document with measurement units set to points.*)
tell application "Adobe InDesign CS5"
    set pageRef to page 1 of document 1
    set polyPoints to {{36, 80}, {{39, 36}, {57, 36},{76, 36}},¬
    {80, 80}}
    tell pageRef
        set polyRef to make polygon with properties {stroke weight:2,¬
        fill color:"None", stroke color:"Black"}
        set pathRef to path 1 of polyRef
        set entire path of pathRef to polyPoints
    end tell
end tell
```

A path that is closed can be a container.

Figure 18.2: Shape with rounded point created with CurvePoints script.

Pathfinder Operations

Methods that combine paths of page items are called pathfinder operations. From a scripting perspective, each operation is a separate command expecting an object or list of object references for its **with** parameter. You will need to have two or more page items selected for the example script. The target object (*objRef*) will be the most recent page item created.

intersect path - Combines objects whose paths intersect. If paths do not intersect, an error is generated.

add path - Combines object with objects that intersect. Deletes items if paths do not intersect.

exclude overlap path - Creates a new path by excluding the areas of the front-most object with that of the other objects.

minus back - Creates a new path by reverse subtracting overlapping areas of the front-most object with other paths.

subtract path - Creates a new path by subtracting overlapping areas of the front-most object from other objects.

The effect of each of these pathfinder operations can be demonstrated with the following generalized script. In the script statement indicated substitute one of the following: **subtract path, intersect path, exclude overlap path, minus back, make compound path**. Select two or more page items that intersect before running script.

Test Pathfinder

```
set itemList to {}
tell application "Adobe InDesign CS5"
    set selList to selection
    set objProp to {fill color:"Black", fill tint:50}
    if length of selList > 1 then
        set objRef to item 1 of selList
        tell objRef
        (*Change make compound path command in the following to one of the
        pathfinder methods listed above.*)
        set newObj to make compound path with item 2 of selList
        end tell
        set properties of newObj to objProp
    end if
end tell
```

Remember

When working with selection lists, the items in the list are arranged according to their item id. The first item selected will be the first item in the list.

Zero Winding Rule

InDesign supports the zero winding rule for a path that intersects itself. Should you want the effect of an even-odd fill rule, the following script will perform the magic. (Figure 18.3)

Odd Rule Fill

```
(*Using the pen tool, draw a path that intersects itself (see Figure 18.3).
Select the path and run the script.*)
tell application "Adobe InDesign CS5"
    set selList to selection
    if length of selList > 0 and class of item 1 of selList = polygon then
        set objRef to item 1 of selList
        if name of fill color of objRef is "None" then
            set fill color of objRef to "Black"
        end if
        set dupItem to duplicate objRef
        tell objRef to add path with dupItem
    end if
end tell
```

Text on a Path

While still on the subject of paths, take a short detour and look at the subject of text on a path. To place text on a path, a text path object is created from a path which can be open or closed. Once the text path object is created, there are a number of properties which need to be set to determine how the text will be displayed: **path alignment, text alignment, path effect, start bracket, end bracket, flip path effect**, and **path spacing**. The following example uses text defaults for styling the text. Change some of the properties to see how they effect the display of the text.

Text on Path

```
(*Assumes selected path, oval, rectangle, graphic line, or text frame. Change
value for path effect in script below for testing. Path effects can be rainbow
path effect, gravity path effect, ribbon path effect, skew path effect, or
stair step path effect.*)
set textContent to "This is an example of text on a path"
tell application "Adobe InDesign CS5"
    set selList to selection
    if length of selList > 0 then

        try
            set pathRef to item 1 of selList
            tell document 1
                set point size of text defaults to 18
                set justification of text defaults to center align
            end tell
            tell pathRef
                set textPathRef to make text path
            end tell
            tell textPathRef
                set contents to textContent
                --change value for path effect in following for testing
                set path effect to rainbow path effect
```

Figure 18.3: Shape before and after running Odd Rule Fill script..

```
                set text alignment to descender text alignment
                set flip path effect to not flipped
            end tell
        on error errStr
            activate
            display dialog errStr
        end try
    end if
end tell
```

Transparency and Effects

The subject of transparency (opacity) and effects in InDesign could fill a book of its own. One would think that setting a property such as opacity would be simple. Not quite. But with the challenge comes the ability to set transparency for fill, content, and stroke. Within each of these classifications you now have **bevel and emboss settings, blending settings, directional feather settings, drop shadow settings, feather settings, gradient feather settings, inner glow settings, inner shadow settings, outer glow settings**, and **satin** settings.

This is one place where you might want to spend some time experimenting in the user interface with the Preview checkbox checked (Object > Effects > Transparency). Once you get the look you want, transferring the settings to a script is fairly easy. The following two demonstration scripts should give you a head start in figuring out the syntax.

Transparency

```
(*Demonstrates creating objects where one has transparency set. Assumes
active document with measurements set to points with swatches "C=0 M=0 Y=100
K=0", "C=100 M=0 Y=0 K=0", and "Black".*)
tell application "Adobe InDesign CS5"
    set docRef to document 1
    set pageRef to page 1 of docRef
    set rectBounds to {36, 36, 144, 144}
    set rectProps to {fill color:"C=0 M=0 Y=100 K=0"}
    set ovalBounds to {56, 56, 124, 124}
    set ovalProps to {fill color:"C=100 M=0 Y=0 K=0", stroke type:"Solid", ¬
    stroke color:"Black", stroke weight:4}
    tell pageRef
        set rectRef to make rectangle with properties {geometric bounds:¬
        rectBounds} & rectProps
        set ovalRef to make oval with properties {geometric bounds:¬
        ovalBounds} & ovalProps
    end tell
    tell ovalRef
        set properties of blending settings of fill transparency settings ¬
        to {opacity:50, blend mode:multiply}
    end tell
end tell
```

Drop Shadow

```
(*Creates a rectangle with a drop shadow. Assumes a document exists with
measurements set to points and swatch "C=0 M=0 Y=100 K=0".*)
tell application "Adobe InDesign CS5"
    set pageRef to page 1 of document 1
```

```
      set rectProps to {fill color:"C=0 M=0 Y=100 K=0", geometric bounds:¬
      {36, 36, 144, 144}}
      tell pageRef
         set rectRef to make rectangle with properties rectProps
      end tell
      tell rectRef
         set properties of fill transparency settings to {drop shadow ¬
         settings:{mode:drop, distance:10, angle:135, spread:0, blend ¬
         mode:multiply, opacity:75, honor other effects:false, x offset:7, ¬
         y offset:7, knocked out:true, use global light:false}}
      end tell
   end tell
```

To help you determine how to set up a property record for some of the many fill transparency settings, you will want to work through the project **Transparency Settings** in the "Make Scripts Work for You" section of this chapter.

Once you get the hang of it, you may wish to set up some object styles with drop shadow and other transparency effects included. Put your favorites in a style sheet or library while you are at it.

Transformations

There are a number of properties available to page items that allow setting flip, scale, rotation, and shear angle. These values can be relative to the object's container (absolute), as in:

```
      set absolute rotation angle of pageItemRef to 45
```

Or the values can be relative to the pasteboard, as in:

```
      set rotation angle of pageItemRef to 45
```

For ultimate transformation power, you will want to get familiar with using the transformation matrix.

Transformation Matrix

New as of InDesign CS3 is the ability to set up transformation "styles." This capability is found in InDesign's dictionary under the class **transformation matrix**. You can give a matrix a name, and assign it any number of properties for translating (moving horizontally and/or vertically), rotating, shearing, and scaling. Once the matrix is defined, apply the matrix to an object to perform one or more translations with one statement. The following demonstrates establishing a transformation matrix with a single property: counterclockwise rotation angle.

Transformation Matrix
```
(*Creates transformation matrix and applies to page item.*)
tell application "Adobe InDesign CS5"
   --create the matrix
   set matRef to make transformation matrix with properties ¬
   {name:"RotateLeft45", counterclockwise rotation angle:45}
   --create rectangle and apply transformation
   tell page 1 of document 1
      set rectRef to make rectangle with properties {geometric bounds:¬
      {"3p", "3p", "15p", "15p"}}
   end tell
```

```
    transform rectRef in inner coordinates from center anchor with ¬
    matrix matRef
end tell
```

Other transformation properties that can be set are **clockwise shear angle**, **horizontal scale factor**, **vertical scale factor**, **horizontal translation**, and **vertical translation**. These should be self-explanatory. There may be some question as to the values to use for the following parameters used in applying transformations:

in - Can be `pasteboard coordinates`, `parent coordinates` (measurement coordinates for parent of item), `inner coordinates` (coordinates for item), or `spread coordinates`.

from - Supply a list of two values, or any one of nine anchor point values (refer to anchor point in InDesign's dictionary for a complete listing).

r**eplacing current** - Set to true if you need to replace the current transformation matrix applied to the object.

considering ruler units - With this property set to true, the measurement units in effect are used. The default is false, in which event points are used. The parameter has no effect unless the reference point is relative to a page.

The following script uses a handler which can prove to be useful for general purposes. It allows the value of the **from** parameter (*transPoint* variable) to be either an integer or a list of coordinate points. In using an integer value, this relates to the transform reference point grid (*proxy point grid*). If you mentally number the cells of the grid from left to right, top to bottom, the number of the cell is the number value you will use. In the following, the value 5 is used, referring to the center proxy reference point.

Transform Item

```
set transPoint to 5 --proxy point cell referenced for transform
--set transPoint to {200, 300} --can be list of x,y coordinates, in points
tell application "Adobe InDesign CS5"
    set selList to selection
    if (length of selList > 0) and ¬
    (class of item 1 of selList = rectangle) then
        set itemRef to item 1 of selList
        set matRef to make transformation matrix with properties ¬
        {name:"Diagonal72", vertical scale factor:0.5, ¬
        horizontal scale factor:0.5, counterclockwise rotation angle:45, ¬
        clockwise shear angle:0, horizontal translation:0, ¬
        vertical translation:0}
        (*Parameters: item, matrix, coordinate, transformation point or list.*)
        set coordRef to parent coordinates
        my transformItem(itemRef, matRef, coordRef, transPoint)
    end if
end tell

(*Transforms item using matrix referenced, in coordinates, using
transPoint.*)
on transformItem(itemRef, matRef, coordRef, transPoint)
    tell application "Adobe InDesign CS5"
        if class of transPoint = integer then
            set transList to {top left anchor, top center anchor, ¬
            top right anchor, left center anchor, center anchor, ¬
            right center anchor, bottom left anchor, bottom center anchor, ¬
            bottom right anchor}
            set transRef to item transPoint of transList
```

```
        else
            set transRef to transPoint
        end if
        transform itemRef in coordRef from transRef with matrix matRef
    end tell
end transformItem
```

The interesting thing about transformations is they are remembered by the page item so you can tell the object to **transform again, transform again individually, transform sequence again**, or **transform sequence again individually**. The transformations remain with the document until closed. This works whether the page item is moved manually or using a transformation matrix. Try it. The project **Test Transform** contains two scripts which can be used with the document "TestTransform.indd."

Select the rectangle on page 1 of the document "Test Transform.indd" and run the script **Test Transform**. Notice that the rectangle moves 72 points even though the ruler units are set to picas. Now run the second script **Transform Again**. Even though another page item is created, the original item remembers its last transformation. You can clear the transformation information from the page item using the command **clear transformation**.

Transform With Rotate

With this chapter's scripts are example scripts that demonstrate using transformations along with transform again: **Duplicate With Transform**, **Gradient Fill Flower**, and **Spirograph**. The first two use the handler **duplicateWTrans** shown below:

```
(*Transforms item with option to group.*)
on duplicateWTrans(objRef, matrixRef, coordSpace, transPoint, numTrans, ¬
groupIt)
    set groupRef to missing value
    tell application "Adobe InDesign CS5"
        set pageRef to parent page of objRef
        set dupRef to duplicate objRef
        select dupRef existing selection add to
        transform dupRef in coordSpace from transPoint with matrix matrixRef
        repeat numTrans times
            set dupRef to duplicate dupRef
            select dupRef existing selection add to
            tell dupRef to transform again
        end repeat
        if groupIt then
            set selList to selection
            tell pageRef
                set groupRef to make group with properties {group items:selList}
            end tell
        end if
        return groupRef
    end tell
end duplicateWTrans
```

Transform Page

Your script can transform pages within a document using a transformation matrix. The **Transform Page** script in the **Master Transform** project demonstrates. It sets the horizontal scale factor for the matrix to 0.5 (50%). The **transformItem** handler performs the transformation. Use the script with the document "Master Transform.indd" to test. Save the resulting document for testing with the next script.

Transform Page

```
tell application "Adobe InDesign CS5"
    set pageRef to page 2 of document 1
    set matRef to make transformation matrix with properties ¬
    {name:"ScaleX50", horizontal scale factor:0.5, vertical scale factor:1}
    set coordRef to parent coordinates
    set transPoint to 5
    my transformItem(pageRef, matRef, coordRef, transPoint)
end tell
(*Add transformItem handler here (Transform folder).*)
```

Note

When setting scale factors for a transformation matrix, make sure to define both the horizontal and vertical scale factors, even if one dimension remains 100% (value of 1).

Master Page Transform

Because versions CS5 and above for InDesign now allow multiple page sizes within a document, a page can be a different size than its applied master page. Setting the **master page transform** for a page allows the Master Page Overlay to be transformed within the Page. Here is one place that scripting gives you more power than working manually as you can scale, rotate, and shear in addition to moving (**horizontal translation** and **vertical translation**). Use with document transformed using script above.

Transform Master Overlay

```
tell application "Adobe InDesign CS5"
    tell layout window 1 of document 1
        set transform reference point to center anchor
    end tell
    set pageRef to page 2 of document 1
    set matRef to make transformation matrix with properties ¬
    {counterclockwise rotation angle:270, horizontal translation:214, ¬
    vertical translation:-30}
    set master page transform of pageRef to matRef
end tell
```

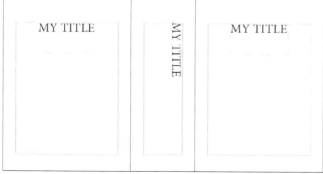

Figure 18.4: Spread created after running Transform Page script to change the size of page 2 and Transform Master Overlay to transform the appearance of the master page on its associated page.

Save the transformed document with a new name as you will want to use the original document ('Master Transform.indd") for testing resize and reframe statements.

Resize and Reframe

The resize and reframe commands allow your scripts to resize page items as well as pages. (See page 219 for list of coordinate spaces to use with the **in** parameter.)

Resize

When resizing a page, the page margins do not resize with the page. Your script needs to make sure that the size of the resized page will not exceed the margin settings. You have the option of resizing using multipliers as demonstrated in the following:

```
tell application "Adobe InDesign CS5"
    tell page 2 of active document
        resize in inner coordinates from center anchor by ¬
        multiplying current dimensions by values {.5, 1}
    end tell
end tell
```

Alternatively, you can **resize** pages using fixed values. These need to be in point measurements.

```
tell application "Adobe InDesign CS5"
    tell page 2 of active document
        resize in inner coordinates from center anchor by replacing current ¬
        dimensions with values {200, 504}
    end tell
end tell
```

To **resize** a page item, the syntax is similar to resizing a page. Add a rectangle on page one of the document. Substitute the following in the code above:

```
tell page 1 of active document
    resize rectangle 1 in spread coordinates from top left anchor by ¬
    replacing current dimensions with values {72, 36}
end tell
```

Reframe

The reframe command changes the bounding box for the page item without changing its content or stroke weight. When used with a page, it changes the page size by changing its page bounds. In using **reframe**, be aware that measurement units in effect for the document are used.

```
--assumes page item on page 1 of active document; measurements set to points
tell application "Adobe InDesign CS5"
    tell page 1 of active document
        set gBounds to geometric bounds of page item 1
        set y0 to (item 1 of gBounds) - 36
        set x0 to (item 2 of gBounds) - 36
        set y1 to (item 3 of gBounds) + 36
        set x1 to (item 4 of gBounds) + 36
        set dupItem to duplicate page item 1
```

```
        reframe dupItem in inner coordinates opposing corners {{y0, x0}, ¬
        {y1, x1}}
        set newBounds to geometric bounds of dupItem
    end tell
end tell
{gBounds, newBounds}
```

You can use multipliers with reframe to resize a page item without changing its content.

```
--assumes active document with page item on page 1
tell application "Adobe InDesign CS5"
    tell page 1 of active document
        resize page item 1 in inner coordinates from top left anchor by ¬
        multiplying current dimensions by values {1.5, 1.5}
    end tell
end tell
```

Try this script using different values for the anchor point: center anchor, top right anchor, left center anchor, bottom right anchor, and so on.

Make Scripts Work for You

Figuring out exactly how a property record is put together can result in some head scratching. One way to solve the problem is to create the object manually and get the properties using a script. Depending on the complexity, this can be a simple task or become somewhat involved. We will work with an example before introducing the project **Transparency Settings**.

Procedure:

1. Start by creating a rectangle on a page. Give it a fill and/or a stroke. Select it and run the following:

```
tell application "Adobe InDesign CS5"
    set selList to selection
    if length of selList > 0 and class of item 1 of selList = rectangle then
        set selItem to item 1 of selList
        get properties of selItem
    end if
end tell
```

2. Open the Result panel for AppleScript Editor. You will most likely need to expand it to see all of the properties listed.

   If you just want to get the settings for a few items, you can browse the list to find the properties you are interested in. Use the Find capability of the script editor to find the properties you are looking for (Command + F).

3. For this example, look for the properties for fill color, stroke color, stroke weight, and stroke type. For stroke weight you can cut and paste the value into a property record:

```
set propRecord to {stroke weight: 0.0}
```

4. For fill color and stroke color, you will want to get the name of the swatch. You will also want to get the name value of the stroke type. Replace the get properties statement in the script above with the following:

```
set fillColor to name of fill color of selItem
set strokeColor to name of stroke color of selItem
set strokeType to name of stroke type of selItem
set strokeWt to stroke weight of selItem
```

```
    set propRecord to {stroke weight:strokeWt, stroke type:strokeType, ¬
        stroke color:strokeColor, fill color:fillColor}
```

5. Run your script with your page item selected. View the result. Use the property record returned in a script to create a similar page item.

Properties such as **content transparency settings, fill transparency settings,** and **stroke transparency settings** are themselves defined by a record.

6. Open the document "TestTransparency.indd" in the **Transparency Settings** project folder. Select one of the items at the top right of the page. Run the following:

```
tell application "Adobe InDesign CS5"
    set selList to selection
    if length of selList > 0 and ¬
    class of item 1 of selList is in {oval, rectangle, text frame} then
        set selItem to item 1 of selList
        set test to properties of fill transparency settings of selItem
    end if
end tell
```

7. View the result in the Result panel. You will see that fill transparency settings are comprised of other records defining **blending settings, drop shadow, feather settings,** and so on. Add the following below the statement that defines the variable *test* in the script from Step 6 above:

```
    set shadowSettings to properties of drop shadow settings of test
```

You have now drilled down to see the settings that can be used for a drop shadow.

8. Now that you have some idea of how to create a property record using values of a selected item, open the script **Get Property Record**.

9. With one of the page items in the document "TestTransparency.indd" selected, run the script. The script should create a rectangle with the transparency fill settings gathered from the selected page item.

This little exercise was intended to give you some idea of working with object properties that involve nested records.

19

Automation Arsenal

To round out your arsenal of solutions for automation, this chapter covers a variety of workflow techniques. You will be exposed to working with libraries and assets, anchored and inline objects, and text variables. You will also work with storing information in an object and extracting the information when needed. That's a lot of ground to cover, so let's get to it.

Insert/Extract Label

Every object in InDesign's hierarchy that supports the **label** property can store and retrieve data using the **insert label** and **extract label** commands. For the purpose of this discussion, the information stored will be referred to as a **custom label**. A custom label consists of two parts:

- key: A string identifier.
- value: The data to store which must be a string value.

This is demonstrated in the following which stores the place point for an item in its label. It assumes there is a page item on page 1 of an active document with measurements set to points.

```
tell application "Adobe InDesign CS5"
    set docRef to document 1
    set objRef to page item 1 of page 1 of docRef
    set gBounds to geometric bounds of objRef
    set y0 to item 1 of gBounds as string
    set x0 to item 2 of gBounds as string
    insert label objRef key "PlacePoint" value (y0 & "|" & x0)
    set storedLabel to extract label objRef key "PlacePoint"
end tell
```

In using **extract label**, if an object does not have a custom label stored as anticipated, the script will not throw an error, but returns an empty string as the result. Select the page item targeted in the previous script, and test with the following:

```
tell application "Adobe InDesign CS5"
    set selList to selection
    if (length of selList > 0) and (class of item 1 of selList is in ¬
    {rectangle, oval, text frame, group}) then
        set storedLabel to extract label (item 1 of selList) key "PlacePoint"
    end if
end tell
```

One technique that can be used for automation is to store scripts, serialized as a string, in a custom label. Extract the script when needed and use **do script** to run. Examples of how this can be used to an advantage will be explored later in this chapter.

In the following discussion covering libraries and assets, we will use a custom label with a library asset.

Libraries and Assets

Libraries are typically used to store often-used page elements: graphics, logos, and other resources. When adding a page item or items as an asset to a library, InDesign saves all page, text, and image attributes with their relationships maintained in the following ways:

- Grouping is maintained.
- Text retains formatting.
- Styles (paragraph, character, and object styles) are converted to the destination document's styles if they have the same name. If not the same name, they are added to the document.
- Original layers of the object are preserved if the **paste remembers layers** property for the clipboard is set to true.

```
tell application "Adobe InDesign CS5"
    tell clipboard preferences to set paste remembers layers to true
end tell
```

The way libraries work in CS5 and 5.5 has changed for the better. There is now a **library panel** object to which a library is associated. When you create a library with a script, add the ".indl" extension for the name. The associated library panel will be created by default with the same name as the library but without the extension.

Library Panel

The listing for a library panel is part of the UI Suite of InDesign's dictionary. To get a reference to the library panel that is open and active, the every reference can be used. If you don't have any libraries open, run the script **Get Library** from InDesign's Scripts panel (Automation).

```
tell application "Adobe InDesign CS5"
    try
        set libList to name of every library panel where visible is true
    end try
end tell
```

Having the name of the panel, you can get the name of the asset, or assets, selected within it. If there is a asset selected, the following will return its name.

```
tell application "Adobe InDesign CS5"
    set assetName to missing value
    try
        set panelName to name of every library panel where visible is true
        tell library panel panelName
            if exists selection then
                set assetName to name of item 1 of selection
            end if
        end tell
        {panelName, assetName}
    end try
end tell
```

If more than one asset is selected, selection will be a list. Your script could later check for this use the information as needed.

```
tell application "Adobe InDesign CS5"
    set panelName to missing value
    set listLen to 0
    try
        set panelName to name of every library panel where visible is true
        tell library panel panelName
            set selList to selection
            if selList is not {} then
                set listLength to length of selList
            end if
        end tell
    end try
end tell
{panelName, listLength}
```

A reference to the library displayed in the visible panel is returned using the **associated library** property of the panel. You can set the order in which the assets are displayed using the **sort order** property for the library panel. Enumeration values for sort order are by name, by oldest, by newest, and by type. You can also set the panel to display by list view, thumbnail view, or large thumbnail view using the property **view**.

```
tell application "Adobe InDesign CS5"
    if exists library panel "MyLibrary" then
        set panelRef to library panel "MyLibrary"
        set visible of panelRef to true
        set libRef to associated library of panelRef
        set view of panelRef to large thumbnail view
        set sort order of panelRef to by newest
    end if
end tell
```

Libraries

A list of the names of open libraries is returned using the following:

```
tell application "Adobe InDesign CS5"
    set theList to name of libraries
end tell
```

The path to where a library is stored is returned using its **full name** property.

```
(*Assumes that the ButtonLibrary is active.*)
tell application "Adobe InDesign CS5"
    set libRef to library "ButtonLibrary.indl"
    set libPath to full name of libRef
end tell
libPath --file "Macintosh HD:Applications:Adobe InDesign CS5:Presets:Button
Library:ButtonLibrary.indl"
```

The button library has its own folder. For the libraries used with this book's scripts, the path to the folder can be constructed using the file path for the application:

Get Library

```
set libName to "MyLibrary.indl"
set libRef to getLibrary (libName)
```

```
(*Returns alias reference to library; otherwise attempts to open it.*)
on getLibrary (libName)
    tell application "Adobe InDesign CS5"
        if exists library libName then
            set libRef to library libName
            return libRef
        end if
        set appPath to file path as string
        set libPath to appPath & "Presets:Libraries:" & libName
        try
            set libAlias to libPath as alias
            set libRef to open libAlias
            return libRef
        end try
        error "Library " & libName & " not found"
    end tell
end getLibrary
```

The **getLibrary** handler is used in the scripts **Place Asset To Doc** and **Place Asset To Text** which are found in the Chapter Scripts folder for this chapter.

Since it can be assumed that the only files in the Libraries folder will be libraries, you can get a list of the library names using list folder (see Chapter 1).

```
tell application "Adobe InDesign CS5"
    set appPath to file path as string
    set libPath to appPath & "Presets:Libraries:"
end tell
set libList to list folder libPath without invisibles
```

Alternatively, you can get the file list from the Finder using the same library folder path (the variable *libPath* in the script above). This is used in the following which allows the user to select a library to open from the list of libraries available:

Choose Library

```
set libType to "IDl4" --may change with InDesign versions
tell application "Adobe InDesign CS5"
    set appPath to file path as string
    set libPath to appPath & "Presets:Libraries:"
end tell
tell application "Finder"
    set libList to name of every file of folder libPath where file type is ¬
    {libType}
end tell
set theFile to choose from list libList without multiple selections allowed ¬
and empty selection allowed
if theFile is not false then
    set fileName to item 1 of theFile
    tell application "Adobe InDesign CS5"
        if not exists library fileName then
            open file (libPath & fileName)
        end if
    end tell
end if
```

To create a library, the handler **checkLibrary** can come in handy. It tests to see if the library named is active. Next it verifies if a library file as named is in the Library folder ([application folder]":Presets:Libraries"). If the tests are false, the user is given the option of creating the library file. From the script **Create Library** the handler is shown below:

```
set libName to "TestLibrary.indl"
set libRef to checkLibrary(libName)

on checkLibrary(libName)
    tell application "Adobe InDesign CS5"
        if exists library libName then
            return library libName
        end if
        set appPath to file path as string
        set libPath to (appPath & "Presets:Libraries:")
        try
            set libAlias to (libPath & libName) as alias
            set libRef to open libAlias
            return libRef
        end try
        set userPrompt to "Library " & libName & " not found."
        set userPrompt to userPrompt & "Do you want to create it?"
        set userResponse to my getBoolean(userPrompt, true)
        if userResponse = true then
            set libRef to make library with properties {name:libName, ¬
            file path:libPath, full name:(libPath & libName)}
            open file (libPath & libName)
        else
            error ("Cannot continue without library reference")
        end if
    end tell
    return libRef
end checkLibrary
(*Add handler getBoolean (Dialogs folder) to complete the script.*)
```

Assets

Once you have a reference to a library, you can use this reference for creating and accessing its assets. The following code is from the script **Concentric Circle** which is in the Chapter Scripts folder for this chapter.

```
(*Partial script. Requires library "MyLibrary.indl."*)
set colorList to {{"Blue", {100, 50, 0, 0}}, {"myYellow", {0, 0, 100, 0}}}
set cx to 200
set cy to 200
set tryName to "ConcentricCircle"
set libName to "MyLibrary.indl"
set assetDesc to "oval centered in square"
try
    set libRef to checkLibrary(libName)
    set assetName to checkAssetName(libRef, tryName)
on error
    return beep
end try
tell application "Adobe InDesign CS5"
    set docRef to make document
    set {orighm, origvm, origro} to my setMeasures(docRef)
    set existingList to my createProcessColors(docRef, colorList)
    tell docRef
```

```
            set layerRef to make layer with properties {name:"Graphics"}
            set pageRef to page 1
        end tell
        set objRef to my createGraphic(docRef, pageRef, layerRef, cx, cy)
        tell libRef
            set assetRef to store using objRef with properties {name:assetName, ¬
            description:assetDesc, asset type:geometry type}
        end tell
        tell docRef
            set active layer to layer 1
        end tell
    end tell
    resetMeasures(docRef, orighm, origvm, origro)
    (*Add handlers: setMeasures, resetMeasures (Environment folder),
    createProcessColors (Colors folder), createGraphic (create your handler).*)
```

To access a library asset, the handler **placeAssetToDoc** checks if the asset exists before attempting to place it on the target object. The handler has two optional parameters: *pageRef* and *placePoint*. If the page reference (*pageRef*) is not missing value, the asset is moved to the page. If the place point (*placePt*) is not missing value, the asset is moved to the coordinates defined. See how the handler is used in the **Place Asset to Doc** script (in Chapter Scripts folder).

```
set assetName to "ConcentricCircle"
set placePt to missing value
set pageRef to missing value
set placedObj to my placeAssetToDoc(docRef, libRef, assetName, pageRef, ¬
placePoint)

(*Verifies asset and then places to document; otherwise throws error.*)
on placeAssetToDoc(docRef, libRef, assetName, pageRef, placePt)
    tell application "Adobe InDesign CS5"
        tell libRef
            if exists asset assetName then
                set assetRef to asset assetName
            else
                error "Asset " & assetName & " not found"
            end if
        end tell
        set placedObj to place asset assetRef on docRef
        if pageRef is not missing value then
            move placedObj to pageRef
        end if
        if placePt is not missing value then
            move placedObj to placePt
        end if
    end tell
    placedObj
end placeAsset
```

Move

When you move an asset onto a page using a script the place point will be {0,0}. For this reason you should also provide a place point.

To get a listing of the names of all assets in a library:

```
--assumes library "MyLibrary.indl" is open
tell application "Adobe InDesign CS5"
    set libRef to library "MyLibrary.indl"
    set assetNames to name of every asset of libRef
end tell
assetNames
```

To get a listing of every asset in every active library;

```
tell application "Adobe InDesign CS5"
    tell every library
        set assetNames to name of every asset
    end tell
end tell
assetNames
```

If you want other information about all available assets, place a reference to the libraries in a list, then parse the list to get a report of asset names and any other information. This can be quite extensive especially if you have the Sample Buttons library open. For this reason, the following excludes that library.

Asset Info

```
tell application "Adobe InDesign CS5"
    set libList to libraries
    set theCounter to 1
    repeat with i from 1 to length of libList
        set fName to full name of item i of libList as string
        if (offset of "ButtonLibrary.indl" in fName) = 0 then
            set assetList to assets of item i of libList
            repeat with j from 1 to length of assetList
                set assetRef to item j of assetList
                set assetName to name of assetRef & ": " & date of assetRef
                if theCounter = 1 then
                    set str to assetName
                else
                    set str to str & return & assetName
                end if
                set theCounter to theCounter + 1
            end repeat
        end if
    end repeat
end tell
str
```

Another property of the assets you may want as part of your report might be **description**. The property **asset type** is an enumeration value which cannot be coerced to a string.

Create Asset

The script **Three Rings** demonstrates creating a library asset with a fun routine for a graphic using transformations (see Figure 19.1). The size of the asset is stored as a custom label as part of the creation process. The script is found in the Chapter Scripts folder for this chapter. The handler **createAsset** from the script is shown below.

```
set libName to "TestLibrary.indl"
set assetName to "Three Rings"
```

```
            set assetDesc to "Graphic of 3 rings"
         on createAsset(docRef, layerRef, libRef, assetName, assetDesc)
            tell application "Adobe InDesign CS5"
               tell libRef
                  if exists asset assetName then
                     error "Asset " & assetName & " exists"
                  end if
                  set objRef to my assetRoutine(docRef)
                  set gBounds to geometric bounds of objRef
                  set wid to (item 4 of gBounds) - (item 2 of gBounds)
                  set hgt to ((item 3 of gBounds) - (item 1 of gBounds)) as string
                  set sizeStr to (wid as string) & " " & (hgt as string)
                  set assetRef to store using objRef with properties ¬
                  {name:assetName, description:assetDesc, asset type:¬
                  geometry type}
                  insert label assetRef key "size" value sizeStr
               end tell
            end tell
         end createAsset
```

Library assets can be used for more than storing graphics. Because styling information is stored with the asset, it can be used as another way of adding text styles and object styles to documents. See how this is done in the following. The entire script, **Asset Styles**, is in the Chapter Scripts folder for this chapter. Select the file "Article.txt" in the Public:Text Files folder when prompted.

```
      (*Partial script is shown below.*)

      set libName to "MyLibrary.indl"
      set assetName to "HeadByDateBody"
      set fileRef to choose file with prompt "Select text file"
      set assetRef to getAsset(libName, assetName)
      tell application "Adobe InDesign CS5"
         place asset assetRef on document 1
         set assetRef to page item 1 of spread 1 of document 1
         set itemID to id of assetRef
         set objStyRef to applied object style of assetRef
         tell page 1 of document 1
            set frameRef to make text frame with properties {geometric bounds:¬
            {"3p", "3p", "45p", "30p"}}
            tell frameRef
               place fileRef
               apply object style using objStyRef
            end tell
         end tell
         tell document 1
            delete page item id itemID
         end tell
      end tell

      (*Returns asset reference if found; otherwise throws error.*)
      on getAsset(libName, assetName)
         tell application "Adobe InDesign CS5"
            set assetRef to missing value
            if exists library libName then
               set libRef to library libName
               tell libRef
                  if exists asset assetName then
```

```
                set assetRef to asset assetName
            end if
        end tell
    end if
    if assetRef = missing value then
        error "Asset " & assetName & " of library " & libName & " not found"
    end if
end tell
return assetRef
end getAsset
```

Note:

In creating an asset to be used for its text and object styles, create the original text frame on the pasteboard. That way, when the asset is imported, it is placed on the pasteboard, not the page.

When you place an asset to a text item, the asset becomes an anchored object. If actual text is the target of the place operation, the text is replaced. For most purposes an insertion point is used as the object specifier.

Anchored Objects

When a text object is used to place the placed object becomes the most recent page item for the parent text frame. Its anchored position by default is inline (**anchored position:**inline position). Other values for **anchored position** are above line, and anchored. Other properties include **anchor xoffset, anchor yoffset**, and **anchor point**. To see the complete listing, look up anchored object settings in the Text Suite of InDesign's dictionary.

The script **Place Asset to Text** demonstrates placing an asset to a text reference. The script then changes some of the anchored object settings for the placed item to anchor the asset outside of the text frame. It also shows how a custom label could be used to provide information for a script. In the example, the custom label "size" for the library asset holds the values for the width and height of the asset. The script assumes that the library and the asset with a custom label "size" exist. A more robust version of this script is found in the Chapter Scripts folder for this chapter.

Place Asset to Text

```
(*Requires text or insertion point selection.*)
set assetName to "Three Rings"
set labelKey to "size"
tell application "Adobe InDesign CS5"
    set selList to selection
    if length of selList > 0 and class of item 1 of selList is in ¬
    {text, insertion point} then
        set textRef to item 1 of selList
        set libRef to library "MyLibrary.indl"
        set assetRef to my placeAssetToText(textRef, libRef, assetName)
        --get the information stored in the custom label labelKey
        set theInfo to extract label assetRef key labelKey
        set theWid to (word 1 of theInfo as number) / 4
        set xOff to "" & theWid & "pt"
        (*The placed object can now be referenced as the last member of
        the page items collection for the parent frame.*)
```

```
            set frameRef to item 1 of parent text frames of textRef
            set inlineRef to page item -1 of frameRef
            --change properties for anchored object settings
            set ancSettings to anchored object settings of inlineRef
            set anchored position of ancSettings to anchored
            set anchor point of ancSettings to bottom right anchor
            set anchor xoffset of ancSettings to xOff
        end if
    end tell

    (*Places asset if found to text object referenced; otherwise throws error.*)
    on placeAssetToText(textRef, libRef, assetName)
        tell application "Adobe InDesign CS5"
            tell libRef
                if exists asset assetName then
                    set assetRef to asset assetName
                else
                    error "Asset " & assetName & " not found"
                end if
            end tell
            place asset assetRef on textRef
        end tell
        return assetRef
    end placeAssetToText
```

The next chapter provides additional opportunities for working with anchored page items. For now, the attention turns to text variables.

Text Variables

A powerhouse for automation, text variables, can come to your rescue in a variety of ways. To start with, InDesign provides a number of text variables by default. For the most part, your scripts may be involved with updating and using the text variables supplied: **Chapter Number, Creation Date, File Name, Image Name, Last Page Number, Modification Date, Output Date**, and **Running Header**.

A text variable can be created and its properties set at both the application and document level. For your own dynamic text variable you will need to create a **custom text variable**. A text variable in a document is similar to a variable in a script in that its value can change. The type of value that a text variable can display is determined by its **variable type** property. With CS5 there are twelve variable types. The **variable options** property associates the text variable with a preference that determines settings which can be set for the variable. Each variable type has its own preference properties.

Chapter Number Text Variable

As an example, the **variable type** for the default text variable **Chapter Number** is chapter number type. Its variable options are defined in the chapter number variable preference for **variable options**. To get an idea of how to set up a property record for defining a chapter number variable, run the following script.

```
tell application "Adobe InDesign CS5"
    set theVariable to text variable "Chapter Number"
    set propRecord to properties of theVariable
```

```
    tell propRecord
        set newRecord to {variable type:variable type}
        set optRecord to properties of variable options
        tell optRecord
            set newRecord to newRecord & {variable options:{format:format, ¬
            text after:text after, text before:text before}}
        end tell
    end tell
end tell
newRecord
(*Result is: {variable type:chapter number type, variable
options:{format:current, text after:"", text before:""}}.*)
```

To update the chapter number variable, use the property record returned from the previous script as a guide. This should result in a script similar to the following:

```
set varName to "Chapter Number"
tell application "Adobe InDesign CS5"
    set theVariable to text variable varName
    set propRecord to {variable type:chapter number type, ¬
    variable options:{format:arabic, text before:"Chapter: "}}
    tell document 1
        if (exists text variable varName) then
            set varRef to text variable varName
        else
            set varRef to make text variable with properties {name:varName}
        end if
        set properties of varRef to propRecord
    end tell
end tell
```

Custom Text Variable

The listing of properties for a custom text variable is found in the **custom text variable preference** in the Preferences Suite of InDesign's dictionary. It shows only one preference that can be set: **contents**. To create a custom text variable, the following example can be used as a guide:

Custom Text Variable

```
set customVarName to "Book Title"
set varContents to " Book Title Here "
tell application "Adobe InDesign CS5"
    set docRef to document 1
    tell docRef
        if exists text variable customVarName then
            set textVarRef to text variable customVarName
        else
            set textVarRef to make text variable with properties ¬
            {name:customVarName}
        end if
        set properties of textVarRef to {variable type:custom text type, ¬
        variable options: {contents:varContents}}
    end tell
end tell
```

Insert Text Variable

Once the text variable has been created, instances of the variable can be added throughout the document's text using one of the following options:

Manually - Choose Type > Text Variables > Insert Variable from InDesign's menu. This will present a flyout menu from which you can select the appropriate variable. For the example script, this would be Book Title.

Using a Script - Preferably, a script to insert the text variable would be saved in the Scripts panel for InDesign. From there it can be launched using a keyboard shortcut. The script could present the user with a list of text variables from which to select. Or, if there is only one text variable involved, its reference could be hard-coded in the script.

To apply a text variable using a script, the script needs a text reference. This can be a story, an insertion point, text frame, or other text object. As there can be any number of text variables within a text object, a text variable instance is created. Each instance can be identified by **name**, **label**, **id**, or **index**. The **story offset** property for a text variable instance returns its position within its parent story. The following script inserts the text variable at the point of text selection. For this example, the text variable "Book Title" is the variable for the book's title. Later, when the name of the book is determined, the custom text variable can be updated to insert the name throughout the text.

Insert Text Variable

```
set textVarName to "Book Title"
try
    set textRef to textSelection()
    set tvarInstance to insertTVarInstance(textRef, textVarName)
on error errStr
    display alert errStr
    return
end try
on insertTVarInstance(textRef, textVarName)
    tell application "Adobe InDesign CS5"
        set docRef to document 1
        tell docRef
            if (exists text variable textVarName) then
                set textVarRef to text variable textVarName
            else
                error "text variable " & textVarName & " not found"
            end if
        end tell
        tell textRef
            set tvarInstance to make text variable instance with properties ¬
            {associated text variable:textVarRef}
        end tell
        return tvarInstance
    end tell
end insertTVarInstance
(*Add handler textSelection (Selection folder) to complete script.*)
```

Working with Text Variables

Unless converted to text, a text variable is an object. If **Show Hidden Characters** (Type > Show Hidden Characters) is enabled, a text variable object is shown in the user interface surrounded by a box.

You will also discover that it is impossible to access individual characters within a text variable. If you convert the text variable to text (Type > TextVariables > Convert Variable to Text), the box disappears and the text within the variable is accessible. Your script can convert a text variable to text using the **convert to text** command for a text variable instance.

You may want to keep your text variable instances as objects, however, as once converted to text, they no longer can be accessed as text variables and will not update when the text variable to which it is associated updates.

All text variable instances for a particular text variable type can be returned using code similar to the following:

```
tell application "Adobe InDesign CS5"
    tell document 1
        set textVarRef to text variable "Book Title"
        set textVarList to associated instances of textVarRef
    end tell
end tell
```

You could then iterate through the list (*textVarList* in example above) to get information about the individual instances such as **parent** (the text object it resides in) as well as its **story offset**.

To get the text variable associated with a text variable instance, use the **associated text variable** property.

The following shows the name and default variable options set for each text variable type:

Variable Type	Name	Default Variable Options
chapter number type	Chapter Number	format:current, text after:"" text before:""
creation date type	Creation Date	format:"MM/dd/yy" text after:"", text before:""
file name type	File Name	include extension:false, include path:false, text after:"", text before:""
last page number type	Last Page Number	format:current, scope:section scope text after:"", text before:""
modification date type	Modification Date	format:"MMMM d, yyyy h:mm aa" text after:"", text before:""
output date type	Output Date	format:"MMMM d, yyyy h:mm aa" text after:"", text before:""
match paragraph style type	Running Header	applied paragraph style:"[Basic Paragraph]", change case:none, delete end punctuation:false, search strategy:first on page, text after:"", text before:""

Variable Type	Name	Default Variable Options
match character style type	Running Header	applied character style:"[None]" change case:none, delete end punctuation:false, search strategy:first on page, text after:"", text before:""
custom text type	(No default)	Only option is contents

Do Script Revisited

The following exercise should give you an overview of how a script inserted into a page item using **insert label** can be used as part of an automated process. Scripts are in the **Do Script** folder for this chapter.

Try the following:

```
--create script as string value
set str to "set selList to selection" & return
set str to str & "set fill color of item 1 of selList to \"Black\"" & return
```

Run the script at this point. Ignoring the enclosing quotations and escapes ("\"), the result should look just like a script. Now add to the lines of code from above to the following and test with a page item selected.

```
--insert script into selected page item
tell application "Adobe InDesign CS5"
    set selList to selection
    if length of selList > 0 and class of item 1 of selList ¬
     is not in {text, insertion point} then
        set selItem to item 1 of selList
        set name of selItem to "scriptItem"
        insert label selItem key "script" value str
    end if
end tell
```

To test your script, select the page item and run the following:

Extract Label

```
--extract script and run script inserted above
tell application "Adobe InDesign CS5"
    set objRef to page item "scriptItem" of document 1
    set theScript to extract label objRef key "script"
    do script theScript
end tell
```

Your page item should fill with the color "Black." Imagine a project with page items prepared similarly. A script could parse through the list of page items, extract scripts and run them. The fill color or other attribute used for the object could depend on the contents of the page item. The possibilities are unlimited.

You can pass information into the script using an arguments list. Run the following with a text frame named "textItem" selected.

Label With Arguments

```
(*Creates a label script allowing color values to be passed as arguments.*)
set str to "set itemRef to text frame \"textItem\" of active document" & return
set str to str & "if text 1 of itemRef begins with \"Item\" then " & return
set str to str & "set fill color of itemRef to item 1 of arguments" & return
set str to str & "else" & return
set str to str & "set fill color of itemRef to item 2 of arguments" & return
set str to str & "end if" & return
set str to str & "set fill tint of itemRef to 20" & return

--insert script into selected text frame
tell application "Adobe InDesign CS5"
    set selList to selection
    if length of selList > 0 and class of item 1 of selList is text frame then
        set selItem to item 1 of selList
        set name of selItem to "textItem"
        insert label selItem key "script" value str
    end if
end tell
```

Extract and run the script passing arguments to the script:

Run Script With Arguments

```
--expects document with page item named "textItem" and color "MyRed"
tell application "Adobe InDesign CS5"
    set objRef to page item "textItem" of document 1
    set theScript to extract label objRef key "script"
    set resVar to do script theScript language applescript language with ¬
    arguments {"Black", "MyRed"}
end tell
```

Notice how a variable can be set as part of a label script in the following:

```
--select text frame in document before running script
set str to "if exists selection then" & return
set str to str & "set itemRef to item 1 of selection" & return
set str to str & "set contentType to content type of itemRef " & return
set str to str & "end if"

--insert script into selected page item
tell application "Adobe InDesign CS5"
    set selList to selection
    if length of selList > 0 and class of item 1 of selList is text frame then
        set selItem to item 1 of selList
        set name of selItem to "testMe"
        insert label selItem key "script" value str
    end if
end tell
str
```

The script that extracts the script and runs it can get the values of the variables set in the script:

```
--extract script and run script inserted above
set valList to {}
tell application "Adobe InDesign CS5"
    set objRef to page item "testMe" of document 1
    set theScript to extract label objRef key "script"
```

```
        set testVal to do script theScript language applescript language with ¬
        arguments {"Black", "MyRed"}
    set end of valList to testVal
    end tell
    valList
```

Notice how a list of values for a variable is set as part of the script:

```
    set end of valList to testVal
```

Hopefully, by now, you may be thinking of a project where do script can be used as part of your ammunition for automating a project. If so, see if you can write the script and insert it into a page item. Then, as needed, have a script extract the script and run it.

Hint:

Be sure to test the text contents of the inserted script before you try to run it. Set a variable to the result of the extract label statement and comment out the line that runs the script. Place the result variable at the bottom of the script to verify its contents.

Make Scripts Work for You

The **Newsletter** project for this chapter creates a fairly robust script starting with a script template. Many of the handlers used in the project should be familiar to you by now.

Procedure:

1. Open the **Newsletter** script template. Run the script just to verify its functionality. Save the script as **Newsletter Final**.

2. Add the **addTextVariables** handler (Text folder of the handlers library) to the bottom of the script. Cut the call to the handler and paste just before the my resetDefaultMeasures statement at the end of the PROCESS section of the script. Add my to the call and change the variable *tableWid* to *docWid*. The call should read as follows:

    ```
        my addTextVariables(docRef, slugFrame, docWid)
    ```

3. Add the **addMetadata** handler (Documents folder) to the bottom of the script. Cut the variable declarations and paste after the first try statement block at the top of the script. Change values for variables as needed. The value for *mAuthor* is set to use a fixed value. To set the value to the name of the current user, you might use the following:

    ```
        set AppleScript's text item delimiters to ":"
        set mAuthor to item -2 of (text items of homeFolder)
        set AppleScript's text item delimiters to ""
    ```

4. You will also want to change values for variables inside the **addMetadata** handler. The variables inside the handler, once set, are expected to be consistent. Cut the call to the handler and paste just below the call to **addTextVariables** (Step 2). Add the word my to the call if needed.

5. Because you will be saving the document created with this script as a template, you will want a **text variable** to be used instead of the fixed variable *dateString*. Remove the declaration for this variable at the top of the script. Instead you will change the values for the *leftFooter* and *rightFooter* variables as follows:

    ```
        set leftFooter to ¬
    ```

```
"Page " & «data utxt0018» & «data utxt2003» & pubName & «data utxt2003»
set rightFooter to "" & «data utxt2003» & pubName & «data utxt2003» ¬
    & "Page " & «data utxt0018»
```

The raw code «data utxt0018» is the current page number character; «data utxt2003» is an em space (see Chapter 14).

6. Instead of using an insertion point to add the current page number character, this script will use it to insert an Output Date **text variable instance**. For this you will need to establish the format for the text variable. Inside the `tell application` block in the PROCESS section, insert the following after `tell docRef`:

```
--set text variable "Output Date" format for document
set format of variable options of text variable "Output Date" to ¬
"MMMM d, yyyy"
```

7. The footers will need to have access to the Output Date text variable after its format has been set. For this reason, move the calls to **doFooter** after the lines added in Step 6 above. To avoid confusion, change the name of the handler to **doFolio**. The calls are now inside a tell statement to the application, so you will need to add the word *my* before each call. The location of the insertion point to place the text variable also changes. Make sure the calls read as follows:

```
my doFolio(docRef, masterRef, 1, layerRef, 12, 24, leftFooter, ¬
styleRef, -1, lAlign)
my doFolio(docRef, masterRef, 2, layerRef, 12, 24, rightFooter, ¬
styleRef, 1, rAlign)
```

8. Find the handler **doFooter** in the HANDLERS section. (Command+F for Find dialog.) Change its name to **doFolio**. In the handler set up a reference to the Output Date text variable. After `tell docRef` add:

```
set printDate to text variable "Output Date"
```

9. Next, inside the same handler replace the statement that sets the contents of the insertion point to auto page number using the following:

```
tell insertion point pageInsert of frameRef
   make text variable instance with properties {associated text ¬
   variable: printDate}
end tell
```

The PROCESS section of the script should now read as follows:

```
--FOR COLORS
--uncomment to add process colors to document; see colorList variable
--set existingList to createProcessColors(colorList)
--FOR FOOTER STYLE
(*If style not found, it is created using styleProps record.*)
set styleRef to getParastyle(docRef, paraStyleName, parastyleProps)
set layerRef to createLayers(docRef, layerNames, "Footer")
tell application "Adobe InDesign CS5"
    tell docRef
        --set text variable "Output Date" format for document
        set format of variable options of text variable "Output Date" to ¬
        "MMMM d, yyyy"
        (*Master spread, page number, layer name, offset, height, text, ¬
        style, page number insert, alignment.*)
        my doFolio (docRef, masterRef, 1, layerRef, 12, 24, leftFooter, ¬
        styleRef, -1, lAlign)
```

```
            my doFolio (docRef, masterRef, 2, layerRef, 12, 24, rightFooter, ¬
            styleRef, 1, rAlign)
            --import styles
            set stylesheetRef to my getStylesheet(stylesheetName)
            --booleans indicate styles to import: object, text, table
            my importStyles(docRef, stylesheetRef, true, true, false)
            --add container frames
            set frameProps to {applied object style:"[Basic Text Frame]"}
            set rectProps to {fill color:"None", stroke weight:0}
            set masterPageRef to page -1 of master spread 1
            set docWid to page width of document preferences
            set layerRef to layer "Furniture"
            set imageLayer to layer "Images"
        end tell
        set frameBounds to {-30, 24, 0, docWid - 24}
        set slugFrame to my namedPgItem(masterPageRef, text frame, ¬
        layerRef, frameBounds, frameProps, "Slug")
        set pageRef to page 1 of docRef
        set mHeadBounds to {topMargin, leftMargin, mHeadHgt, docWid - rightMargin}
        set mHeadFrame to my namedPgItem(pageRef, rectangle, imageLayer,¬
        mHeadBounds, rectProps, "Masthead")
        --add text variables to slug of document
        my addTextVariables(docRef, slugFrame, docWid)
        --add metadata
        my addMetadata(docRef, metaTitle, metaDesc, metaName, metaKeys, mAuthor)
        my resetDefaultMeasures(orighm, origvm, origro)
    end tell
```

10. Refer to **Newsletter_Final** in the project folder if you have problems.

11. Make changes to the commented description at the top of the script for future reference.

12. Test the script. Examine the document to make sure the result is as anticipated. Do the text variables display correctly? Were text styles imported? Notice that the first item in the slug is named "Untitled." This will change once the document is saved (assuming you give the document a name other than "Untitled").

13. Save the resulting document as a template in the Templates folder for InDesign. Name the template "Newsletter.indt."

20

Experience XML

Whatever your scope of automation, XML can be a key ingredient. If you are not familiar with XML, it is a method of using plain text to markup and store information. It is routinely used for exchanging data between applications and/or systems that would otherwise be incompatible. In essence, it defines what the individual elements of the data are and how they relate to one another. How XML works with InDesign is not a trivial subject. To cover all of the ways in which XML can be incorporated into an automated workflow would require a book of its own. This chapter will attempt to provide an overview to get you started.

As you will see, XML is all about structure: the structure of the data (content) and the structure of the document (layout). The separation of data from structure allows the same information to be displayed in diverse layouts and/or repurposed for display on other devices in addition to print. The best thing about XML is the support built into InDesign. In this chapter you will:

- Populate structured documents with text marked up using XML to style the import.
- Be introduced to scripts that can be used to build a structured document.

To view the structure for a document, the Structure bay for InDesign needs to be opened. Either select Structure > Show Structure from the View menu or type the keyboard shortcut Command + Option + 1.

XML Basics

XML data is hierarchal. Just like objects in InDesign, there is one parent object at the top of the parent/child family tree. The XML parent is usually referred to as the **root**. Under the root are branches or nodes (XML elements). Each node can be both a parent and child of other nodes in the structure. XML elements that are contained within the root element are said to be nested within the root. An element that is enclosed by another is called a child of the containing element. Conversely, the containing element is called the parent of its enclosed elements.

Nodes are related to corresponding objects in an InDesign document using XML tags. Tags provide the link between the XML element and the document. Tags can be related to styles (paragraph and character styles) to provide text styling. If for no other reason, the relationship of structure-to-tag-to-style in InDesign should be the basis for using text styles exclusively when developing a project. You never know when a "one-off" project may turn into a "let's do this again campaign." If your document uses styles exclusively, incorporating an XML workflow is a piece of cake. Structure your document and import the XML.

So where does XML data come from? Many databases and applications can generate an XML file for end use in publishing and for the web. InDesign's Story Editor (Edit > Edit in

XML Basics

Tags

Use angle brackets (< >) to set off tags from content. Every XML element must have an associated opening and closing tag to be valid.

<myTag>Will be styled using myTag if using tag to style mapping.</myTag>

Case

XML is a case-sensitive language: <myTag>, <MyTag>, and <MYTAG> are separate unrelated elements because of case.

Naming Convention

Element names in XML may only start with either a letter or underscore character. The rest of the name may consist of any mixture of letters, numbers, underscores, dots or hyphens. Spaces are not allowed in element names, nor can the name begin with the letters *xml* which is reserved for the XML specification.

Attributes

XML elements can contain one or more attributes which define values that are relevant to that element. Each attribute has a name and a value assigned with the assignment (=) operator. The naming convention for attributes follows that of element names. All attribute values must be enclosed in quotation marks to be valid.

Elements

Every valid XML document must have one single element that entirely encloses all the other elements in the document. This element is often called the *root* element.

Comments

Comments can be added to any source code to make the purpose clear when read by a third party, or when the source code is revisited after a period of time. XML uses the same syntax as HTML for comments so that any text that is inserted between "<!--" and "-->" is ignored by the XML parser.

Character Entities

There are five characters in the XML language that must use a special syntax to prevent the XML parser from interpreting the character as code. These character entities are represented in XML content as follows:

- &lt - the left angle bracket (<)
- &gt - the right angle bracket (>)
- &amp - the ampersand character (&)
- &apos - the single quote aprostrophe (')
- &quot - the double quotation mark (")

Prolog

An XML file must begin with a prolog that looks similar to the following. Notice that quotation marks are straight quotes.

```
<?xml version="1.0" encoding="UTF-8" standalone="yes"?>
```

Story Editor) can be used for those operations where editors have access to InDesign. Assign an XML tag to the story and export as XML. Otherwise, for the best editor-to-InDesign integration, Adobe InCopy CS5 (or CS5.5) is recommended. Databases as well as some data management applications such as FileMaker Pro work well with XML. For the web designer, Adobe Dreamweaver may be an excellent choice as it provides an easy method for creating, tagging, and editing XML data. Then, of course, there are the dedicated applications such as Syncro Soft oXygen and Altova XMLSpy. You can even create forms in Acrobat that can be emailed to your client for their completion. When the Submit button in an Acrobat form is clicked, the information can be sent back to you as XML. The bottom line: as long as you can get structured data, there is a way to automate it into InDesign.

Tagging

XML tags define what data elements are. If you have worked with InDesign Tagged Text or HTML, shifting gears to work with XML will make sense as similar tagging formats are used for mark up. All of these mark up methods identify data in a meaningful way, using angle brackets to identify tags as with <h1></h1> in HTML. In one way XML is the most flexible of the three markup languages in that it is not constrained by a required set of tag names. XML only defines a set of rules (see sidebar on facing page). For the rest it is up to you, your organization, or your industry, to determine what the tags will be and how the data will be structured. This extensibility is what gives XML its name (Extensible Markup Language). You extend the language by defining your own code words (tags) and determining how the data will be structured.

Note:

The naming convention for XML tags must conform to XML guidelines.

Structure

Structure defines how data elements relate to one another. You might think of XML structure as a topical outline of the elements that will be used for your document. A simplified structure could look similar to the following:

```
<document>
<article>
<headline>This is a headline</headline>
<byline>I wrote the story</byline>
<body>This is the text for the story. Working with XML is a cool way to work
with data as it separates content from structure.</body>
</article>
<article>
<headline>Headline for second article</headline>
<byline>Reported by John Doe</byline>
<body>This is the text for the second story.</body>
</article>
</document>
```

It is important to note that all elements have a beginning and ending tag, and must be correctly nested by using a closing inner tag before the closing tag of the outer parent element.

An XML file also needs to have an introductory statement at the top (*prolog*) that announces what kind of document it is. In its most basic form, a prolog looks like the following, showing the version of XML and Unicode encoding supported. The designation standalone="yes" indicates that no support files are required.

```
<?xml version="1.0" encoding="UTF-8" standalone="yes"?>
```

Add this header (prolog) to the structure above, and you have an XML file that InDesign should recognize.

But enough for theory. Let's take XML for a test drive. In the folder for this chapter you will find a number of projects that are based on XML. The projects include an XML file along with the resources needed to work with the included document. The first project to explore is the one called **Merge Import**. It demonstrates working with a simple XML structure.

Hands-On XML

Merge Import

From the **Merge Import** project folder, open the file "SimpleStructure.xml" in your favorite text editor. You will see that it includes a prolog at the top followed by the XML data. Notice the line returns at the end of paragraphs. These will be part of the paragraph when imported. The line return forces the ending tag to be on the following line. Study the structure to understand how tags nest inside one another.

Your first task will be to import this file manually into an InDesign document. For this, the document "SimpleStructure.indd" is provided. Open the document. From the File menu choose Import XML. Select the file "SimpleStructure.xml." For import options make sure Mode is Merge Content. With exception of "Do not import contents of whitespace only elements," all check boxes should not be checked. Click OK to continue the import.

View the XML structure in the Structure bay to the left of the document window. If not open, open it from the View menu (View > Structure > Open Structure), or use the keyboard shortcut (Command + Option + 1). Expand the Root element in the bay by clicking on the twisty triangle to its left. You will see that the structure for this document allows two articles inside the Root node. Inside of these nodes are three elements (see Figure 20.1).

If not already opened, open the Tags panel for InDesign (Window > Utilities > Tags). If you click on a frame for one of the articles, you will see its tag highlighted in the Tags panel. Enable Show Frames from the View menu (View> Structure > Show Tagged Frames) and the tagged frames will be colored to match the color of its tag. Although rudimentary, we can say

Figure 20.1: Structure panel with file "SimpleStructure.xml" imported.

that the document is structured. Later, you will learn how to structure a document with tags and XML elements defined. For now, let's look at importing an XML file using a script.

Importing an XML File

To import an XML file into InDesign with a script, you first need to set up some import preferences for the document (**XML import preferences**). These preferences are critical and need to be set appropriately depending on the automation technique used. If you set these preferences up incorrectly, the process may not complete satisfactorily, or worse, InDesign may quietly quit without warning. For now, the only property you need to be concerned with is **import style**, which has two options:

merge import - Clears out existing structure in document. The imported XML will be the only structure remaining.

append import - Adds the structure for the XML file to the existing structure in the document.

You will get an opportunity to work with some of the other preferences later in this chapter.

To set up XML preferences for a merge import, you may wish to use the handler **xmlImportPrefs**. The handlers provided for working with XML are in the folder XML in the Handlers Library (see Chapter 1). To import the XML file, the handler **importXMLFile** assumes that **XML import preferences** have been set up appropriately for the document. See how these two handlers are used in the script for the **Merge Import** project :

Merge Import

```
set doRepeat to false
set homeFolder to path to home folder from user domain as string
try
    set dLocation to homeFolder & ¬
    ("AppleScripts for CS5:Chapter 20:Merge Import") as alias
    set docRef to getDocRef()
    --set up XML import preferences
    xmlImportPrefs(docRef, doRepeat)
    --second parameter is an alias reference to file or missing value
    importXMLFile(docRef, missing value, dLocation)
on error errStr
    display alert errStr
end try

(*User chooses file if fileRef is missing value. File is then imported.*)
on importXMLFile(docRef, fileRef, dLocation)
    if fileRef = missing value then
        set fileRef to choose file with prompt "Select XML file to import" ¬
        default location dLocation without invisibles and ¬
        multiple selections allowed
        set theInfo to info for fileRef
        if name extension of theInfo is not "xml" then
            error "XML file not chosen"
        end if
    end if
    tell application "Adobe InDesign CS5"
        tell docRef
            import XML from fileRef
        end tell
```

```
        end tell
    end importXMLFile
    (*Sets up XML import preferences for merge import*)
    on xmlImportPrefs(docRef, doRepeat)
        tell application "Adobe InDesign CS5"
            tell XML import preferences
                set create link to XML to false
                set allow transform to false
                set import style to merge import
                set repeat text elements to doRepeat
                set import to selected to false
                set ignore whitespace to true
                set ignore unmatched incoming to false
                set import CALS tables to false
                set import text into tables to false
                set remove unmatched existing to false
            end tell
        end tell
    end xmlImportPrefs
    (*Add handler getDocRef (Document folder) to complete the script.*)
```

To test the script, open the document "SimpleStructure.indd." Run the script and select the file "Simple Structure.xml" when prompted. Keep the document open for a later test.

Next test the script with the document "MappedStructure.indd" choosing the same XML file when prompted. The reason for the difference is the layout for the "SimpleStructure" document has not had the XML tags mapped to correspond to paragraph styles. The easiest way to do this is to use tag-to-style mapping. This requires the name for the paragraph styles in the document to be the same as the tags in the imported XML file. In setting up a document for XML import you can save yourself a lot of work if you make sure that your text style names match the tags used in the XML file.

Switch back to the "SimpleStructure.indd" document. Run the **Map Tags** script from the project to have the following handler map the tags for you.

Map Tags

```
    set docRef to document 1 of application "Adobe InDesign CS5"
    mapTags(docRef)

    (*Uses XML tag to style to map styles.*)
    on mapTags(docRef)
        tell application "Adobe InDesign CS5"
            tell docRef
                set tagList to XML tags
                repeat with i from 1 to length of tagList
                    set tagName to name of item i of tagList
                    if (exists paragraph style tagName) then
                        set styleRef to paragraph style tagName
                        make XML import map with properties {mapped style: ¬
                            styleRef, markup tag:item i of tagList}
                    end if
                end repeat
                map XML tags to styles
            end tell
        end tell
    end mapTags
```

Adding Images

In an XML file, any text outside of the tag's angle brackets is considered literal text.

An image has no literal text so the content portion of its tag is empty. Elements that do not enclose any child elements or textual data are called empty elements. The path to an image is defined inside an empty element using markup borrowed from HTML: *href*.

```
opening tag with href        relative file reference        closing tag

<Photo href = "file//filename.ext"></Photo>
```

To reference a file using XML, either a relative or absolute path to the file can be used. An absolute path defines the entire path from the server down to the file.

```
<photo1 href="file:///serverName/folderName/images/imageName.jpg"></photo1>
```

The more flexible reference, a relative path, defines the path to the image relative to the XML file.

```
<photo1 href="file://images/imageName.jpg"></photo1>
```

Although either a relative or absolute reference can be used, it is often best to reference image files relative to the XML file. The slashes indicate the relative reference to the folder containing the XML file. From there the file's path can be built. In the example below, images are located in a folder called Images residing at the same level as the XML file. Notice that an empty element can have a closing tag, as above, or can use a shorthand method that combines both opening and closing tags, adding the closing slash at the end of the opening tag:

```
<photo1 href="file://Images/Picture 1.psd"/>
```

To get some experience using an image, the project **XML With Photo** provides a sample document, "XMLwPhoto.indd", as well as resources for XML import. Open the document and examine the Structure bay for InDesign, the Paragraph Styles panel, and Tags panel. Notice that paragraph styles have been defined for the document, but tags have not been mapped to the styles. The script **XML With Photo** is almost the same as the **Merge Import** script, with the exception that code has been added to reference the XML file from the script's path. In order for this to work, you will need to create an alias to the script and place it in one of InDesign's script folders. Run the script from the Scripts panel using the document for testing. Part of the script is shown below:

```
set xmlFileName to "XMLwPhoto.xml"
set doRepeat to false
try
    set docRef to getDocRef()
    --set up XML import preferences
    xmlImportPrefs(docRef, doRepeat)
```

```
        set folderPath to scriptParentPath()
        set filePath to folderPath & xmlFileName
        importXMLFile(docRef, filePath, missing value)
        mapTags(docRef)
    on error errStr
        display alert errStr
    end try

    (*Returns path to parent folder of active script.*)
    on scriptParentPath()
        tell application "Adobe InDesign CS5"
            set scriptPath to active script as string
        end tell
        set theOffset to offset of ":" in (reverse of (characters of scriptPath) ¬
        as string)
        set folderPath to text 1 thru -theOffset of scriptPath
        return folderPath
    end scriptParentPath
    (*Add handlers xmlImportPrefs (XML folder) mapTags (XML folder) importXMLFile
    (XML folder) and getDocRef (Document folder) to complete script.*)
```

XML Attributes

Other than the tag name itself, text inside tag brackets are attributes of the element. In
addition to the href attribute (used to define the file path for an image), an XML element
can have any number of attributes. Attributes are not well suited for containing explicit data,
and are more typically used to supply information about the element's content. This data is
called meta-information.

Each attribute for an XML element must have a name and a value. The attribute value is
defined using the assignment operator (=) and is enclosed in quotes. When the value of the
attribute is a string, it needs to be enclosed by quotes (single quotes inside of double quotes
or vice versa).

This example uses the shorthand method for the end closer of an element with an attribute.

```
<Image href="file://images/fileName" credit="'James Taylor'"/>
```

Attributes that Style Text

Interestingly, you can use attributes with text content to designate the paragraph and/or
character style to be applied to the element's contents when placed in InDesign. For this
an aid:pstyle attribute is used to define the paragraph style name and an aid:cstyle
attribute is used to define a character style. To add the aid attributes to the XML document,
the Adobe InDesign version 4.0 XML namespace needs to be defined as an attribute for a
node in the XML. This definition needs to occur in a parent element before the aid attribute
is used. For this, the root node is generally used.

```
<?xml version="1.0" encoding="UTF-8" standalone="yes"?>
<Root xmlns:aid="http://ns.adobe.com/AdobeInDesign/4.0/">
<Story1>
<Category aid:pstyle="Category">Large Animal Anesthesia</Category>
<Description aid:style="Description">The Z100 by <Bold
aid:cstyle="Bold">Northland Medical</Bold> is a support system for large
animals equipped with the reconfigured <Italic aid:cstyle="Italic">Draper
</Italic> ventilator. </Description></Story1></Root>
```

Notice that the name of the element may or may not be the same as the name of the style. You will find an XML file and a document for testing in the project **Aid Text Attributes** (in the folder for this chapter). The tags and styles have been defined for this document. The script to use for importing the XML is **Aid Attributes**.

Place XML

For a simple layout where all text elements can be contained by a single text frame (or one text frame link), you can forego the need for tagging frames and use a page or spread to place the contents of the XML. What makes this possible is the **Place XML** command. When the page (or spread) places XML, there are three parameters provided:

using - The XML element whose content will be used.

place point - The y-x coordinate on the page (or spread) to use for placement. Notice that the place point coordinates are opposite from other place coordinates (y, or vertical, is the first list item).

autoflowing - True or false indicating whether to autoflow the story.

The project, **Biz Card_1up**, demonstrates. The script **Biz Card_1up** uses place XML with a place point defined by the master text frame. It introduces the handler **placeXMLFile**, which uses a y-x coordinate to place the file. If missing value is supplied for the file reference, the user is asked to choose the file from the folder defined by the variable *dLocation*. Following is the handler **placeXMLFile** from the script.

```
(*parameters:document, page, XMLElement, place point, autoflow, file
reference, default location*)
placeXMLFile(docRef, pageRef, rootElement, placePt, doRepeat, missing value,¬
dLocation)

(*User chooses file if fileRef is missing value. File is then imported.*)
on placeXMLFile(docRef, pageRef, XMLElement, placePt, useAutoflow, fileRef, ¬
dLocation)
    if fileRef = missing value then
        set fileRef to choose file with prompt "Select XML file to import" ¬
        default location dLocation without invisibles and ¬
        multiple selections allowed
        set theInfo to info for fileRef
        if name extension of theInfo is not "xml" then
            error "XML file not chosen."
        end if
    end if
    tell application "Adobe InDesign CS5"
        tell docRef
            import XML from fileRef
        end tell
        tell pageRef
            place XML using XMLElement place point placePt autoflowing ¬
            useAutoflow
        end tell
    end tell
end placeXMLFile
```

Run the **Biz Card_1up** script with the "Biz Card_1up.indd" document open. Select the XML file "Biz Card_1up.xml" when prompted. Do not save the document. You will need the original for the next discussion.

Note:

Place point for XML lists the coordinates in the order y,x (vertical before horizontal), which is different from most other point coordinates in InDesign which list the coordinates in the order x,y.

The **placePtMasterFrame** handler can be used when you need to have the master text frame on the master page define the point at which to place a file . It is written to use A-Master (the first master page of the document), but could be modified to accept any master page.

```
(*Uses Master Frame or page margins to determine place point*)
on placePtMasterFrame(docRef)
    tell application "Adobe InDesign CS5"
        tell docRef
            if master text frame of document preferences is false then
                error "Requires master text frame"
            end if
            tell page 1 of master spread 1
                if (exists text frame "Master Frame") then
                    set gBounds to geometric bounds of text frame "Master Frame"
                else
                    tell margin preferences of it
                        set gBounds to {top, left}
                    end tell
                end if
            end tell
            set y0 to item 1 of gBounds
            set x0 to item 2 of gBounds
        end tell
    end tell
    return {y0, x0}
end placePtMasterFrame
```

Other Place Commands

When a page item places XML (**place XML** command), there is only one parameter: **using**.

An XML element is similar to a page item in that it can place an XML file using the **place XML** command. In this case, the value of the **using** parameter can be a page item, a story, a graphic, movie, or sound object.

An XML element also has the following commands that allow its contents to be placed:

place into copy - Creates a copy of a page item as the content is placed. Parameters are: **on** (page, spread, or master spread), **place point**, **copy item**, and a boolean, **retain existing frame**, which, if true, associates the XML element with the existing page item and moves the page item to the place point.

place into frame - Creates a rectangular page item to hold contents as part of the XML being placed. Parameters are: **on** (page, spread, or master spread) and a list for geometric bounds.

place into inline copy - Similar to **place into copy,** this command has only two parameters: **copy item** and **retain existing frame.**

place into inline frame - Similar to **place into frame** but has only one parameter: **dimensions** a list which describes the width and height of the inline frame.

When you need to repeat a layout within a document or on a page, you may find using one of the place XML commands indispensable.

Multiple Items

Suppose you are asked to create the business card used in the **Biz Card_1up** project for each name in a database. For this you need to understand the database concept of records and fields. If you have ever worked with a database, you know that each row in a data table is a record. Data elements within a row are separated into table columns (fields). For instance, you could have a data table called Employees. Inside of this table is a number of rows—one row for each employee. For each employee (record), data fields (columns) could include name, title, email address, and so forth.

The data for the Biz Card_1up business card has the following XML structure:

```
<Root>
<Employee>
<name>data</Name>
<Title>data</Title>
<Email>data</Email>
</Employee>
</Root>
```

The parent node for each record in this structure is Employee. Ideally, when a document needs to work with a number of data records, you will want to confine the data fields to a single story flow. In the following example, a separate page in the InDesign document will be created for each record as the result of the **autoflow** parameter being set to true and the **repeat text elements** property of **XML import preferences** being set to true (*doRepeat* variable). Although the times that you might need a one-up business card may be next to none, the same general principle can be applied to a project where page formatting is the same, just the data changes.

Biz Card 1up_Multiple

When no text frame is designated to contain the XML, placing data to a place point places the data on the page. The frame for the data is defined by the margins and/or columns of the page. When you need to repeat the same layout on a number of pages, using place XML with the page (or spread) allows the autoflow parameter to be set as part of the place XML method. With autoflowing, the text is free to flow from page to page with pages created as needed.

To use autoflow, the following guidelines are required:

- A single story flow is used for all data records.
- Data fields for a record are child elements of a single XML node.
- The place point used must be inside of the margins for the page.
- The **start paragraph** property for the first paragraph of each record needs to be next column or next page as appropriate. This forces each record to be on a separate page or column.

Change the value of the *doRepeat* variable for the **Biz Card_1up** script to true. Run it with the "Biz Card_1up" document. Choose the file "Biz Card_Multiple.xml" when prompted.

Creating a Template for XML from Original

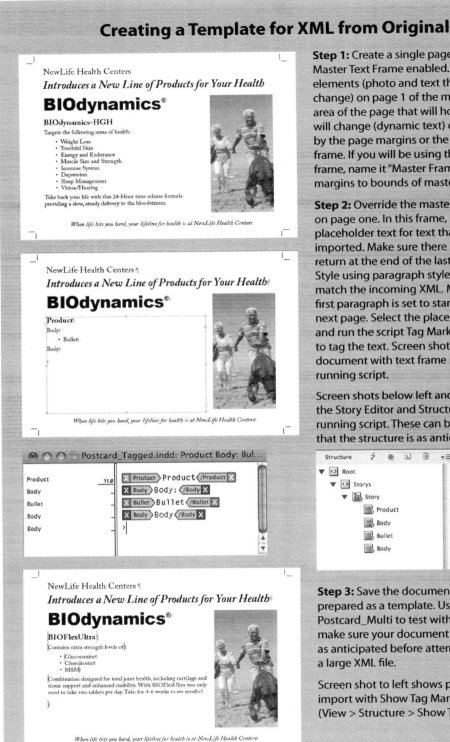

Step 1: Create a single page document with Master Text Frame enabled. Place all static elements (photo and text that does not change) on page 1 of the master spread. The area of the page that will hold the text that will change (dynamic text) can be identified by the page margins or the master text frame. If you will be using the master text frame, name it "Master Frame." Match margins to bounds of master frame.

Step 2: Override the master text frame on page one. In this frame, substitute placeholder text for text that will be imported. Make sure there is a paragraph return at the end of the last paragraph. Style using paragraph styles named to match the incoming XML. Make sure the first paragraph is set to start paragraph on next page. Select the placeholder text frame and run the script Tag Markup Paragraphs to tag the text. Screen shot to left shows document with text frame selected before running script.

Screen shots below left and below show the Story Editor and Structure panel after running script. These can be used to verify that the structure is as anticipated.

Step 3: Save the document you have prepared as a template. Use the script Postcard_Multi to test with sample data to make sure your document and script work as anticipated before attempting to import a large XML file.

Screen shot to left shows page after XML import with Show Tag Markers enabled (View > Structure > Show Tag Markers).

Using Placeholder Text

For layouts that require a more restricted structure, you will want to use placeholder text to set up a format model to represent how the data will be styled. For this workflow you set the **repeat text elements** property of XML import preferences to true. As the name of this property implies, a value of true allows the format model to be repeated on one page and/or over a series of pages.

The placeholder text for a format model is styled with paragraph styles and defines the structure for the XML record's fields. The actual text for placeholders can be anything, but common practice is to use the name of the tag and/or paragraph style used for the data field.

Suppose you have a product sheet that you have prepared and the client now wants to use the same layout for a number of products. The data for the products will be supplied as XML. The procedure for preparing the layout is demonstrated in the project **Postcard_NoImage**. The resources for this project are referenced in the following discussion.

To prepare the layout to receive XML, you will want all of the dynamic text to be contained by the master text frame. Make sure the page margins match the bounds of the master text frame (see the sample document "Postcard_Orig.indd"). Text and images that don't change are placed in other frames on the master page.

Override the master text frame on page one. In this frame, create a placeholder for each text field. Even though some of the text fields may have more than one paragraph, you will want only one placeholder to represent each field. Make sure that there is a paragraph return at the end of the last placeholder and that there are no empty paragraphs. Placeholders need to be styled with paragraph styles named to conform to the XML tags used in the XML file. The paragraph style for the first paragraph will need to have **keep options start paragraph** set to in next column or on next page (see the sample document "Postcard_Ready.indd").

With this accomplished, select the container that will receive the XML data, and run the script **Tag Markup Paragraphs**. Accept the default name for the tag ("Story"). The script tags and marks up the frame, as well as each of the paragraphs in the frame. Check out the Structure bay when the script completes. (The result should be like the sample document "Postcard_Tagged.indd.") Notice that the script creates a parent XML element with the same name as the frame's tag only, with an "s" appended.

See how this works using the document "Postcard Tagged.indd." Run the script **Postcard_Multi** to import the XML file provided ("Postcard_NoImage.xml"). Select this file when prompted.

In a real world situation, you might want to export the document as XML after tagging. The exported XML file produced can be used as a guide for structuring the data for import.

Anchoring Elements in Text Flow

So, you may be thinking, this is well and good for a layout that uses text only, but what about images? If you will recall, anchored objects allow graphics to be "tied" to a text frame or text, and as such will flow with the text. Additionally, you are not limited to using anchored objects just for graphics. Text can also be placed in an anchored container. For imported XML that includes images, use a single text frame for the XML text, and anchor frames for those items that need to be in separate containers.

There are a few points you need to remember in using this type of layout:

- Add the anchored objects after the text is tagged. If you add the objects manually, you will need to create the XML tag and associate it with the anchored object's container.

- Using a text frame to place XML breaks the ability of the XML data stream to flow between pages. You will need to use one of the place into XML commands, such as **place into frame**, to place the XML after it is imported.

- The physical anchor marker must be outside of any XML tags. Show tag markers (View > Structure > Show Tag Markers) to make sure that you don't place an anchor inside of a tag. You can double check the story in the Story Editor if needed. (With insertion point in the story flow, use the keystroke combination Command + Y.)

- Using an object style for anchored objects assures consistency.

Postcard With Image

The **Postcard_Image** project demonstrates using an anchored object to hold the image that will change with each data record. Open the document "Postcard_Image.indd." Place the insertion point inside the story flow. Use the keyboard shortcut to open the Story Editor window (Command-Y). Notice that the container tag (*Story*) does not display, just the contents of the story. The anchor marker is outside of the first XML tag. Close the Story Editor and save the document using a different name.

Run the script Postcard_Image to import and place the XML. Choose "Postcard_Image.xml" when prompted. The script targets the second page of the document for placement. Other than that, it is similar to the one used for **Postcard_NoImage**. The big difference is in how the XML structure is modeled, and in the XML file itself. Run the script **Postcard_Image** and select the file "Postcard_Image.xml" when prompted.

Creating a Template with Anchored Items

The document "Postcard_Image.indd" is typical of a document prepared to receive repeating XML data that includes images. To work through the procedure for creating a similar document, open the document "Postcard_Image Orig.indd." Follow the procedure for tagging and marking up placeholder text as outlined for the **Postcard_noImage** project. When you run the script **Tag Markup Paragraphs**, use the name "Story" for the placeholder frame.

Note

Make sure there is a return character at the end of the last placeholder paragraph before running the Tag Markup Paragraphs script.

Once you have tagged and marked up the text placeholders, you will want to add the anchored element to the structure. To assist you, the script **Anchor Placeholder** is provided.

With the placeholder text frame selected, run the **Anchor Placeholder** script. You will be asked to choose an image. Choose one of the images from the Images folder inside the project folder. The script places the image, anchors it, removes the image from the anchored frame, and tags it. Save the completed document. If you anticipate using this document on more than one occasion, save it also as a template. Now you are ready to add the XML.

Run the script **Postcard_Image**. Select the file "Postcard_Image.xml" when prompted. Because the Images folder is in the same folder as the XML file, the images place along with the text in the XML file.

Repeating XML Items

For those situations that require more than one item (*data record*) on a page, the procedure is similar to the postcard projects, but involves an additional step: creating text frames for each XML item on a page and linking to create a single text flow.

The next example project, **Biz Card_4up**, demonstrates. Open the document "Biz Card_4up.indd." The document has a format model in the first linked text frame. The model frame has placeholder text defined for each of the data fields. A container for the image is anchored to the text frame. This way, all elements for each record are contained within a single text frame (the *data record container*). The data record containers are linked and the first frame named "Employee" for identification.

Run the script **Biz Card_4up** and select the file "Biz Card_4up.xml" when prompted. The script populates the cards with the XML. Notice in the script that the first text frame in the linked frames (named "Employee") places the XML using the root element (*elementRef*). To perform the magic, **autoflowing** needs to be set to true. In addition to the handlers **getDocRef**, **XMLClonePrefs**, and **chooseFileExtTest**, the script introduces the handler **framePlaceXML**:

```
(*Boolean value determines autoflow*)
framePlaceXML(docRef, frameName, fileRef, true)

(*Text frame places XML after file is imported to the root element*)
on framePlaceXML(docRef, frameName, fileRef, doAutoflow)
    tell application "Adobe InDesign CS5"
        tell docRef
            set frameRef to text frame frameName
            set elementRef to XML element 1
        end tell
        tell elementRef to import XML from fileRef
        tell frameRef
            place XML using elementRef autoflowing doAutoflow
        end tell
    end tell
end FramePlaceXML
```

Setting up a Multiple Item Template

The secret to having the import XML procedure work in the **Biz Card_4up** project is in how the template is set up. Refer to the step-by-step on the next page. Make sure that the text frame for the XML imported text is as large as needed to accommodate the text and the anchored item, if used.

Create the document with Master Text Frame enabled. Set number of pages to 1. On Layer 1 of A-Master resize the master text fame and/or page margins as needed to accommodate the dynamic text and anchored objects for the first data record. Run the script **Grid Items_Dlg** with the text frame on the master page selected to create and link the text frames for each of the other corresponding containers on the master page. Return to page one. Add and style

Template for Multiple Items on Multiple Pages

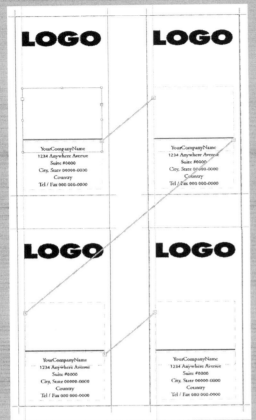

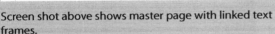

Step 1: Create the document with Master Text Frame enabled. Set number of pages to 1.

Step 2: On master spread A-Master, resize the master text frame as needed to accommodate the dynamic text for the first item.

Step 3: Create text frames for each of the remaining items to be placed on the page. Link the frames. Use the script Grid Items_Oride to automate this for you.

Step 4: Return to the first page. If the first master frame is not overridden, Command+Shift click on the first frame on the page to override it.

Step 5: In the overridden frame add placeholder text for each XML field to be imported. Make sure there is a paragraph return after the last paragraph. Style placeholder text with paragraph styles matching tags for the incoming XML. The style for the first paragraph needs to have Start Paragraph set to In Next Frame.

Screen shot above shows master page with linked text frames.

Step 6: Select the text frame that holds the placeholder text. Run the script Tag Markup Paragraphs.

Step 7: You will be asked to enter the name for the repeating data record. It must match the tag for the incoming XML.

Step 8: If an anchored frame is required, place the insertion point next to the placeholder to which it will be associated (outside of the tag for the placeholder). Alternatively, select the frame for the placeholders.

Step 9: Change settings if needed for the script Anchor Placeholder. Run the script and enter the tag name for the anchored object to match the tag of the incoming XML. Select the image to be associated when prompted.

Step 10: Verify that tags are created correctly and save the document as a template.

placeholder text in the first master frame using style names to match the incoming XML. Be sure there is a paragraph return after the last placeholder, and the first placeholder's style is set for Start Paragraph: In Next Frame. With the placeholder text created, select its parent text frame and run the script **Tag Markup Paragraphs** to tag and markup the placeholder text. Add anchored objects as needed. Check your structure in InDesign's Structure pane to make sure it matches the structure of your XML file.

Line Returns and Whitespace

When working with placeholder text, the subject of line returns and whitespace becomes a critical issue. Realize that InDesign replaces the content between tag markers in the document with the content between the tags in the XML file.

If you insert a line return at the end of the content before the element's ending tag, the line return will be interpreted as part of the XML text. This is true for both the story structure and the XML file. Static text is not replaced by incoming XML. This can cause problems in the XML not flowing as expected. If you use the **Tag Markup Paragraphs** script to markup text, you will notice that the line returns for the paragraphs are not included inside the tags. When attaching an anchored object, make sure that the insertion point is outside of the adjacent tag before adding the anchored object. You may wish to use either the **Anchor Placeholder** or **Anchor Placeholder_Dlg** script to create an anchored placeholder for the image.

There is a bright side to the line return/whitespace dilemma. You can put text or anchored objects outside of tags in the story structure for text that you don't want replaced by the XML. A typical example would be a product page where a static headline is used to separate sections such as Ingredients and Description in a recipe, or for subheadings as in the next example.

Static Text Inside XML Record

To allow for static text within each imported XML record you will want to set XML import preferences **ignore whitespace** to true, and **ignore unmatched incoming** to false. The project **Wines**, demonstrates. Open the **Wines** script in this project. The handler **xmlStaticPrefs** sets the following XML import preferences to true; all others (except import styles) are false.

```
set repeat text elements to true
set ignore whitespace to true
```

Open the document "Wines.indd" and look at the Structure bay as well as the contents of the Story Editor (Command+Y with insertion point in text frame). Run the **Wines** script and select the file "Wines.xml" when prompted.

Notice the similarity of the script to the other demonstration scripts in this chapter. The big difference is in the values for XML import preferences and how the XML model structure is set up.

Ignore Missing Elements

When working with placeholder text, you need to create a model structure that matches the structure of the XML content you plan to import. Right? Well, mostly. The structures do not need to be an exact match. But the sequence of elements in the model and the sequence of elements in the incoming XML file must match.

Let's look at an example. Suppose your model structure is as follows:

```
<Root>
<Books>
<Book>
<Category>Category here</Category>
<Author>Author here</Author>
<Title>Title here</Title>
</Book>
</Books>
</Root>
```

The problem is that you only want the content of the element <Category> to appear over the first book in each category. InDesign XML import preferences has an answer for this: **ignore unmatched incoming**.

```
tell application "Adobe InDesign CS5"
    tell XML import preferences of document 1 to ¬
    set ignore unmatched incoming  to true
end tell
```

In the folder for this chapter, the project **Book Catalog** is designed to demonstrate this concept. First, open the XML file in your favorite text editor. Notice only a few items actually have the Category element tag. Open the document "Book Catalog.indd" and look at the structure for the XML model. With the document open, run the script **Books** and select the XML file "Books.xml" when prompted. Sit back and watch the magic.

Make Scripts Work for You

For more experience working with some of the scripts in this chapter, the **Business Card** project uses the scripts **Tag Markup Paragraphs**, **Anchor Placeholder_8up**, and **Biz Card_8up** to automate an 8-up business card layout for an XML import. Scripts are in the **Business Card** project folder as well as in the XML folder for InDesign's Scripts panel.

1. Start with the document "Business Card_8up.indd" open. Run the script **Biz Card_8up**. When prompted select the file "Biz Card_8up.xml."

2. Using "Business Card_8up.indd" as a guide, see if you can prepare a similar document using the scripts with the project. For this you will start with the document "Business Card_8up Dieline.indd."

3. In the document's master page, create a text frame for the dynamic text (Layer 1). Make sure the frame is large enough to accommodate the anchored image file. With the frame selected, run the script **Grid Frames_8up**. Use default value presented in the dialog.

4. Switch to the first page of the document. Override the first master text frame. In this frame, create text placeholders for Name, Title, and Cel using paragraph styles of the same name. Make sure there is a paragraph return after the last paragraph.

5. With the text placeholder frame selected, run the script **Tag Markup Paragraphs**. Set the tag for the story element name to "Employee."

6. With the text placeholder frame still selected, run the script **Anchor Placeholder_8up**. Select one of the images from the Images folder for the project. Save your prepared document.

7. Run the script **Biz Card_8up** and select the file "Biz Card_8up.xml" when prompted.

You should be convinced by now that XML definitely gives you a leg up when it comes to an automated workflow. This discussion has only scratched the surface of what can be done with XML. The subject is huge.

21

M is for "Multi"

M is for multiple and multipurpose, that is. Which goes to say that a multitude of automation techniques can fall into this classification. This chapter will explore a few. The projects you will be working with in this chapter share the following:

- They work with multiple documents.
- They depend on resources saved in pre-determined folders on the desktop.
- More than one script is involved. Each script automates a discrete step (module) within the project's workflow. Working with modules is similar to building scripts using handlers. It is easier to build a workflow one step at a time as there are fewer issues to deal with; and consequently, fewer things can go awry. Furthermore, once built, a module can be used without major modification in any number of workflows.

Before we jump headlong into the chapter's projects, you need to have a heads-up on some issues dealing with multiple documents.

Multiple Documents

Throughout the book, scripts have made reference to the document using one of the following:

```
document 1

active document
```

These statements can be used interchangeably and for most purposes will be all you need. On the other hand, there are some instances you may need to refer to the document using some other reference.

As of version CS5.0, InDesign refers to documents by their id. This can be seen by running the following with a document open:

```
tell application "Adobe InDesign CS5"
    set docRef to active document
end tell
--document id 6 of application "Adobe InDesign CS5"
```

In earlier versions of InDesign the reference is to the document by name. Because of this, scripts can run into a problem when working with more than one document. The value of a variable that references document 1 can change. This is demonstrated in the following.

```
set publicFolder to path to public folder from user domain as string
set folderPath to publicFolder & "Test:"
set docName to "TestDoc.indd"
set docPath to folderPath & docName
tell application "Adobe InDesign CS5"
    make document
```

```
        set docRef to document 1
        save docRef to docPath with force save
        make document
        set test to name of docRef
    end tell
```

The result of running the script above in CS5 results in the name of the first document ("TestDoc.indd"). In earlier versions, the result would be the untitled document because the variable *docRef* points to document 1 and document 1 is the untitled document at the end of the script.

When working with multiple documents your script can make sure the first document will be the active document (document 1) in the code above by adding the following before the statement that tests the document's name.

```
        set active document to docRef
```

A problem with multiple documents open can arise when it comes to a selection reference. This occurs when the application is the specifier of a selection statement. A selection in any other than the front-most document (document 1) is not recognized. Your script needs to make sure the document in question is the active document. To see this in action, close the two documents created with the previous script. Change the code to read as follows:

```
    set publicFolder to path to public folder from user domain as string
    set folderPath to publicFolder & "Test:"
    set docName to "TestDoc.indd"
    set docPath to folderPath & docName
    tell application "Adobe InDesign CS5"
        make document
        set docRef to active document
        save docRef to docPath
        set docRef1 to make document
        tell docRef
            set rectRef to make rectangle with properties {geometric bounds:¬
            {"6p0", "3p0", "9p0", "10p0"}}
            select rectRef existing selection replace with
        end tell
        set selList to selection --this is the statement in question
        set test to length of selList
    end tell
    test
```

Although the rectangle is selected in the first document, the variable *test* has the value of zero (0). Move the highlighted statement (sets the value of *selList)* inside the tell block for the document and the problem is solved.

Books

The book object is not just for books. It does wonders when it comes to combining multiple documents into one book publication. But the book object does more. It ties the documents together so they can share attributes, formats, and page numbering. Even if you do not need the page numbering and indexing capability, you will want to take advantage of a book's ability to share formats between its documents.

Suppose you have a number of documents that need to update formatting. Rather than painstakingly updating each document manually, you can book them and use synchronizing to update them all in one fell swoop.

Book Project

The **Book** project includes a script that may make your book projects a little easier on your time budget. For whatever reason you may need to create a book, the script **Create Book** can be used. To book a number of documents the following procedure may be followed.

1. Place the files to be booked and possibly synchronized in a single folder.

2. If you want the files to book in order, you will want to make sure that they are named alphabetically. (Remember: a space comes before any alpha or number character.)

3. If you will be synchronizing the documents, you may want to name the file that will serve as the style source so it will be the first in the book list.

Note

Files in a book are ordered alphabetically. If you do not want to rename the Style Source document to make it appear first, you can always designate the style source once the book is created.

---

4. You may want to copy the **Create Book** script to one of InDesign's designated script folders so you can run the script from InDesign's Scripts panel.

5. If you have books and/or documents open, you will be asked to close the documents before running the script.

6. When prompted, select the folder with the files for booking.

7. A second prompt will have you designate the folder and name for the book file.

8. Once the book is created, you will want to verify (or designate) the style source document.

9. Select synchronizing options from the Book menu (small down arrow at top right of Book panel). Click the Synchronize button from the synchronize Options dialog. Alternatively, you might create a script that synchronizes the documents for you. The following statement will be needed as part of that script: (See the script **Create And Synchronize** that is part of the Chapter Scripts for this chapter.)

Table of Contents

Undoubtedly you know how to create a table of contents manually. It's not a big deal. But should you consistently produce documents all with similar setups, you could save some time and user effort with a script. The script, **Create TOC Style**, included in the **Book** project creates a TOC style from fixed values hard-coded in the script. The script imports the TOC paragraph styles from a style sheet. It references three levels using a list of lists: *entryList*. Each item in *entryList* lists the name of the document style, the TOC paragraph style, the separator character (tab), and the name of the character style to use for the separator. The fifth value can be `missing value` indicating that the style for the page number will use the same styling as for the entry. The last value in the list can be "None" or `missing value`. If "None" the page number will not be included with the entry.

The *entryList* reads as follows. Note the tab character ("\t") which is one of the list items.

```
set entryList to {{"Chapter Title", "Level_1", "\t", "Leader", missing value,
    "None"}, {"Head 1", "Level_2", "\t", "Leader", "PageNum", missing value}, ¬
    {"Head 2", "Level_3", "\t", "Leader", "PageNum", missing value}}
```

When you run the script, the Table of Contents style ("TOCstyle") is created. You can then open the Table of Contents dialog (Layout > Table of Contents) and tweak your style if needed. Click OK in the dialog to create the table of contents. The resulting text is loaded to InDesign's place gun for placement. You will want to have the document for the table of contents open when you run the script. If this is to be a separate document, make sure it is has the same text styles as the other documents in the book. Add it to the book's contents.

Index

Depending on the project, creating an index can be an arduous task. You might consider getting a head start by creating the index topics first using a script. With topics pre-created, adding entry references becomes easier and more consistent. For this you have two options:

- Read the topics from an existing text file.
- Import topics from a standing document such as a style sheet.

The script **Index Topics** gives the user the option of using one or both of the above options from within a custom dialog. The dialog returns the index of the file chosen for the option or missing value. From the script we read:

```
--define path for text index topic file
set homeFolder to path to home folder from user domain as string
set folderPath to homeFolder & "AppleScripts for CS5:Chapter 21:Book:"
--define path to style sheets
set appPath to path to applications folder as string
set stylePath to getStylePath()
--get lists of files
tell application "Finder"
    set fileList to name of files of folder folderPath where file type ¬
    is {"text"}
    set styleList to name of files of folder stylePath
end tell
try
    set docRef to getDocRef()
    set userResponse to userDialog(docRef, "Search Preferences", true, ¬
    "Dialog Label", fileList, styleList)
    if item 1 of userResponse is not missing value then
        set fileIndex to item 1 of userResponse
        set fileName to item fileIndex of fileList
        set fileAlias to (folderPath & fileName) as alias
        set delimChar to return
        set topicList to readTextFile(fileAlias, delimChar)
        set indexRef to indexWTopics(docRef, topicList)
    end if
    if item 2 of userResponse is not missing value then
        set styleIndex to item 2 of userResponse
        set styleFileName to item styleIndex of styleList
        set stylefileAlias to (stylePath & styleFileName) as alias
        tell application "Adobe InDesign CS5"
            set indexRef to my indexWTopics(docRef, {}) --list can be empty
            tell indexRef
```

```
                    import topics from stylefileAlias
                end tell
            end tell
        end if
    end try

    (*Checks for index by property indexName; creates index if needed; adds
    topics from list.*)
    on indexWTopics(docRef, topicList)
        tell application "Adobe InDesign CS5"
            tell docRef
                if exists index indexName then
                    set indexRef to index 1
                    set indexAlert to "Adding to current index " & name of indexRef
                else
                    set indexAlert to "Creating new index"
                    set indexRef to make index with properties {name:indexName}
                end if
                activate
                display alert indexAlert
                tell indexRef
                    repeat with i from 1 to length of topicList
                        if not (exists topic (item i of topicList)) then
                            make topic with properties {name:item i of topicList}
                        end if
                    end repeat
                end tell
            end tell
        end tell
        return indexRef
    end indexWTopics
    (*Add handlers getDocRef (Document), userDialog (Dialogs), getStylePath
    (Files Folders) and readTextFile (Files Folders) to complete script. You will
    find the script in the Book project for this chapter.*)
```

For adding a simple one-level entry to your index, you may want to take advantage of the script **Index Entry**. It should be one of the scripts found in the User folder for InDesign's Scripts panel (see Chapter 1). Assign a keyboard shortcut to the script. Then, when you need to add an entry, select the text to reference, and enter the keyboard shortcut.

Index Entry

```
tell application "Adobe InDesign CS5"
    tell document 1
        set indexRef to index 1
        set selList to selection
        if length of selection > 0 then
            set textRef to item 1 of selList
            set textStr to contents of item 1 of selList
        else
            return beep
        end if
        tell indexRef
            if not (exists topic textStr) then
                set topicRef to make topic with properties {name:textStr}
            else
                set topicRef to topic textStr
```

```
            end if
        end tell
        tell topicRef
            set topicPage to make page reference with properties ¬
            {page reference type:current page, source text:textRef}
        end tell
    end tell
end tell
```

You might also want to allow the script to assign a character style to the selected text for visual reference. You can always remove the attribute for the style when no longer needed.

When you have completed indexing you can remove any unused topics using the **remove unused** topics command.

```
    tell indexRef to remove unused topics
```

Small Ads

The problem with small ads is that the variety of sizes possible makes using templates almost impossible. Undoubtedly, when your work group receives an order for an ad, the information is stored somewhere. Depending on the size of your organization, this could be a database, a spreadsheet file, or even a return-delimited text file. The data might include the name and id for the ad, the salesman, the page placement (column and vertical coordinates), the column width for the ad, its height, run dates, and so forth.

If you produce a number of publications with small ads, you can save yourself some headache by using a script to start the ad layout. Begin by importing the information for the ad from your database or spreadsheet. Present the person creating the ad a dialog to get some basic styling information. Let the script create the ad, layers, background, border, and import styles. Our **Small Ads** project is designed to get you thinking in this direction.

Ad information for two sample ads is read from a text file and placed in a variable (*adInfoList*). The ad information lists the following information for each ad: ad name, client, salesman, column begin, columns wide, column depth (in inches), a number indicating vertical positioning, and page number.

The custom dialog gets information for the background, border, and text frame for the ad. It then creates the ad and saves it to a pre-determined location in a sub-folder named for the publication month.

The **Small Ads** script is pretty hefty so you will want to spend a little time looking over the handlers included.

Once the script creates the ad structure, the designer enters and styles the ad. To help in this process, a series of paragraph styles are imported based on a "BasicSans" and "BasicSerif" style. The time savings in document creation is trumped by the consistency and accuracy of the ad created including:

- File naming and layer structure are consistent.
- The ad border is set to inside alignment (does not exceed column width).
- Required information is added to the slug.
- Metadata is added to the file.

See the section Making Scripts Work for You for working with this project.

When it comes to placing the ads, the ad document can now be used. No more saving the ad as an .eps file. The big benefit comes when the advertiser calls with a last minute change and you can take advantage of Edit Original.

Edit Original

One of the powerful features of later versions of InDesign is the ability to live link between applications. You have probably enjoyed this feature in working with Photoshop files, but have you worked with it using InDesign documents? With your ads saved and placed as InDesign documents, Edit Original can switch you into the ad document with a simple keystroke. Make the change(s). When you save and close the ad you are taken back to your publication with the ad updated. To make Edit Original a one-keystroke task, set up a keyboard shortcut that is easy to remember.

Working With Multiples

Multiple Resources

Workflows for magazines, newspapers, and some newsletters can be similar in that they work with multiple stories, multiple ads, as well as multiple columns. For publications having multiple columns, the terms *columns wide* and *column depth* are common terms in the newsroom. These are used to describe the size of stories and ads within the document. Because of their complexity, these publications are often pre-planned in "budget" sessions. The information from the budget session is stored in some type of formalized data storage: a database, a spreadsheet, or even a delimited text file. From there, a script can incorporate this information into an automated workflow.

The editor for an institution's newsletter might provide the following information for each ad to be included in an edition: a name for the ad, the client's name, the salesman, the beginning column, the width of the ad (*columns wide*), the height of the ad (*column inches*), and page number. From there a script could build the document's skeleton using the information provided to create placeholder frames. Labels for the frames contain the information for the ad. This could be a delimited string, or even a script that imports the ad at a later date after being created. The script, **Newsletter Setup**, could be a good beginning. It creates the document from a standing template, and creates the placeholder frames. It is a fairly extensive script, so only parts of the script are shown below. The complete script is in the Newsletter folder of InDesign's Scripts panel (see Chapter 1). To edit the script, Control-click on its entry in the panel and select Edit Script from the menu.

For working with columns, the live page bounds for the page and column coordinates for the designated column(s) is returned from the **getColumnCoords** handler.

```
(*Returns live page bounds and column positions for columns indicated.*)
on getColumnCoords(docRef, pageRef, beginColIndex, endColIndex)
    tell application "Adobe InDesign CS5"
        set pgHgt to page height of document preferences of docRef
        tell margin preferences of pageRef
            set colPositions to columns positions
            copy {top, left, bottom, right} to {my0, mx0, my1, mx1}
        end tell
        tell pageRef
```

```
            set colLeft to item ((beginColIndex * 2) -1) of colPositions
            set colRight to item (endColIndex * 2) of colPositions
            if side = left hand then
                set x0 to mx1 + colLeft
                set x1 to mx1 + colRight
            else
                set x0 to mx0 + colLeft
                set x1 to mx1 + colRight
            end if
        end tell
        set px1 to item -1 of colPositions
    end tell
    return {x0, x1, my0, mx0, (pgHgt - my1), px1}
end getColumnCoords
```

The geometric bounds for the placeholders are calculated in the **adPlaceholder** handler which then calls the **createPageItem** handler.

```
(*Creates text frame to act as ad placeholder.*)
on adPlaceholder(docRef, pageNumber, adInfo, mx0, my1, colPositions)
    tell application "Adobe InDesign CS5"
        copy adInfo to {adName, clientName, salesmanName, colIndex, adWid,¬
        adHgt, yPos}
        set pageRef to page pageNumber of docRef
        set x0 to (item ((colIndex * 2) - 1) of colPositions)
        set endColIndex to colIndex + (adWid - 1)
        set x1 to (item (endColIndex * 2) of colPositions)
        set y1 to my1 - (yPos * 72)
        set y0 to y1 - (adHgt * 72)
        set gBounds to {y0, x0, y1, x1}
        set adInfoStr to adName & return & clientName & return & salesmanName
        set itemProps to {name:adName, item layer:"Ads", contents:¬
        adInfoStr, label:adInfoStr}
        my createPageItem(docRef, pageRef, text frame, gBounds, itemProps)
    end tell
end adPlaceholder
```

Multiple Columns

As you can see from the handlers above, the **columns positions** property of a page's **margin preferences** is invaluable for working with multiple columns. It returns the left and right x-position for each column on a page. If there are no columns set for the page, the value returned will be a list of two items (0.0 for the left margin and the value for the x-position at the right margin). With columns established for the page, you get a single list of the left and right x-positions for the columns. The last value of the list is often calculated in a script using the page's width minus the width of the right margin. There are a number of ways you can use columns positions as part of an automation script. The script **Rule Gutters** uses columns positions to calculate the center horizontal coordinate for columns on a page. Taking advantage of **rest of** list, it then rules the page gutters using the information returned from the handler **calcGutterCenters**. Open the script **Rule Gutters** in the Chapter Scripts folder for this chapter to see how handlers are used in this script. A portion of the handler that calculates the center horizontal coordinates for the gutters is shown below.

```
set centerList to {}
tell application "Adobe InDesign CS5"
```

```
set pgHgt to page height of document preferences of docRef
tell margin preferences of pageRef
   set colList to columns positions
   if length of colList = 2 then
      return centerList
   end if
   copy {top, left, bottom, right} to {my0, mx0, my1, mx1}
end tell
tell pageRef
   if side = left hand then
      set px0 to mx1
   else
      set px0 to mx0
   end if
end tell
repeat while length of colList > 2
   set x0 to item 2 of colList
   set x1 to item 3 of colList
   set cx to (x1 - x0) / 2 + (px0 + x0)
   set end of centerList to cx
   set colList to rest of colList
   set colList to rest of colList
end repeat
return {centerList, {my0, px0, pgHgt - my1, px1}}
```

Multipurposing

The thrust of the 5.5 release for InDesign is to support the burgeoning world of handheld devices. If you browse InDesign's scripting dictionary for 5.5, you will see the number of listings having to do with export have all but doubled from previous versions. Much of this is to support export for HTML and EPub. Among the new classes added are:

- Style export tag map - For mapping paragraph styles to HTML styles.
- Article object - Allows content and order of export to be determined by user.

If your document is structured using XML, you have the option of using the XML structure when exporting to EPub, HTML, and tagged PDF.

Export

To get a glimpse of the many ways an InDesign CS5.5 document can be multipurposed, you may want to explore the following classes.

- Export for web preference
- InCopy export preference (new)
- InCopy export options
- Interactive PDF export preference
- EPS export preference
- JPEG export preference
- PDF export preference and PDF export preset
- SWF export preference

- XFL export preference
- XML export preference

Chapter 23 will look at some of the ways an InDesign document can be multipurposed for electronic display.

Style Export Tag Map

New for CS5.5 is the **style export map** object which is an element for both paragraph and character styles. By default, a map named "EPUB" is provided. Styles are tagged using the Export Tagging panel for the text style. Open the Paragraph (or Character) Style Options panel. At the bottom of the option list is the new addition: **Export Tagging**. Here you can assign the HTML tag that will represent the style selected when the document is exported for HTML or EPUB. (For paragraph styles, this includes h1 through h6 and p). As of this writing, support for working with the style export map on the scripting side is not complete. You can get a reference to the map assigned to the style using the following:

```
--assumes document with paragraph style "Head_24" assigned to a tag map item
tell application "Adobe InDesign CS5.5"
    set docRef to document 1
    set parastyleRef to paragraph style "Head_24" of docRef
    set stylemapRef to style export tag map 1 of parastyleRef
end tell
```

HTML

Support for HTML returned as of CS4 in the guise of Export to Dreamweaver (File > Export > Export For...). This was a good beginning but left a lot to be desired. Although the support for HTML improved as of CS5, unless you can take advantage of CSS, anything other than a one-column layout can involve a little work in Dreamweaver. The good news is in CS5.5 for a simple layout you can go direct from InDesign to web using the style export tag map and, optionally, the Article panel. These two new features make working with a simple layout a breeze, but you will still need to get to know CSS for any layout other than a simple single column layout. For an automated solution, set up your text style mapping as part of a template or import styles with mapping established from a style sheet.

EPub

New in CS5.5 is the **EPub export preferences** class which can be a property of a book or document. Many of its properties are the same as those for HTML export preferences. For EPub there is currently support for XHTML and DTBook formats. The list of properties for EPub export preferences is considerable but should not require explanation.

SWF and FLA

InDesign CS4 opened the door to support for SWF but it was not pretty, especially when it came to working with text in linked frames. With CS5 all that is history.

Make Scripts Work for You

To acquaint you with some methods for automating documents that would reside in other documents, this section will walk you through the creation of two small ads using scripts in the **Small Ads** project. These ads will be used in the **Newsletter** project in the next chapter.

The idea behind the small ads project is based on a workflow where some method for storing ad information is part of the process of the ad being ordered. This could be a database, or even just a text file. Ad information would include its size (in column widths and column inches), the client, the salesman, its position on the page, color, and page number, among others. For this project this information is read from a text file found in the Newsletter folder (in user's Public folder). The first ad (Entrada_125) relies on XML for creating the ad contents. The second ad (Entrada_222) will have the contents entered by hand using styles that are chained. Scripts for the project are found in the Newsletter folder of InDesign's Scripts panel as well as in the Small Ads folder for this chapter.

Small Ads - The resources for the small ads are found in the User's Public:Newsletter folder. The script presents the user with a dialog from which to select the ad, and to enter pertinent information. It then builds the basic structure for the ad and saves it in a folder named for the publication month inside the same folder. The ads are saved in InDesign document format (.indd). The script relies on files being located in pre-determined locations:

- Style sheet - SmallAds.indd in the Styles folder inside the Presets folder for InDesign.
- Entrada folder - Inside the user's Pubic folder ([HardDrive]:Users:[User]: Public:Newsletter:Entrada).

Entrada_125

1. Run the **Small Ads** script. Select Entrada_125 from the dropdown in the user dialog. Select the publication month.
2. Enter the following information into the dialog: Border Width: 4 pt, Corner Type:Rounded Corner, Corner Radius: 18 pt. Check the Add Text Frame checkbox and change Bottom to 6. All other settings can be left as is. Click OK.
3. The basic structure of the ad is created. You can close the ad (it has been saved), or leave it open for the next script.

Style Ad_XML - This script populates the ad with XML. It is designed for those ads, such as contract ads, that repeat periodically where only the content of the ad changes. The size and styling of the ad remains constant but the text and image can change.

1. With the Entrada_125 document open, run the script.
2. When prompted select the XML file Entrada_125.xml inside the Entrada folder which is part of this project.
3. Make whatever modifications you may want to the ad and save .

Entrada_222

1. Run the **Small Ads** script. Select Entrada_222 from the dropdown in the dialog. Select the month for publication.
2. Check the option for Background. It is set by default to Black. Leave as is.
3. For the Border options, set the following values: Border Width: 10, Border Style: Thin-Thick, Border Color: Paper, Corner type: Rounded Corner. Leave Corner radius set at 24.
4. Check Add text frame option. Set the value for Top to 24; all others: 18. Click OK.

With the framework for the ad created, the text will be added manually using chained paragraph styles. This relies on styles loaded from a style sheet named "AdStyles.indd."

1. Look for the paragraph style group HeadBodyTrailer_paper30c. It should be near the bottom of your style list. Click on its triangle to open the group.

2. Place your cursor in the text frame and select the paragraph style Head from the style group.

3. Enter the following using a return or soft return (Shift-Return) where indicated:

```
LASER HAIR[soft return]
REMOVAL[return]
Get the Information[soft return]
You Need[soft return]
Before You Buy[return]
www.laserhairtruth.com [return]
```

4. Make any adjustments needed for the ad and save.

This project was designed simply to give you some ideas of what you could do to automate creating small ads. If small ads are part of your workflow, modify the scripts to work for you.

Figure 21.1: Entrada_125 ad created from scripts in the Small Ads project.

Figure 21.2: Entrada_222 ad created using Small Ads script.

22

Workflows

When considering a workflow, an automated process may not begin and end with InDesign. You may or may not have control over how some of the resources for your project are created. From text to images, and from tables to diagrams, your workflow may depend on other applications working in concert with InDesign. Text may be created in a program such as Microsoft Word, and images most certainly may come from Adobe Photoshop, and artwork may come from Adobe Illustrator. It goes without saying that InDesign works well with the other applications in the Creative Suite especially with **Edit Original** in the mix.

Edit Original

```
(*Demonstrates using Edit Original to open a selected image in Photoshop.*)
tell application "Adobe InDesign CS5"
    set selList to selection
    if class of item 1 of selList is in {image} then
        set theImage to item 1 of selList
        if image type name of theImage is in {"Photoshop"} then
            edit original item link of theImage
        end if
    else
        set theClass to class of item 1 of selList
    end if
end tell
```

With AppleScript as your scripting language, you may want to take advantage of some of the automation provided by applications on the Macintosh. If so, poke around in the dictionaries for some of the applications that show up when you select Open Dictionary... from AppleScript Editor's File menu.

The following discussion will look at some of applications your script may include as part of a project's workflow.

Bridge

To automate Bridge with a script you will need to either learn ExtendScript (or acquire the help of someone to write the script for you). Aside from that, there is some functionality built into Bridge that you may want to take advantage of. So get familiar with Bridge's Tools menu.

When you need to add metadata to your files, you don't need to launch Photoshop; you can do it in Bridge. First, you will want to create (or edit) a Metadata Template. In Bridge select Tools > Create Metadata Template. You can append or replace existing metadata in files with the information established in your template. Once you have created a Metadata Template, select files from Bridge's Content panel, and choose the appropriate metadata option from the

Tools menu. The information in your template will be added to (or will replace) the metadata in the selected files.

You might also want to look at using the Batch Rename option in the Tools menu. This can be especially handy if you need to add an incremented number to filenames. But be advised, the files will be numbered in alphabetical order.

Word Processors

For a small project, the InDesign user can compose copy in the document entering text directly into text frames. More efficiently, the Story panel can be used for composing copy (Edit > Edit in Story Editor). For projects that require the power or remote status of a word processor, the options are all but without limit as InDesign supports a wide variety of file formats. Some of the more popular are discussed in the following.

Buzzword

For a workflow that involves persons in diverse locations, you will want to get familiar with Buzzword. Buzzword is an online word processor that is perfect for working in a collaborative environment. Documents created in Buzzword are pixel-perfect on screen. Buzzword requires that you have an Acrobat.com account. Check it out.

With Buzzword you can:

*   Write, edit, and comment on documents with the people you choose.
*   Control access levels and document versions and track edits by contributor.
*   Designate the role of each participant as co-author (full edit privileges), reviewer (add comments only), or reader.
*   Avoid editing and reviewing conflicts because everyone works with the same version of the document.
*   Import Buzzword documents into InDesign and export InDesign documents for Buzzword (File > Export for > Buzzword).

With a document open, select Place from Buzzword from InDesign's File menu. Sign in with your account name and password, and select a document from the list presented. If you have a text frame selected, the file is placed in the frame. Otherwise, place the file using the loaded cursor (place gun).

When imported into InDesign, you can style the document using object and paragraph styles. The beauty of using Buzzword is there is no software requirement; the software and files are stored on the web. Buzzword supports a variety of file types for import and export including Open Document format, Microsoft Word, PDF, HTML, EPUB, TXT, and RTF. You can print directly from Buzzword or output to PDF. Once you have an Acrobat.com account, you can use it for more than just Buzzword. Web conferencing, presentations, and more are at your disposal.

InCopy

InCopy is Adobe's answer to a text editor front end for InDesign. The beauty of InCopy is that it uses the same text engine as InDesign. The user can write and edit stories taking advantage of InDesign's paragraph and character styling with the assurance that copyfitting will be exact. The InDesign-InCopy workflow is ideal for workgroups involved in creating books, small newspapers, and magazines. The combination of the two applications provides an easy-to-use, integrated solution where users can work collaboratively without the fear of overwriting copy or otherwise stepping on each other's toes. Whether connected by an intranet or working remotely, the versatility of the two applications working together makes it possible to design a workflow ideal for any situation. As InCopy is also scriptable, you can further customize or automate steps within the process as needed.

The typical InCopy workflow starts the document in InDesign where containers for content are created and styling is established. To keep styling consistent, use text, table, and object styling exclusively. Story containers should be styled with object styles that include chained text styles when possible. Image placeholders can be styled using object styles that pre-determine the fitting for the image. If the project will include tables, use table and cell styles.

Once exported as an InCopy document, the file can be opened in InCopy. If not assigned, the document can be opened and worked on by any editorial member. Alternatively, individual stories or spreads can be assigned to different members of the editorial group using Assignments (see next page). If connected by an intranet, work can be done on the document concurrently. Editors can be editing stories while the layout is still being designed.

For the remote editor, assignments can be saved as packages. Like a StuffIt archive, all the resources for the story are part of the package. When the story is completed, the story is returned as a package.

Having the luxury of a pre-planned layout is often not an option. A reporter working remotely may be writing a story close to publication deadline. If anything, the only information she may have is the column inches the article needs to fill. If this user has InCopy to work with, you might want to set up his or her laptop with a style sheet and a script. The script is used to create the story framework and can optionally include static information (reporter's name, affiliation, and so forth). As the script relies on a style sheet for importing styles, you will want to make sure the style sheet is available on his or her computer. The following script demonstrates. It requires a style sheet named "ForInCopy.indd" to be located in the Presets:Styles folder for InCopy.

InCopy Setup

```
--change variable values as needed
set reporterName to "Reporter Name, Reporter"
set columnWidth to "14p4" --publication column width
set presetName to "InCopy Basic"
set stylesheetName to "ForInCopy.indd"
set doObject to false
set doText to true
set doTable to true
set textContent to "Headline here" & return & reporterName & return
set textContent to textContent & "Quickread here" & return & "Story:"
set styleList to {"Head_24", "Byline", "Quickread", "Body"}
set userPrompt to "Enter story depth"
set defaultAnswer to "10" --default depth for text
set dialogTitle to "InCopy Story Depth"
try
    set stylesheetRef to getStylesheet(stylesheetName)
    (*Prompts user to enter a number; traps entry if not number or user
    cancels.*)
```

InDesign-InCopy Assignment Workflow

In this workflow a story starts with the designer who creates the document and lays out the frames for each story and its supporting resources. The styling of the contents for the containers can be determined by applying object styles. Many workgroups prefer this workflow as it can optionally provide a dummy layout which can be approved before actual production (see the Newsletter project with this chapter). If the document is exported as an InCopy document (.icma file), all editors can have access to the file for reviewing and commenting.

When it comes time to work on the project, either individual page items belonging to a story, or entire spreads can be assigned to individual members of the editorial group. This process is accomplished in the Assignment panel (Window > Editorial > Assignment). You might want to think of an assignment as a container for stories. The assignment file (.icml) provides the link between the content files and the InDesign document.

To identify the members within the collaborative workflow, it is a good idea to set up each user with a user name and color. This makes it easy to identify the person involved at the various stages of production. Choose File > User in InDesign to open the User dialog.

To create an assignment, open the Assignment panel. Click on the New Assignment button at the bottom of the panel. First give your assignment a name. The Assigned To field is optional. If you have assigned a color to the user, you may want to fill in the color field. The panel will identify Assignments with a tint of the user's color for ease of identification. Activate the radio button that indicates the scope of the assignment: Placeholder Frames, Assigned Spreads, or All Spreads. For most purposes Placeholder Frames is all that is required and yields the fastest performance. Click OK.

Although you have created an assignment, it is empty. You now need to select the frames you wish to assign, and go to Edit > InCopy > Add Selection to Assignment. Choose the assignment you just created from the list presented. You will be prompted to save your document if you have not done so.

When you have completed creating assignments, choose Update All Assignments from the Assignments panel flyout menu.

Layout integrity is preserved in this workflow as only the contents of the linked frames and designated image containers can be edited. While users can apply local formatting, the text styles associated with the stories cannot be changed. If the designer makes a change to the layout while it is being worked on, the editor is notified. Choosing File > Update will refresh the layout without losing any edits.

InCopy provides three modes in which copy can be written, edited, and viewed: Story, Galley, and Layout. The latter option is only available if the story is linked to the InDesign document using an assignment.

With Enable Tracking turned on, edits made in either InCopy or InDesign can be tracked. These can be viewed in Galley or Story view while in InCopy, or in Story Editor in InDesign. Changes can be accepted or rejected using the Changes menu.

When working with an Assignment workflow, users need to check in assigned articles before editing, and check out before closing.

```
        set textDepth to getNumber(userPrompt, defaultAnswer, dialogTitle)
    on error errStr
        display alert errStr
        return
    end try

    tell application "Adobe InCopy CS5.5"
        set presetProps to {name:presetName, facing pages:false, page height:¬
        "11 in", page width:"8.5 in", text area depth:textDepth, ¬
        text area width:colWidth}
        set presetRef to my getPreset(presetName, presetProps)
        set docRef to make document with properties {document preset:presetRef}
        my importStyles(docRef, stylesheetRef, doText, doTable)
        set storyRef to story 1 of docRef
        tell docRef to load XML tags from stylesheetRef
        tell storyRef
            set contents to textContent
        end tell
        repeat with i from 1 to length of styleList
            set styleName to item i of styleList
            set styleRef to paragraph style styleName of docRef
            set applied paragraph style of paragraph i of storyRef to styleRef
        end repeat
        tell storyRef
            select paragraph i existing selection replace with
        end tell
    end tell

(*Imports styles from style sheet referenced given boolean values for object,
text, and/or table styles.*)
on importStyles(docRef, stylesheetRef, doText, doTable)
    tell application "Adobe InCopy CS5.5"
        tell docRef
            if doText is true then
                import styles format text styles format from stylesheetRef
            end if
            if doTable is true then
                import styles format table styles format from stylesheetRef
            end if
        end tell
    end tell
end importStyles

on getStylesheet(fileName)
    tell application "Adobe InCopy CS5.5"
        set appPath to file path as string
    end tell
    set stylePath to appPath & "Presets:Styles:"
    try
        set stylesheetRef to (stylePath & fileName) as alias
        return stylesheetRef
    end try
    error "Style sheet " & fileName & " not found"
end getStylesheet

(*Handler tests for number response from user.*)
on getNumber(userPrompt, defaultAnswer, dialogTitle)
    set userResponse to display dialog userPrompt default answer ¬
    defaultAnswer with title dialogTitle
```

```
            if length of text returned of userResponse is 0 then
                error ("No value entered")
            else
                --this statement will throw an error if not a number value
                set theNumber to (text returned of userResponse) as number
            end if
            return theNumber
        end getNumber

        on getPreset(presetName, presetProps)
            tell application "Adobe InCopy CS5.5"
                if not (exists document preset presetName) then
                    set presetRef to make document preset with properties presetProps
                else
                    set presetRef to document preset presetName
                end if
                return presetRef
            end tell
        end getPreset
        (*Change the target application reference to your version as needed.*)
```

The reporter saves the content as an InCopy document (.icml). When received by the graphic designer, the file is placed in the document. At this time the story and its related graphics can be given an assignment. If assigned, editorial can now check in the article and give it its OK or make last-minute changes. Once editorial checks out and closes the document, the designer preflights the document and sends it off to be printed.

The paragraph and character styles in the sample style sheet are assigned to HTML tags. Depending on the method for export, the document is all but ready for multipurposing using export for HTML, EPub, PDF tagged, or XML.

If reporters do not have InCopy (perish the thought!), editors can import Microsoft Word documents into InCopy or InDesign.

Microsoft Word

Microsoft Word's .doc and .docx files use Rich Text Formatting (RTF), which supports text styling including style sheets. If paragraph styles are set up with the same naming convention as that used in the InDesign document, the workflow can be made much simpler. For this reason, encourage the people who supply your Word documents to use style sheets. For those that use a consistent style pattern, you may want to supply a template.

For importing Word documents, InDesign has a number of properties you can set to make sure files import as anticipated. The handler below can be a start.

```
        (*Sets preferences for importing Microsoft Word RTF format.*)
        on mWordImportPrefs()
            tell application "Adobe InDesign CS5"
                tell word RTF import preferences
                    set convert bullets and numbers to text to false
                    set convert page breaks to none --none, page break or column break
                    set remove formatting to false
                    set import endnotes to true
                    set import footnotes to true
                    set import index to true
                    set import TOC to true
                    set import unused styles to false
```

```
            set preserve graphics to true
            set resolve character style clash to resolve clash use existing
            set resolve paragraph style clash to resolve clash use existing
            set use typographers quotes to true
            --note: the following are valid if remove formatting is true
            --set convert tables to Unformatted Table--Unformatted Tabbed text
            --set preserve local overrides to true
        end tell
    end tell
end mWordImportPrefs
```

The settings established above work best if the receiving InDesign document has paragraph styles defined with names corresponding to Microsoft Word's: "Headline 1", "Normal", and so forth. The incoming text will pick up the style definitions for the styles in the receiving document.

Even with this, the document may end up having numerous style overrides in the form of local formatting. You may decide to replace style overrides with character and paragraph styles. The following is from the script **Place Microsoft Word_Style**. The script expects an active document. Use with the sample "ForWord.indd." Select the file "Text Overrides.doc" when prompted. The complete script is in the **Microsoft Word** project folder for this chapter.

```
set homePath to path to home folder from user domain as string
set dLocation to (homePath & ¬
"AppleScripts for CS5:Chapter 22:Microsoft Word:") as alias
set tablestyleName to "GrayHead"
set headerRow to true --if true first row will be header
set rowHgt to "1p4"
set storyIndex to -1
try
    set docRef to getDocRef()
    mWordImportPrefs()
    set fileRef to chooseFileExtTest("Select Microsoft Word file", {"doc"}, ¬
    dLocation)
    tell application "Adobe InDesign CS5"
        set pageRef to page 1 of docRef
        tell margin preferences of pageRef
            set placePt to {left, top}
        end tell
        tell pageRef
            place fileRef place point placePt
        end tell
        --style tables
        my styleTables(docRef, storyIndex, tablestyleName, headerRow, rowHgt)
        my findChangeTextOptions()
        --find/replace Normal styles with overrides
        my initTextPrefs()
        set findAttrib to {applied paragraph style:"Normal", bullets and ¬
        numbering list type:bullet list}
        set styleName to "Bullets"
        my styleFoundText(docRef, findAttrib, styleName, false)
        set styleName to "DropCaps"
        set dropAttrib to {applied paragraph style:"Normal", drop cap ¬
        characters:1}
        my styleFoundText(docRef, dropAttrib, styleName, false)
        my initTextPrefs()
    end tell
```

```
on error errStr
    activate
    display alert errStr
    return
end try

(*Creates paragraph style based on properties of found text and applies.*)
on styleFoundText(docRef, findAttrib, styleName, overrideStyle)
    initTextPrefs()
    tell application "Adobe InDesign CS5"
        set properties of find text preferences to findAttrib
        tell docRef
            set foundSet to find text
        end tell
        if length of foundSet > 0 then
            set pstyleProps to properties of item 1 of foundSet
            --overrideStyle indicates style will be overwritten if existing
            set parastyleRef to my getParastyle(docRef, styleName, ¬
            pstyleProps, overrideStyle)
            set applied paragraph style of change text preferences to ¬
            parastyleRef
            tell docRef to change text
            my initTextPrefs()
            return pstyleProps
        end if
    end tell
    initTextPrefs()
end styleFoundText

(*Add handlers to complete script: initTextPrefs (Find Change), getDocRef
(Documents), chooseFileExtTest (File Folder), mWordImportPrefs (Import
Export), importStyles (Styles), styleTables (Table Cell), getParastyle
(Styles).
```

You might question the setting used above for the **set preserve graphics property** of **Word RTF Import Preferences**. Image files embedded in Word documents are imported as anchored page items of the parent story. As part of placing a story an object style can be applied to establish text wrap and anchor style settings. The script **Import Word_Images** creates a document from a preset "Ltr_FacingAuto." If the preset does not exist, it is created. Paragraph styles "Heading 1" and "Normal" are also created as well as the object style "InlineAnchor." You will find the complete script in the **Microsoft Word** project folder. When you run the script, select the file "Text With Image.doc" when prompted.

Spreadsheets

For tabular data, outside of having information stored in a database, you can have clients submit information as a Buzzword table, an Acrobat form, or from any number of applications. Of all, Microsoft Excel has been around forever and is widely used.

Microsoft Excel

For Microsoft Excel **excel import preferences** includes settings to indicate the worksheet and range name, as well as table formatting. Supplying `missing value` to the **excelImportPrefs** handler will import the entire table. When an Excel file is placed, the **file linking** property in

text preferences for the document csan be set to true as shown below. This allows the table to be updated in the event of a last-minute change to the data.

```
tell text preferences of docRef
    set link text files when importing to true
end tell
```

The handler, **excelImportPrefs**, is part of the script **Place Linked Table** in the **Microsoft Excel** project with this chapter's files. The script expects an active document with the table style "GrayHead." Use with the sample document "Import Excel.indd" and select the file "MS4Workbook.xls" when prompted. Save the document for further testing.

```
set showOptions to false
set sheetName to "Sheet1"
set rangeName to missing value
excelImportPrefs(sheetName, rangeName)

on excelImportPrefs(sheetName, rangeName)
    tell application "Adobe InDesign CS5"
        tell excel import preferences
            if rangeName is not missing value then
                set range name to rangeName
            end if
            set table formatting to excel unformatted table
            set alignment style to spreadsheet
            set sheet name to sheetName
            set decimal places to 2
            set preserve graphics to true
            set show hidden cells to true
            set use typographers quotes to true
        end tell
    end tell
end excelImportPrefs
```

As much as having the Excel file linked to the InDesign document can be a great idea, there are some problems that must be dealt with. When you update the table, for example, your table formatting is lost. This is a minor problem, as using a script to open the document with a linked Excel file can take care of updating the table and restoring the styling. A greater problem is the Excel file must be in a frame by itself. If you want it to be part of a text flow, you will need to anchor its container to the text.

To update and restore formatting for Excel tables, the script **Update Excel Table** looks at all links for the document. If the link is an Excel file and the file is linked and out of date, the link is updated and the object style restored. To test, place the "MS4Workbook.xls" file in the Original Spreadsheet folder. Drag the file of the same name from the Changed Spreadsheet folder to replace the original. Run the **Update Excel Table** script to open the document and update the table. Select the document you saved from the previous script when prompted. The **updateExcelLinks** handler from the script is shown below.

```
tell application "Adobe InDesign CS5"
    set docRef to open fileRef
    myUpdateExcelLinks (docRef)
end tell

on updateExcelLinks(docRef)
    tell application "Adobe InDesign CS5"
        tell docRef
            set linkList to every link
```

```
            repeat with i from 1 to length of linkList
                set linkRef to item i of linkList
                if link type of linkRef = "Microsoft Excel Import Filter" ¬
                and status of linkRef = link out of date then
                    set parentRef to parent of linkRef
                    update linkRef
                    tell table 1 of parentRef
                        set row type of row 1 to header row
                        clear table style overrides
                    end tell
                end if
            end repeat
        end tell
    end tell
end updateExcelLinks
```

Note

If using file linking when working with Excel tables, place the table in a text frame of its own. You can anchor the text frame into the story flow as needed.

As you can see, InDesign supports a wealth of import options to accommodate a variety of file formats. If you consistently receive information in a particular file format, save yourself trips to the import file format dialog by setting the import preferences up as a script. Additionally, the script can perform any number of functions to keep operators on track and help eliminate errors.

Apple Applications

AppleScript scripts can take advantage of added functionality provided by applications written exclusively for Macintosh. Among the applications, Address Book and Mail can play a substantial role in automated workflows. The following script imports information from Address Book that could be used as part of a data merge script.

Save Address Book Data

```
(*Demonstrates pulling information from Address Book into a tab-delimited
file for data merge. Requires entries having first name, last name, and
address fields. The address field needs to have street, city, state, and
zip.*)
property theTab : (ASCII character 9)
set groupList to "Accountants" --put name of group here
set masterString to ""
tell application "Address Book"
    set theGroup to groupList
    tell group theGroup
        set theEntries to every person
        set theCount to count of theEntries
        if theCount > 0 then
            set masterString to "fullName" & theTab & "streetAddress" & ¬
            theTab & "cityAddress" & theTab & "firstName" & return
        else
            activate
            display alert("No information returned from group")
            return
```

```
          end if
          repeat with i from 1 to theCount
              set theString to ""
              set theName to first name of item i of theEntries
              set fullName to theName & " " & last name of item i of theEntries
              set theProperties to (properties of address of item i of ¬
              theEntries)
              set theAddress to item 1 of theProperties
              set theString to theString & fullName & theTab
              set theString to theString & my getVal(street of theAddress) &¬
              theTab
              set cityString to ""
              set cityString to cityString & my getVal(city of theAddress)
              set cityString to cityString & ", " & my getVal(state of theAddress)
              set cityString to cityString & " " & my getVal(zip of theAddress)
              set theString to theString & cityString & theTab
              set theString to theString & theName
              if i < theCount then
                  set masterString to masterString & theString & return
              else
                  set masterString to masterString & theString
              end if
          end repeat
      end tell
  end tell
  if (count of paragraphs of masterString) > 1 then
      writeFile(masterString)
  end if
  masterString

  (*Converts data in field to string value.*)
  on getVal(theField)
      if theField is not missing value then
          set thisString to theField
      else
          set thisString to " "
      end if
      return thisString
  end getVal

  (*Writes string to file. No option for merging to existing information.*)
  on writeFile(masterString)
      set theFile to choose file name with prompt ¬
      "Select location for data file"
      set fileRef to open for access theFile with write permission
      set eof fileRef to 0
      write masterString to fileRef
      try
          close access fileRef
      on error
          close access fileRef
      end try
  end writeToFile
```

The file created is ready for use as the Data Source for Data Merge. With a document open, open the Data Merge panel (Window > Utilities > Data Merge). Follow the directions in the panel using the file you just created for the first step. A list of the fields created will appear in the panel. Add these to your document as placeholders for the actual data (usually on the master page for the document). Apply styling to the placeholders as needed. Click on the Preview checkbox in the Data Merge panel to see how your files will look when merged. When you have your template document prepared the way you want it, click the button in the lower-right corner of the panel to create the merged documents. To create a PDF of the merged documents, choose Export to PDF from the panel's menu.

Running Scripts

For some workflows you may not want your user to run the script from inside InDesign's Script panel. In fact, you might not want your user to have to run the script at all. With AppleScript you have several options. Your script can be run from AppleScript's Script menu, or your script can be triggered into action by some other event.

Application or Droplet

When you save a script as an application it can respond when double-clicked or, as a "droplet" when a file is dropped onto its icon. The code inside an on run block will execute when the file is double-clicked. To have the script respond when a file is dropped on it you need to include an on open handler. Your script can have both handlers so it can respond to either event.

Test Droplet

```
property fileTypes : {"IDd7", "ID7t"}
property fileExtensions : {"indd", "indt"}

--triggers when file is double-clicked
on run
    set fileList to choose file with prompt "Choose InDesign file" of type ¬
    {"IDd7", "ID7t"} without multiple selections allowed
    processFiles(fileList)
end run

--triggers when file is dropped on its icon
on open (aliasList)
    processFiles(item 1 of aliasList)
end open

--handler processes the file
on processFiles(eachItem)
    tell application "Adobe InDesign CS5"
        activate
        set oldPrefs to user interaction level of script preferences
        set user interaction level of script preferences to never interact
        if my checkType(eachItem) then
            try
                open eachItem
                --do whatever processes you need done here
            on error errStr
                --make sure preferences are set back in case of error
                set user interaction level of script preferences to oldPrefs
                return errStr
            end try
        end if
        set user interaction level of script preferences to oldPrefs
    end tell
end processFiles
```

```
--returns true if file type or file extension is in a property list
on checkType(fileRef)
    set theInfo to info for fileRef
    set theType to file type of theInfo
    set theExt to name extension of theInfo
    return (theType is in fileTypes) or (theExt is in fileExtensions)
end checkType
```

Script Menu

If you don't see an AppleScript icon somewhere on the right side of the computer's menu bar, you will want to add it. For most versions of the OS prior to Snow Leopard, you will find an application called "AppleScript Utility" in the AppleScript folder inside the Applications folder. Run the utility and check the checkbox next to "Show Script Menu in menu bar." With Snow Leopard, access to the menu is in the General tab of AppleScript Editor's preferences. While in the General tab you may also want to enable Show Computer Scripts.

To add your script(s) to the menu bar, add them to the Scripts folder inside the hard drive's Library folder. You might want to create a folder or folders for your own individual scripts.

iCal

Among all of the things that iCal can do to keep you on track, it can run a script just for a reminder or to perform a defined function at a particular time of day. Launch iCal and create a new event (File > New Event). Name the event and set the time when you want the script to run. Click on the word *alarm* and choose Run Script from its pop-up menu. Click on the pair of arrows below to select your script. If not in the list, select Other and browse to the script desired. Now click on the pair of arrows below and select a time option (on *date* for example).

Folder Action

Scripts attached to a folder as a **folder action** run when the designated state for the folder changes. The following instructions are for Snow Leopard. For earlier versions, you will need to seek out the AppleScript Utility in the AppleScript folder (Applications folder).

Start by creating your script as normal and test to make sure everything works as planned. If you are anticipating having the folder action trigger when a file (or files) are dropped on the folder, use a choose file statement temporarily while writing your script and testing. When your script is ready for real time, remove the choose file statement. When your script is ready, select the code and control-click. Choose Folder Actions Handlers from the contextual menu, then choose the trigger option to use for running the script. Your code will be enclosed in a folder action wrapper. Save the script in the following file path:

```
[hard drive]:Library:Scripts:Folder Action Scripts.
```

Next you will want to create the folder that will trigger the script when files are dropped onto its icon. Control-click on the folder and select your script from the list of scripts. Make sure Enable Folder Actions is clicked. Close the dialog. Drag a file to the folder to see the folder action script go into action. You might want to try the following, script. The folder, with the this script attached, will sort image files dropped onto it by file extension

.

```
on adding folder items to this_folder after receiving added_Items
    repeat with thisItem in added_Items
        set fileExt to name extension of (info for thisItem)
        tell application "Finder"
            if fileExt is not in {missing value, ""} then
                if (not (folder fileExt in this_folder exists)) then
                    make new folder in folder this_folder with properties ¬
                    {name:fileExt}
                end if
                move thisItem to folder fileExt in this_folder
            end if
        end tell
    end repeat
end adding folder items to
```

Automator

Apple has put a lot of energy into its Automator application to make it easy for the user to tie action presets and scripts together into a useful workflow. Working with Automator is like working with handlers in a script. Each action preset provides for input, process, and output. You just need to make sure that the output of an action is of the type required by the action following. When you click on an action in the Library, you will see a short description of the action in the box at the bottom of the list. Drag actions you want to use, in order, to the action list. If you want to see the result of an action, place a "View Results" action between two actions to see the data being passed. The "View Results" action is in the Automator's Utilities folder.

You can move actions around to reorder as needed. After creating a workflow, save it, and use it, and share it with others. You can run your workflow from within Automator, or save it as a standalone application.

Just for fun and to introduce you to working with Automator, do the following. Instructions are for Snow Leopard but will be similar in earlier versions of the OS.

1. Launch Automator and select Application from the workflow type. (Choose Custom in earlier versions.) Click Choose.
2. From the Library, select Files and Folders > **Get Specified Finder Items**. Drag it into the work area.
3. Click the Add button and browse to an InDesign file. You might try FormalInvite.indd in the Public:Test folder installed from the book's support site (see Chapter 1).
4. From Automator's Files & Folders folder, add the **Filter Finder Items** action preset. In the first dropdown choose **File Extension**. In the second, choose **is**. In the text field, type *indd*.
5. From the Utilities folder add the **Run AppleScript** action preset. Inside the on run code, enter:

```
tell application "Adobe InDesign CS5"
    open input
    set docRef to document 1
    set theContents to contents of text frame 1 of page 1 of docRef
    return theContents
end tell
```

6. From the Utilities folder add the **Speak Text** action preset and choose a voice from the Voice dropdown.

7. Run the workflow using the Run button. Click OK to dismiss the warning dialog.

8. Once you get your Automator automation working, remove the **Get Specified Finder Items** action from the top of the workflow by clicking the "x" in the upper right corner.

9. Save your workflow to the desktop as "Speakfile_indd."

10. Test your workflow by dragging an InDesign file to its icon.

While following the steps above, take a look at some of the preset actions provided. You may see some very good reasons for letting Automator organize your workflow.

Make Scripts Work for You

In this section you will pull together a number of scripts and the result of several projects to explore workflow options for automating a newsletter project. The **Newsletter** project uses the Newsletter template created in Chapter 19 ("Newsletter.indt"). The scripts should all be in the Newsletter Scripts folder of InDesign's Scripts panel (see Chapter 1). The scripts are also included in the Newsletter project folder for this chapter. The scripts involved are:

*   **Newsletter Setup** - Creates document from Newsletter template (in Templates folder for InDesign). It creates ad placeholders for ads that have been planned for the edition. The information for the ads is read from a text file in the project folder ("AdInfo.txt").

*   **Image With Caption** - Places image chosen by user and adds caption frame with credit and caption information from images metadata (Author and Description fields). The image and caption frame are grouped and moved to center of page.

*   **Place Gun** - Allows user to select a number of images to place. Images layer is activated and default graphic object style is set for Image style to assure that images are placed on the correct layer and assigned the style as part of being placed.

*   **Story Placeholder_InCopy** and **Story Placeholder** - Creates story placeholders in the Newsletter for stories that have been planned. The information for the planned stories is hard-coded in the script.

*   **Place Ads** - Replaces placeholders in document with completed ads. When this script is run, the user selects the appropriate month for the publication. The month chosen should correspond to the month designated when working with the **Small Ads** project in Chapter 21. If you completed the **Small Ads** project, the ads should be located in the following path:

        users:[user]:Public:Newsletter:[Month]

The project will be using an InCopy workflow. If your work includes creating small newspapers or periodicals, such as newsletters, and you don't use InCopy, it is suggested that you get a trial copy of InCopy (www.adobe.com) and try out the following workflow. There are a number of ways you can automate a workflow such as this. The outline below is just one and is limited in scope. It uses a text file for ad information.

To check a story in or out, you will need the Assignments panel open (Window > Editorial > Assignments). The check in/out button is at the bottom of the panel. When you check a story in, you will be presented a confirmation dialog. Click OK to close.

1. Run the **Newsletter Setup** script from InDesign's Script panel (Newsletter folder).

2. Run the **Story Placeholder_InCopy** script.

3. Select the story "Ancient Cultures" from the list presented. The story information is hard-coded in the script. In a real world situation, the information would come from a database or other resource.

4. Run the **Image With Caption** script. The script sets the default location for choosing images to the Images folder inside the User's Public folder. Select the file "Petroglyphs_1col.jpg." Control click on the image to move it to your desired location.

5. Although an assignment was created as part of the **Story Placeholder_InCopy** script, you will need to add the text frame and the image to the assignment. Marquee-select the text frame for the story and the image. Choose InCopy from InDesign's Edit menu. From the flyout menu, select Add Selection to Assignment and select "Ancient Cultures" from the list.

6. In the Assignment panel select your story and select Update Selected Assignments from the menu. Alternatively, you can wait until all stories are assigned and use Update All Assignments. Assignments are saved to the following path:

    ```
    Users:[User]:Public:Newsletter:[Publication folder]:Assignments
    ```

    Assignments have the extension: icma. The content folder (.icml files) acts like a book in that it associates the assignments for the publication.

7. You can continue assigning stories using the procedure outlined above. For the story "Rock Art" place two or more image files from the Images:Capitol Reef folder using the script **Place Gun**. (These images have nothing to do with the story, but are simply for demonstration.)

8. From within InCopy, the user will choose Open File from the File menu to open an assignment (.icma file extension). The story is checked out by clicking on the Check Out Selection button at the bottom of the Assignment panel. Alternatively, the user can start to type inside the story and respond "Yes" to the dialog displayed.

9. The "Ancient Cultures" and "Rock Art" stories have been submitted as .rtf files. After checking in the appropriate assignment, a text file can be placed in InCopy by selecting the story's dummy text and using the keyboard shortcut Command + D to navigate to the file. The placed story is then edited to copy fit. When editing is complete, the story is saved (Save Content or Save All Content), checked back in, and closed.

10. The "Looking Forward" story will require the story to be input directly in InCopy. Open this story assignment and add text to see how the user is given a warning and then a cut-off point for copy fitting.

11. At any time within the editing process, the user can click on the Layout tab to see how the story will look when it is updated in InDesign.

12. Back in InDesign, open the document from the File menu if you closed it and confirm updating links. Otherwise, update assignments in the Assignment panel. Check in stories to edit. When through, check out any stories that are checked in, update assignments as needed, and save.

13. When you are ready to place ads, run the **Place Ads** script to replace the ad placeholders with the finished ads. The script looks for text frames on the "Ads" layer of the document. If a frame is found matching a file name in the month folder designated by the user ([hard drive]:Users:[user name]:Public:Newsletter:[month name]), it is placed in the page placeholder.

14. Preflight your document, save, and proceed to print.

23

Interactive

Now that you have had your fill of static printed documents, move up to interactive. This chapter focuses on working with documents designed to be viewed electronically as PDF, Flash, HTML, or ePub. As you progress, you will be introduced to scripts using handlers provided in the Interactive folder of the Handlers Library (see Chapter 1).

In case you haven't noticed, InDesign CS5 and CS5.5 have a whole new focus on publishing for electronic devices. As of CS5 there is a new option for export to PDF. Choose File > Export… and select Adobe PDF (Interactive) from the Format list. You will be presented a completely new dialog dedicated to interactive PDF. Under the Buttons and Media heading, select Include All to activate buttons, movies, sounds, hyperlinks, bookmarks, and page transitions in the exported document.

While in the Export Format dropdown menu, you may notice entries for Flash CS5 Professional (FLA) and Flash Player (SWF). You will be pleased to know that as of CS5, page transitions, hyperlinks, animation, text, and most button behaviors now transfer beautifully when documents are exported to Flash Player. For Flash CS5 Professional, pages are exported as keyframes in the Flash timeline.

Interactive PDF

Be aware that interactive PDF documents need to be viewed in Adobe Acrobat for functions such as page flipping and page transitions to be effective.

Setting Up for Electronic Media

Before you can export your interactive project, you will need to build it. For that purpose you might want to create a document preset or two just for interactive media. Some of the properties you may want to set for your preset are:

- intent – Web intent.
- page size – You can use any one of the page sizes that appear in the New Document Page Size dropdown when Web is selected for Intent. Or add your own custom size.
- page height – Supply measurement value in pixels (as in "600 px").
- page width – Supply measurement value in pixels (as in "800 px").

For creating documents to use for testing there are two scripts in the Chapter Scripts folder for this chapter. They are also in the Interactive folder of the Scripts panel.

- **Web Doc Choose Preset** - Presents user a list of existing document presets which have intent set for web.
- **Web Doc With Dialog** - Includes a custom dialog for selecting a document preset, style sheet for import, and layers.

These scripts are also in the Interactive folder of InDesign's Scripts panel.

CMYK to RGB

You can export documents created for print (CMYK) for output to web (RGB). Set **blending space** of **transparency preferences** to RGB. (In the user interface choose Edit > Transparency Blend Space > Document RGB.)

Movies

Use one of the above scripts to create a document. With the document structure built, you may want to include a movie. Adding movies is similar to placing images with the exception that the movie does not display on the page. To give the user a visual movie indicator, add a poster file. It will help if you know the dimensions of the movie when you write your script. You could have the user select the movie using **choose file**, or supply a fixed path. In the following, the movie and its poster are assumed to be in the user's Movies folder. You will need to change the values for the movie name, height, and width, as well as file paths as appropriate. Scripts for movies are in the **Movies** project folder for this chapter.

Place Movie

```
(*Requires active document with "Interactive" layer.*)
set movieWid to 432
set movieHgt to 235
set placePt to {72, 72}
set movieName to "myMovie" --change this and the following 3 lines as needed
set movieFolder to path to movies folder from user domain as string
set moviePath to movieFolder & movieName & ".flv"
set posterPath to movieFolder & movieName & ".jpg"
set gBounds to {item 2 of placePt, item 1 of placePt, ¬
item 2 of placePt + movieHgt, item 1 of placePt + movieWid}
tell application "Adobe InDesign CS5"
    set docRef to document 1
    set layerRef to my checkLayer (docRef, "Interactive", true)
    set pageRef to active page of layout window 1
    tell pageRef
        set frameRef to make rectangle with properties {name: "Movie", ¬
        geometric bounds:gBounds, fill color: "None", stroke weight:0, ¬
        item layer: layerRef}
    end tell
    tell frameRef
        place file moviePath
        fit given frame to content
        set movieRef to movie 1 of frameRef
    end tell
    --set movie properties
    tell movieRef
        set embed in PDF to false
```

```
            set show controls to true
            set movie loop to false
            set play on page turn to false
            set controller skin to "SkinOverAllNoCaption"
            --add poster image
            set poster file to posterPath
        end tell
    end tell
    (*Add handler checkLayer (Document Structure folder) to complete script.*)
```

Test your movie in InDesign's Preview window (Command + Shift + Return). Keep your document open for testing the next two scripts.

Buttons

If the movie does not include a controller, you may want to add some simple buttons for your movie. You can make any page item, with the exception of a movie or sound, into a **button**. To use buttons provided in the Sample Buttons library, just drag a button from the library and set its behavior in the Buttons panel (Windows > Interactive > Buttons). You can also create buttons with a script.

Creating a button as part of a script is not as difficult as you might think. Just remember that a button is a container that contains the elements that make up the button (shape and possibly text). First, create the button with its geometric bounds property. The part of the button that is visible (the contained object) can be a page item having any number of properties including stroke and fill, as well as its geometry. The geometry can be either geometric bounds (for a circle or rectangle), or a path describing any shape.

In the following example, paths are used to define the shape of each button's contained object: a triangle (for start), and a rectangle (for stop). Most of the work involved is in defining the properties for the various button states (normal, roll over, and clicked). To make the script flexible, the bounds and paths describe points relative to center coordinates. That way, you just need to change the center coordinate to place the buttons anywhere on the page.

To define a path, each point is a list of two values: the x coordinate followed by the y coordinate. And yes, x (horizontal) comes before y (vertical) in the list.

The following assumes that a document exists with a movie placed in a rectangle named "Movie" (see **Place Movie** script above). Color swatches "RGB Red" and "RGB Gray" will be created if not found.

Three State Buttons

```
(*Expects a rectangle named "Movie" on page 1 of document with measurements
set to pixels.*)
set radx to 12
set rady to 12
set homeFolder to path to home folder from user domain
set projPath to homeFolder & "AppleScripts for CS5:Chapter 23:Buttons:"
try
    set docRef to getDocRef()
    set grayColor to checkSwatch(docRef, "RGB Gray", {230, 230, 230})
    set redColor to checkSwatch(docRef, "RGB Red", {255, 0, 0})
    --if last parameter is true, layer will be created if not found
    set layerRef to checkLayer(docRef, "Interactive", true)
```

```
      on error errstr
         display alert errstr
         return
      end try
   tell application "Adobe InDesign CS5"
      --for buttons
      set dShadowProps to {mode:drop, angle:90, x offset:0, y offset:0, size:4}
      set pageRef to page 1 of docRef
      set rectRef to rectangle "Movie" of pageRef
      --calculate bounds and path for buttons using center points
      set rBounds to geometric bounds of rectRef
      set cy to ((item 3 of rBounds) - (item 1 of rBounds)) / 2 + ¬
      (item 1 of rBounds)
      set cx0 to ((item 2 of rBounds) - (2 * radx))
      set cx1 to ((item 4 of rBounds) + (2 * radx))
      set btnBounds to {cy - rady, cx0 - radx, cy + rady, cx0 + radx}
      set btnPath to {{cx0 - radx, cy - rady}, {cx0 - radx, cy + rady}, ¬
      {cx0 + radx, cy}}
      set rectBounds to {cy - rady, cx1 - radx, cy + rady, cx1 + radx}
      set rectPath to {{cx1 - radx, cy - rady}, {cx1 - radx, cy + rady}, ¬
      {cx1 + radx, cy + rady}, {cx1 + radx, cy - rady}}
      set movieRef to movie 1 of rectRef
      set btnProps to {fill color:grayColor, stroke color:"None", ¬
      stroke weight:0}
      set ROProps to {fill color:grayColor, stroke color:"None", ¬
      stroke weight:0}
      set clkProps to {fill color:redColor, stroke color:"None", ¬
      stroke weight:0}
      set playBtn to my poly3StateBtn(pageRef, "PlayBtn", btnBounds, ¬
      btnPath, btnProps, ROProps, clkProps, dShadowProps)
      --add behavior to buttons
      tell playBtn
         set movStartBehavior to make movie behavior with properties ¬
         {movie item:movieRef, behavior event:mouse up, operation:play}
      end tell
      set stopBtn to my poly3StateBtn(pageRef, "StopBtn", rectBounds, ¬
      rectPath, btnProps, ROProps, clkProps, dShadowProps)
      tell stopBtn
         set movStopBehavior to make movie behavior with properties ¬
         {movie item:movieRef, behavior event:mouse up, operation:stop}
      end tell
   end tell

(*Creates shape and states for button.*)
on poly3StateBtn(pageRef, btnName, btnBounds, btnPath, btnProps, ROProps, ¬
   clkProps, dShadowProps)
   tell application "Adobe InDesign CS5"
      tell pageRef
         set btnRef to make button with properties {geometric bounds:¬
         btnBounds, name:btnName}
         tell btnRef
            set polyRef to make polygon with properties btnProps
         end tell
         set entire path of path 1 of polyRef to btnPath
         --add roll over State
         tell btnRef
            set roState to make state
```

```
          end tell
          tell roState
             set roPoly to make polygon with properties ROProps
          end tell
          set entire path of path 1 of roPoly to btnPath
          if dShadowProps is not missing value then
             set properties of roPoly to {fill transparency settings:¬
             {drop shadow settings:dShadowProps}}
          end if
          --add click state;
          tell btnRef
             set clkState to make state
          end tell
          tell clkState
             set clkPoly to make polygon with properties clkProps
          end tell
          set entire path of path 1 of clkPoly to btnPath
       end tell
    end tell
    return btnRef
 end poly3StateBtn
 (*Add handlers: getDocRef (Document folder), checkSwatch (Colors folder), and
 checkLayer (Document Structure folder) to complete the script.*)
```

Sound

The only thing that might be missing in your project at this point is sound. Perhaps you would like the computer to make an audible click when a button is clicked. The script **Movie With Btns** places a movie along with adding buttons and sound. You will find it in the project folder **Movie**. Open the script and find the code that adds the sound.

With variable declarations at top of script:

```
set sndPath to movieFolder & "click.mp3"
set placePt to {24, 24} --place point for sound, can be anywhere on page
```

In the main section of script after the --add sound comment:

```
tell pageRef
   set soundObj to place file sndPath place point placePt
end tell
set soundRef to item 1 of soundObj
tell soundRef
   set embed in PDF to true
   set do not print poster to true
   set sound loop to false
end tell
```

Inside playBtn tell block:

```
make sound behavior with properties {enable behavior:true, ¬
sound item:soundRef, behavior event:mouse down, operation:play}
```

Inside stopBtn tell block:

```
make sound behavior with properties {enable behavior:true, ¬
sound item:soundRef, behavior event:mouse up, operation:play}
```

Make changes to names of files and file paths at the top of the script as needed to identify your movie, poster file, and sound file. After running the script, view the page in InDesign's Preview panel. Roll over a button. Click on the run button, then the stop button. Finish the page as you desire and export to Flash Player (SWF) or Interactive PDF with View After Exporting clicked. Make sure the checkbox for Buttons and Media, Include All is enabled. For SWF you need to check Create HTML in order to be able to view after export.

Multistate Objects

Multistate objects are like having a slideshow inside of a page item on your document page. A multistate object can have any number of states. Each state can have more than one object. Using a script can take all of the hassle out of creating a multistate object. For a scripted solution you may want the images to be displayed in a predetermined order. For this you may decide to identify image files using an incremented naming convention. Alternatively you could use a list, matching names in the list to the names of the files. The **Multistate** project uses two folders of files: one for the images and the second for the corresponding text. Files in both folders are named using an incremented naming convention. Text files are named the same as the images with just the extension changed. From the **Multistate Object** script, the following shows the handler that creates the multistate object. The complete script is in the **Multistate** project folder.

```
(*Creates Multistate object with image and text frames.*)
on makeMSO(docRef, msoName, MSOBounds, imageBounds, layerRef, objstyleRef,
projectPath, fileNames)
    set imagePath to projectPath & "Images:"
    set textPath to projectPath & "Text:"
    set statesToAdd to (length of fileNames) - 2
    tell application "Adobe InDesign CS5"
        tell docRef
            set MSORef to make multi state object with properties:{name:¬
            "MultiImages", geometric bounds:MSOBounds, item layer:layerRef}
            repeat with i from 1 to statesToAdd
                tell MSORef to make state
            end repeat
        end tell
        set txtBounds to {item 3 of imageBounds, item 2 of imageBounds, ¬
        item 3 of MSOBounds, item 4 of imageBounds}
        repeat with i from 1 to length of fileNames
            set nameStr to item i of fileNames
            set fileAlias to (imagePath & nameStr & "." & imageFileExt) as alias
            set txtAlias to (textPath & nameStr & ".txt") as alias
            tell state i of MSORef
                set rectRef to make rectangle with properties ¬
                {geometric bounds:imageBounds, name:("State" & i), ¬
                fill color:"None", stroke weight:0}
                set txtRef to make text frame with properties {geometric ¬
                bounds:txtBounds, name:("State" & i), applied object style:¬
                objstyleRef}
            end tell
            tell rectRef to place fileAlias
            tell txtRef
                place txtAlias
                clear object style overrides
            end tell
```

```
            end repeat
        end tell
        return MSORef
end makeMSO
```

Note

Multistate objects only work with Flash SWF export. If you want a multistate object in an interactive PDF project, export it to SWF and import the SWF into your document for export to PDF.

Hyperlinks

Hyperlinks give readers the option of jumping to points of interest in the document or of viewing additional information in other documents or web links. A hyperlink is a type of button in that it performs an action when clicked. Unlike buttons, however, hyperlinks can be applied to text. Naming hyperlinks is optional.

Bookmarks

When you create a table of contents for your document (Layout > Table of Contents…), clicking the **Create PDF Bookmarks** checkbox in Options creates bookmarks for items in the table of contents when you export to PDF interactive. If you don't want all of the items in the Table of Contents to appear as bookmarks, or you don't necessarily want to create a table of contents, you can work with the Bookmarks panel (Window > Interactive > Bookmarks) or use a script. The **Create Bookmarks** script, adds bookmarks for pages where a designated paragraph style is used (most likely for a page head). It does this by creating page destination hyperlinks. The handler that does the work is listed below.

```
(*Creates page destination bookmarks using text items styled with
styleName.*)
on createBookmarks(docRef, styleName)
    set numBookmarks to 0
    set foundSet to {}
    tell application "Adobe InDesign CS5"
        tell docRef
            set parastyleRef to paragraph style styleName
            set attribRecord to {applied paragraph style:parastyleRef}
            set foundSet to my findByAttribute(docRef, attribRecord)
            if length of foundSet > 0 then
                delete bookmarks
                repeat with i from 1 to length of foundSet
                    set textItem to item i of foundSet
                    set frameRef to item 1 of parent text frames of textItem
                    set pageRef to parent page of frameRef
                    set destContent to contents of textItem
                    set destName to "Page " & name of pageRef
                    if not (exists hyperlink page destination destName) then
                        set markDest to (make hyperlink page destination with ¬
                        properties {destination page:pageRef, name:destName, ¬
                        view setting:inherit zoom})
                    else
                        set markDest to hyperlink page destination destName
                    end if
                    if not (exists bookmark destContent) then
```

```
                  make bookmark with properties {name:destContent, ¬
                      destination:markDest}
                end if
            end repeat
            set numBookmarks to count of bookmarks
          end if
        end tell
      end tell
      return numBookmarks
    end createBookmarks
```

Interactive PDF Project

The project **Interactive PDF** uses bookmarks and hyperlinks to provide navigation for an interactive PDF project. Working through this project will give you the opportunity to get familiar with the **Create Bookmarks** script introduced above as well as two other scripts: **Hyper Glossary**, and **Hyper Buttons**. The scripts are in the Scripts folder inside the project folder. Open the document "TravelTreasures.indd" and run the **Bookmarks** script. Select Destination from the list presented. Keep your document open.

Hyperlink Glossary

Perhaps your PDF has a glossary page or pages defining terms used throughout the document. An automated workflow for adding text hyperlinks would be to read in a list of hyperlinks from a text file or to get the list from the glossary page itself. From there, a script could parse the list to find references to text in the story and create the hyperlinks. At the same time, you might want to assign the text a character style to identify it as a hyperlink.

The **Hyper Glossary** script can be a real labor saver for this process. It relies on glossary items in a text frame named "Glossary." It gets a list of all of the glossary entries identified by their assigned character style. It then uses a **find** operation to parse this list to locate matching text in the document set with the "Body" style. The text found is styled with a character style, and a hyperlink is created to the glossary page.

Hyperlink Buttons

The **Hyper Buttons** script references all of the rectangles on the master page named with a specific naming convention (file name, underscore, page number). The script hyperlinks the rectangles to pages designated in the button's name. Although the rectangles act similar to a button, they technically are not buttons as they do not have states and behaviors.

After running the scripts for the project, export as Adobe PDF (Interactive). Check the box for View After Exporting, and for Buttons and Media select the radio button Include All. Disable all others. If opened in Acrobat, your interactivity should be enabled.

Export for Interactive

InDesign CS5.5 made some vast improvements when it comes to export, especially for EPub and HTML. You may want to set up a few scripts just to set the export preferences for the different document types you will be exporting to. In this section we will look at a few. For the purpose of our discussion here, we will be looking at the export preferences for version CS5.5.

Structure Tags

When you output your document to PDF (either for print or interactive), you may notice that you have an option to create a tagged PDF. For a script, this option is the property **include structure** of **interactive PDF export preferences**. (Similar preference settings are available for HTML and EPub export.) A tagged PDF can be a major bonus for your readers as it improves document navigation. This is especially important for longer, more complex documents, and for documents being read on mobile devices or with assistive software. Most assistive software depends on document structure tags to determine text reading order and to convey the meaning of other content. Reflowing a document for viewing on the small screen of a mobile device relies on structure tags. If your document is not structured, and you export with include structure set to true (Create Tagged PDF in the user interface), Acrobat tries to tag the document for you, but the result may not be exactly as you want. For version CS5.0 you can use XML structure; with CS5.5 you have the option of using XML or a structure created using the new **articles** object (Articles panel in the user interface).

Exporting to Interactive PDF

For exporting to interactive PDF, the properties you will need to define are listed in the **interactive PDF export preferences** class (Preference Suite of InDesign's Dictionary). In the following, the **export_IAPDFPrefs** handler sets the properties for the interactive PDF export preferences for a slideshow. This is part of the **Export Slideshow** script. The complete script is found in the **Slideshow** project for this chapter. See the section Making Scripts Work for You for instructions on working with this project.

```
(*TransitionIndex is index of transition in transitionTypeList returned from
custom dialog.*)
--set up export preferences
export_IAPDFPrefs(docRef, docName, transitionIndex, viewAfter)

on export_IAPDFPrefs(docRef, docName, transitionIndex, viewAfter)
    tell application "Adobe InDesign CS5"
        set transitionTypeList to {from document, none, blinds transition, ¬
        box transition, comb transition, cover transition, ¬
        dissolve transition, fade transition, page turn transition, ¬
        push transition, split transition, uncover transition, ¬
        wipe transition, zoom in transition, zoom out transition}
        tell interactive PDF export preferences
            set view PDF to viewAfter
            set page range to all pages
            set page transition override to item transitionIndex of ¬
            transitionTypeList --can be from document
            set open in full screen to true
            set flip pages to true
            set flip pages speed to 5
            --default settings for export PDF interactive document
            set export layers to false
            set export reader spreads to true
            set PDF JPEG quality to high
            set PDF raster compression to lossless compression
            set raster resolution to seventy two ppi
            set include structure to false
            set pdf magnification to default
```

```
            set interactive PDF interactive elements option to ¬
                include all media
            set pdf magnification to fit page
            set pdf page layout to default
            set test to flip pages
        end tell
    end tell
end export_IAPDFPrefs
```

EPub and HTML

Documents designed for export to EPub and HTML share similar issues. New with CS5.5 is the ability to tag paragraph styles with standard HTML tags (H1, and so forth). Alternatively, you can rely on CSS3 for HTML5. For images, you can designate how they will repurpose in the HTML or EPub file. As part of the export preference properties you can establish settings for all images. In CS5.5 you can determine settings for individual images to be treated otherwise. You can save your designers a trip to the menu bar (Object > Object Export Option), by providing a script triggered by a keyboard shortcut. As part of the object export options you can have alternate text created automatically using image file metadata.

For many layouts, structuring the document for export is a necessity. A script could save some work here. If page items are added to the document in the order of intended output, a script could use that order to create articles automatically. Version CS5.5 also makes it super easy to anchor page items in text. With the export property **respect anchors** set to true, the image anchoring placement will be honored in the export.

Export for EPub and HTML in CS5.5 share many of the same export preference properties, many of which are exclusive to CS5.5. For an example that saves a document to HTML in CS5.5, you will want to look at the script **HTML Export**. This script starts out by giving the user a choice of three options: Structure the document, Export to HTML, and Both. The Structure segment creates an **article** for each page item in the document in the order placed, from first to last. When the file is exported, the article panel order is used. The HTML segment of the script sets the export to use the article panel order if there are articles in the document. Otherwise, the old method of ordering items from left to right, top to bottom will be used. This can make a huge difference in how the HTML will display. Additionally, the export HTML settings honor anchor placements.

The bottom line is, if you are careful in how items are added to the page and use anchors wisely, you can go directly from InDesign to a simple HTML page. The **HTML Export** script demonstrates creating articles in addition to export to HTML. It also uses a simple method for sorting list items. The handlers from the script follow:

```
(*VERSION 5.5 ONLY.*)
on doStructure(docRef, articleBaseName, willExport)
    tell application "Adobe InDesign CS5.5"
        set pageRef to active page of layout window 1
        tell pageRef
            set pageItemList to page items
        end tell
        --reorder page items by item id
        set sortList to my sortList (pageItemList)
        --create an article for each item in the reordered list
        repeat with i from 1 to length of sortList
            set articleName to articleBaseName & "_" & i
```

```
                set pageItemRef to page item id (item i of sortList) of docRef
                my createArticle(docRef, articleName, pageItemRef)
                if (exists image 1 of pageItemRef) then
                    tell object export options of pageItemRef
                        set alt text source type to source xmp title
                    end tell
                end if
            end repeat
        end tell
    end doStructure

    on createArticle (docRef, articleName, pageItemRef)
        tell application "Adobe InDesign CS5.5"
            tell docRef
                if not exists (article articleName) then
                    set articleRef to make article with properties ¬
                    {name:articleName, article export status:true}
                    tell articleRef
                        set artMember to make article member with properties ¬
                        {itemRef:pageItemRef}
                    end tell
                end if
            end tell
        end tell
    end createArticle

    (*Sorts list of items in pageItemList by item id.*)
    on sortList (origList)
        tell application "Adobe InDesign CS5.5"
            set newList to {id of item 1 of origList}
            repeat with i from 2 to length of origList
                set myId to id of item i of origList
                if myId < item 1 of newList then
                    set the beginning of newList to myId
                else if myId > item -1 of newList then
                    set the end of newList to myId
                else
                    repeat with j from 2 to length of newList
                        if myId < item j of newList then
                            set firstSnip to items 1 thru (j-1) of newList
                            set lastSnip to items j thru -1 of newList
                            set newList to firstSnip & myId & lastSnip
                            exit repeat
                        end if
                    end repeat
                end if
            end repeat
        end tell
        return newList
    end sortList
```

You will find the complete script in the Chapter Scripts folder for this chapter and in the Interactive folder of InDesign's Scripts panel.

Flash Export

When you export to flash (FLA) each spread becomes a separate key frame in the timeline. Both SWF and FLA support buttons, multistage objects, page transitions, hyperlinks, animation, and media. For FLA, only the poster is included in the file. Supported media is saved in a resources folder. Be aware that CMYK and LAB are converted to sRGB. To avoid unwanted color changes for artwork with transparency choose Edit > Transparency Blend Space > Document RGB, or add the following to your export script:

```
set blending space of transparency preferences to RGB
```

Make sure objects with transparency do not overlap over interactive objects. You may want to flatten transparency before export.

Animation

You can apply animation to objects in your scripts with or without **motion presets**. InDesign provides a number of presets by default which you can use as is, or modify by overriding some of the settings in the preset. You can also define a preset in Flash and import it into InDesign. To apply a motion preset to a page item the following handler can get you started.

```
(*Presents user with list of presets to apply to item referenced.*)
on applyPreset(itemRef, defaultChoice, dTime)
    set thePrompt to "Choose preset from list"
    tell application "Adobe InDesign CS5"
        set choiceList to name of Motion Presets
        set userChoice to choose from list choiceList with prompt thePrompt ¬
        default items defaultChoice without multiple selections allowed
        if class of userChoice is not list then
            error "User cancelled"
        else
            set presetName to item 1 of userChoice
        end if
        set presetRef to Motion Preset presetName
        tell animation settings of itemRef
            set plays loop to false
            set duration to dTime
            set preset to item 1 of presetRef
            set design option to to current location
        end tell
    end tell
end applyPreset
```

Alternatively, the script can define a motion path for the animation. The **animation settings** property for a page item controls the animation to be applied. The duration of the animation for an object is controlled by its **duration** property as in the example above. The point at which animation starts is relative to the event that triggers it. In the example above, the animation will be triggered when the page is loaded, which is the default.

Basic animations do not require timing to be set. To set timing, you work with the **timing settings** object for the page item or one of its parents. **Timing settings** contain **timing lists**. Each timing list is triggered by a separate event. For each timing list, you create one or more

timing groups. Page items are "affiliated" with a timing group using the **dynamic target** property of the timing group. You can see how this works in the following which assumes an active document with swatches "RGB Blue", "RGB Red", and "RGB Green." The animation is triggered the first time the page is clicked.

Multi Animation

```
property mPathPoints: {{{{72, 100}, {72, 100}, {72, 100}}, {{500, 100}, ¬
{500, 100}, {500, 100}}}, true} --motion path
set cx to 36
set cy to 36
set xRad to 18
set yRad to 18
set gBounds to {cy - yRad, cx - xRad, cy + yRad, cx + xRad}
tell document 1 of application "Adobe InDesign CS5"
        set pageRef to active page of layout window 1
        set itemList to {}
        set itemColors to {"RGB Blue", "RGB Red", "RGB Green"}
        tell pageRef
            repeat with i from 1 to length of itemColors
                set itemRef to make oval with properties {geometric bounds:¬
                gBounds, fill color:item i of itemColors, stroke color:"None"}
                set end of itemList to itemRef
            end repeat
        end tell
        --set animation preferences for items
        repeat with i from 1 to length of itemList
            tell animation settings of item i of itemList
                set duration to 2
                set motion path points to mPathPoints
            end tell
        end repeat
        tell timing settings of parent of pageRef
            --remove default list
            delete timing list 1
            --timing list triggers when page is clicked
            set timingListRef to make timing list with properties ¬
            {trigger event:on page click}
        end tell
        --add page items to timing group
        tell timingListRef
            set timingGroupRef to make timing group with properties ¬
            {dynamic target:item 1 of itemList, delay seconds:0}
        end tell
        tell timingGroupRef
            repeat with i from 2 to length of itemList
                make timing target with properties ¬
                {dynamic target:item i of itemList, delay seconds:2}
            end repeat
        end tell --timing group
    end tell --document
```

A more robust version of this script is found in the **Animation** project folder for this chapter.

Key Frames

For to-the-second control of your project's animation, use **key frames**. Key frames are motion path points in time (in seconds) within the length of the animation. If the rate of the movie is 24 frames per second, then a 2 second movie would have 48 frames. Notice in the following how points of the motion path are lists of lists nested inside of a list (*mPath*) with the first list item defining frames as a point in time—0 (start), 23 (1 second), and 47 (end}.

Key Frames

```
(*Assumes document with colors "RGB Blue", "RGB Red", and "RGB Green."*)
property mPath: {{0, {{0, 0}, {0, 0}, {0, 0}}}, {23, {{234, 0}, {234, 0}, ¬
{234, 0}}}, {47, {{468, 0}, {468, 0}, {468, 0}}}}
set cx to 36
set cy to 36
set xRad to 18
set yRad to 18
set gBounds to {cy - yRad, cx - xRad, cy + yRad, cx + xRad}
tell document 1 of application "Adobe InDesign CS5"
    set pageRef to active page of layout window 1
    set itemList to {}
    set itemColors to {"RGB Blue", "RGB Red", "RGB Green"}
    tell pageRef
        repeat with i from 1 to length of itemColors
            set itemRef to make oval with properties {geometric bounds:¬
            gBounds, fill color:item i of itemColors, stroke color:"None"}
            set end of itemList to itemRef
        end repeat
    end tell
    (*For each of the 3 key frames (0, 23, 47) lists in list are for scale
    percentages of each of the 3 page items at key frame 0, 23, and 47.*)
    set itemScales to {{100, 200, 100}, {200, 300, 50}, {50, 200, 400}}
    --each list defines opacity of page item at key frame 0, 23, and 47
    set alphaList to {{100, 20, 100}, {10, 80, 60}, {100, 40, 80}}
    repeat with i from 1 to length of itemList
        set scaleList to {{0, item 1 of item i of itemScales}, ¬
        {23, item 2 of item i of itemScales}, ¬
        {47, item 3 of item i of itemScales}}
        tell animation settings of item i of itemList
            set duration to 2
            set motion path to mPath
            set scale x array to scaleList
            set scale y array to scaleList
            set opacity array to {{0, item 1 of item i of alphaList}, ¬
            {23, item 2 of item i of alphaList}, ¬
            {47, item 3 of item i of alphaList}}
            set plays loop to true
        end tell
    end repeat
end tell --document
```

A more robust version of this script is found in the **Animation** project for this chapter. You will find some other examples of animation in the same folder. Read the description and instructions at the top of the scripts.

Animation in EPub and HTML

You can place movies and sound in your EPub and HTML documents, but animation is not supported; at least not directly. You can export your animated InDesign document to FLA. Then, using an experimental technology, Wallaby, you can convert artwork and animation from Flash Professional (FLA) files into HTML. At this point, animations are set for infinite loops. If this is not what you want your animation to do (and most likely you won't), you will need to set the number of times to repeat. This can be done easily in a text editor: Open the CSS file and search for "infinite." Replace this value with the number of times to repeat. For more about Wallaby, see labs.adobe.com/technologies/wallaby/.

Make Scripts Work for You

Slideshow

This project will use a script to create a slideshow document. Alternatively, you may want to use a template such as the one included in the project folder. Scripts for the project are in the Slideshow folder of InDesign's Script panel as well as in the project folder.

1. Prepare images for the slideshow. The project relies on images located in the Images folder for the project. A few very low resolution files have been provided. If you use your own files, they should be sized consistently and have metadata information added to identify the image:
    Name: Document Title field for name or title of the image.
    Description: Description field provides a short description of the image.
    Author: Author field is for credit or creator of image.

2. Prepare the **Export Slideshow_PDF** script. Open the **Export Slideshow_PDF** script and view the code. The value defined for *dLocation* establishes the default folder location for the choose file name command. You may want to change the value for this variable.

3. Create your document. Run the **Web Doc Choose Preset** script from the Interactive folder of InDesign's Scripts panel. Or use the "Gallery.indd" document provided with the project. If using this document, skip step 4 below.

4. Add a rectangle for your images. In the document, switch to the master page (A-Master). Create a rectangle of the size desired for your images. Leave at least an inch below to allow for a caption text frame.Select the rectangle. When you run the **Prepare Slideshow** script (step 5 below), the script names the selected rectangle, adds a caption text frame below, and creates styles for the document.

5. Add Images. Run the script **Prepare Slideshow**. The script checks for a rectangle named "Image" and a text frame named "Caption" on the "A-Master" spread of the document. If these are not found, the script expects a rectangle to be selected on the master page (see step 4 above). It gets a list of the images found in the Images folder for the project and adds them to the document in file-naming order. As part of placing the image, it gets the image's metadata and uses it to populate the caption frame.

6. Save the document. If needed, switch back to page one of the document. Save the document.

7. Export as Adobe PDF (Interactive). Run the script **Export Slideshow**. If you select to view the PDF (check the checkbox control "View PDF"), the slideshow will open when you dismiss the dialog. Acrobat may ask for permission to take over the screen. If so, reply OK and watch your slideshow.

If the pages of your slideshow don't flip, check the values for *flipPages* and *flipSpeed* in the **Export Slideshow** script. Also, make sure you have Adobe Acrobat chosen to view PDF files in your computer system (see sidebar below).

Setup Acrobat for PDF View

To set Adobe Acrobat Professional as the application for viewing interactive PDF files, use the following procedure: Click on a representative PDF file in the System Finder and Get Info for the file (Command + I). In the dialog presented, select Adobe Acrobat Professional in the Open With dropdown.

Figure 23.1: Screen from slideshow created with Slideshow script and document template.

24

Only the Beginning

Assuming you worked through the chapters to arrive at the end of the book, congratulations! Hopefully, you found the journey fun, informative, and rewarding. You have been introduced to a wide range of subjects, but there is much left for further study. So where to go from here?

Onward and Upward

Like any language, the more you use AppleScript, the more adept at using it you become. Start small. If nothing more, use scripts to help organize the way you work and to eliminate those repetitive nasty little tasks that, when added together, can be the difference between having time for an extra round of golf or for creative endeavors, and having to keep grinding away at repetitive taks in order to get your work out.

As you may have discovered, there are as many ways to write an InDesign script as there are ways to work with the program manually, and Adobe loves to give users at least two or more ways to accomplish a particular task. The method that works best for you is up to you. Keep this book and Adobe's excellent documentation handy for reference. Review the scripts with this book, and work through the scripts in the Sample scripts folder (Adobe's sample scripts).

- Sign up for the AppleScript list that supports this book: http://tech.groups.yahoo.com/group/applescriptingindesign.

- Keep in touch with Adobe's scripting forum: http://forums.adobe.com/community/indesign/indesign_scripting.

- Keep your eyes out for scripts that may be posted to the web. When you find a handler or a routine you think you may use, follow the instructions below to add it to your library.

- As you work, keep an open mind on ways you can improve your work process, perhaps with a script or two. Write your ideas down. Then when the time or the need arises, put your script together using your library of handlers.

Adding Handlers to Library

1. Write your handler so it can be used in as many scripts as possible. (It doesn't make much sense to have a handler that can only be used once.)

2. Of course, you are going to test and re-test your handler to make sure it works. Place a comment before the handler to describe its functionality with the parameters required.

3. Using AppleScript Editor, open the file "ScriptLibTemplate.scpt" found in your Handlers Library.

   ```
   (Hard Drive:Library:Preferences:Scripts:Script Editor Scripts:[your version
   of the handlers folder].
   ```

4. Copy the handler from your script. Paste it into the script template ("ScriptLibTemplate. scpt"), in place of the comment "--put handler here." Be careful not to disturb any of the other code, especially the ending quotation mark. Remember, these handlers are scripts that are converted to text and need to be enclosed in quotes. The enclosing quotes are part of the template.

5. Add some line spaces above the handler. Cut the call to your handler and paste above your handler.

6. Use Script Editor's Find dialog (Command + F) to search for quotation marks.

7. Place a backslash (\) in front of each quotation mark.

8. Compile the script. If you get a message that reads as below, you missed a quotation mark.

    ```
    Syntax Error:
    Expected expression but found unknown token.
    ```

9. When the script template compiles successfully, save the template using the name of your handler and place it in the appropriate folder of your Handlers Library.

10. Create a sample script that will use your handler. Add the handler to the script along with values and variables that will be passed to the script. Make sure your variables match those required for the call to the handler.

Troubleshooting

When you start putting handlers together to create a script, and/or start writing your own code, you are bound to get errors.

compile error - You get an error when you click the compile button in your script editor.

runtime error - You or your user gets an error or unexpected result when the script is run. This means that something about the script or data supplied is incorrect.

As much as you try to avoid errors, they will happen, and maybe a little more frequently than you would like.

Compile Errors

Before you look any further, make sure the application reference is to your version of InDesign. Other compile errors are usually easy to spot: you misspelled a word, forgot an ending quotation mark, or failed to close a code block (end tell, end if, end try, etc.). The error message you get should point you to the problem. Here are a few of the more common:

*   "Expected end of line, etc. but found identifier."

    Look for a misspelled word or missing end quote.

*   "Expected end of line but found end of script."

    Look for missing (unmatched) end if or end tell.

*   "[…] doesn't match the parameters […] for [name of handler]."

    Look for missing required parameter in call to handler.

*   "Expected "," or "}" but found number."

    Look for missing comma in a list or unmatched curly brace at end of a list.

Runtime Errors

Runtime errors often don't raise their heads until you hand the script off to someone else. These often happen because the environment in which the script runs is different than your testing environment, or the user has done something you failed to anticipate. Remember that users often don't read instructions, and will often fail to provide the environment or data on which the script depends (dependencies). Some errors you may encounter are listed below:

- "Adobe InDesign CS got an error. Can't get [missing object here]."

  You have anticipated an existing object, and it does not exist.

- Script runs but nothing seems to happen.

  Check measurement units and colors (point units anticipated but inches being used, paper color text on paper background, etc.).

- "Adobe InDesign CS5 got an error: Can't continue [handler name here]."

  You forgot to put a **my** qualifier in front of the call to the handler.

- "Import failed."

  Your script may be trying to place text into a linked text frame that contains text.

- "Adobe InDesign CS5 got an error: Connection is invalid" (and InDesign quits).

  Your script tried to get the value of an item of a selection without an existing selection. Always have your script check for the length of selection of if selection exists before attempting to get the class or reference to an item of a selection.

Trapping Errors

The effort you put into trapping errors is often the difference between a successful script and one that fails. The sample scripts in this book use a minimum of error trapping simply to make scripts easier to read and to cut down on redundancy. Also, the only information returned from an error that was used was the text of the error. This is what the user will see in an on error block such as in the following:

```
try
    --statements that can cause an error
on error errStr
    activate
    display alert errStr
end try
```

While working with your script, you may want to capture more information about the error than just the text of the error. For this you can use the following:

```
try
    --statements that can cause an error
on error errMsg number errNumber from errSubject to typeExpected ¬
    partial result resultList
    set testResult to {errMsg, errNumber, errSubject, typeExpected, ¬
    resultList}
    testResult
end try
```

Only the error message (errMsg) and error number (errNumber) can be coerced to a string for display in a display alert statement, and the error number is not meaningful to the user. For this reason, most scripts will only handle the text of the error returned.

The error number can come in handy should you need to test for multiple errors. Try the following. First, use a value for the variable *folderName* that you know does not exist. Then test using the name of a folder that does exist but already contains the file chosen.

```
set folderName to "Test" --name of folder
set publicFolder to path to public folder from user domain as string
set folderPath to publicFolder & folderName
set theFile to choose file "Choose a text file"
try
    tell application "Finder"
        duplicate file theFile to folder folderPath
    end tell
on error errStr number errNumber
    if errNumber = -10006 then
        display alert "File or folder specified does not exist"
    else if errNumber = -15267 then
        display alert "Folder already has a file with the same name"
    else
        display alert "Error: " & errMsg
    end if
end try
```

For a list of error numbers, look up the following reference. You will find a comprehensive list of errors and error numbers in Appendix B at this address along with a wealth of other information..

```
http://developer.apple.com/library/mac/#documentation/AppleScript/
Conceptual/AppleScriptLangGuide/reference/ASLR_error_xmpls.html
```

Unhandled Errors

One caveat on working with errors is that unhandled errors travel up the execution trail until an on error statement is found. This can be a good thing, or possibly dangerous. Here is a short example.

```
set numList to {12, 24, 36, 48}
try
    set testValue to getTotal(numList)
on error errStr
    set testValue to errStr
end try
testValue

on getTotal(numList)
    set theTotal to 0
    repeat while length of numList > 0
        set theTotal to theTotal + (item 1 of numList)
        set numList to rest of numList
    end repeat
    set theTotal to addAnotherValue(theTotal)
    return theTotal
end getTotal
```

```
on addAnotherValue(theTotal)
    set myList to {}
    set theTotal to theTotal + (item 1 of myList)
    --error occurs here as there is no number result
end addAnotherValue
```

Notice that the error generated is not caught until it filters back to the `try` statement at the top of the script.

Finding Bugs

If you have an error, but can't figure where the problem occurs, try one or more of the following:

- Use AppleScript Editor's Event Log to your advantage. See what statements executed and what the results were. The Event Log History is enabled in the History panel for AppleScript Editor's preferences. You can also set the maximum number of entries for the log in this panel.

- Isolate code. Comment out all of the code with the exception of a single call to a handler, or a group of statements.

- Track code execution. Put a global tracking variable at the top of your script. Update the variable throughout the script. Use a single `try`/`on error` trap that encompasses the entire script, then test the value of your tracking variable in the `on error` statement. This will narrow you in on where the error occurred.

- Use display alert statements. Periodically throughout the script, add display alert statements to indicate value of variables and/or where code execution is taking place.

- Serious users will want to investigate using Script Debugger (http://www.latenightsw.com).

Testing

When it comes to testing, remember that you can never do enough.

- Purposely try to anticipate errors by failing to follow the instructions for your script, such as not having a document open or failing to provide resources on which the script depends.

- Have someone else test your scripts, preferably in a different computer environment.

- If you think you know the script best, give it to a novice user. This person is bound to find an error or dependency you failed to anticipate.

Most importantly, should you encounter an error with one of the scripts or handlers supplied with the resources for this book, don't be shy. We make mistakes too. Let us know and learn fromour mistakes. Suggestions and questions are always welcome. Feel free to email the author at: shopkins@xmission.com.

Index